The
Status of
Muslim
Women
in Medieval India

The
Status of
Muslim
Women
in Medieval India

Sudha Sharma

 **SAGE** www.sagepublications.com
Los Angeles • London • New Delhi • Singapore • Washington DC

First published in 2016 by

 SAGE Publications India Pvt Ltd
B1/I-1 Mohan Cooperative Industrial Area
Mathura Road, New Delhi 110 044, India
www.sagepub.in

SAGE Publications Inc
2455 Teller Road
Thousand Oaks, California 91320, USA

SAGE Publications Ltd
1 Oliver's Yard, 55 City Road
London EC1Y 1SP, United Kingdom

SAGE Publications Asia-Pacific Pte Ltd
3 Church Street
#10-04 Samsung Hub
Singapore 049483

Published by Vivek Mehra for SAGE Publications India Pvt Ltd, typeset at 10/12 pts Sabon by Zaza Eunice, Hosur, Tamil Nadu and printed at Chaman Enterprises, New Delhi.

Library of Congress Cataloging-in-Publication Data Available

ISBN: 978-93-515-0566-2 (HB)

The SAGE Team: Aditi Chopra, Neha Sharma, Kritika Vashist and Anupama Krishnan

Contents

Preface

Woman has been considered, through ages, as the prime mover of family and the society alike. The term 'status' refers to the position of woman as a person in the social structure, defined by her designated rights and obligations. Each 'status-position' is explained in terms of a pattern of behaviour expected of the incumbent. The role and status assigned to women in the society have always been a yardstick to assess the level of progress of civilisations. The book traces the status of Muslim women in medieval India in terms of their social, economic, political and cultural roles.

At its inception, the book traces the status of women in pre-Islamic Arabic tribal society during its dark age where women had no recognised place except that they were considered a mere property. Islam improved their position and instituted many reforms, effecting a marked improvement in their status. However, the Islamic religious text, like in other spheres, laid down the minutest code of conduct for women, the slightest deviation from which was considered irreligious. Such rigidity, coupled with the apathy of the *ulemas* (Muslim religious scholars/the Muslim theologians, who were considered competent to interpret the holy Quran and *Sunnah* (traditions of Prophet Mohammad)[1] for any change, made the fort of Islam almost impregnable, resulting in the static status for Muslim women within the Islamic fold. The subsequent historical developments, however, brought different clans within its fold, comprising mainly Arabs, Turks, Mongols, Tartars, Afghans and Persians. Each group had its own clannish traits and norms concerning women. As a result, assimilation of different ethnic groups influenced the Islamic society, even though they retained some of their own customs and traditions. Such group interactions were different in different countries; hence, there also appeared regional diversity within the Islamic fold. Accordingly, the early dicta were now understood in the light of the new experience and, thus, the Quran was subjected to many interpretations, including about the status of women.

Islam came to India loaded with influences of other ideologies and underwent further changes after intermixing with the Hindu way of life at that point of time. Most of the Muslim invaders, who came to India, were not accompanied by women, and hence they took local women for wives. Thus, the forcible conversions by the attackers or the intrusion through marriages with Indian women, combined with intermingling with the local culture and the varying policies of different kings at different points of time, brought about a change in the status of Muslim women from time to time. Women in India in the contemporary period had fallen very low from the exalted position they once enjoyed. It did not take many years for Muslims to adopt new ways for their own women as well.

The literature on women during medieval period is scanty and, therefore, studies on Muslim women are only a few. Some authors deal with individual aspects and problems of Muslim women in contemporary India. However, the study of their status in medieval India had, more or less, remained peripheral in the contemporary chronicles and the modern works. Since Muslim women remained in seclusion, public reference to them was avoided unless someone played a significant role in politics, literature or any other field. We find references in the memoirs of the contemporary Indian kings, diaries and dispatches of Christian missionaries, travel accounts of foreign travellers, contemporary Hindi and Persian writers and Edicts from the harem that throw light on the attitude of that society towards Muslim women. However, whatever references are found, these have to be interpreted and analysed in the light of the background and limitations of the contemporary chroniclers. Modern works primarily focus on the role of women connected with royalty and nobility of that time.

This book is an attempt to analyse the changing socio-economic-politico-cultural status of Muslim women of all classes in medieval India (13th–18th century). It is divided into six chapters, followed by a conclusion and a bibliography.

Each chapter is followed by 'references' in the endnotes that are related with the aspects discussed within the chapter.

Chapter 1 gives the background. It dwells on the status of women in the pre-Islamic Arabic society and then further discusses the tenets of Islam as to how and to what extent did it improve the status of women. The chapter further traces the spread of Islam, different clans joining Islam and the status of women within these respective clans, which ultimately led to new interpretations about position of women within the Islamic fold.

Chapter 2 deals with the social profile of Muslim women during the period of this study. It discusses at length as to how the degenerating status of women in the contemporary Indian society was also adopted by the Muslims and how, ultimately, Muslim women, in general, became totally subservient to their menfolk and, except an exception here and there, became victim of social apathy and neglect. Due light has also been thrown on the position of special classes of ladies like dancing girls, prostitutes, widows, female relations, slave girls, besides morality of women and general social attitude towards them.

Chapter 3 discusses the economic rights and privileges of the Muslim ladies of different economic standing—royalty, nobility and common classes. It narrates how the royal and high-strata ladies were very well provided for through different means, varying according to their status within the harem, their importance in the political set-up and the financial resources of their masters. The chapter also narrates the concern of the royalty for female subjects of all classes and they all were given sufficient grants, in different forms, for their maintenance Their *mahr* (obligatory bridal money/possession paid/promised for marriage contract), ownership and inheritance rights have been discussed. The economic activities of different sections of unprivileged classes have also been elaborated in this section.

Chapter 4 dwells on harem and purdah. It narrates how a large harem had become a status symbol and how Mughals added to the number of harem inmates by following the policy of seeking peace and strengthening relations through matrimonial alliance. The Muslim jealousy about their wives was proverbial. A detailed narration has been made as to how they guarded them, provided for their dwellings and expenses and worked out, during the time of Mughals, an elaborate system of internal management for the security and maintenance of the harem inmates. The chapter gives a detailed account of activities of the ladies of royalty and nobility in harems and also their life of splendour, pomp and luxury, which, in fact, impacted their status negatively. The practice of purdah, which had become common and came to be regarded as symbol of honour, has also been discussed in this section. It has been made clear with examples as to how different stress was laid on observance of purdah during different periods in history. The role of purdah in the lower strata of the society has been reviewed distinctly. It is interesting to observe how the rigidity with which purdah was adopted reduced the status of Muslim women and had varying adverse impact on ladies of different classes.

Chapter 5 discusses the role of Muslim women on political platform. In this respect, important role played by different ladies of royalty, nobility and high birth or even concubines and dancing girls at different points of time—as active participators or regents of the minor kings or as manipulators behind the scene—has been discussed. The influence of these ladies varied from time to time according to their personality, family connection, political situation and the character of the sultan or the emperor. The chapter contains a detailed description of such participation by different ladies, which depicts how with the weakening of the empire and the royalty falling into debauchery, the ladies of low birth like dancing girls and concubines gained greater sway in court machinations in the later period in contrast to the positive role played by royal ladies like Razia or Nur Jahan in the earlier period.

Chapter 6 focuses on cultural achievements and pursuits of Muslim women during the period under study. In this domain, the common Muslim women had little to contribute because of their educational backwardness and prevalence of early marriage and purdah. The narration brings out that as the kings of the sultanate period were conservative, their ladies did not make a mark, except a few like Razia, who patronised education. However, Mughals made arrangements for education of harem ladies. Instances have been explored wherein Mughal ladies made a mark in different fields like education, writing, fine arts, designing, laying beautiful gardens, architecture, etc. Their acts of charity and religious piety have also been highlighted, which did enhance the social status of the Muslim women.

The last chapter gives, in conclusion, an overview of the status of Muslim women as it changed during the course of history in medieval India. It is further followed by a list of references titled 'Bibliography'.

The literature in this book largely emanates from my Doctoral thesis with the title 'Changing Status of Muslim Women in Medieval India Till 1761', which was accomplished under the guidance of renowned scholar of history, late Dr R.C. Jauhri, then Professor of History, Panjab University, Chandigarh. Additional material and latest references have been induced to make the reading more contemporary. Thus, this book holds authentic reference for those studying the position of Muslim women from all aspects in medieval India.

A pointed research, an analysis and interpretation of the literature of medieval India could not be accomplished without reference to the archival works, most of which are available in Persian. It warrants assistance from authorities in Islamic Studies, besides experts in Persian language, to read and assimilate. Many learned scholars, especially Dr Madhukar Arya of Persian Department of Panjab University, Chandigarh, and Dr Mohammad Afzal Khan of History Department of Aligarh Muslim University, rendered valuable assistance in my endeavour to understand the subject in its right perspective. I extend my gratitude to all of them.

I am grateful to the authorities of Aligarh Muslim University; National Archives, New Delhi; Indian Institute of Islamic Studies, Tughlaqabad; Khuda Bakhsh Oriental Public Library, Patna; U.P. Archaeological Department, Lucknow; Panjab University, Chandigarh; Central Library, Chandigarh; Dwarka Dass Library, Chandigarh; Vishveshwara Nand Library, Hoshiarpur; Government College, Hoshiarpur; Lajpat Library, D.A.V. College, Jalandhar; Doaba College, Jalandhar; Lyallpur Khalsa College, Jalandhar and host of other institutions for permitting me to use their libraries for collecting the research material. I thank Dr K.L. Sachdeva, former Lecturer at D.A.V. College, Jalandhar, for allowing me an access to his rich personal library.

My husband, S.M. Sharma, provided me with much-needed moral support. I am also thankful to my children, Himani, Garima and Kinshuk, who smiled away the deprivation of motherly care during this research and also provided technical support.

My profuse appreciation and thanks are due to SAGE Publications for bringing this book to the readers in a lucid and presentable form.

Sudha Sharma

Note

1. Sultans in medieval India often allowed the *ulemas* to act as religious and legal arbiters.

1

Islamic Heritage: A Background

Islam—The Religion

The changing status of Muslim women in India cannot be discussed without considering the tenets of the Muslim religion and also the Middle Eastern ethos that existed during the contemporary period. In Islam, the Quran is a perennial source of reference for interpretation and validity of almost every conceivable human act and situation. It is the code that contains all procedures and practices, be they religious, political, civil, commercial, military or judicial—all of which are of importance to a Muslim. It regulates everything: from the elaborate ceremonies of religion to mundane activities of daily life, from the salvation of the soul to the health of the body, from the rights of the community to those of each individual, from morality to crime and from punishment here to that in the life to come.[1]

As Islam moved out beyond the borders of Arabia, the people of varied cultures joined its fold. This brought new ideas and also new problems in its trail. Consequently, to meet the demands of the changing times, the simple early dicta of the Quran were subjected to new interpretations and additions. The new issues were solved with the help of the 'traditions' of the Prophet, known as hadith, rules of law deduced from the hadith called *sunna*, the consensus of the scholars called the *ijma* and the analogical deductions known as the *qiyas*. Prophet Mohammad was realistic enough to foresee that Islam and its followers must keep pace with the changing times if Islam had to continue till eternity. According to a hadith, Muadh, on being appointed ruler of Yemen, was questioned by Mohammad as to how would he deliver justice. 'I will judge matters according to the Book of God', replied Muadh. 'But if the Book of God contains nothing to guide you?' asked Mohammad. 'Then', replied Muadh, 'I will act on the precedent of the Messenger of God.' 'But', persisted

Mohammad, 'if the precedents fail?' 'Then I will endeavour to form my own judgement', replied Muadh. On hearing this, Mohammad is reported to have expressed the greatest satisfaction.[2] In the *fatihah*, the very opening chapter of the Quran, Muslims pray to the Almighty to 'guide us on the right path', indicating concern for the future eventualities. Had it not been so, Muslims would not pray for future guidance but would offer thanks for guidance already received. Some of the laws made by the Prophet were later on annulled or modified according to the needs of the time. Intermarriages with non-Muslims, for example, were first permitted but as the war tension increased, such marriages were prohibited.[3] Prophet Mohammad's vision of future is best reflected by Ameer Ali:

> The great Teacher, who was fully conscious of the exigencies of his own time, and the requirements of the people ... foretold that a time would come when the accidental and temporary regulations would have to be different from the permanent and general. Ye are in an age, he declared, in which, if ye abandon one-tenths of what is ordered ye shall be ruined. After this, time will come when he who shall observe one-tenth of what is now ordered will be redeemed.[4]

Status of Women in Pre-Islamic Arabic Society

In pre-Islamic Arabia, women had an exalted position. They enjoyed great freedom and exercised much influence over the fortune of their tribes. They were not the symbol of weakness, but the embodiment of strength and action. It was the young bride of Haris bin Auf, the powerful chief of the Banu Murra, who brought about the settlement of a long-standing feud between the two rival tribes of Abs and Zubjan.[5] The women accompanied the warriors to battle and inspired them to heroism. The cavaliers fought singing the praises of sisters, wives or lady loves. The chastity of women was honoured the most. An insult inflicted on a woman of a tribe set in flame the desert tribes from one end to the other of the peninsula. The 'Sacrilegious Wars', which continued for 40 years before Mohammad brought them to an end, had the root cause in an insult to a young girl at one of the fairs of Okaz.[6]

Such chivalrous customs continued for quite some time among some of the nomads of Arabia. The condition of women among the Arabs settled in the cities and villages, who had adopted the loose notions of morality prevalent among the Syrians, Persians and Romans, gradually deteriorated to an abysmal level with the contemporaneous political degeneration. Ultimately, the portrait of free, courageous woman, with an independent will of her own, vanished and in its place, the image of women as captives of the harem, immersed in toilet, trifles, sensual pleasures and short of all dignified pride, emerged.[7]

In the tribal society, loyalties were totally for the interests of the kinship groups, tribes and classes. Theirs was the patriarchal society. As such, in the social set-up, as it developed with the passage of time, women came to have no recognised place.[8] The birth of a daughter came to be regarded as a matter of shame. The custom of female infanticide crept in. This gets revealed from *ayat*s (verse of the Quran) 16:58–59 of the Quran, which read as follows:

> When if one of them receiveth tidings of the birth of a female, his face remaineth darkened, and he is wroth inwardly. He hideth himself from the folk because of the evil of that whereof he hath had tidings, (asking himself): Shall he keep it in contempt, or bury it beneath the dust! Verily evil is their judgement.[9]

As per the acknowledged authorities on the social order of Islam, the root cause of female infanticide was the poverty of the parents. There was also fear of the possibility of disgrace and loss of prestige in having one of their flesh and blood married to a stranger. The prevalence of female infanticide among the Arabs seemed to be guided more by the latter factor than by economic considerations. The rough geographical conditions forced them to become nomadic and to indulge in constant fight for survival. Under such life of perpetual struggle, these Bedouins desired sons, especially when the size and strength of the male members of a tribe determined its status and well-being. In their social order, marriage by capture was common and it was considered honourable to take away the wives and concubines of the enemies. Contrarily, seduction of their women was considered a great disgrace. Their intense feeling in this regard can be gathered from the prevalent sayings like the ones which said that 'the grave is the best bridegroom' and that 'burial of daughters is demanded by honour'.[10]

Even when a girl was allowed to live, she was forced to get married at an early age of 7 or 8. A form of endogamy, expressed in the marriage of cousins, prevailed amongst a majority of Arabian tribes. A man's father's brother's daughter was, as a rule, his first wife who remained mistress of the household, even when other women, who might be greater favourites, were introduced into it. Such a marriage within the tribe was preferred probably to keep control over the bridegroom, to prevent the loss of any property of the tribe and to keep their children within its fold.[11]

In pre-Islamic Arabia, a variety of different marriage practices were prevalent; the more common were: marriage by agreement, marriage by capture, marriage by purchase, *beena* marriage, *baal* marriage and *Muta* marriage. The marriage by agreement consisted of an agreement between a man and his future wife's family. The marriage could be within the tribe or between two families of different tribes. Marriage by capture most often took place during times of war, whereby women were taken captive by men from other tribes.[12] In marriage by purchase, a sum of money (known as *mahr*) was paid by a man to the father or nearest kinsman of the woman whom he wished to marry and the other sum (the *sadaq*) to the girl herself. [13] In *beena* marriage, a number of men, 10 or less, would be invited by a woman in her tent to have intercourse with her. If she conceived and delivered a child, she had the right to summon all the men and they were bound to come. She would then say, 'O, so and so, this is your son'. This established paternity conclusively and the man had no choice to disclaim it. The children were brought up by the clan of the wife.[14] In *baal* marriage, the wife used to come to husband's house and her children were given the name of father's clan. The Hebrew word *baal* denoted 'lord', 'master' or 'possessor' and the term was used in the Old Testament for 'husband'. It, thus, substituted *beena* marriage by which women lost their independence and the supremacy of man was established.[15] As for *muta* marriage, it was a totally personal arrangement for temporary fixed period between the two parties, without any intervention from woman's kin. At the end of the period, both the parties were free to depart, without any further ceremony, provided that the woman had received the dower or the fee due to her.[16] Another type of marriage that was prevalent was one in which a man desiring noble offspring would ask his wife to send for a great chief and have intercourse with him. During the period of such intercourse, the husband would stay away and return to her after pregnancy was well advanced.[17] Above all, common prostitutes were well known. If a prostitute conceived, the men who frequented her house were assembled and the physiognomists decided as to whom the child belonged.[18] Most of these conjugal relations, however, could hardly be termed as marriages. They are aptly been termed as 'legalized prostitution or common sexual behaviour recognized by custom'.[19] Even polyandry was practised by some of the tribes.[20] In all such arrangements, woman was never a free agent to make a choice. It was the *wali*, the father or the male guardian, who gave her in marriage and her consent for the same was of no importance. There was no limit to the number of wives a man could have, besides having a number of concubines.[21] In fact, wife was looked upon as a kind of chattel. She could even be lent to a guest as a mark of hospitality for which the Arabs were well known.

The powers of divorce possessed by the husband were also unlimited.[22] Hence, divorces were common. A man, having purchased his wife, could be discharged of his total obligation to her by payment of a portion of the *mahr* that might remain due to her father or *wali* and be rid of her by pronouncement of the formula of dismissal. This required him to repeat his intention of divorcing his wife three times at one go or at intervals.[23] A woman did not have corresponding right of divorce except in case of marriage by purchase where she could buy her freedom from the husband by relinquishing her *mahr* to him. This kind of divorce was known as *khul*.[24]

Closely linked with the subject of marriage is the veiling and seclusion of women. Regarding veiling, customs appear to have varied between the Arab nomads and the city dwellers. While women of desert dwellers went unveiled, associating themselves freely with men, women in cities were veiled. Amongst Prophet's own tribe of the Quraish, veiling was the rule, in general. It is reported that in ancient Mecca, citizens used to dress their daughters and female slaves beautifully and parade them unveiled around Kaba with a hope of attracting some suitors or buyers. If they succeeded in their mission, then the women used to resume their veil again.[25] Possibly, a reference of this also appears in a passage of the Quran where Mohammad exhorted his wives to remain in their houses and not to go out decked in public as in the 'time of barbarism'.[26]

In the Arabian Law of Inheritance, a female could not inherit; the usage was that only he could inherit who could ride on the back of the horse and take the field against the enemy and guard the tribal property. Even among males, only agnates could inherit while the cognates (males through females) were debarred from succession.[27] A woman formed an integral part of the estate of her husband or her father, and the widows of a man descended to his eldest son by right of inheritance, like any other portion of his patrimony. There are references of matrimonial unions between stepsons and stepmothers.[28] Some of the old Arabian proverbs like 'women are the whips of Satan' or 'trust neither a king, horse nor a woman' or 'our mother forbids us to err and runs into error' or 'what has a woman to do with the councils of a nation' or 'obedience to a woman will have to be repented of' speak eloquently as to how the Arabian women were regarded as malign beings and greatly inferior to men.[29]

Islam and Women

With the advent of Islam in Arabian Peninsula, the social institution of the *Jahiliya* (the age of ignorance) underwent significant changes. For restoring the dignity of women, one of the laudable acts of the Prophet was to denounce the practice of female infanticide and to forbid it strictly through the authority of Quranic injunctions; some of these injunctions are quoted as followed:

> 6:140: They are losers who besottedly have slain their children without knowledge.... They indeed have gone astray and are not guided.

> 6:151: ... ye slay not your children because of penury—We provide for you and for them....

> 17:31: Slay not your children, fearing a fall to poverty. We shall provide for them and for you.

> 81:8–9: And when the girl-child that was buried alive is asked. For what sin she was slain.[30]

He went a step further and succeeded partly in removing poverty within a short time, which was one of the main causes of such practice, by making *zakat* (almsgiving) compulsory and worthy of praise. Such collections were to be used for specific purposes, including the use for the poor and the needy.[31] The birth of a daughter was not to be regarded as unwelcome. It was ordained that for a man who brought up daughters, the latter would become a covering against Hell.[32]

The Prophet also raised the status of the mother and declared that paradise lay at the feet of a mother. He reminded his followers of the childbearing pain a mother undergoes and the way she nurses the child with her milk for 30 months. Hence, the man should be thankful and kind to her.[33] Checking the pre-Islamic custom, he forbade marrying mothers.[34] He also raised their economic status by giving mothers a share in the inheritance.[35] A well-known 'tradition' of *Al-Bukhari* clearly shows the exalted position to which mothers were raised by the Prophet. A man came to the Prophet and asked him as to whom he should be kind to. The Prophet replied, 'Your mother'. 'Who next?' 'Your mother', was the reply. The man asked again, 'Who after that?' He again said, 'Your mother'. And it was only when he repeated this question for the fourth time that the Prophet replied, 'Your father'.[36]

The Quran enjoined the pursuit of knowledge by all Muslims regardless of their sex. It repeatedly commanded all readers to read, to recite, to think, to contemplate as well as to learn *ayats*. The very first revelation to the Prophet concerned knowledge and it reads:

96:1–5: Read: In the name of thy Lord who createth,

Createth man from a clot.

Read: And thy Lord is the Most Bounteous,

Who teacheth by the pen,

Teacheth man that which he knew not.[37]

Commands for the equal rights of women and men to pursue education can be found in the hadith literature. It, however, made a difference regarding the type of education meant for a man and that for a woman. A woman's sphere of activity was the home; she should be trained primarily in those branches of knowledge that make her more useful in the domestic sphere.[38]

The Prophet also upgraded the woman's position in the society by bringing many improvements in marriage rules. As per 'traditions', the *muta* marriage was forbidden in the third year of Hijra.[39] Marriage was made not only a contract but a sacred covenant. Being a contract, it gave the man no power over the woman's person beyond what the law defined. Nevertheless, it was regarded as an institution that led to the upliftment of man and was a means for the continuance of the human race. Hence, marriage was considered to be essential for everybody.[40] Spouses were enjoined to honour and love each other.[41] Mohammad asked men to see their brides before marrying them.[42] He taught that nobility of character was the best reason for marrying a woman.[43] He observed, 'It is not lawful for you forcibly to inherit the women (of your deceased Kinsmen)....'[44] He exhorted women to be very careful in choosing a suitable partner for themselves, 'Vile women are for vile men, and vile men for vile women. Good women are for good men and good men for good women....'[45] It was imperative to seek 'free consent' of the lady for solemnising a marriage. No person, a relative or otherwise, could compel her to marry a person against her will.[46]

As an economic obligation, a husband was obliged to pay his wife a sum of money known as *mahr* or marriage settlement. The Quran commands:

> 4:4: And give unto the women, (whom ye marry)
> free gift of their marriage portions...)[47]

Such money was supposed to provide for her in the difficult times, besides preventing the husband from a thoughtless and capricious divorce. The significance attached by the Prophet to this aspect is evident by his repetition of the idea at several places and during different times. He went to the extent of commanding that *mahr* should be paid even to a captive married woman and maids taken in wedlock by a Muslim:

> 4:24: And all married women are forbidden unto you save those (captives) whom your right hands possess.... And those of whom ye seek content (by marrying them), give unto them their portions as a duty.

> 4:25: And who so is not able to afford to marry free, believing women, let them marry from the believing maids ... so wed them ... and give unto them their portions in kindness....[48]

He emphasised that the dower (*mahr*) of her marriage should belong to her alone. Thus, *mahr* and *sadaq* of Arabian times became inter-changeable terms. The Quran forbade husband from taking back his gifts save in exceptional circumstances like *khul* divorce or a case where the wife was guilty of 'flagrant lewdness'.[49] In *surah* 2 (chapter of the Quran; the Quran is divided into *surahs* and further into *ayats* [verses]), *ayat* 237, he has described the act of forgoing the dower as that 'nearer to piety'. Since any religious woman could aspire to do a pious act, *mahr* was likely to be given up by her almost as a sacred duty. Further, he laid down that the wife might remit all or part of it, if she so desired, 'but if they of their own accord remit unto you a part thereof, then ye are welcome to absorb it (in your wealth)'.[50]

Another important reform was to restrict the number of lawful wives to four, with an overriding clause that such plurality of wives was possible only in a case when the four were treated alike materially as well as emotionally. There was also a universally accepted hadith that proclaimed that a husband should not show greater preference for one wife or another.[51] Even Mohammad believed that such absolute equality in matters of feelings and attachment was impossible:

> 4:129: Ye will not be able to deal equally between
> (your) wives, however much ye wish (to do so).[52]

The authorities are, therefore, of the view that in reality, it propounded monogamy and meant prohibition of polygamy.[53]

There was no age limit for marriage in Islam. The Quran held it to be a time when a person was capable of exercising his/her choice in the matter of sexual liking or decision. Accordingly, he/she was in a position to take a decision before giving 'consent' for marriage.[54] Child marriage though not enjoined in the Quran or the 'tradition', yet, it was in vogue; Mohammad himself had married Ayisha when she was just six to seven years of age.[55]

The Prophet gave to women many rights within the family framework. In his behaviour towards his wife, the Quran directed the man:

> 4:19: O Ye who believe! it is not lawful for you forcibly to inherit the women (of your deceased kinsmen), nor (that) ye should put constraint upon them that ye may take away a part of that which ye have given them, unless they be guilty of flagrant lewdness. But consort with them in kindness....[56]

Quranic expression 'retain them in kindness or release them in kindness' appeared several times in relation to the conduct of the husband towards his wife.[57] These *ayat*s were interpreted to mean that a husband should make a choice between two alternatives when he embarked on marriage: either he must retain his wife honourably and with fairness or let her go kindly. These Quranic phrases were revealed in connection with divorce and the period of *iddat* (waiting period). However, hadith shows that the phrase was taken as a general rule, as it was used in circumstances other than *iddat* or divorce also. One such hadith in Al Kafi related about Imam Sadia having said that whenever a man wanted to marry, he should say, 'I acknowledge the promise which God has taken from me, that, I will retain the woman honourably or shall set her free with kindness'. Another hadith from Prophet Mohammad illustrated Prophet's emphasis on treating one's wife courteously. He declared to Muslims, 'O people, keep *Allah* in mind and fear him in respect to women because you have taken them as a trust from *Allah*'.[58] Still, another 'tradition' of Ibn-i-Majah mentioned that once Hazrat Umar complained against the women having grown insolent and sought permission to have resort to beating to set them right. The prophet granted this permission. As a result, 70 women got thrashing from their husbands. These women represented against this treatment to the Prophet. At this, the Prophet declared, 'The best among you are those who are good to their wives and kind to their people'. One of Al-Bukhari's 'traditions' brought out how the Prophet highlighted women's emotional nature and stressed on kind treatment to them. He had said, 'The woman is like a rib. If you try to straighten her, you would break her. But if you employ her usefully, you will benefit from her in spite of her crookedness'.[59]

The Quran gave a married woman the right of maintenance from her husband as a part of his legal obligation:

> 5:87: Men are in charge of women ... because they spend of their property (for the support of women).[60]

A wife had a right to sexual relation. An oath of sexual abstinence, consequently, was vehemently condemned in Islam:

> 4:34: O ye who believe! Forbid not the good things which *Allah* hath made lawful for you, and transgress not.[61]

The women were obliged to make the married life a success. They were to obey the husband and guard their chastity in his absence, 'So good women are the obedient, guarding in secret that which *Allah* hath guarded'.[62] She was expected to give sexual company to her husband at all reasonable times and appropriate places, consistent with her health and decency. She was obliged to reside and live with her husband at his abode and also follow him to any place unless there was a reasonable cause for contrary conduct. Al Bukhari is quoted to have written that a woman was responsible for keeping and running the house of her husband and was answerable for the conduct of her duties.[63] Mohammad had emphasised the interdependence of husband and wife for a smooth marital life. The wife and husband were likened as garments of each other and as mates, living and dwelling in tranquillity.[64] Men and women were directed to complement each other and not to compete with each other. They were, thus, made the protectors of each other.[65]

Islam prohibited adultery for married women by declaring, 'And all married women are forbidden unto you save those (captives)....'[66] For the rest of women, practising adultery was a hateful activity, 'And come not near unto adultery. Lo! it is an abomination and an evil way'.[67] For adulterer and adulteress both, Mohammad provided the punishment of 100 stripes each, once the guilt was proved.[68] He also laid down that an adulterer could marry an adulteress or an idolatress alone and no one else and vice versa.[69] There was, however, another surah whereby only adulterous wives were mentioned and they were to be kept confined to houses until they died.[70] This gave a basis to some authorities on Islam for explaining the practice being followed in early days of Islam when adulterous ladies were literally imprisoned and which later on was changed to stoning to death. However, other experts, like Muhammad Ali, consider it un-Islamic, because death was never prescribed by the Quran, as in such cases, the punishment could not be halved for the slave girls, as stipulated.[71] However, lest this power was misused, he commanded that those who accused honourable women of adultery must bring four witnesses in support, failing which they would be punished by 80 stripes. Further, the testimony of such persons would not be accepted afterwards except for those who repented and made amends.[72] Such witnesses were practically impossible to collect. And by recommending forgiveness for them in case of repentance, Mohammad allowed such persons to go scot-free. But, when a husband accused his wife of adultery but had no witness except himself, his testimony was to be taken equivalent to that of four persons and along with this, he had to invoke the curse of Allah on him if he was telling a lie. The wife could avert punishment in such a case only if she bore a witness before Allah four times that the charges levied by her husband on her were false and by further invoking wrath of Allah upon her if her husband was speaking the truth.[73] Here again, the woman was discriminated against. While the man was given the privilege of being equivalent to four witnesses in case of charge of adultery on wife, no such privilege was given to the wife in case of charge of adultery on the husband. Above all, if the man was unhappy with his wife, then, by levying such charges, he was capable of hurting her emotionally.

The Prophet prohibited those men and women from marrying each other who were bound by nature to live together in a close relationship. The following relations could not marry each other: mother and son, father and daughter, brother and sister, paternal aunt and nephew, paternal uncle and niece, maternal aunt and nephew, maternal uncle and niece, stepfather and stepdaughter, stepmother and stepson, mother-in-law and son-in-law, father-in-law and daughter-in-law, wife's sister and brother-in-law (during sister's lifetime) and foster relations.[74]

The Quran legitimised husband's pre-Islamic right to divorce his wife, without assigning any cause, which undermined the position of women.[75] The Prophet was, however, liberal in conceding divorces to the ladies too, at their initiation. He allowed divorce even on grounds of mental incompatibility. The ugly Sabit-bin-Qais was repulsive to his wife, the beautiful Jamila. She went to the Prophet and said, 'I am not annoyed with my husband nor do I see anything objectionable in his conduct but I don't love him'. She was granted a divorce.[76] Nevertheless, the Prophet did not favour it and emphatically stated that of the many things that God made permissible for men, the most displeasing to him was divorce.[77] But considering conjugal differences, it was considered better to wreck the unity of the family than to wreck the future happiness of the couple. Under strained conditions, it was most relieving for the wife to get a separation from the husband. The Prophet, therefore, made a new departure by giving wife the power to seek divorce on reasonable grounds, say, impotence of the husband, cruelty perpetrated by him on the wife or his inability to pay her *mahr* amount or to provide for her maintenance. For all this, she had to forgo her dower unless she showed solid grounds for demanding separation.[78]

A man could break the marriage ties by pronouncing *talaq* (divorce) thrice. But the process of this pronouncement was made complicated, spreading it over a period of roughly three months (once every month), known as period of *iddat* or waiting.[79] *Iddat* is an innovation made by Islam. In the *Jahiliya* (age of darkness), the divorced woman could remarry immediately after divorce even if she was pregnant and such a child belonged to the new husband.[80] This served the dual purpose of allowing tempers to cool down and for pregnancy to be established. If, during this period, intercourse took place even once, the divorce was annulled. In the case of pregnancy, this period of waiting extended till the birth of the child or termination of pregnancy.[81] But if the husband decided to repeat *talaq* for the third time too, then he was ordained to free the woman with kindness and retain her 'not to their hurt'.[82] Under such circumstances, the maintenance of a wife during the period of waiting was the duty of the husband.[83] Besides, since mothers were required to suckle their children for more than two years, the duty of feeding and clothing a nursing mother rested upon the father of the child. For nursing his child, he was required to provide for the maintenance of his divorced wife too.[84] The Prophet went to the extent of saying that even if the marriage had not been consummated nor a *mahr* fixed, the husband should 'provide for them, the rich according to his means, and the straitened according to his means, a fair provision'. For those whose marriages were not consummated but where a portion was fixed, he directed to pay 'half of that which ye appointed, unless they (the women) agree to forgo it, or he agreeth to forgo it in whose hand is the marriage tie'.[85] Thus, the Muslim law made divorce a financial burden on the husband, requiring him to maintain his wife in a prescribed manner at least for a limited period.

To discourage indiscriminate divorces, it was provided that once a man divorced a woman, he could not take her back lawfully until she married another man, had her second marriage consummated and then was divorced by her second husband. Remarriage in this case could take place after she had three 'courses' following her second divorce from her second husband.[86] The Prophet also laid down that for a widow, the period of *iddat* was four months and ten days and in case of a pregnancy, till the birth of the child. After that, like a divorced woman, she was free to do anything she liked, including getting authority to remarry.[87] Towards the end of his life, Mohammad made a further change. He forbade the exercise of the power of divorce by men without the intervention of arbiters or a judge.[88]

Economic rights conferred on women raised their status. Meeting their necessities was the responsibility of father before marriage and of husband after marriage. However wealthy the wife might be, the husband was in no case absolved of this responsibility. Mohammad also called upon dying husbands to leave behind some wealth for their widows so that they could support themselves even if they did not get remarried.[89]

The Quran granted women very extensive rights of inheritance. After the battle of Uhad, in which one Aws Ibn Samit had fallen, his widow complained to Mohammad that two cousins of her husband claimed his estate and that if they were permitted to have it, then she and her three young daughters would be left destitute. Thereupon, the Prophet received the revelation:

> 4:7: Unto the men (of a family) belongeth of a share of that which parents and near kindred leave, and unto the women a share of that which parents and near kindred leave, whether it be little or much—a legal share.[90]

Further instructions were given in the same chapter for disposal of the property of a man dying intestate:

> 4:11: *Allah* chargeth you concerning (the provision for) your children: to the male the equivalent of the portion of two females, and if there be women more than two, then theirs is two thirds of the inheritance, and if there be one (only) then the half. And to his parents a sixth of the inheritance if he have a son; and if he have no son and his parents are his heirs, then, to his mother appertaineth the third; and if he have brethren, then to his mother appertaineth the sixth, after any legacy he may have bequeathed, or debt (hath been paid).[91]

Surahs 4: 12 and 4:176 also referred to this aspect. After payment of bequests and debts, the son inherited half of the total property and the rest was divided among other relatives. If there were two or more daughters, two-thirds of the property was to be divided equally between them. If only parents survived the deceased, the father would inherit two-thirds of the property and the mother one-third. If, however, there were living children, each of the parents would inherit one-sixth of the property and the remainder would go to the children. If there were no surviving children but only brothers, sisters and parents, then the mother received one-sixth instead of one-third. The wife got one-eighth of her husband's property, if there were children and one-fourth, if there were none. Regarding succession of wife's property, the husband was entitled to a half of what his wife left behind if she had no child, otherwise he got only one-fourth. If either of the husband or the wife left behind neither parents nor children but distant sister or a brother (from mother's side), then each of them shared one-sixth and if they were more than two, then all of them shared one-third.[92] When there were no issue nor parents, then a single sister (of a male deceased) or brother (of a female deceased) was entitled to one-half, two or more sisters to two-thirds and if brother also existed, then they inherited the whole property, the male having double the share of the female.[93] The privilege of making testamentary bequests was also provided to women along with men, although it was limited only to one-third of the total heritage.[94]

From all these Quranic injunctions, many fundamental principles regarding inheritance have been drawn. Thus, the husband or wife was made an heir. Females and cognates were made competent to inherit. Parents and ascendants were given the right to inherit even when male descendants existed. As a general rule, female, might be wife or daughter, was given one half of the share of a male. In other words, wife got half of the share of husband and daughter, half of that of the son. No distinction was made between movable and immovable property. The right of will up to a limited level was given to women also. There was no concept of the birth right, the right of inheritance arose only on the death of a certain person. There was no community of property between husband and wife. The husband and wife retained full possession and control of their respective individual belongings. Nobody—father, husband or any other relative—could interfere in a woman's financial matters. If she invested her money in business or earned with her own hand, she was the sole owner of the fruit of her labour. Similarly, each woman was absolute master of her share of inheritance.[95]

The fact that women were entitled to only half of what their menfolk received was taken as an example of low status of women in Muslim society. Nonetheless, this distribution was not considered inequitable by some of the writers. They argued that women had the right to be maintained throughout their life while a man always had the obligation to support her along with other dependents. Besides, since it was almost a matter of religious obligation for every woman to marry, she received inheritance from many sources. She would not only have half as much property as her brother, but would also inherit from her husband, offspring and other near relatives besides having her own self-acquired property. Thus, she would enjoy a much higher financial standing than her brother. She also had the right to enjoy in her husband's property, whereas a husband had no legal power to touch his wife's money or property. If she let him use any part of it, it was only at her instance. In view of all this, the economic position of a woman had become so secure economically in Islam that more often than not, she was better off than her husband.[96]

In the religious domain, the Quran propounded male–female equality in matters such as origin of humanity, religious obligations and rewards and punishments. There is nothing in the Quran to show that the first woman created by God was a creature of lesser worth. Instead, the first human couple was made from a single soul to complement each other. It was envisaged that the noblest creature would be the one who, irrespective of sex, conducted himself the best.[97] Being born equal, it implied equal treatment, wherever possible, with regard to reward and punishment. It was observed that God could observe even the smallest good or evil deed done by male or female and the value of every person was based on his/her own actions.[98] All persons, irrespective of sex, doing good works would be rewarded and those doing evil works would not be acquitted.[99]

In the realm of worship, the obligations of Muslim men and women were identical. There were five 'pillars' of Islam. The first three were made obligatory for Muslims, rich and poor, and male and female. These were: confession of faith, the five compulsory prayers performed daily and fasting (*roza*) in the month of Ramzan. The remaining two 'pillars' were made compulsory only for the rich: the hajj (pilgrimage to Mecca) and *zakat* (giving of alms). Since the Quran recognised women's independent rights over property, they were expected to pay alms on their own behalf. Regarding hajj, a woman could not go there alone but if she had resources, she could arrange to be accompanied by a male relative. However, she should not mix with men, as far as possible, while moving around the Kaba. Maududi has narrated many 'traditions' which revealed that during Prophet's time, women used to go to Kaba at early hours of the day when it was still dark. Also, when women moved around the Kaba along with men, they did not mix with the latter.[100] With regard to prayers, the Quran did not forbid women from praying in mosques. There are many 'traditions' that bring out this fact. According to an early 'tradition', Mohammad himself was not averse to allowing women to pray in his company. He declared that they could go to the mosques regularly if their husbands permitted. This is corroborated by another 'tradition' in which the Prophet was depicted disapproving any hurdle placed in the way of women who wished to pray in the mosque.[101] However, according to these 'traditions', many conditions were laid down that needed to be observed by women. First, the women were required to go to mosques during 'night prayers' and 'dawn prayers'. According to Ibn Umar, the Prophet said, 'Let the women come to the mosque at night' (*Al-Tirmizi; Al-Bukhari*). Second, women were to avoid adornment and perfuming themselves while coming to mosques. Otherwise, the Prophet was reported to have declared that their prayers would not be rewarded by Allah (Muaata, Muslim and Ibn Majah). Third, they should stand separately behind the rows of men, the place considered best for women by the Prophet (*Al-Tirmizi, Al-Bukhari* and Nasai). Hazrat Umar even provided separate doors for women in the mosques (Abu Daud). Fourth, they should not raise their voice during prayers. Even if Imam was to be told about an error, while the men were to say '*Subhan Allah*', the women could only tap their hands (Al Bukhari and Abu Daud). Fifth, though the Prophet himself used to take his daughters and wives to the Id congregations, yet the Id and Friday prayers in mosques were made optional for women (Al Tirmizi, Ibn Majah and Abu Daud).[102] All these restrictions show that men were given preferential treatment. Even amid the serene atmosphere of a mosque, a woman was not regarded as a devotee but only as a woman. Some authorities even go still further. Quoting Mohammad, 'Best Mosque for women is their own houses', they opine that women were not allowed to go out of their houses even for prayers, much less for anything else.[103]

In Mohammad's days, women participated openly in congregations. His own wife Khadija played a decisive role in early Islam. It was she, who stood at the fountain of this 'Faith', supported her husband, kept alive his enthusiasm, consoled him in defeat and rejoiced with him in success.[104] Fatima, the daughter of Mohammad, was another protagonist. She lectured openly to the mixed gatherings of both sexes, often in the courtyard of her house and some times in the public mosque.[105] Ayisha, another wife of Mohammad, played an important role in the propagation of his religion. It is said that two-thirds of the 'Faith' was narrated by her and it was also incorporated in the form of hadith.[106] Thus, theoretically, within the sphere of religion, equal status was granted to men and women in Islam.

The Quranic position on purdah (veiling of women) is ambiguous. Did Mohammad advocate purdah at all, as we take it today, and if so, was the veiling of women meant only for the female relatives of the Prophet or it was an essential attire for all pious Muslim women? Relevant *ayat*s are:

24:27: O ye who believe! Enter not houses other than your own without first announcing your presence and invoking peace upon the folk thereof. That is better for you, that yet may be heedful.

24:28: And if ye find no one therein, still enter not until permission hath been given. And if it be said unto You: Go away again, then go away for it is purer for you.

24:30: Tell the believing men to lower their gaze and be modest. That is purer for them.

24:31: And tell the believing women to lower their gaze and be modest, and to display of their adornment only that which is apparent, and to draw their veils over their bosoms, and not to reveal their adornment save to their own husbands or fathers or husbands' fathers or their sons, or their husbands' sons, or their brothers or their brothers' sons or sisters' sons, or their women, or their slaves, or male attendants who lack vigour or children who know naught of women's nakedness. And let them not stamp their feet so as to reveal what they hide of their adornment.

24:60: As for women past child-bearing, who have no hope of marriage, it is no sin for them if they discard their (outer) clothing in such a way as not to show adornment. But to refrain is better for them.

33:53: O, ye who believe! Enter not the dwelling of the Prophet for a meal without waiting for the proper time, unless permission be granted you. But if ye are invited ... when your meal is ended, then disperse. Linger not for conversation.... And when ye ask of them (the wives of the Prophet) anything, ask it of them from behind a curtain. That is purer for your hearts and for their hearts.

33:55: It is no sin for them (thy wives) (to converse freely) with their fathers, or their sons, or their brothers, or their brothers' sons, or the sons of their sisters or of their own women, or their slaves.

33:59: O Prophet! tell thy wives and thy daughters and the women of the believers to draw their cloaks close round them (when they go abroad). That will be better, so that they may be recognised and not annoyed.[107]

These *ayat*s indicated that a woman must not exhibit her adornments, except those that were apparent, to anybody other than her near relatives who were identified and described therein. Men and women should look downwards while speaking with members of other sex. Both men and women should be modest in their behaviour. The women were to cover their bosoms. The list of men, a married woman could converse with, was given. All of them were incorporated within prohibited degree, as per the Quran, for purpose of marriage except the eunuchs and children too young to be conscious of difference of sex. No man other than a near relative was entitled to step into a house, either when there was no response to call or when he was asked to go away. Whenever a woman was to go out of the house, she was to cover herself with a cloak so that she would be recognised as a respectable woman and not a lewd one, and therefore nobody would think of molesting her. But it was not necessary for a middle-aged woman to cover herself, since her youth and charm were on the decline, provided she did not have the desire of showing her adornment. Besides, regarding himself, the Prophet requested his followers not to make familiar use of his house and not to enter it except by his permission. If they had any request to make to his wives, they were to ask it from behind a veil.

After going through these *ayat*s and analysing them, Maulana Abul Ala Maududi opined that purdah was established by the Prophet in his own days as an Islamic institution, even though the word *naqab* (veil) is not mentioned in the Quran and that the Prophet ordained both sexes to hide the parts of the body called *satr*, that is, that part of the body which is to be kept covered. For men, it is the part of the body between the pit of the stomach and the knee. For women, it is the whole body except the face and hand.[108] However, in implementation, it was enjoined on women to hide their faces from the other people through a veil, which was made a regular part of their dress outside the house, to obviate sexual anarchy and emotional dispersion in the society. However, uncovering of face under genuine needs, say, visiting a doctor, appearing before *qazi* (the theologians of Islam) for witness or in the case of a fire or war, was permitted. The Prophet had not given the woman an absolute command in respect of covering the face as in respect of covering the *satr* and hiding the decorations, because such covering did not restrain her from attending to the needs of life. It seems that veiling and segregation of women developed out of the Quranic precepts, although their subsequent forms and rigidity were not in consonance with the original intent.

The other important institution resulting from the seclusion of women is the harem. The Arabic word 'harem' simply means the 'women's quarters'. It denoted the apartments in the house or the palace reserved for the female members and children of the family.[109] The *zanana* or harem was unknown during Mohammad's time. The houses or dwellings of the early Muslims were not divided into male and female units within a kinship cluster of families. Such an idea was totally inconceivable and impracticable in the tents of the nomadic desert dwellers. Their houses consisted of a room or two around a common space, open or roofed, the latter being used by the clan for congregations and deciding important matters. It is considered that the early Muslim institutions like *shura* came into being out of such social background only.[110] But the Prophet's sayings regarding veiling contained within them the germs of future genesis of harem as an institution.[111]

Mohammad found slavery as an essential element of society of his times. He struck at the very root of it by dispensing with the practice of keeping prisoners of war. According to his command, when the war ceased and peace was established, all war prisoners would have to be set free.[112] A slave was required to provide for the *mahr* on his marriage, like a free man, which he must earn by his own labour. Such a *mahr* would become the property of the wife's owner if she was a slave. The Quran gave permission to the free Muslim man to marry his own slave girl, if she was of his own faith, with the permission of her folks. He should also give her *mahr* in kindness. The Muslim authorities, however, opined that in such a case, the man had to first emancipate her, before seeking her 'free consent' that was a prerequisite for marriage.[113] In fact, by making marriage compulsory for slave girls, as was for free women, Mohammad checked two pre-Islamic evil practices, namely sexual misuse of slave girls by masters and forced prostitution for monetary gains. The reflection of this and also of the abolition of prostitution appeared in the very Quranic *ayat*s, which read as follows:

24:32: And marry such of you as are solitary and pious of your slaves and maid-servants.

24:33: Force not your slave girls to whoredom that ye may seek enjoyment of life of the world, if they would preserve their chastity.[114]

The interpretation of this *ayat* is a subject of controversy as to whether in Islam, prostitution was abolished or not. The controversy is created by the qualification attached with the word 'if' appearing in *ayat* 24:33. According to Levy, it indicated that in Arabia, Prostitution was so deeply rooted that it was difficult to eradicate it outrightly. However, Muhammad Ali, another authority, considered such conclusion totally a 'misinterpretation of the Quranic word'. As per him, if this view is accepted, then it would mean that if the women did not have intention to keep chaste, they would be compelled to prostitution which is self-contradictory. He, therefore, interpreted the *ayat* to mean that since 'it is the very nature of woman, whether free or slave, that she would remain chaste, slave girls who are under the control of their masters, should not be compelled to prostitution by not allowing them to marry'.[115] Nonetheless, the plain reading of this along with *ayat* 24:32 makes it ample clear that by giving the injunction for slave girls to get married, the Prophet indicated that he was against prostitution.

Connected with it was the question of concubinage—a regular connection with a female who did not possess the legal status of a wife. Quranic expressions in some *ayat*s indicate its existence.[116] But these expressions were early Mecca revelations and were superseded by the reforms introduced at Madina, when the clear injunction was given that all slaves should be married. With this, the practice of concubinage died its own death. Later on, the Prophet himself made concubinage unlawful for men:

> 5:5: And so are the virtuous women of the believers and the virtuous women of those who received the Scripture before you (lawful for you) when ye give them their marriage portions and live with them in honour, not in fornication, not taking them as secret concubines.[117]

It was provided that if a master took his own slave for a concubine by virtue of his right of ownership and she begot children from him, she was then termed as *Umm Walad* and her children by him were free, although her children, if any, from any other man continued to be slaves and property of her master. This was an improvement upon the norm prevalent before Islam wherein the usage followed was that 'the child followed the womb'. It was the sweet will of the master to recognise such children as his own or not. If he accepted them, then they were free. Otherwise, they too continued to be his slaves.[118] It was also provided that he could not sell, pledge or give *Umm Walad* away as a gift, although he could demand service from her and could give her in marriage to another man, even against her will. She was freed from him along with her children on his death. However, if one wished to marry his slave himself, he had to first free her and then had to seek her consent for such marriage, as she was now a free woman, and also had to give dower to her.[119]

The Quran and the hadith made it a commendable act for masters to free slaves as a penalty for certain misdeeds done by themselves or as a fulfilment of the desire of slaves to be free, if they were worthy of it.[120] The slave who became possession of one with whom he was related, either through ascendant or descendant, was free. For example, if a father who was a free man got his slave son by a master's bequest, then the son was free. A slave could also be freed by the promise of the master, verbal or in writing, to free him/her after his death. Such slaves were classified as *mudabbar*.[121]

With all these rights to woman, the Prophet still placed man at a higher pedestal and maintained man's supremacy over woman. He propounded that basically a man was made superior to a woman by Allah.[122] *Ayat* 4:34 propounds that man was made provider of the family, with responsibility to earn a living for the family and arranging for it the necessities of life. Hence, a man was superior to a woman; the *ayat* reads as follows:

> 4:34: Men are in charge of women, because Allah made the one of them to excel the other, and because they spend of their property (for the support of women)....

In interpreting this passage, commentator Baydawi of the 13th century, whose word is held valid by Sunnites to the present day, enumerated different ways wherein men were considered superior to women. Men were superior in mental ability, good counsel, in their power for performance of duties and for carrying out divine commands. Hence, prophecy, religious leadership, saintship, pilgrimage rites, the giving of evidence in law courts, the duties of the Holy war, worship in mosque on Friday, the privilege of electing chiefs, a bigger share in inheritance and an upper hand in divorce had been confided to men.[123] He was given authority to admonish and punish his wife. He was also given the unilateral power to divorce while a woman was allowed this only in exceptional circumstances and that too after sacrificing her *mahr* rights. The property rights of a woman were half of those of a man. In the matter of marriage, a man was allowed polygamy, while the woman had to follow monogamy. Besides, a man could marry a non-Muslim (*Kitabia*) while a woman could not do so.[124] A wife was to obey her husband implicitly.[125] As testimony before a *qazi*, the evidence of two women was taken as equal to that of a man. The supremacy was also expressed clearly in the description of paradise. In the material that heaven prepared for the men of Muslim faith, even the poorest man was rewarded with 72 beautiful brides, termed as *hurris*. Besides possessing these heavenly spouses, a man might renew his marriage with the wives who had preceded him into elysium (in Greek mythology, place of ideal happiness). To Muslim women, paradise offered no such allurements. She would dwell there, as she dwelt on earth, one of many wives.[126]

The Quran gave a special treatment to the Prophet and his family. Against allowing maximum four wives to a Muslim man, in general, he himself married ten more women after Khadija, his first wife, and also sought the Quranic sanction for the same.[127] He repudiated a long-established custom of regarding an adopted son as equal to a real son in all respects, when he married Zeyd, the divorced wife of his own adopted son.[128] He ordained that nobody should marry his widows, although he wanted his followers to marry widows and protect orphans.[129] Different reasons have been given by the authorities for more than four wives of the Prophet. As per E.W. Lane, this might be because of Prophet's desire to have a son, which also gets reflected from *ayat* 33: 40 of the Quran. According to W. Sheowring and C.W. Thies, this might be because of the magnanimity of the Prophet to protect the widows of his persecuted followers. Ameer Ali, besides giving both these reasons, further wrote that by marriage alliance, Prophet united the warring tribes and brought some degree of harmony within them.[130]

Expansion of Islam and New Equations

Mohammad took to arms and brought the whole of Arabia under his sway before his death in 632 A.D. After him, Islam embarked on an era of change. The conquests in battles transformed a small religious community into a mighty political empire. People of different races came within the fold of Islam; a majority of them were Arabs, Persians, Turks, Mongols, Hebrews, Romans, Egyptians and Afghans. Along with them, they brought their respective beliefs and customs as well.

Persian women had a very low social status. The prevalent Persian saying like 'women and dragons are dangerous creatures, fit only to be destroyed'[131] is suggestive of their attitude towards women. They had degraded moral values. There was no recognised law of marriage and even if there was any, it was mostly ignored. In the absence of any fixed rule in the Zend Avesta with regard to the number of wives a man could possess, the Persians practised polygamy besides keeping a number of concubines.[132] Adultery was common and it was not considered a crime that would attract penalty. Similarly, term marriages or temporary unions, like *muta* marriage, were also prevalent.[133] Seclusion of women was in vogue. They were guarded very closely in their harems. Even in the inscriptions and sculptures of ancient Persia, reference to a woman was avoided.[134] The Persians were notorious for sodomy.[135] The only positive attitude, however, was towards the mothers and grandmothers who were greatly respected.[136]

The Turks,[137] in general, gave their women a fair measure of freedom. Marriage in ancient Turkey was a matter of negotiation and arrangement and not of capture, as was among the Arabs and some Eastern tribes. But they too were polygamous and like all the martial races of the ancient times, they sought pleasure in warfare, extension of territory, capture of women, slaves and spoils. The respect for mother was observed by them also.[138]

The Society of the Mongols was based on patrilineal clans (*obok*). Different clans from a common ancestor were considered as kin. Intermarriages among such clans were not permitted. A group of kindred clans was known as *yasun*. Clans of different *yasun* mutually agreed for exogamous marriages. At times, exogamy was observed by forcefully taking a girl of other *yasun* as bride.[139] Polygamy was practised by those who could afford it and they also kept concubines.

For instance, Yesukai, father of Changez Khan, had two wives, Yulun Eke and Suchigil. Changez Khan himself had five wives besides five hundred 'accessory wives and servant-maids'.[140] But the first wife of a ruler was the chief wife. She enjoyed a special status. She alone had the right to sit on throne by the side of the ruler. Changez Khan's first wife, Bortei, enjoyed this privilege. Only her children had the right to inherit the ruler's worldly empire.[141] In matters of legitimacy, the children of a concubine had the same status as those of a legal wife.[142] When fathers died, the sons took over their widows except their own mother. Similarly, the living brothers took over the widows of the deceased brothers. But this rule was not followed always. Han-Sadeh, the widow of Taimur's son, Jahangir, was remarried to Miran Shah, her brother-in-law. But Changez Khan's mother, Yulun Eke, remarried Munlik, her husband's friend, an outsider, after Yesukai's death.[143] Adultery was punishable with death.[144] The women were not confined to houses and enjoyed quite a bit of freedom and authority. They lived the same outdoor life as their male counterparts. The highest duty of women was to work for the upliftment of their respective husbands. They were solely responsible for management of their households including family flocks, herds and possessions. This duty included works like milking cows and preparing milk products, cooking, preparing stores for winter, driving carts, setting up and dismantling tents, sewing clothes and footwears, upbringing and educating children. Another important duty was to keep their respective husbands' things always ready to enable them to march to the battlefield in no time at the call of the Khan.[145] The women were also expert riders and learnt the art of shooting with bow.[146] They accompanied their husbands in wars and worked as their auxiliaries. Changez Khan's mother and wives accompanied him in the battlefield.[147]

They played significant role in politics as advisers, regents or as participants in court machinations, supporting the cause of their respective wards. Changez Khan was frequently advised by his mother Yulun Eke and wife Bortei in many of his political moves. Turakina, widow of Ogatai, worked as regent from 1241 to 1246 A.D. till she succeeded in getting her son Kuyuk chosen as *Khakan* (a title to Khan, means-the Chief Khan. A Tartar (Mongol) ruler was called *Khakan*). From 1248 to 1251 A.D., Kuyuk's widow, Ogul Gaimish, worked as a regent. Suyurkuk Teni, widow of Tuli (youngest son of Changez Khan), showed great political acumen. She manoeuvred to snatch the

Khanate from family of Ogatai when her son Mongu was chosen the Khakan in 1251 A.D. and regent Ogul Gaimish was executed.[148] Being the martial race, however, the Mongols showed no compassion towards the ladies of their enemies. They not only inflicted insults but also did not spare them in the merciless killings that followed each of their victories, might be in Khwarizm, Balkh, Ghazni, Herat, Persia, Baghdad or any other place. It is reported that once Changez Khan was asked as to what, in his view, was the greatest happiness of life. His reply was, 'to vanquish your enemies, to chase them before you, to rob them of their wealth, to see those dear to them bathed in tears, to ride their horses, to clasp to your bosom their wives and daughters'. In another incident, Ogatai once intended the Uirats to marry their daughters to men of other tribes. But, to ward this off, Uirats immediately betrothed them. At this, Ogatai ordered all girls above 7 of that tribe, including those married during the year, to be collected. They numbered 4000. He chose best of them for himself, his officers and the brothels, the remaining were sent to his soldiers to be scrambled for in front of their fathers, husbands and brothers.[149]

The Hebrews had patriarchal society where the women were legally under the control of their husbands. They had no right of inheritance. They were debarred from commercial and political activities. They were required to cover their bodies fully and also to support veil. A Hebrew husband could divorce his wife for any reason while the wife did not have any right to seek divorce. However, except for some pressing reasons, such as adultery or sterility, the Hebrew community did not favour divorces. They disapproved adultery, especially on the part of married women, for which they prescribed death penalty. Sex relations on the part of the bachelors were also considered a sin. Virginity was a must for a 'bride-to-be'. Violation led to severe punishment including death penalty. Virtually for all sex offences, infringement by women was viewed more seriously than that committed by the men.[150]

The women among other Eastern nations like Assyrians, Athenians and Romans were equally degraded.[151] But in Egypt, a woman enjoyed a very respectable and high position. She moved freely without purdah. Marriage appeared to be a legal contract where all her rights were guarded. She had right to divorce. Monogamy was generally practiced except among the royalty. She was free to follow any career. All properties descended on the female line and she could manage them of her own as per her own wish.[152]

The social life of the Pathans of Afghanistan revolved round the family, the clan and the tribe. *Pukhtunwali* or *Pushtunwali*, that is, the code of Pathans guided their way of life. They were very proud people and were very sensitive with regard to their *Zan*, that is, women. Chastity and seclusion of women were rigidly observed, so much so that they avoided talking of women, whether of their own or of anyone else. The women were totally confined to their houses and were a part of the background only. They had no role to play in the daily life of the community. It was taken as a dishonour for a married Pathan woman to work, for whatever reason, for anyone else other than her husband. The Pukhto proverbs like 'For a woman either the house (*kor*) or the grave (*gor*)' and 'Husband is another name for God' summed up the secluded and dependent life of the Pathan women. The women were conceptualised in two types: *mor* or mother and *tor*, literally meaning 'black'. The *mor* or the mother held high respect in that society. On the contrary, where the chastity of a woman was compromised and the honour of her close agnatic kin—father, husband or brothers—was at stake, she was considered a *tor*. In such a case, both the actors, particularly the woman, were killed by the closest male kin as per the Pathan code. The tribal custom of 'money for the head' (*sar paisey*) or 'bride-price' suggests that the daughters were literally bought and sold. Another tribal custom shows that a boy's mother booked a girl at the time of her birth and it was considered to be a formal engagement. Backing out from this at a later date involved all revenge and *tor* consequences as if the girl were actually married.[153]

In the beginning, Arabs dominated the Islamic fold. Later on, the Persian influence transformed the character of Islam. Slowly, the cultural heritage of Persia percolated into every facet of the Muslim life. During the 11th century, the Persian influence was replaced by the Turkish ascendancy.

The need of the hour was to adapt the Islamic ordinance to new conditions that were not contemplated by the Prophet. The first effort in this regard was the collection of the 'traditions' of the Prophet practised during the time of four Caliphs with the intention to get solutions to most of the problems out of them. There were six popular books of 'traditions': (a) Abu Abdullah Mohammad bin Ismail Al Bukhari, a Persian who collected 600,000 'traditions', of which he rejected all but 7,276; (b) Muslim bin Hajjaj of Khorasan (204–260 A.H.) who collected 30,000 of them but kept only 4,000 'traditions'; (c) Abu Daud of Seistan (202–275 A.H.) had 4,800 'traditions' (legal 'traditions'); (c) *Kitabus Sunan* of Ibn-i-Majah (209–333 A.H.) had 4,000 'traditions' (legal 'traditions'); (e) *Jammy* by Abu Mussa Mohammad Trimidhi of Tirmidh (f) *Al-Mujtaba* by Abu Abdur-Rehman Nasai of Khorasan (214–303 A.H.) whose 'traditions' were about rituals. These 'traditions' were so important that throughout the reign of Seljukides and decline of Abbasids, particularly in India and Iran, they superseded even the Quran.[154] A woman once came to Abu Bakr claiming her share of inheritance from her deceased grandson. The Caliph pronounced the judgement that as per the Quran, she could not receive any share. Thereupon, Mughira, son of Shoba, got up and said, 'I have seen the Prophet granting one-sixth share to a grandmother'. This was recorded and accordingly the judgement was delivered.[155] The Shariat was interpreted and elaborated theoretically, by different schools of interpretations, keeping in mind the requirements of the people and the necessities of the time. There were four main schools, basing their interpretation on different principles, namely Abu Hanafi on *istehsan* (equity), Malik on *istislah* (consideration of public interest), Shafi on *qiyas* (analogy) and Hanbal on 'traditions'. Besides these, there were many other schools but they did not become popular.[156] The judgement delivered by *Muftis* (Juris Consults) were accepted as rules for *qazi*s for deciding similar cases in the future.[157] Two groups, Shia and Sunni, emerged within Muslim community with distinct approaches towards Islamic developments.[158]

The different schools explained the Quranic commands regarding women in their own way. For example, *muta* marriage was forbidden by all schools except the Akhbari Shias.[159] Similarly, the minimum dower fixed by different schools did not tally with one another. While Shafiites and Shiites had no fixed minimum, the Malikis fixed it at three *dirhams* and the Hanafis at ten *dirhams*.[160] The minimum dower fixed by the law could hardly be deemed to be an adequate provision for the wife. Hence, the check that dower was supposed to have on reckless divorces by husbands lost its meaning. Regarding slave girls, in spite of the Quranic acceptance of the marriage of a free man with a female slave, the Hanafi code forbade a free man from marrying his own or his son's female slave and a (free) woman from marrying her male slave.[161] When a wife swore chastity against the charge of adultery levied by her husband, the marriage was still considered annulled as per Shafiites, although, as per Hanafis, this was a case that would be decided by a judge.[162] There was a wide difference between Sunnite and Shiite laws of inheritance also. While the Sunnite law of inheritance kept intact the ancient tribal structure and made agnates (related through males) the most important heirs, the Shiite law placed cognates (related through females) on an equal footing. The Shiites, thus, raised the position of the daughter's children from class III to class I. For example, in the case of a daughter's son, father's mother and full brother, as per Hanafi law, the daughter's son being a uterine heir is excluded; father's mother, as a Quranic heir takes one-sixth and the full brother, as agnatic heir, takes five-sixth. But in Shiite law, the daughter's son, being of class I, succeeds in preference to the other two, who belong to class II.[163] Imam Husain was son of Prophet's daughter. Therefore, the Shiite law, apparently, paid special attention to this relationship and made the interpretation such that all females, howsoever remotely related, inherited on the analogy of inheritance by a daughter or a sister. This right to women was, probably, the most important legal reform introduced by Islam.

Notwithstanding the incorporation of non-Arab practices and changing interpretations of different schools affecting the position of women adversely, there were examples of great women in every walk of life from the early days of Islam. The roles played by Khadija and Fatima are well known. Similarly, Aiysha (granddaughter of Caliph Abu Bakr and niece of the Prophet's wife Ayisha) never wore the veil, even though her husband insisted on it.[164] There was no check on remarriages of women. Aiysha (niece of Ayisha) got married thrice, each time getting a big amount of dower. Atiqa, belonging to one of the noblest families of Mecca, also married three times. Sakina, the granddaughter of Fatima, married several times and made complete freedom of action a condition precedent to her marriages.[165] She was the leader in fashions and set the tone for cultured society of her age. Her house was the meeting place for poets, scholars, jurists and other distinguished people of both sexes. Her overflowing generosity towards learning and her appreciation of scholarly pursuits left deep impact on the intellectual development of the Islamic people.[166] Women enjoyed freedom of choice of husband. There is a case, on record, of a widow of the Caliph (Saffah) who married a private gentleman of a distinguished lineage, though poor.[167] The freedom of divorce was also there. Umm Salma left her husband when she found that he had connections with a slave girl.[168]

The women had freedom of education. They flocked to the sermons of the Caliphs and other disciples. Umar is said to have appointed Quran reader, especially for ladies at public worship.[169] They studied theology and law and many of them educated their children without any outside help. Rabia-ur-Rai, one of the greatest jurists of early Islam, was educated by his mother.[170] The famous Sufi saint Rabia was so popular that she invited the jealousy of men who argued that since a woman on the path of God becomes a man, she can't any more be called a woman.[171] Shuhda, another lady, was known for her profound knowledge of hadith.[172] The narration of the 'traditions' at the time of their compilation was mainly done by the ladies. Among the Prophet's widows, Hafsa, daughter of Umar, the second Caliph, narrated 60 pieces; Ayisha, 164 pieces (Bukhari and Muslim, while Raw gave credit to her for 2200 pieces); Zainab, several other pieces and Safiyya and Umm-Salma narrated 378 pieces, respectively.[173] Umm-ul-Khair Fatima and Umm Ibrahim Fatima Alyezdani taught theology and the 'traditions' to men as well as women. Shafi, one of the great interpreters of Muslim Jurisprudence, learnt the elements of Jurisprudence from a lady named Syeda Nafisa.[174]

In the field of public affairs, their influence was evident. During Umayyad's time, Umm-ul-Banin, the queen of Walid I, possessed great influence over her husband and frequently interfered in affairs of the state. During the early Abbasids, women wielded great influence on the state affairs. Umm-Salma, the queen of Abul Abbas Saffah, the first Abbasid Caliph, had such an influence over her husband that he decided nothing without her advice. Khaizuran, the consort of Mahdi, the third Abbasid Caliph, had so much influence that courtiers, powerful dignitaries, ministers, poets and scholars flocked to her. She was revered for her generosity towards the poor and the needy. Zubaida, the wife of Harun-al-Rashid, had much influence in administration and her tomb is venerated even to this day. Qatr-un-Nada, mother of Caliph Muqtadar, held the reins of government with perfection as the mother regent.[175]

In cultural sphere, many women were keenly interested. They remained engaged in poetry, singing, dancing, fashion and games for their own amusement. Princesses and ladies of rank gave musical programmes.[176] The famous singers of the time were Baze, a contemporary of Harun-al-Rashid, Neem and Ubayadah-at-tamburia, of the times of Mamun besides Mutasim, Olayya, Zatul, Khal, Rayya, Soda and Sahiqa, who were adept musicians of the Abbasid dynasty.[177] Ladies influenced the world of fashion too. Zubaida, as referred to earlier, introduced jewelled girdles, jewelled shoes and sedan chair. Olayya, the half-sister of Harun-al-Rashid, introduced head dress.[178] Women of the middle class also used a head ornament, a kind of fillet set in jewels. They also used anklets and bracelets. Different types of cosmetics were also in use.[179] Women played different kinds of games, and thus kept them amused.[180]

The women of this period possessed military skill as well. For instance, Zainab, the granddaughter of Hazrat Ali and sister of Husain, showed her skill while guarding her nephew from the Umayyads after the butchery at Karbala.[181] During battles, these women helped in various ways. At times, they fought actively in battles. During Mansur's time, two of his lady cousins fought in the Byzantine war clad in mail. Safaih, Umm-Salet and Umm-Saleem were some of the ladies who distinguished in this field.[182] Apparently, there existed some sort of military training for women. They were taught not only the use of arms but also horse riding.[183]

Turkhan Khatun, the wife of Saad II, *Atabeg* of Shiraz, was known for her accomplishments. After the death of her husband in 1260 A.D., she ruled the principality as mother regent for her infant son with wisdom and tact. She patronised art and learning and made her court 'one of the most polished and cultured in that unhappy age when the gloom of night had settled on Western Asia'. Another princess of the *Atabeg* family was Aiysha Khatun. She ruled Shiraz soon after Turkhan Khatun. She encouraged poets and scholars. These two ladies, Turkhan and Aiysha, did a lot for beautifying and embellishing Shiraz.[184] Ibn Khallikan's *Biographical Encyclopedia* is full of instances of women belonging to the lower ranks of society, reading, reciting and improvising.

The jurists expressly acknowledged the woman's right to bind her husband before marriage and to not take a second wife during her lifetime. Also, the right of women to pray in the mosques continued to be recognised till the 3rd century A.H. Afterwards, it fell into disuse. Two reasons have been given for the same. Firstly, it was disapproved by the *qazi* as Von Kremer held and secondly, because of the degenerating social values, father and husband apprehended that their womenfolk might not, by some lapse of conduct, disgrace them.[185]

Notwithstanding the exalted position, with passing of time, the condition of Muslim women also suffered a successive degradation. This downfall became quite glaring by the 13th century. There were many factors responsible for this. The foremost among them was the negative role of the *qazis*. Umar is usually credited with having been the first to appoint them to assist him in discharging duty of settling disputes; however, with their interpretation of law, they did great disservice to women. Although they had well-stocked harems, yet, outside their little paradise, they showed contempt for the worldly things and the 'levity of the fair sex'. They interpreted many of the Quranic commandments related to women against the interests of the women and in favour of men. One such example is the women's right to pray in mosques, as narrated above. They also twisted the meaning of the hadith deliberately so as to depict women as downtrodden and mean and hence, for the most part, fit only for hell. For instance, Baydawi, while commenting on surah 16:11 of the Quran, adduced a hadith and thereby explained that while innumerable men had attained religious perfection with the resultant reward of paradise, only four women have ever done so.[186]

The gradual decline of the old Arab aristocracy also dealt a serious blow to the dignity of Muslim women. The mixed race that replaced them lacked both purity of descent and the refinement of feelings. There is not a single instance in the beginning of the Caliphate of a son of a concubine succeeding to the Caliphate. But, mother's descent was totally ignored subsequently. Consequently, the rule of the mistresses and courtesans set in, over-shadowing the legitimate wives.[187] The slave trade also led to the degradation of the position of women. After the shifting of the Caliph's seat to Baghdad, numerous girls were brought to Baghdad to be sold as slaves. It became a profitable business to purchase young women, to train them in music and dance and then to sell them at fabulous prices to rich merchants. The house of such merchants became dens of sensual pleasures.[188] Simultaneously, the Persian vice of sodomy gradually expanded to an extent that by the time of Caliph Harun-al-Rashid, it no longer was taken as a vice at all. It is informed that a boy, who became the centre of jealousy between his sons, had to be shut up in the seraglio, fearing his abduction.[189]

The emergence and expansion of the institutions of polygamy, purdah and harem also led to the degeneration of the status of Muslim women. The Arabs conquered large territories. In order to control these multitude of vanquished races, they required large military establishments. For this, they needed to enlarge their population rapidly. Consequently, they propounded polygamy, resulting in marriages even with non-Arab women. This not only destroyed the purity of the race but also resulted into an effeminate race of bastards and rule of mistresses and concubines.[190] With such moral laxity all around, the Muslim men of the age insisted on the fidelity of their women and sought to achieve that by force, by putting restrictions on them. This resulted into the gradual development of purdah and the harem.

Authorities have different views about the origin of purdah. To some (S.M. Ahmad), purdah owes its origin to Al-Hakim, the Fatimid Caliph of Egypt, who made the wearing of veil compulsory for the women in his kingdom. Since he swayed spiritual power in Persia too, it became a permanent injunction throughout the Muslim world including India. Qurratulain Hyder, on the contrary, considered its origin during the reign of Umayyad Caliph Walid II (743–744 A.D.) when the Arab ruling class was thoroughly corrupted and courtesans and local and foreign dancing girls flocked to Baghdad and the respectable citizens started secluding their women from public gaze. According to her, it was the difference between the professional entertainer and the responsible housewife that laid the foundation of the system of purdah. As per Mazhar-ul-Haq Khan, purdah as a system of female segregation from social life first appeared among the ruling aristocratic families of later Umayyads. The genesis of the system lay in the desire of the aristocracy to conceal their innumerable wives and concubines from public eyes. Gradually, it diffused downwards among the middle, rural and lower classes in the Abbasid society. The policies of the Abbasid Caliphs of 9th and 10th centuries led to the development of purdah into a regular social institution of the Muslim society. Still, another authority (Mikhail) opines that purdah took form in the 2nd century of the Islamic era, first among the rich and the powerful as a status symbol and then percolated among the less affluent through emulation. He links the development closely to the influence of Byzantine and Persian customs with which the Arabs came in contact in the new territories conquered by them.[191]

As for the origin of system of the harem, no precise date can be given. Khuda Bukhsh considered its origin sometimes between the end of the Umayyad rule and the Caliphate of Harun-al-Rashid. Reuben Levy seemed to be agreeing to this view, since as per him, the system was fully developed by the time of Caliph Harun. K.S. Lal also agrees to this. According to Qurratulain Hyder, it originated during the reign of Umayyad Caliph Walid II (743–744 A.D.). As per

Mazhar-ul-Haq Khan, the bifurcation into male and female quarters was not there in the palaces built by early Umayyads, as Qusayr Amra or Hammam-as-Sarakh were built by the Umayyad Caliph Walid I (705–715 A.D.) in the deserts of Syria and Jordon. These palaces had only an audience hall for the Caliph to hold court and two bed rooms adjacent to it. The first 'Zanana-like apartments' appeared, for the first time, in the palaces built by Umayyad Walid II (743–744 A.D.), namely Mshatta and Qasr-at-Tuba in Trans-Jordon. These palaces had the usual audience hall, but had four, instead of two, bayts or households for his harem. These bayts were, though, still located in the centre and not pushed to the rear, as in the latter-day harems. The change became more glaring during the Abbasid regime. Isa bin Musa, the nephew and heir apparent of as-Saffa, the founder of Abbasid dynasty, built the palace of Ukhaidir of Iraq in 778 A.D. during his governorship of that place. He further modified the 'four-bayts' design of the Umayyad palaces and pushed these bayts in more 'isolated and self-contained sets of vaulted chambers, each with its own courtyard'. Half a century later in 836 A.D., when Mutasim founded the new capital city, Samara, north of Baghdad, the medieval harem system fully came into being. It was, now, divided into several households, unlike the 'four-bayt' design, and was secluded from the male and the public portion of the palace. This division into two distinct parts became the standard pattern of the Muslim domestic architecture, both the houses of common people and of the royal palaces, ever since then till the present day.[192]

In this background, Al-Mutawakkil (847–861 A.D.), the last of the Abbasids, decreed the segregation of the sexes at feasts and public ceremonies. Finally, Abbasid Caliph Qadir-b'lllah (991–1030 A.D.) forbade women's entry to mosques, colleges or to appear in public without supporting a burqa. Yet, almost to the end of 12th century, women mixed with men with dignity and self-respect. It was by the end of the Abbasid Caliphate in the middle of the 13th century, when the political decadence of Caliphate was complete and the society had disintegrated under the attacks of the Tartars, that the segregation of women had become so complete that the propriety of public visibility of female hands or feet was hotly discussed by the ulemas.[193]

The foreign Muslim immigrants to India during the medieval period comprised of the Arabs, the Turks, the Afghans, the Mughals and the Persians.[194] They were further joined by a multitude of Indian Muslims who were the Hindu converts to Islam and formed the majority of Muslim population in India.[195] The different immigrant groups had their own distinct cultures and concepts about women, as already discussed above. They retained their racial and tribal identities and ethnic customs and traditions, and also imbibed the traditions of the other group, in due course, because of pressures, promiscuity and interactions. The Indian Muslims also did not change their social set-up and outlook with the change of their religion. Mandelslo's observations vouch for this when he wrote,

> All the Mahumetans (Muslims) of these parts (i.e. of Hindustan) may be said to profess the same Religion; but they have among them certain superstitions, and particular Manners of life, whereby they are distinguished into several sects, though it may be also alleged, that they are to be accounted rather so many Nations then (than) different sects.[196]

The position of Hindu women was not good during the time and the Hindu converts carried with them their general attitude towards women to the Muslim fold.[197] The immigrants tried to adjust the social and religious structure of Islam to Indian conditions. These new interactions on the Indian soil led to further adjustments and emergence of the Indianised Muslim culture, different from that of Turks and Persians. About this new evolved changed culture, Mandelslo, who had extensively travelled throughout the Muslim world, has aptly observed, 'we shall ... treat of the manner of life of the Mahumetans of the Indies, which is much different from that of the Turks and Persians'.[198]

Thus, Islam came to India in a changed form, after being influenced by the Persian, Turkish and other foreign ideologies. The general status of Mohammadan women was on the wane at that time. The ensuing assimilation of Hindu–Muslim cultures under Indian conditions did not promise much change for the better in the status of Muslim women in India.

Notes

1. John Davenport, *Mohammad and Teachings of Quran*, ed. Mohammad Amin (Lahore: Sh. S.M. Ashraf, 1944), 45–46; M.R.A. Baig, *The Muslim Dilemma in India* (New Delhi: Vikas Publishing House, 1974), 18; Shibani Roy, *Status of Muslim Women in Northern India* (Delhi: B.R. Publishing Corp., 1979), 3; Barbara E. Ward, ed., *Women in the New Asia* (Paris: UNESCO, 1963), 67–68.
2. Baig, *The Muslim Dilemma*, ix.

3. K.A. Nizami, ed., *Politics and Society During the Early Medieval Period*, vol. 1 (New Delhi: People's Publishing House, 1974), 35.

4. Syed Ameer Ali, *The Spirit of Islam* (London: MacMillan & Co., 1953), 183.

5. S. Khuda Bukhsh, *Studies: Indian and Islamic* (Delhi: Idarah-i-Adabiyat-i-Delli, 1978), 80–81 (on the authority of *Kitabul-Aghani*); Imtiaz Ali, ed. *Ameer Ali on Islam* (Delhi: Amar Prakashan, 1982), 51.

6. Ameer Ali, *The Spirit*, 253.

7. Khuda Bukhsh, *Studies: Indian and Islamic*, 79.

8. Mazhar-ul-Haq Khan, *Social Pathology of the Muslim Society* (Delhi: Amar Prakashan, 1978), 1–17.

9. *Quran*, trans., M. Pickthall, *The Meaning of the Glorious Quran*, vol. 16 (Delhi: Taj Company, 1986), 58–59.

10. W.R. Smith, *Kinship and Marriage in Early Arabia* (London: Cambridge University Press, 1885), 279; Reuben Levy, *The Social Structure of Islam* (London: Cambridge University Press, 1957), 91–92; Demombynes M. Gaudefroy, *Muslim Institutions*, trans. J.P. Macgregor (London: Allen & Unwin, 1950), 127–130.

11. Levy, *The Social Structure*, 102.

12. W.N. Gallichan, *Women Under Polygamy* (London: Holden & Hardingham, 1914), 212.

13. Tatiel E.T. Moganan, *The Arab Woman* (London, 1937), 36.

14. M.M. Siddiqi, *Women in Islam* (New Delhi: New Taj Office, 1991), 143; Gallichan, *Women Under Polygamy*, 209.

15. Levy, *The Social Structure*, 115.

16. Smith, *Kinship and Marriage*, 67–69; Levy, *The Social Structure*, 115; Gallichan, *Women Under Polygamy*, 209; Ameer Ali, *The Spirit*, 227.

17. K.M. Kapadia, *Marriage and Family in India* (London: Oxford University Press, 1959), 187–188.

18. Levy, *The Social Structure*, 118; Siddiqi, *Women in Islam*, 142–143.

19. A.A.A. Fyzee, *Outlines of Muhammadan Law* (London: Oxford University Press, 1964), 8.

20. Levy, *The Social Structure*, 91.

21. Ameer Ali, *The Spirit*, 222; S.M.H. Zaidi, *Position of Women Under Islam* (Calcutta: Book Tower, 1935), 151.

22. Ameer Ali, *The Spirit*, 243; Smith, *Kinship and Marriage*, 83.

23. Levy, *The Social Structure*, 121.

24. Smith, *Kinship and Marriage*, 92; Ameer Ali, *The Spirit*, 241.

25. Levy, *The Social Structure*, 124 (on the authority of historian Fakihi). See also E.W. Lane, *An Account of the Manners And Customs of The Modern Egyptians*, vth ed. (London: John Murray, 1860), Ch. VI, 'Domestic Life–continued (Women of the Higher and Middle Orders)', on marriage customs.

26. *Quran*, 33:33: And stay in your houses. Bedizen not yourselves with bedizenment of the Time of Ignorance.

27. Fyzee, *Outlines of Muhammadan Law*, 10; Maulana Muhammad Ali, *The Religion of Islam* (New Delhi: S. Chand & Co., n.d.), 640; also Levy, *The Social Structure*, 95–96.

28. Ameer Ali, *The Spirit*, 227–228.

29. T.P. Hughes, *Dictionary of Islam* (New Delhi: Rupa & Co., 1988), 677.

30. *Quran*, 6: 140; 6.151; 17: 31; 81: 8–9.
31. *Ibid.*, 98: 5; 9: 60.
32. S.A.A. Maududi, *Purdah and the Status of Woman in Islam*, trans. and ed. Al-Ash' Ari (Delhi: markazi Maktaba Islami, 1974), 159, Siddiqi, *Women in Islam*, 15–16.
33. *Quran*, 46: 15–17, 17: 23–24. Also see Syed Mahmud-un-nasir, *Islam, Its Concept and History* (Delhi: Kitab Bhavan, 1981), 395; A.M.A. Shushtery, *Outline of Islamic Culture* (Banglore: The Banglore Printing and Publishing Co., 1954), 529; S.M.N. Kidwai, *Women under Different Social and Religious Laws* (Delhi, 1976), 78.
34. *Quran*, 4: 22–23.
35. *Ibid.*, 4: 11–12.
36. Maududi, *Purdah and the Status*, 159.
37. *Quran*, 96: 1–5
38. Maududi, *Purdah and the Status*, 156.
39. Ameer Ali, *The Spirit*, 229.
40. *Quran*, 4: 1, 24: 32.
41. *Quran*, 49: 13, 30: 21.
42. Maulana Muhammad Ali, *A Manual of Hadith*, No. 7 (Lahore: Ahmadiyya Anjuman Ishaat Islam, 1944), 271.
43. Maulana Muhammad Ali, *A Manual*, No.11, 272–273.
44. *Quran*, 4: 19.
45. *Ibid.*, 24: 26.
46. Moganan, *The Arab Woman*, 38, note 2; Ameer Ali, *The Spirit*, 256.
47. *Quran*, 4: 4: And give unto the women, (whom ye marry)
    free gift of their marriage portions....
48. *Quran*, 4: 24; 4: 25.
49. *Ibid.*, 2: 229, 4: 19, 4: 21.
50. *Ibid.*, 4: 4.
51. *Quran*, 4: 3; A.J. Wensinck, Chapter on Marriage (for hadith), in *A Handbook of Early Muhammadan Tradition* (Leiden: E. J. Brill, 1971).
52. *Quran*, 4: 129: Ye will not be able to deal equally between
    (your) wives, however much ye wish (to do so).
53. Ameer Ali, *The Spirit*, 229–230; Elizabeth Cooper, *The Harim and the Purdah: Studies of Oriental Women* (Delhi: Bimla Publishing House, 1983), 28; Mazhar-ul-Haq Khan, *Social Pathology*, 27–28; Shushtery, *Islamic Culture*, 523–524; Hughes, *Dictionary of Islam*, 462.
54. *Quran*, 4: 6; Muhammad Ali, *The Religion*, 618–620. See also Levy, *The Social Structure*, 107–108. As per him, it was not the age but the physical fitness for matrimony which was the decisive factor.
55. V.R. Bevan and L. Jones, *Women in Islam: A Manual with Social Reference to Conditions in India* (Lucknow: The Lucknow Publishing House, 1941), 91; Ameer Ali, *The Spirit*, 234 (as per him, she was only seven at that time). Another authority says that she was six years of age at the time of *Nikah* (A Muslim marriage) but the actual departure to husband's house took place when she turned nine (Abdul Qadir Al-Badaoni, *Muntakhabu-t-Tawarikh*, trans. W.H. Lowe, vol. 2 (Delhi: Idarah-i-Adabiyat-i-Delli, 1973), 349).
56. *Quran*, 4: 19.
57. *Ibid.*, 2: 229, 231.

58. Anonymous, 'Marriage in Islam', *Mahjubah* 4, no. 7(1986): 31.
59. Maududi, *Purdah and the Status*, 159–160; see also Siddiqi, *Women in Islam*, 56–58.
60. *Quran*, 4: 34.
61. *Ibid.*, 5: 87.
62. *Ibid.*, 4: 34.
63. Maududi, *Purdah and the Status*, 149.
64. *Quran*, 2: 187; 33: 21, 7: 189.
65. *Ibid.*, 9: 71.
66. *Ibid.*, 4: 24.
67. *Ibid.*, 17: 32.
68. *Ibid.*, 24: 2.
69. *Ibid.*, 24: 3.
70. *Ibid.*, 4: 15.
71. Levy, *The Social Structure*, 120; Muhammad Ali, *The Religion*, 753. See *Quran*, 4: 25 (for half punishment to female slaves).
72. *Ibid.*, 24: 4–5; also Hughes, *Dictionary of Islam*, 476–477; Levy, *The Social Structure*, 119.
73. *Quran*, 24: 6–9.
74. *Ibid.*, 4: 22–23.
75. *Ibid.*, 2: 226, 228; also Robert Roberts, *The Social Laws of Quran* (New Delhi: Adam Publishers, 1978), 20–21; Kapadia, *Marriage and Family*, 191–192.
76. Jamila BrijBhushan, *Muslim Women in Purdah and Out of it* (New Delhi: Vikas Publishing House, 1980), 66.
77. Ameer Ali, *The Spirit*, 243; Hughes, *Dictionary of Islam*, 87.
78. Ameer Ali, *The Spirit*, 245; Levy, *The Social Structure*, 122–123; Indu Menon, *Status of Muslim Women in India* (New Delhi: Uppal Publishing House, 1981), 75.
79. *Quran*, 2: 228.
80. Levy, *The Social Structure*, 122, note 2. See also Ameer Ali, *The Spirit*, 246–247.
81. *Quran*, 65: 4, 2: 228.
82. *Ibid.*, 2: 231.
83. *Ibid.*, 65: 1.
84. *Ibid.*, 2: 233.
85. *Ibid.*, 2: 236, 237.
86. *Ibid.*, 2: 230.
87. *Ibid.*, 2: 232, 234.
88. *Ibid.*, 4: 35; also see Ameer Ali, *The Spirit*, 244–245; Kapadia, *Marriage and Family*, 190.
89. *Quran*, 2: 240.
90. *Ibid.*, 4: 7; Levy, *The Social Structure*, 96–97.
91. *Quran*, 4: 11.
92. *Ibid.*, 4: 12.
93. *Ibid.*, 4: 176. Also Muhammad Ali, *The Religion*, 708, see also 702–707.
94. *Quran*, 4: 12.
95. Fyzee, *Outlines of Muhammadan Law*, 381–384; F.B. Tyabji, *Muhammadan Law* (Bombay: N.M. Tripathi, 1940), 603, 822.
96. Maududi, *Purdah and the Status*, 154–155, note 1; BrijBhushan, *Muslim Women in Purda*, 84; Siddiqi, *Women in Islam*, 48–49.

97. *Quran*, 7: 189, 49: 13, 4: 1.
98. *Ibid.*, 33: 35, 3: 195.
99. *Ibid.*, 4: 124, 16: 97, 40: 40, 24: 2.
100. Maududi, *Purdah and the Status*, 211-212.
101. Muhammad Ali, *The Religion*, 390–391; Levy, *The Social Structure*, 131(on the authority of Al Bukhari [Author/compiler and details: *Sahih*, ed. M. Ludolf Krehl, Leiden, 1862–8. For first 'tradition' and Tabari [Abu Jafar Muhammad ibn Jarir al-Tabari, *Tafsir al-Tabari*, 30 parts, Cairo, A.H. 1320–1321], I, 2649 for second 'tradition' narrated).
102. Roy, *Status of Muslim Women*, 113. See also Maududi, *Purdah and the Status*, 210–212.
103. Bevan and Jones, *Women in Islam*, 250.
104. Imtiaz Ali, *Ameer Ali on Islam*, (Delhi: Amar Prakashan, 1982), 52.
105. Ameer Ali, *The Spirit*, 250; Alfred De Souza, ed., *Women in Contemporary India* (New Delhi: Manohar Book Service, 1975), 114.
106. Levy, *The Social Structure*, 132.
107. *Quran*, 24: 27, 28, 30, 31, 60; 33: 53, 55, 59.
108. Maududi, *Purdah and the Status*, 177, 184–203.
109. Cooper, *The Harim and the Purdah*, 25–27; Hughes, *Dictionary of Islam*, 163.
110. Mazhar-ul-Haq Khan, *Social Pathology*, 34–35.
111. Malladi Subbamma, *Islam and Women*, trans. M.V. Ramamurty (New Delhi: Sterling Publishers, 1988), 104–105.
112. *Quran*, 47: 4; Muhammad Ali, *The Religion*, 586.
113. *Quran*, 4: 25, 3. See also Levy, *The Social Structure*, 111–112 (for emancipation before marriage on the authority of Aghani).
114. *Ibid.*, 24: 32, 33.
115. Levy, *The Social Structure*, 118; Muhammad Ali, *The Religion*, 662, note 1.
116. *Quran*, 23: 5–6, 70: 29–30.
117. *Ibid.*, 5: 5; see also Ameer Ali, *The Spirit*, 247.
118. Levy, *The Social Structure*, 78–79, note 8. See also P.K. Hitti, *History of the Arabs* (New York: Macmillan & Co, 1956), 76. For definition of *Umm Walad*, see Hughes, *Dictionary of Islam*, 655.
119. Levy, *The Social Structure*, 80, 111–112 (on the authority of the Khalil b. Ishaq, E. Sachau and Aghani). See also D.R. Banaji, *Slavery in British India* (Bombay: Taraborevala Sons & Co., 1933), 228–229.
120. *Quran*, 4: 92, 5: 89, 24: 33.
121. Levy, *The Social Structure*, 80; Banaji, *Slavery in British India*, 228.
122. *Quran*, 2: 228.
123. *Ibid.*, 4: 34. See Levy, *The Social Structure*, 98–99, 132 (for Baydawi comments on the authority of Ibn Khaldun).
124. *Ibid.*, 5: 5, 60: 10.
125. *Ibid.*, 4: 34.
126. Gallichan, *Women Under Polygamy*, 44–45. Compare Z. Bhatty 'Status of Muslim Women and Social Change', in *Indian Women from Pardah to Modernity*, ed. B.R. Nanda (New Delhi: Vikas Publishing House, 1976), 102–104; Mohammad Yasin, *A Social History of Islamic India 1605–1748)* (Lucknow: The Upper India Publishing House, 1958, 120 for dwelling on inequalities. Contrarily, compare Mohammad Qutb, (*Islam: The*

Misunderstood Religion (Delhi: The Board of Islamic Publications, 1964), 183) and Ameer Ali, (*The Spirit*, 229) who considered that Islam gave equal status to men and women.

127. *Quran*, 33: 50.
128. *Quran*, 33: 4, 33: 37. Also see Levy, *The Social Structure*, 100–101; Baig, *The Muslim Dilemma*, 8.
129. *Ibid.*, 33: 53.
130. Lane, *The Modern Egyptians*, Chapter III, On Religion and Laws; W. Sheowring and C.W. Thies, *Religious Systems of the World* (New Delhi: Ajay Book Service, 1982), 256; Ameer Ali, *The Spirit*, 233–238.
131. Afif, *Tarikh-i-Firoz Shahi*, ed. Maulvi Vilayat Husain (Calcutta: Bibliothica Indica, 1891), 352.
132. Ameer Ali, *The Spirit*, xxxiii, 222–223, 227; P.M. Holt et al., ed., *The Cambridge History of Islam*, vol. 2: 515.
133. Gallichan, *Women Under Polygamy*, 209, 236–237.
134. Ameer Ali, *The Spirit*, 248; H.G. Rawlinson, *Five Great Monarchies*, vol 3 (London: John Murray, 1871), 222; Levy, *The Social Structure*, 129, note 5; Qurratulain Hyder, 'Muslim Women in India', in *Indian Woman*, ed. Devaki Jain (New Delhi: Ministry of Information and Broadcasting, 1975), 191; Mona N. Mikhail, *Images of Arab Women* (Washington, D.C.: Three Continents Press, Inc., 1979), 3; M.Z. Siddiqi, *Sir Abdullah Memorial Lectures* (Calcutta: Calcutta University, 1971), 66–67.
135. Khuda Bukhsh, *Studies: Indian and Islamic*, 102.
136. Rawlinson, *Five Great Monarchies*, vol. 3: 220; Gallichan, *Women Under Polygamy*, 217.
137. The Turks along with Mongols and Manchus are known as Tartars. For detailed study, see W. Erskine, *History of India under the Two First Sovereigns of the House of Taimur*, vol. 1 (Delhi: Idarah-i-Adabiyat-i-Delli, 1973), 9–11, 533–536.
138. Gallichan, *Women Under Polygamy*, 139, 161, 151(respect for mother).
139. E.D. Phillips, *The Mongol* (London: Thames and Hudson, 1969), 26. Also see David Morgan, *The Mongols* (Oxford: Basil Blackwell, 1986), 40; Jacob Abbott, *Makers of History—Genghis Khan—Life and Conquests* (New Delhi: Heritage Publishers, 1975), 56.
140. Michael Prawdin, *The Mongol Empire, Its Rise and Legacy*, trans. Eden and Cedar Paul (New York: The Free Press, 1967), 28, 61, 229; also Michel Hoang, *Genghis Khan*, trans. Ingrid Cranfield (London: Saqi Books, 1990), 91–92, 97.
141. Prawdin, *The Mongol Empire*, 63, 86, 88; Morgan, *The Mongols*, 40.
142. Phillips, *The Mongol*, 27.
143. Prawdin, *The Mongol Empire*, 51, 485; also Phillips, *The Mongol*, 23.
144. Pringle Kennedy, *History of the Great Moghuls* (Calcutta: Thacker Spink & Co., 1968), 44; Prawdin, *The Mongol Empire*, 94.
145. Prawdin, *The Mongol Empire*, 94–96; Morgan, *The Mongols*, 40; Bertold Spuler, *The Mongols in History* (London: Pall Mall Press, 1971), 9.
146. Phillips, *The Mongol*, 32.
147. Abbott, *Makers of History*, 54–55, 237. Also see Ameer Ali, *A Short History of the Saracens* (London: MacMillan & Co., 1953), 383; Spuler, *The Mongols in History*, 9.

148. Prawdin, *The Mongol Empire*, 28–30, 43, 64–66, 91–92, 98–99, 275–278, 286–288, 290–293, 297, 487–488; also Spuler, *The Mongols in History*, 19–21; Morgan, *The Mongols*, 40; Phillips, *The Mongol*, 85.

149. Kennedy, *History of the Great Moghuls*, 13, 15, 16, 21, 22, 23, 28, 41–43, 74–75. See also Hoang, *Genghis Khan*, 229, 240, 244–245, 247.

150. Edward Humphrey et al., ed., *The Webster Family Encyclopedia*, vol. 7 (Webster: Webster Publishing Co., 1984), 33–34.

151. Ameer Ali, *The Spirit*, 222–223, 242, 253; Edward Gibbon, *The Decline and Fall of the Roman Empire*, vol. 2 (Chicago: Encyclopaedia Britannica, 1978), 83–86.

152. Humphrey et al., *Encyclopedia*, vol. 2, 322; Douglas W. Downey et al., ed., *New Standard Encyclopedia*, vol. 17 (Chicago: Standard Educational Corp., 1987), 278; Siddiqi, *Sir Abdullah*, 15–16.

153. Akbar S. Ahmed, *Discovering Islam: Making Sense of Muslim History and Society* (New Delhi: Vistaar Publications, 1990), 187–189; James W. Spain, *The Way of the Pathans* (London: Robert Hale Ltd, 1962), 46, 143–152; Humphrey et al., *Encyclopedia*, vol. 1, 106.

154. S.M. Ahmad, comp., *Islam in India and the Middle East* (Allahabad: Abbas Manzil Library, n.d.), 146–151.

155. Shushtery, *Islamic Culture*, 461.

156. Shushtery, *Islamic Culture*, 464–466; Levy, *The Social Structure*, 165–186.

157. Imtiaz Ali, *Ameer Ali on Islam*, 224; Qurratulain Hyder, *Indian Woman*, 190.

158. Sheikh Abrar Husain, *Marriage Customs Among Muslims in India* (New Delhi: Sterling Publishers, 1976), 4–5; S.V. Mir Ahmad Ali, *Husain, the King of Martyrs* (Karachi: Grenich Pub. Co., 1964), 216; Levy, *The Social Structure*, 171.

159. Ameer Ali, *Mahommedan Law*, vol. 2 (New Delhi: The English Book Store, 1985), 317–318, 398–404; Levy, *The Social Structure*, 247; Fyzee, *Outlines of Muhammadan Law*, 112–113, 115. It is asserted that *Quran* (4: 24) regulated and sanctioned the practice of *muta* marriage.

160. *Dirham* is a word derived from Greek. It is the name of the silver coin, 2.97 grams in weight (M.T. Houtsma et al., ed., *Encyclopaedia of Islam*, vol. 1 (London: Leyden, 1927), 978.) Ten *dirhams* have been valued at 6 s. (shilling). and 8 d. (pence; it is the plural of penny) and 3 *dirhams* at 2 s. (V. Fitzgerald, *Muhammadan Law—An Abridgement* (London: Oxford University Press, 1931), 63).

161. Levy, *The Social Structure*, 105.

162. Levy, *The Social Structure*, 120–121, note 1.

163. Tyabji, *Muhammadan Law*, 605 (5) and (6), 898, 926–929; Fitzgerald, *Muhammadan Law*, 145; Fyzee, *Outlines of Muhammadan Law*, 396. For illustration, see D.F. Mulla, *Principles of Mahomedan Law*, Illustration No. (a) (Calcutta: The Eastern Law House, 1961), 88.

164. Khuda Bukhsh, *Studies: Indian and Islamic*, 82 (on the authority on Aghani, X, 54).

165. Khuda Bukhsh, *Studies: Indian and Islamic*, 82–83.

166. Imtiaz Ali, *Ameer Ali on Islam*, 54; Ameer Ali, *Saracens*, 201–202.

167. Khuda Bukhsh, *Studies: Indian and Islamic*, 83 (on the authority of Aghani, IV, 89).

168. Levy, *The Social Structure*, 93 (on the authority of Aghani, IV, 89).

169. Levy, *The Social Structure*, 126 (on the authority of Tabari, I, 2649); Imtiaz Ali, *Ameer Ali on Islam*, 53).

170. Imtiaz Ali, *Ameer Ali on Islam*, 53.

171. Farid-ud-Din Attar, *Tadhkirat-al-Auliya*, ed. Reynold A. Nicholson, vol.1 (Leiden: Luzac & Co, 1905), 59. See also Levy, *The Social Structure*, 132.

172. Levy, *The Social Structure*, 133; Ameer Ali, *The Spirit*, 255.

173. Shushtery, *Islamic Culture*, 461.

174. Imtiaz Ali, *Ameer Ali on Islam*, 59.

175. Imtiaz Ali, *Ameer Ali on Islam*, 55–58. For other instances, see Holt et al., *The Cambridge History*, vol. 1: 188, 209–210, 349, 408–411.

176. Ameer Ali, *Saracens*, 203, 246, 456–457, 459.

177. Ameer Ali, *Saracens*, 456–457; Shushtery, *Islamic Culture*, 590–591.

178. Ameer Ali, *Saracens*, 454, note 1; Hitti, *History of the Arabs*, 302.

179. Ameer Ali, *Saracens*, 454–455; Hitti, *History of the Arabs*, 334.

180. S.M.H. Zaidi, *The Muslim Womanhood in Revolution* (Calcutta: S.M.H. Zaidi, 1937), 15.

181. Ameer Ali, *The Spirit*, 250.

182. Imtiaz Ali, *Ameer Ali on Islam*, 58–59; Ameer Ali, *Saracens*, 143, 246, 455; Kidwai, *Social and Religious Laws*, 159.

183. Ameer Ali, *Saracens*, 455.

184. Imtiaz Ali, *Ameer Ali on Islam*, 60. A number of petty feudal lords ruling in Western Asia as Prince-Governors were known as *Atabegs*.

185. Khuda Bukhsh, *Studies: Indian and Islamic*, 83; Levy, *The Social Structure*, 126, 131.

186. Khuda Bukhsh, *Studies: Indian and Islamic*, 85. See also Levy, *The Social Structure*, 129–130 (for Baydawi comments on surah 16:11), 338.

187. Khuda Bukhsh, *Studies: Indian and Islamic*, 85.

188. Khuda Bukhsh, *Studies: Indian and Islamic*, 89–90.

189. Khuda Bukhsh, *Studies: Indian and Islamic*, 103; P. Thomas, *Indian Women Through the Ages* (New York: Asia Publishing House, 1964), 249.

190. Thomas, *Indian Women*, 93, also see 90–92, 94, 95.

191. Thomas, *Indian Women*, 249. Ahmad, *Islam in India*, 145; Qurratulain Hyder, *Indian Woman*, 191; Mazhar-ul-Haq Khan, *Social Pathology*, 32; Mikhail, *Images of Arab Women*, 3.

192. Khuda Bukhsh, *Studies: Indian and Islamic*, 87; Levy, *The Social Structure*, 127; K.S. Lal, *Early Muslims in India* (New Delhi: Books and Books, 1984), 141; Qurratulain Hyder, *Indian Woman*, 191; Mazhar-ul-Haq Khan, *Social Pathology*, 34–36; Mikhail, *Images of Arab Women*, 3.

193. Mazhar-ul-Haq Khan, *Social Pathology*, 32–33; Imtiaz Ali, *Ameer Ali on Islam*, 51, 59.

194. Yasin, *A Social History*, 1–13 (makes a good reading in this regard).

195. Imtiaz Ahmad, ed., *Caste and Social Stratification Among Muslims in India* (New Delhi: Manohar Publications, 1978), 13; K.S. Lal, *Growth of Muslim Population in Medieval India, A.D. 1000–1800* (Delhi: Research Publications in Social Sciences, 1973), 204; Lal, *Early Muslims*, 114.

196. J.A. De Mandelslo, *The Voyage and Travels of J. Albert de Mandelslo … into the East Indies*, trans. John Davies (London: Printed for John Starkey, and Thomas Basset, 1669), 65. Also see Yasin, *A Social History*, 3, 14–16; H.G. Rawlinson, *India, A Short Cultural History* (Great Britain: The Cresset Press, 1948), 244.

197. For the condition of Hindu women, A.L Altekar's *The Position of Women in Hindu Civilization*, 3rd ed. (Delhi: Motilal Banarasidass, 1962) and P. Thomas's *Indian Women* provide a good reading.

198. Yasin, *A Social History*, 87–93; Holt et al., *The Cambridge History*, vol. 2: 67, 569; Mushirul Hasan, 'Some Aspects of the Problems of Muslim Social Reform', in *Muslims in India*, ed. Zafar Imam (New Delhi: Orient Longman, 1975), 217; Qurratulain Hyder, *Indian Woman*, 192; Mandelslo, *The Voyage and Travels*, 62.

2

The Social Profile

An Overview

The social status of the Muslim women underwent many changes as a result of their interaction with Indian environment. Since both Hindu and Muslim cultures existed simultaneously in the same region, their values and norms got assimilated. Muslims married Indian girls. They also converted Hindus into their fold. These factors resulted in infiltration of the Hindu thought into the Muslim mind and brought a transformation in their thinking about their own women and a consequential change in their customs also. The status and public respectability of women also underwent modification with changing moral values of the society. Since these values came down to the lowest ebb during the time of later Mughals, the dignity of womanhood also suffered most during that period. The changing policies of different rulers also affected their status. While on the one hand, Sultan Qutb-ud-din Mubarak Shah's fondness for the company of harlots provided an environment favourable to the prostitutes and the inclination of kings of later Mughal period towards amorous life gave the dancing girls and ladies of lower birth a sway in the royal court, on the other hand, the honourable concern and the respect shown by some kings like Sher Shah Suri or Akbar or Alivardi Khan or Sayyid brother Hussain Ali towards womanhood brought a few salutary royal pronouncements and actions, restoring some dignity to them. However, in an overall lustful and degrading environment, which affected Akbar also equally, women were generally looked down upon, with the exception of some relations, and held a deteriorating position in the social gamut. The status of Muslim ladies belonging to different social classes also altered differently. Since the upper class was most affected by the degenerating values, the women of these strata suffered most in their social standing over the period of time. For the women belonging to middle and lower classes, the change was not so marked.

Barring the respectability of motherhood or female blood relations and individual examples of marital affinity, women, as a class, suffered discernible discrimination vis-a-vis men, from birth till death. They were regarded not only subservient to men but also as second-rate citizens. Having been cut off from the outer world, they were confined within the four walls of harem (separate compartments for women), with duties to bear and rear children and to perform all sorts of household chores. Right from their unwelcome birth, different social customs and ceremonies, besides the social response they received, made them conscious of their subservient position. In the contemporary perspective, some of the ladies might have carved out a place for themselves by dint of their own qualities, but the very fact that their recognition depended on their appeal to their masters shows that Muslim women of that time were destined to play a secondary role in the contemporary social set-up and remained an object of neglect, apathy and despise.

Unwelcome Birth

The life of a girl began with an unwelcome note. The birth of a girl was considered something inauspicious. Amir Khusrau lamented over the birth of his daughter, 'I wish you were not born and if you were, it would have been better if you had been a boy'. Amid such moroseness, he consoled, 'But my father was born of a woman and I am also born of a woman'.[1] His craving brings out the psyche of his times. This becomes all the more glaring when contrasted with his equally intense desire to have a son, a desire that was universal. For instance, it is informed that after the birth of sons, Muslims dressed them like girls in order to avoid the evil eyes and jealousy of the people. The custom amply throws light on importance of male child and also the undesirability of baby girls and the social apathy towards them.[2]

In the medieval society of warring factions, when men were required to fight the battles, the longing for a son could be visualised. The undesirability of a daughter was also understandable, considering a *purdah nashin* (staying behind the curtain, which screens women from the sight of men) female of the time whose very presence was a constant security hazard and a permanent liability on her kith and kin. Equally marked was the sensuality of the age. During this period, the mutual assimilation of Hindu–Muslim cultures was also taking place. Hindus always craved for the birth of sons in preference to the daughters. A verse in the Atharva veda echoes the general longing for a son: 'स्त्रैषूयमन्यत्र दधत्पुमांसमु दधदिह'(May He [the Lord of creatures] put elsewhere woman birth, but may He put here a male).

Gradually, a female child came to be considered as a misfortune, especially after the advent of the Muslims. In some of the sections of the Rajputs, whenever a girl was born, she was killed soon thereafter or during her infancy.[3] The practice was imbibed by some sections of the Muslim population also. Jahangir confirmed its prevalence among the Mohammadans of Rajaur who were basically Hindu converts. He writes:

> Also when a daughter is born, to a man without means, they put her to death by strangulation. They alley themselves with Hindus and both give and take girl.... I gave an order that hereafter they should not do such things and whoever was guilty of them, should be capitally punished.[4]

In fact, Infanticide among Muslims was not practiced when they came to India. No migrant group—Turk, Afghan, Mongol, Mughal, Persian—was familiar with this evil, and therefore it did not become common among them even after their settlement in India. Also, the yearning for a boy did not influence the Muslim psyche to the same extent as that of a Hindu. Nonetheless, the desire for having a son in preference to girls was there among Muslims too, so much so that people approached holy men and visited tombs of the saints to ask for sons. The royalty also was not free from this practice. Gulbadan's reference of Babur's eagerness for a boy before Hindal was about to be born or *Akbar Nama and Tuzuk-i-Jahangiri* writing about Akbar's vow to undertake journey on foot to the shrine of Muin-ud-din Chisti at Ajmer in the event of the birth of a son, which he fulfilled after the birth of Salim (Jahangir) or Shah Jahan's journey to the tomb of Chisti for praying for the birth of a son are a few examples.[5] The undesirability of a female child gets reflected from an anecdote of the time of Sultan Muzaffar of Gujarat, when one of his confidants, Malik Allah Dia (Faridi read it as Mli-Kul-Hidaya), was very sad because he did not have any son. Similarly, another incident is narrated by Abul Fazl as per which the mother of Amir Saif Khan had only daughters and when he was still in womb, his father had threatened to divorce his mother if she again got a daughter. Akbar showed his displeasure when the matter was reported to him. Luckily a son, Saif Khan, was born to ward off the threat.[6] Social undesirability of girls had become common to both Hindus and Muslims. Social discrimination against girls and in favour of boys was very open. The only ceremony enjoined upon by Prophet Mohammad at the birth of a child was *aqiqah* and its celebration began with discrimination. On this day, goats were sacrificed, two for the boy but only one for the girl.[7] There were many other ceremonies that owed their origin either to the 'traditions' or other Mohammadan works on ethics or to the local customs of India. Many of them were meant only for the boys. The rejoicing and festivities that followed these celebrations were marked only if the child was a male and not otherwise. There are innumerable instances of rejoicing and feasting on the birth of a son, an invariable occurrence in every 'blessed' house, but there were no such rejoicing on the birth of a daughter. In the royal households, only women rejoiced and feasted on the birth of a daughter while the whole court participated in the celebrations when a prince was born. There are many paintings depicting rejoicings at the birth of a prince.[8] But when Akbar ordered general rejoicing on the birth of Affat Banu, daughter of prince Salim, it surprised all, including Abul Fazl, since this was 'contrary to the custom of contemporaries'.[9]

Under such conditions, every married woman, in spite of the fact that she bore equal pain for the birth of a girl or a boy, always yearned for becoming the mother of a son, which added to her respectability instantly. Conversely, the birth of a daughter saddened her instinctively. The birth of a girl was, however, not universally condemned as a curse by Muslims in the beginning. Social norms of Islam that were still existing and liberal attitude of persons like Akbar and Nur Jahan also contributed to this. Therefore, even though bride money or dower was gradually turning from instant to deferred, it had not been replaced by dowry in Muslim families by that time.[10] But with the increase in dowry demands by the Muslims also, daughters' birth became undesirable. Besides, as the moral values of the society fell, the honour of a woman was always in peril. Consequently, the birth of a girl became woeful and a matter of great concern for the Muslim parents as well.

Early Marriage

In such an unfavourable atmosphere, the girl was not destined to enjoy the parental care for long. Born and brought up under the close parental supervision, the greatest worry of her guardians was to get her married as soon as possible. Therefore, early marriage had become, more or less, a distinctive and universal trait of the Medieval Indian society, of both Hindus and Muslims. Mushtaqi has narrated an incident of the time of Bahlol Lodi wherein a Sayyid begged of help for getting his daughter married and visualising his worry, a person named Jamal Khan gave him a horse, his only possession.[11] The event shows the worry of a daughter's father to get her married. It was believed that a girl not married before the age of puberty would bring social disgrace for the parental family. Therefore, the girls seldom crossed the age of 9 or 10 and the boys 16 or 17 before they were tied in wedlock during the sultanate and early Mughal periods. Thus, during the time of Firoz Shah, the girls got married at *Khurd salgi*, that is, a very early age and the king is reported to have laid down the age of marriage of girls at 9.[12] The Bahmanis in the South also followed the custom of early marriage for both princes and princesses. Nizam Shah (1461–1463 A.D.) and Muhammad III (1463–1482 A.D.) got married very early. Prince Ahmad, aged 14, the son of Mahmud Shah Bahmani (1482–1518 A.D.), got married to the infant daughter of Sultan Adil Khan.[13] This age came further down as the laxity in social norms increased. Fitch (1583–1591), writing during the time of Akbar, wrote about marriages being solemnised of boys of 8 or 10 and girls of 5 or 6 years, although consummation did not take place before they were 10 years old. Similarly, Terry (1616–1619 A.D.), writing during the times of Jahangir, mentioned, 'They marry for the most part at the ages of twelve or thirteen'. De Laet also mentions about the prevalence of child marriages during Jahangir's time. Orme (1659 A.D.) wrote that they all got married before 13 invariably. But Manucci, writing at a later date, reported a girl of Sind giving birth to a male child when she aged only 9. Thevenot gave the marriage age as 4–6. Many other foreigner travellers corroborated practice of early marriage.[14] For the Mughal princesses, the marriageable age was a little higher than the general Muslim public. They, generally, got married at 14 or 15, although there are examples when they got married even at 5. Thus, Aesha got betrothed to Babur at the age of 5, although the marriage got solemnised later on when she became 16; Babur's daughters Gulchehra Begam and Gulrang Begam got married between 13 and 15 and 15 and 19, respectively; Hamida Banu got married to Humayun at 14; Humayun's daughter Bakshi Banu Begam got betrothed at 10; Gulbadan Begum's marriage with Khizr Khan took place when she was 14 and Arjumand Banu Begam was betrothed to Shah Jahan in 1607 at the age of 14 and married in 1612 when she was 19 years of age.[15] The average age for marriage of the princes was also low, ranging between 16 and 18. At the time of his first marriage, Salim was 16, Murad was 17, Auranzeb was 18 years and 7 months, Dara was more than 18, Muhammad Azim was 14, Kam Bakhsh was about 14 and Prince Muhammad Sultan was of 20 years. Manucci recorded that princes were brought up in palaces up to the age of 16 and then they were to be married.[16]

The writings of the contemporary travellers show that the arrangement of marriage was totally a parental affair. The parents were constrained by many considerations, like family status, traditions, social honour, interests, reports, similar trade and the like, before taking a decision in this regard.[17] As such, marriage being more of a family question than a personal concern of the marrying couple was arranged even at the cost of the interests and feelings of the latter. The greatest sufferer, invariably, was the girl. She was supposed to go like a dumb, driven cattle behind the bridegroom, irrespective of his unsuitability. The only respite the society could offer to these hapless girls was that even after the marriage was solemnised, they allowed some more years to lapse before they were allowed to enter the actual conjugal life. During this period, they remained under the care of their parents. The case of Aesha, Babur's wife, has been discussed above. Some other instances are: the daughter of Sultan Adil Khan, although married as an infant to Prince Ahmad Bahmani, was delivered to him only at the age of 10. There was similar practice prevailing during the time of Akbar and Jahangir among Muslims of Bengal, wherein the females were betrothed at a very early age, but the actual marriage and consummation took place only after they attained the age of puberty.[18]

Child marriages were bound to affect both physical and mental development of the girls. Because of early marriage, they became mothers of many children at a very young age, which resulted in the deterioration of their health and aging before time. Thevenot writes, 'but the women who have children so young soon leaves off child bearing and commonly do not conceive after thirty years of age, but become extremely wrinkly....'[19] In the inquisitive age of learning and playing, they were dumped into the four walls of the house of in-laws, burdened with the heavy responsibilities to bear and rear children, to run the house and to be attuned to the commands of all elders present in the husband's family. Consequently, the growth of their own personality got restricted and their individuality was nipped in the bud. No doubt, a boy was also married at an early age, but in that man-dominated society, his status remained unruffled since he was always to remain the master of his house. Women were considered as emotionless machines to procreate, to satisfy the sensuality of their masters and to rise to every command they were given.

Emperor Akbar visualised the injustice done to female children by these arranged early marriages. Abul Fazl writes in *Akbar Nama*,

> In the extensive country of India men are active to form this union at a tender age and this introduces the leaven of evil. The world's lord will on no account admit of it before puberty, and will not anticipate the proper time for it.

Again, in *Ain-i-Akbari*, he penned,

> He (Akbar) abhors marriages which take place between man and woman before the age of puberty. They bring forth no fruit, and His Majesty thinks them even hurtful; for afterwards, when such a couple ripens into manhood, they dislike having connexion, and their home is desolate.

Badaoni confirmed Akbar's open disliking for the child marriage and also for the early marriage of Ayisha with Mohammad.[20] He, therefore, promulgated regulations that recommended the minimum age of marriage for girls and boys as 14 and 16 years, respectively. He also made the consent of the bride and the bridegroom and the permission of the parents absolutely necessary in marriage contracts. He appointed two officers named *Tu-i-begi* (master of marriages) in order to investigate the circumstances of the bride and the bridegroom before the marriage was actually solemnised.[21] However, since social habits die hard, Badaoni's narration shows that this regulation could not create much impact, except in increasing corruption.[22] Nor could the regulation regarding the compulsory consent of the boy and the girl for marriage have any relevance since the brides and bridegrooms were too young to have any decisive power. The innocent bride would have done nothing except giving her consent for marriage, as the Quran envisaged, by following the dictates of

her *wali*. Marriage had come to be regarded as the be-all and end-all
of the lives of these tiny hapless females before the period of Akbar
and even thereafter. The practice could not be checked and it also
continued subsequently.

Unmatched Marriages

Another serious problem of the day was unmatched marriages, which
had become very common by the time of Akbar. The poor ladies tried
to avoid it but could not escape. Such marriages were not voluntary,
but these took place under pressure, put on the poor victim girls,
giving the bait of money, confirms Manucci.[23] The social insecurity
and their poverty forced them to succumb. As for the royalty and
nobility, they considered themselves fit to marry the tender girls at
any age. Humayun was 33 when he married Hamida Banu, aged 14.[24]
Alamgir II, at the ripe age of 60 and with a shattered health, was
fascinated by Hazrat Begam, daughter of Muhammad Shah, who was
just 16, and demanded her hand for himself. She, however, declined
the offer replying, 'I prefer death to (such a) marriage.... I regard you
as my father and you too should look upon me in the same light....'
For that she had to suffer the punishment of forced isolation.[25] The
like of her were only exceptions. By and large, in the eagerness to
get their daughters married, their parents often compromised with
the age of the groom.

There was another prevalent practice of wealthy women marrying
men much younger to them and men accepting the same, as it
promised wealth and prosperity. Sher Shah, for instance, married
Lad Malika, who was almost of his mother's age, for the sake of
her property. He himself was 44 years of age at that time.[26] This
practice seems to have become so common by the time of Akbar that
it did not miss his attention. Badaoni informs that Akbar passed a
law wherein a man could not marry a girl more than 12 years elder
to him. Such unmatched marriages, as per him, were regarded by
Akbar to be 'against all modesty'.[27] However, the sensuality of the
age and Akbar's apathy towards women becomes apparent when
he thought of bringing regulations against unmatched marriages
of old heiresses with young destitute boys but left undisturbed the
prevalent menace of old and decrepit men tying nuptial knots with
innocent young girls.

The Dowry

The system of dowry, which is not sanctioned by the Quran, yet Muslims imbibed it in India, resulting in further deterioration of status of Muslim women. It was an old custom in the Hindu society, which gradually became rigorous. With close association with the Hindus, dowry gradually became a part of the Muslim society as well. It was popularly known as *jahej* among them.[28] Among the royalty and nobility, it comprised of cash, pearls and jewels, animals like elephants and horses with golden saddles and strings, valuable robes and vessels, territories and many more articles besides male and female slaves and singing and dancing girls. There are numerous instances showing that the sultans and Mughal emperors gave and took dowry in the marriage of their daughters and sons, respectively. The only difference was that, as compared to the sultanate period, it had become very extensive and ostentatious during the time of the Mughals, although it varied according to the status of bride's guardians. The dowry of Devaraya's daughter to Firoz Bahmani comprised of 5 maunds of pearls, 50 elephants, cash indemnity, territory of Bankapur and 2,000 male and female slaves, singers, dancers and musicians. Similarly, Amir Khusrau mentions about huge dowry having been given in the marriage of Dewal Rani and Khizr Khan.[29] But, it got settled at a figure of 20 million *tankas* (a coin of copper with a small silver alloy) in the marriage of Man Bai with Jahangir that included 100 elephants, several strings of horses, all sorts of golden vessels set with jewels and precious stones, utensils of gold and silver and all sorts of stuffs, the quantity of which was beyond all computations, besides male and female servants of Indian, Circassian and Abyssinian origin. Along with this, all the nobles who were members of the imperial party were presented with Persian, Turkish and Arabian horses with golden saddles.[30] Similarly, in Farrukhsiyar's marriage with daughter of Ajit Singh, dowry consisting of a cash of ₹5 million besides 10 elephants with litters studded with gold and silver worth ₹5 million and 50 horses of Iraqi and Arabian breed with gold and silver trappings was given. We have references of huge dowry given by Sultan Ali Khan of Kashmir in his daughter's marriage, of Aurangzeb's son prince Sultan Muhammad getting fortress of Ramgiri in dowry while marrying the princess of Golkunda and dowries received in the marriages of prince Muhammad Akbar, Muhammad Azim and Kam Bakhsh, sons of Aurangzeb.[31] The custom continued unabated.

Following the example of the Kings and the nobles, who were the leaders and ideals of the society, the system of dowry percolated down among the general public as well, and the writings of the contemporary European travellers stand testimony to this.[32] In order to save the poor girls from forced celibacy for want of dowry and getting them married in time, many of the nobles, sultans and royal ladies came to their rescue by extending them financial help for this purpose. Some of the noteworthy among them were Fakhr-ud-din of Balban's time, Sultan Firoz Tughlaq, Amir Zain-ud-din of Sikander Lodi's period and Nur Jahan. Fakhr-ud-din, Kotwal of Balban, was estimated to have provided dowry to about 1,000 poor girls every year.[33] Sultan Firoz Tughlaq established a department, *Diwan-i-Khairat*, for this purpose. It examined the genuine financial needs of each case and accordingly gave them grants of 50, 30 or 25 *tankas* each, as per the three grades of grants provided therein.[34] It is reported about Zain-ud-din that whosoever asked him for financial help for daughter's marriage, he gave him all items of dowry including clothes, beds and even *palki* (palanquin/sedan chair. It was a mode of transport of higher strata women).[35] As for Nur Jahan, she met the expenses of marriage and dowry of 500 girls during her 16 years of authority and power.[36]

Dowry brought a great financial burden on the parents and guardians of the girls. As it had a bearing on the social status of bride's family, the guardians of the brides were forced to manage dowry even beyond their capacity. Being worried about the welfare of their daughters and aspiring for a better deal for them from their in-laws, the girls' parents tried their best to fulfil the capricious demands of the bridegrooms and their families. The girls came to be regarded as a burden under such circumstances. Dowry demand was less in the beginning. But as the time passed and the moral values of the society became lax, the avarice of the people and their demand for dowry also increased. Consequently, the status of women suffered.

The Divorce

The study of contemporary history shows that divorces did take place in medieval India among Muslim population, although such occurrences were only few and far between, and wise and honourable

persons always disapproved of it. Barbosa confirmed about the prevalence of divorce among the Mohammadans of Cambay and that the
Muslim women also enjoyed the same liberty in this regard.[37] The son
of *Qazi* Nasir-ud-din divorced his wife at her request. She was the
sister of Sultan Muizz-ud-din Bahram Shah.[38] Similarly, the daughter
of Ali Khan, the ruler of Kashmir (1563–1578 A.D.), also sought
divorce from her husband, Shaikh Arif-i-Husaini, for which she even
asked back her dowry.[39] Sometimes a person was forced to divorce
his wife for not her fault but because of pressure of others. Abdul
Wasi, for instance, divorced his beloved wife because Akbar's lustful
eyes fell on her and he wanted to marry her. Wasi had to surrender
before the Emperor's wish. He divorced his wife and, in frustration,
left the city and went to Bider.[40] Among the Mughal ladies, some
instances of divorce were those of Aesha Sultan Begam, Babur's wife
who left him; Khanzada Begam, Babur's sister and Gulbarg Begam,
Humayun's wife after her divorce from Shah Husain Arghun, her
first husband.[41] Another example is of Misri Begam, daughter of Asaf
Jah, who was married to Jarullan, son of Asaf Khan. Somehow, the
marriage did not consummate. Jahangir, therefore, ordered Jarullan
to divorce his wife so as to get him remarried.[42]

The lesser number of divorces in no way reflected any respect or
reverence shown towards women. This might be because Muslim
religion did not favour divorce by men or women seeking it, which
was considered as the last resort. It propounded reconciliation.[43]
That is why, from the description of Badaoni, it appears that even
if a woman moved to the *qazi* for seeking divorce from her spouse
for a valid reason, the *qazi* tried to dissuade her. He wrote:

> If woman prayed for a separation from her husband on the ground of
> his absence from her, he (Shaikh Muin, *Qazi* of Lahore) would provide
> her with means of livelihood to the extent of his ability, and would
> say, 'take this much for your subsistence and await your husband's
> return: do not separate from him'.[44]

Under the circumstances, it was not possible for these ladies to use
their legal power to seek divorce, in spite of neglect and disregard of
their husbands. In the higher strata, the ladies, with a few exceptions,
always remained in the waiting for their masters who were maintaining
large harems and were also indulging in extramarital relations. But
because of their subservient position, they could not think of divorcing

them on this ground. What to talk of divorce, even airing resentment for their absence was unsavoury to their menfolk. Humayun's wife Bega Begam, being beloved of the Emperor, once gathered courage only to convey the resentment of the harem ladies for his absence from the harem. For this, not only had she to face a shut up call but all ladies were also made to give in writing that they would not make such complaints in the future. The ladies obeyed his command.[45] Such dominance, in fact, was maintained by males of all strata of the society. Therefore, Badaoni's reference that ladies also sought divorces can be construed only as an exception and not the rule and they became all the more rare in the subsequent period. As for men, they did not have the necessity to have recourse to a divorce because once the ladies became their stooges and came under their total command, the harmonious family life got ensured. For the richer few, it was perhaps not required at all. Not recognising the sanctity of religion, they had as many wives as they wished, without having any need of divorcing the earlier ones in order to restrict their number to 4. Even within the religious sanctions, they could fulfil their desire through *muta* marriages or having concubines. If still some tried to follow the religious injunctions, then they would divorce the earlier one to be in a position to marry a new woman. For instance, an aunt and her niece could not be co-wives as per the Quran. But Shaibani Khan, in order to get married to Khanzada Begam, sister of Babur, divorced her maternal aunt Mihr Nigar Chaghtai.[46] Under such conditions and with successive moral degradation, the institution of marriage lost its significance and so did the practice of divorce, which became exceedingly rare.

For the general Muslim public, the assimilation of the Hindu way of life also had an impact and gradually Muslim society also started abstaining from divorces. Some of the wills of the later Mughal period clearly indicate that divorces by Muslim women were dissuaded.[47] Observing about the Hindu impact on Muslims in 1892, a modern writer wrote that in spite of permission for divorce, they were virtually unknown. This observation along with the record of the contemporary authorities lends credence to the view. Since social changes are very slow, similar situation could also not be ruled out during the period of this study, might be with some variation in degrees. Similarly, The Census Report of 1901 elaborated still another reason for lesser divorces among Muslims. It wrote, 'People are often married among their own relations. A wife who is divorced brings the greatest possible shame on all her people who happen to be the people of her husband'.[48] Although the Report was of a much later period, yet the facts were equally relevant during the period of this study also, with marriages in close relations and with deep sense of clannish attachment.

Treatment to Widows

The widows among the Muslims had a better life than their counterparts among the Hindus. The only check was to observe strictly the period of *iddat* of four months and ten days wherein restrictions were put on women, such as they had to avoid all adorations, wearing of ornaments, new clothes, coming out of the house and even remarriage. Muslim women of the time followed these Quranic injunctions with some exceptions, like, in Multan, this period of *iddat* was not observed by all and some people even married women who were not divorced by their previous husbands.[49] Nonetheless, once the period of *Iddat* was over, they had all social privileges, respect and could arrange and participate in festivities and functions without any social blemish. Gulbadan begam's *Humayun Nama* is full of such narrations. She writes about Maham Begam, widow of Babur, hosting a grand feast in honour of Humayun; widow relations participating in Hindal's marriage and enjoying picnic and going on expeditions. It is also reported that Babur's widow asked Humayun to marry Maywajan, which he respectfully agreed. They also had excursions to Mecca for *Hajj* and were treated respectfully on return.[50]

They were also treated with sympathy and concern and were well provided for. Barani narrates about the consideration of Balban for the widows. Once he gave a judgement against one of his slaves, Haibat Khan, who had murdered the husband of a woman. Visualising the intense grief of the lady, he punished him with 500 lashes and then handed over the murderer to her, to stab him with her own hands. The lady forgave the slave but felt redeemed at heart for having received the justice. *Tuzuk-i-Jahangiri* also narrates an incident wherein a widow complained against Muqarrab Khan, a *mansabdar*, for having taken her daughter and for keeping her in his house. The enquiry revealed that it was done by one of his attendants. At this, the Emperor put the attendant to death and reduced the *mansab* (a *mansab* was a numerically expressed rank denoting the position of a Mughal officer) of Muqarrab Khan by half.[51]

Remarriage

Another redeeming feature of the Muslim society was the permission to the widows and also to the divorcees, of both rich and poor classes, to remarry. In this respect, they were much better off compared to their Hindu counterparts. No social stigma was attached to remarriage. There are many instances to show as to how easily these ladies entered into fresh wedlocks after the old ones were broken by divorce or death. The daughter-in-law of *Qazi* Nasir-ud-din, after being divorced, got remarried to Ikhtiar-ud-din Aitkin, the wazir of Sultan Muizzud-din Bahram Shah, who succeed the throne after ouster of Razia.[52] The mother of Sultan Nasir-ud-din Mahmud, who was widow of Iltutmish, married Qutlugh Khan when her son became the sultan (after Bahram Shah) and she became the Malika-i-Jahan.[53]

As for the Mughal period, all foreign travellers of different periods recorded prevalence of remarriages among Muslims and it was not disapproved till the reign of Aurangzeb. The Mughal rulers rather encouraged widow remarriage and themselves married widows. The Turkish custom of *yangalik* was also followed by them in the beginning, although it was discontinued subsequently. As per this custom, a younger brother was to marry the widow of elder brother. To give a few examples, after the death of Saniz Mirza, one of the Daughlat amirs, his widow was married to Muhammad Haider Mirza, the younger brother of the deceased. Haider Mirza was grandfather of Mirza Haider, the author of *Tarikh-i-Rashidi* and the cousin (maternal aunt's son) of Babur. Similarly, Sultan Nigar Khanam, daughter of Yunus Khan, on the death of her husband Awiq, got married to his brother Qasim. But, when under this custom, Aurangzeb wished to marry Rana Dil, Dara's widow, she refused to agree and the marriage did not materialise.[54] Many royal ladies also remarried. Mahdi Khwaja was the third husband of Khanzada Begam, the first husband Shaibani Khan having divorced her and the second Saiyyad Hada having died.[55] Gulbarg Begam's remarriage with Humayun after divorce has already been discussed. Abul Fazl also wrote about many such remarriages. Thus, Akbar's sister Bakshi Banu Begam was married to Mirza Ibrahim and after his death to Mirza Sharaf-ud-din and Muqim Mirza's daughter, Haji Begam, got married thrice, first to Qasim Koka, then after his death to Mirza Hasan and after having again been widowed, she got married to Muhammad Mirza Isa.[56] Further, Humayun's daughter Fakhr-un-nisa Begam first got married to Shah Abul Ma'ali and after his death, she married Khwaja Hasan Naqshbandi.[57] Humayun's widow Mahchuchak Begam, in all probability, remarried Haider Qasim and there are many other instances.[58] Akbar himself married Salima Sultan Begam, the widow of Bairam Khan, and Jahangir married Nur Jahan, the widow of Sher Afgun.[59] Akbar is reported to have ordered that the widows should not be forbidden to remarry, although a widow whose menstruation cycle had ceased should not wish to have a husband.[60] It is also reported that when prince Daniyal died, his harem of 300 women was placed under the charge of prince Salim. The latter sent a word to these ladies that if any one of them desired to marry, they should inform him along with the name of the noble to whom they wanted to get married. Aurangzeb also permitted maid servants and ladies, other than wives of Shah Jahan, to 'marry freely anyone they pleased'.[61] The prevalence of remarriages and their acceptability in Muslim society gets indicated from the writing of Careri who mentions that the Hindu widows desirous of remarriage got converted either into Christianity or to Islam.[62]

However, the assimilation of the Hindu practices within the Muslim fold did have a gradual impact on the Muslim psyche in matters pertaining to remarriages, and the practice lost popularity. Rather, the widows who refrained from remarriages were respected both in the family and also in the society. When Dara Shukoh's widow, Rana Dil, refused to marry Aurangzeb, the latter gave her more respect.[63] Manucci also confirmed about remarriages among higher strata women becoming rare. He writes, 'The wives of these great men do not marry again, though in no way prohibited'.[64] During the reign of Muhammad Shah (1719–1748), widow remarriage came to be regarded as undesirable, particularly in higher and respectable families.[65] So much so that many religious heads tried to speak against this prejudice. There are some wills of the time, like that of Shah Wali Allah Dihlawi, pertaining to later Mughal period, which exhorted that it was improper to refuse to give Muslim widows in marriage, a bad impact of the Hindus.[66]

Polygamy

The Quran was taken to have given sanction for keeping up to four wives. The Muslim men of the medieval period, particularly of the richer class, enjoyed the luxury of a polygamous life. The royalty often indulged in having a number of legal wives (more than the Quranic sanction) besides many others contracted through *muta* marriage. This was in addition to a number of concubines and slave girls whom they possessed.[67]

The nobility too was polygamous. Ibn Batuta, for instance, was never without wives or slave girls, whom he considered indispensable. Wherever he went, he managed them for himself.[68] The accounts of the contemporary travellers show that in general, the nobles maintained three to four wives and sometimes even more, the most senior being the most honoured one (*harem-i-muhtaram*). She had precedence in all matters of dignity and management of the household except in matters of getting the love of her master where the juniors could be better placed.[69] The richer class of the society also followed this practice. Referring to the Moors of Cambay, Barbosa wrote, 'They have very beautiful, white women, very well clad, and they may marry as they can maintain, in accordance with the law of Mafamede; so many of them have four or five, all recognized and maintained'.[70] Similarly, Ovington, while writing about his voyage to Surat, has mentioned about the 'extraordinary liberty for women' taken by the Muslim men and he wrote:

> The Moora, therefore here, as in other kingdoms, practise the use of concubines, according as their fortunes and abilities can reach towards their maintenance; by which means they fancy not only an impunity to themselves, but something of merit, by propagating the number and increase of the faithful.[71]

It is also reported that in Bengal during the early 17th century, the rich Muslim merchants kept separate wives with complete establishments in each town they visited for their business.[72]

Polygamy had become a way of life of the higher strata of society, even to the extent that in order to meet their desires and intentions, the religious zealots gave new interpretations to the Quranic injunctions, to suit their purposes. The discussion in *Ibadat Khana* (house of worship) was a meeting house built in 1575 A.D. by the Mughal emperor Akbar to hold religious assemblies) regarding the legal number of wives at the time of Akbar can be the best example where the Quranic *ayat* (4:3) was interpreted as permitting nine wives. Some *Mujtahids* (a Muslim Jurist who is qualified to interpret Muslim Law by practising *Ijtihad* (legal reasoning) calculated 18 as the sanctioned number. They reached at the figure of 18 by multiplying each number given in the *ayat* by 2, that is, $(2 \times 2) + (3 \times 2) + (4 \times 2) = 18$ and at the figure of 9 by adding them, that is, $2 + 3 + 4 = 9$. During this discussion, it also came to light that taking recourse to such interpretation, a *qazi* himself had nine wives. Being the employees of Akbar and knowing fully well that the Emperor wanted to find a religious sanction for his plurality of wives, they gave these new interpretations. The ultimate consensus reached at was that a man might marry any number of wives by *muta* marriage but only four by *nikah*.[73] This plurality of wives has been justified in not very serious, but suggestive, way by others. Mirza Aziz Koka, for instance, remarked tersely,

> A man should marry four wives —a Persian woman to have somebody to talk to; a *Khurasani* woman, for his housework; a Hindu woman, for nursing his children; and a woman from Mawarannahr (Transoxiana), to have someone to whip as a warning for the other three.

Another writer, Richard Burton, explained in another amusing way for having four wives, 'One quarrels with you; two are sure to involve you in their squabbles...; and, when you have three, a faction is always formed against her you love best, so as to make her hours bitter. But four find society and occupation for themselves; of course they divide into two parties, but you, oh husband, are comparatively comfortable'.[74]

Akbar, though polygamous himself, visualised the bad effects of polygamy on health and family peace of the general public, and so propounded monogamy. He introduced the practice that a man should have a single legal wife unless he had no child.[75] Such a regulation was bound to have no impact, particularly when polygamy had become a second nature with the upper class Muslims and a symbol of their dignity. Thus, polygamy remained the order of the day with the wealthy Mohammadans, only the number of wives differed according to means, the state of necessity and the fancy of the man.

From the observations of the contemporary European travellers, it can be construed that among common Muslims also, the practice of having more than one wife was followed. Nicoli Conti wrote:

> The inhabitants of central India are only allowed to marry one wife, in the other parts of India polygamy prevails generally, except among those Christians who have adopted the Nestorian heresy, who confine themselves to one solitary mate.

His specific association of the Christians and inhabitants of central India with monogamy shows that during the early part of the Muslim period, the Muslim population followed polygamy. Terry confirmed the prevalence of polygamy during the time of Jahangir and so did Thevenot and Careri about the plurality of wives of the Mohammadans in general during the time of Shah Jahan and Aurangzeb.[76]

However, the people of lower classes even among the Muslims were normally monogamists. They could not afford the luxury of maintaining several wives with their inadequate economic resources.

The position of women was undermined by the prevalence of polygamy. The permission of four wives itself was discriminatory and humiliating for women. The enhancement of number by flouting this rule became all the more derogatory. Confined within the female quarters and lost in their mutual bickering, theirs was a wretched life without much importance that worsened further with the presence of concubines and slave girls. These illegal mates often stole the show by becoming the cynosure of the eyes of their masters, and thus gained precedence over the legal wives. Since their impact increased as the high-ups in the society degraded morally, the plight of the lawful wives became deplorable successively.[77] Compared to the harem ladies, women of middle and lower classes had a better status. They had rarely any rival in their homes. Indirectly though, women, in general, were affected adversely by the polygamy among the higher strata. Their self-respect and modesty were susceptible to the greedy eyes of lustful masters, perpetual saturnalia being the be -all and end-all of their lives, particularly in the later Mughal period.

Woman and Household

In marriage and family life, the woman was man's possession like any other commodity. The references in the writings of the contemporaries subscribe to this view.[78] According to a narration of the time of Al-ud-din Khalji, a husband even sold off his spouse in order to pay off taxes and such practices continued even during the Mughal period.[79] Women were subjected to all sorts of ethical rules. Amir Khusrau wrote that a girl, who had any reflections cast on her chastity, could never expect to find any respectable person to marry her, even though the charges levelled might prove to be totally base-less later on. The poet, therefore, cautioned them that in case they took to life of vices, their death alone would be able to purify them. He advised people against telling secrets to such women who were prone to evil acts.[80] Even for the married women, the social restrictions were so strict that except with their husbands, they could not remain alone in the company of any other male person including their brothers or fathers.[81] The ideals laid down for women were to consider their husbands as God on earth, follow their instructions, tolerate all their excesses and manage the household within the income that their husbands earned.

The women were conscious of their subservient position. They showed all devotion towards their spouses and tolerated all mental and physical tortures perpetrated on them by their husbands or their relations at home. For instance, the wife of Sultan Nasir-ud-din Mahmud was so devoted towards him that she herself did all household work and cooked food for the sultan. Once she pleaded to the sultan for a maid servant because her fingers were burnt while baking bread, but the sultan did not provide the same. His wife never complained thereafter.[82] At times, women were also subjected to torture. The sister of Sultan Muhammad bin Tughlaq was tortured to death by her husband Mughis, son of Malik-ul-Muluk.[83] Mushtaqi narrates yet another incident of the time of Sikander Lodi about the use of force by a husband against his wife on a false charge of her hiding a *lal* (a precious stone) from him. The sultan, however, was able to dig out the truth ultimately.[84] Similarly, Khwaja Muazzam, brother of Hamida Banu, was notorious for ill-treating his wife Zahra (Zuhra) Agha, whom he finally killed.[85]

During the Mughal period, the womanly devotion, particularly in the higher strata, was shaken. They were not trusted and were closely guarded. Having nothing to do, they remained engrossed in adorning and regaling themselves and in making efforts to please, attract and entertain their respective husbands so as to dissuade them from getting distracted to other women. They even developed extramarital relations and some of them even killed their husbands out of frustration because of excessive control and checks. Ismail Quli Khan, a commander of 4,000 in Akbar's reign, was poisoned by his 1,200 women for his ill-treatment. He was said to be so jealous of them that whenever he went to court, he would put his seal over the strings attached to their night drawers.[86]

Women in general, however, did not change much. Born and brought up in their ordinary environment, trained and moulded from the very childhood by the authoritative mothers-in-law and living always under the cover of purdah and domestic restrictions, any recalcitrant behaviour was just not expected of them. They remained docile all through and lived and died like the stooges of their husbands or the servants of their families. Family peace was maintained not because of any sense of comradeship and love between husband and wife but because of the perfect understanding of the subservient role by the wife.

Some women, however, did have a personality of their own. They exercised considerable influence on their husbands in their private and public lives. Bibi Mattu, Shams Khatun, Bibi Ambha, Bibi Raji, Bega Begam (Humayun's wife), Hamida Banu Begam, Salima Sultan Begam, Maham Begam, Nur Jahan and Mumtaz Mahal Aurangabadi Mahal can be cited as examples. They enjoyed a status much better than that of other ladies of their times.

The Mother

The position of woman as a mother was most respectable. Both the rulers and the ruled followed exhortations of Islam in this regard. Poet Amir Khusrau eulogised mother in his poems for all the pains she bears in childbirth and the dominant role she plays in moulding the character of the child.[87] During the sultanate period, the royalty not only showed regards towards their mothers but also allowed them to play prominent role in the state politics. Sultan Muhammad bin Tughlaq, for instance, held his mother Makhduma-i-Jahan in high esteem. Once she travelled along with him and he returned a little earlier than her. Later, when his mother arrived, he proceeded towards her, got down from his horse and kissed her feet in public in order to pay his humble regards.[88] She was his permanent counsel and was allowed to spend as much as she wanted for her charity. He mourned her death for 10 days before resuming his march to Multan.[89] Similarly, Sayyid Sultan Mubarak Shah (1421–1434) also had great respect for his mother. She was also given the title of Makhduma-i-Jahan. Once when he was on his way to his expedition to Samana and then to Panipat, he heard about the illness of his mother in 1432 A.D.

He came back immediately, leaving his army and baggage in the charge of the *Amirs* and *Maliks* (second highest grade of officer, lower than the *Khans* but higher than *Amirs*). His mother died a few days after his return. The sultan stayed for 10 days in order to observe her funeral rites and rejoined his army only after that.[90] It is only because of the exclusive place enjoyed by them that the mothers like Shah Turkan (mother of Rukn-ud-din Firoz), Malika-i-Jahan (mother of Sultan Rukn-ud-din Ibrahim Khalji), Dudu Bibi (mother of Sultan Jalal-ud-din Lohani of Bihar) and Makhduma-i-Jahan (mother of Sultans Nizam Shah Bahmani and Muhammad Bahmani, III) played crucial roles in politics as mother regents, safeguarding the interests of their sons.[91] There were also some unhappy examples. Sultan Shihab-ud-din, son and successor of Ala-ud-din Khalji, showed disrespect towards his stepmother (mother of Khizr Khan), Malika-i-Jahan, by imprisoning her and confiscating her valuable possessions.[92] Mothers who killed their children for selfish ends are also mentioned by the contemporaries. In one such instance, during the reign of Sultan Zain-ul-Abdin of Kashmir, a lady killed her own child and threw his dead body in the house of the lady living in her neighbourhood, because she had a grudge against the latter and wanted to get her punished by insinuating her for the murder of her child.[93] Such references, however, did not reflect the normal behaviour.

With the coming of the Mughals, the position of mother was exalted to its zenith. Stepmothers, foster mothers and even enemies' mothers were equally respected. Babur showed all reverence towards the mother of his enemy, Ibrahim Lodi, by giving her mansion, a *pargana* (an administrative unit, comprising of a group of villages) with an annual revenue of ₹700,000, besides allowing to retain her servants and slaves, in spite of the fact that her son was his arch rival whom he had killed and that she too had conspired to kill Babur. It is reported that he used to call her 'mother' and requested her to take him just like her son.[94] Babur's regard for his own mother, Qutlugh Nigar Khanam, was well known. Mirza Haider wrote that during difficult days, Babur had only one horse suitable for a person of his rank and that was used by his mother.[95] She remained a constant guide and consoler of her son, during all his tribulations, till her death in 1505 A.D.[96] Humayun had great regard for his mother, Maham Begam. Gulbadan, stepsister of Humayun, also loved her intensely for the care with which she had reared her up. She often referred to her as *akam* or 'my lady' with love and regard.[97] Gulbadan spoke very high of her real mother, Dildar Begam, as well.[98]

Hamida Banu was held in highest esteem by Akbar. His going out of the city to receive her whenever she returned from a journey,[99] his abrupt coming back from his hunting trip on hearing about her indisposition,[100] his carrying her palanquin on his own shoulders once during her journey from Lahore to Agra,[101] his heart-felt mourning at her death when he shaved off his head and beard and removed all ornaments and took her bier on his shoulders for a pace:[102] all betray his respect for his mother. His regard extended to his stepmother, Haji Begam. He was so much attached to Haji Begam that many people, as Akbar himself confirmed, mistook her to be his real mother and confused her with Hamida Banu. Badaoni called her 'second mother to the Emperor'.[103] Akbar was equally respectful to his foster mothers like Maham Anaga and Jiji Anaga. To Maham Anaga, he used to call *walida*, that is, mother. She enjoyed the greatest influence on Akbar as well as in the court. On account of it, he showed deepest attachment even to their sons and husbands known as *kokas* and *atkas*, respectively. Adham Khan, son of Maham Anaga, was repeatedly pardoned by Akbar, in spite of his recalcitrant behaviour before he finally punished him. Similarly, Aziz Koka, son of Jiji Anaga, offended Akbar often with his impetuosity, yet, he rarely punished him. He used to say, 'Between me and Aziz is a river of milk which I cannot cross'. Further, Shams-ud-din Atka Khan, husband of Jiji Anaga was made the Prime Minister after the fall of Bairam Khan.[104] The universal respect given to the mothers has also been confirmed by Badaoni. He himself availed of the services of his mother once in an effort to settle his differences with Muqarrab Khan, a chief of the amirs of the Deccan.[105] Even after Akbar, the foster mothers continued to be given kind and considerate treatment in the royal household.[106]

Jahangir was equally respectful towards his mother. Lunar and solar weighing of the Emperor and many royal marriages took place in her palace.[107] During important festivals, the Emperor visited her palace to pay his respect. Hawkins mentioned about Jahangir's visit to his mother on his birthday when each of the nobles accompanying the Emperor presented her a jewel according to his respective estate.[108] He had such great reverence for his mother that in order to perform *kornish* (a recognised mode of salutation, which consisted of putting the palm of the right hand on the forehead and then bending down the head), *sijdah* (prostration/a way of salutation, which consisted of bowing down the forehead to the earth), and *taslim* (Total submission wherein the person placed the back of his right hand on the ground, raised it slowly till he stood erect and then put the raised palm on the top of his head) to her, he travelled all the way to Dahr (near Lahore) where she was staying. There is a Mughal painting of the time, showing Jahangir paying respect to his mother, which is a testimony of his affection for his mother.[109] Such was his regard for mothers that once when Pahar, son of Ghaznin Khan, killed his mother because she had prevented him from evil doings, Jahangir punished him to death.[110] Prince Muhammad Azam, son of Aurangzeb, also had great regard for his mother.[111]

Even during later Mughal period, when the society witnessed general degradation in moral values, to which mothers were no exceptions, the reverence for mother remained untarnished. Udham Bai, the mother of Emperor Ahmad Shah, was morally lax and had objectionable relations with eunuch Javed Khan. Still, she was most revered by her son. She was de facto administrator of his empire. It is reported that during the Maratha attack on the imperial camp, while running away from Sikandrabad, Ahmad Shah took along with him his mother besides his son Mahmud Shah, his favourite wife Inayetpuri Bai and half-sister Sahiba Begam, leaving all other queens and princesses at the mercy of his enemies.[112]

The Mughal mothers played important role as mediators also. Some of them who took an active part in the administration of the empire were Qutlugh Nigar Khanam, Maham Begam, Hamida Banu, Salima Sultan Begam, Mahchuchak Begam, Udaipuri Mahal, *Sahiba-i-Nishwan* (mother of Farrukhsiyar) and Udham Bai.[113]

Female Relations

The Quran propounded justice, kindness and due consideration towards near relations also.[114] The Muslims, in general, followed these ethical rules. During the sultanate period, there was some deterioration in their position. Along with the instances of respect and kindness towards the near relations, those of disrespect and intrigues against them were also observed. While the period witnessed the brothers of Razia Begam working against her interests, it also saw Khudavandzada, the sister of Muhammad bin Tughlaq, being held in great esteem by the latter.

The position of female relations became much better under the Mughals. Babur's respect for his grandmother Ehsan Daulat Begam, sister Khanzada Begam and for his aunts is abundantly testified in *Babur Nama, Humayun Nama* and *Tarikh-i-Rashidi.* After the conquest of north India, he invited his aunts, *begams* and *khanams* (means 'princess' or 'noble woman', title attached to the names of the royal ladies as mark of respect) from Kabul to Agra. In all, 96 of them arrived and all were given presents. A comfortable living was arranged for them. Babur himself visited them on every Friday and continued to do so, even though Maham exhorted him not to come, as it was hot season.[115] Babur's visit to the houses of his aunts at Kabul; his welcome to Maham Begam and his 'honourable reception' to Khanzada Begam, both ladies returning from Kabul to Hindustan at two different occasions; Mirza Haider Dughlat testifying his warm regards for his maternal aunt, Mihr Nigar Khanam, and his extending warm welcome to his lady relations in spite of his mourning on his mother's death are testimony to his regard for his lady relations. It is also reported by Abul Fazl that he pardoned rebel Khan Mirza at the intercession of Mihr Nigar Khanam.[116] Beveridge, therefore, observed, 'Apropos of the aunts of frequent mention, it may be said that both Babur and Mirza Haider convey the opinion that deference to elder women was a permanent trait of their age and set'.[117]

Humayun followed his father. His love for his sisters was so much that during his illness, he remembered them the most.[118] He often visited them and cared for their welfare. He looked after his elderly lady relations so much that it even aroused the jealousy of his wives.[119] Akbar and Jahangir were equally respectful to lady relations. Akbar showed all kindness towards the wife of Mirza Muhammad Hakim, his cousin sister, and so did Jahangir towards his sister Shukr-un-nisa.[120] Aurangzeb's love for Roshanara and Jahanara is well known. He favoured both of them. He rejoiced at Jahanara's recovery from her burns.[121] Aurangzeb showed regard for Qamar-un-nisa, the daughter of his maternal aunt and Prime Minister Asad Khan. He cared for her comforts in spite of the fact that he confined her son, Mirza Tafakhur, for his rowdy behaviour in molesting a Hindu woman.[122] Even during the later period, this regard and love for the female relations continued. One could visualise the good fortune of these Mughal lady relations in contrast to the position prevalent in the neighbouring country. Thevenot found that the King of Persia killed his grandmother because she opposed the occupation of Qandhar from the Mughals, during the time of Shah Jahan. Mughal women did not face such brutality. Even in cases of detected conspiracies, the Mughal kings showed magnanimity of forgiving them or, at worst, confiscated their properties, stopped their pensions and put them behind the bars, like in case of Maham Anaga or Zeb-un-nisa and others.[123]

The respect that the female relations of the royalty got from the nobility was noteworthy. Till the kings maintained their hold, the nobles could not meet the royal ladies directly. Moreover, they dismounted from their horses at a distance and bowed if they happened to pass their way. They showed all respect to the royal ladies and if they were offered betel leaves by them through their eunuchs, the nobles received that with a bow, thus expressing their regard for them.[124] However, in the later period of weak Mughal emperors, all such reverence vanished. The royal guards caricatured Udham Bai's relation with Javed Khan. They tied up a young ass and bitch at the palace gate and when the nobles and courtiers came to attend darbar (King's Court where the king held all discussions regarding the state), they audaciously asked them to bow to these two first, because the ass represented Javed Khan entitled *Nawab Bahadur* and the bitch, Hazrat Qudsia (Udham Bai), the queen mother.[125]

The practice of filial love and concern continued to be observed in Muslim households, in general. Muslim homes remained the abodes of love and regards for the elders and other female relations.[126]

Sati and Jauhar

There were two peculiar practices of Hindus—the primitive custom of sati, that is, burning of the widow along with the dead body of the husband and *jauhar*, that is, self-immolation of the ladies in view of the impending widowhood on the defeat and death of their respective husbands in the battle. Sati was originally a Kshatriya (name of a caste) custom and was mainly followed by the ruling and the warring classes up to about 13th century. Thereafter, it came to be adopted by the commoners as well. Nevertheless, not all Hindu widows committed sati and as per one estimation, when the prevalence of this custom was at its highest, among Rajputs, about 10 per cent and among general population, about one in a thousand widows committed sati. Such cases were both voluntary and coercive.

The foreign travellers have made repeated references of Hindu satis. The practices were not known to other Muslim communities outside India.[127] Sati was highly extolled in Hindu community, particularly Rajputs. Since it was related with the single-minded devotion of the lady towards her husband, even poets like Amir Khusrau praised it and suggested that if his religion permitted this, then many of his co-religionists would die eagerly in that manner.[128] Ibn Batuta narrates that when a rebel, Ain-ul-Mulk, was rumoured to have been killed, his wife refused to save her life by running away along with her other relations. She showed her inclination to be burnt alive, like a Hindu widow, in case his death was confirmed.[129] During the reign of Jahangir, the Muslim population of Rajaur, who were converts from Hindus, were practising it in their own novel way. Instead of burning the widows, they buried them alive, along with the bodies of their deceased husbands. Jahangir recorded, 'I heard that recently they (the people of Rajaur) put alive into the grave a girl of ten or twelve along with her (dead) husband, who was of the same age'.[130] The writings of the contemporary travellers show that such novel burial continued even thereafter.[131] Aurangzeb has also mentioned about Sati when, in his last letter to Kam Bakhsh, he wrote, 'Udaipuri, your mother was with me in my sickness. She intends to accompany me (after my death i.e. she will soon die after me like a Hindu Sati)'.[132] However, the practice did not become popular among the Muslims and it remained limited to only a few of those, who had a Hindu origin or who lived in a Hindu environment.

As for *jauhar*, it was mostly confined to Rajputs. It attracted some followers from among the Muslims also. At the time of the invasion of Timur, Kamal-ud-din, the Governor of Bhatnir, and his retainers burnt their women alive, along with their property before going to the battlefield.[133] Humayun thought of killing all his female kith and kin after his defeat at Kanauj. He repented later for not having killed Aqiqa Bibi in his own presence, who got lost during the battle of Chausa.[134] Mirza Nathan, the author of *Baharistan-i-Ghaybi*, wrote that like Rajputs, the Muslims killed their women and children before going to fight the battle.[135] During his own fight with the Assamese, this author ordered Sadat Khan to stay at the gate of his harem and as soon as he heard about his attaining martyrdom in the battlefield, he should perform the rites of *jauhar* 'with all the inmates of the mahal, big and small and take your (his) journey to the Kingdom of Heaven with eternal honour'.[136] One modern authority is of the view that *jauhar* was frequently resorted to by Muslims as the last weapon to save the honour of their family.[137] However, since there are not many references of Muslim ladies undergoing it in comparison to the Rajput ladies in the contemporary works, it appears that although having an impact, yet, it was not very popular among Muslims who considered the shedding of female blood a heinous crime.

Posthumous Ceremonies

A look at the ceremonies for the dead brings to light the discrimination made in their observance with regard to women. The Quran provided for similar funeral and after-death rites for both men and women.[138] Similar prayers were recited for both at the time of laying the body to rest in the grave and then similarity was observed in the rituals that followed. One of the important ceremonies, for instance, was *siyum* or the ceremony of the third day or the *phool* ceremony. On this day, the friends and relatives gathered at the grave of the dead to recite the Quran for the benefit of the departed soul. Ibn Batuta narrated in detail as to how this ceremony was performed for his deceased daughter. A large gathering collected at her grave, the Holy Quran was read, flowers, dry fruits, coconut and a cloth were placed upon her grave and all the mourners were served with sugar-candy drinks and betel leaves thereafter, besides being sprinkled with rose water.[139] With the passage of time and the fall in the status of women, some of the ceremonies for them were dropped. Manucci has narrated, 'In the case of women they do not call out the commendations to Muhammad as is done for men, for they declare that women have no entry into heaven'.[140] This social discrimination against women was against the Quranic promise of equal treatment for both the sexes with regard to reward and punishment. Apparently, the status of women in society had declined.

Female Slaves

A large number of slaves and maids existed in the medieval society. Ala-ud-din alone had 50,000 slaves. Muhammad bin Tughlaq had so many slaves that as per Ibn Batuta, he set apart three days of the week during Id celebrations to manumit some of them and to get them married. As per Afif, he kept a day of the week for this purpose. During the time of Firoz Tughlaq, their number had risen to 180,000.[141] The slave girls were called *bandis* or *khawas* or *pari-star*.[142] The writings of the contemporary authorities show that they were treated like commodities. Hence, a sultan was asked to pay proper compensation if he desired to get released a slave from the custody of a master.[143] They were purchased and sold in the market; their price varied according to their physique, personal charm and sensual appeal. There were markets for them in India and other countries like China, Persia, Turkistan, Moka (Mocha on Red Sea) and Arabia.[144] During Ala-ud-din Khalji's time, they had fixed prices in the market. The price of an ordinary working female slave, as per Barani, ranged from 5 to 12 *tankas* and for a charming beauty between 20 and 40 *tankas*. Their prices could not be bargained, nor could they be displayed like other commodities. Even the presence of brokers in their case was prohibited. Subsequently, during the 14th century, another set of prices prevailed for the female slaves in Delhi. Umari informed that An ordinary female slave was priced 8 *tankas*, 15 *tankas* for one who was kept as mistress and even 20,000 *tankas* or more for an accomplished one. Their prices were less outside Delhi. Even Ibn Batuta informed about general low price of the slave girls during his time.[145] However, slavery recorded discernible decline after the 14th century. This may be due to the availability of a cheap, free trained hereditary labour in the later period. Babur, in his *Babur Nama*, mentions about the presence of a large number of artisans and workmen organised in hereditary castes, but omits mention of slaves. Similarly, the European travellers although refer to the existence of slaves, they did not, however, notice any large-scale slave market as existed in Delhi during the 14th century.[146]

The replenishment of slaves, however, came from another source. Women of the enemies were captured in the battlefields. This was not only to inflict a great humiliation on the enemy but also to get beautiful damsels for varied purposes. The author of *Mirat-i-Sikanderi* narrated how Hoshang, the sultan of Malwa, captured slaves and slave girls after his victory over sultan of Sonkhera. Similarly, Gulbadan mentions about Babur's capture and distribution of Ibrahim Lodi's dancing girls.[147] Akbar tried to be more humane by banning the practice of capturing prisoners of war.[148] However, the salutary impact of this measure got eroded when he and his successors openly asked for the daughters and other female relations of the vanquished for their harems as a part of the peace treaty, finding mention in *Ain-i-Akbari* and also in *Tuzak-i-Jahangiri*.[149] As a result, along with these ladies, hundreds of their slave girls and maid servants accompanied the brides. They served their mistresses and were to be the 'joy-toy' for the new masters. An interesting story was that of Ganna Begam. She was an accomplished poetess and an exemplary beauty. Her hand was sought by the highest of nobles like Shuja-ud-daulah, the *Nawab* of Bengal and Imad-ul-Mulk, the imperial Wazir. When she was on her way to get married to Shuja, she was surrounded by a contingent of Jawahar Singh Jat. Somehow, she escaped the capture. Thereafter, her mother got her married to Imad-ul-Mulk. Her marriage offended Mughlani Begam whose daughter, Umda Begam, had been betrothed to Imad-ul-Mulk in her childhood. When Abdali captured Delhi in 1757 A.D., Mughlani Begam, being in Abdali's good books, ensured that Imad-ul-Mulk married Umda Begam and forced Ganna Begam to serve as a bondmaid to her for the rest of her life. The poignancy of this lady has been vividly engraved in the epitaph on her grave that reads '*Ah, Gham-i-Ganna Begam*' (Alas! weep for Ganna Begam).[150]

Slave girls and maid servants formed a part of the dowry or were offered as gifts as a mark of respect and love.[151] They were even exchanged mutually. Aurangzeb exchanged Zainabadi for his concubine Chatter Bai.[152] The writings of the contemporary European travellers inform that peasant women along with their men and children were ill-treated and enslaved for non-payment of land revenue. During the Mughal period, it was a practice that if any robbery took place within the jurisdiction of a *Jagirdar* (the holder of a *jagir* [assignment of a land grant bestowed by the King to a feudal superior in recognition of his administrative and/or military service]) or a *Faujdar* (the administrative head of a *Sarkar* (district), he was either required to trace out the culprit and recover loot or compensate for the loss himself. It was under this pretext that these officials sacked any village they chose. They killed the menfolk and carried away their women and children, whom they sold as slaves. It is reported that once a woman having been seized in one of such raids by a *Faujdar* was given to a trooper in lieu of his pay. The latter, however, sold her for ₹40.[153]

The female slaves were broadly of two types: those kept for menial and domestic work and the others who, because of their talent and beauty, were meant for company and pleasure. The former were ill-treated and the latter were treated with kindness.[154] At times, slave girls occupied a dominating position in the household. Many of them became concubines and few even rose to the level of their legal wives. Shah Turkan was a Turkish maid turned concubine of Iltutmish.[155] Mewajan, the wife of Humayun was initially a domestic maid of Gulbadan's retinue.[156] Three *kaneezes* (slave girls) became lawful wives of Hasan, Sher Shah's father.[157] Zainabadi Mahal, the love of Aurangzeb's youthful days was the slave girl of Mir Khalil, his maternal uncle.[158] Udaipuri Mahal was his slave girl turned concubine.[159]

The Prostitutes

Another class of women, who catered to the public need of pleasure and entertainment, was the prostitutes. They were, generally, proficient in dance and music. In that age of sensuality, prostitution had come to stay as a part and parcel of the social life. An anecdote of Ferishta shows how they had become very popular by the time of Ala-ud-din Khalji. Once a courtier named Ain-ud-din Bijapuri pointed out to the sultan his neglect in regulating the most popular commodity, that is, prostitutes, although he had fixed the prices of other items.[160] It is also recorded that once an ordinary citizen complained to Delhi Kotwal about the disturbance of public peace, one of the reasons for which was the opening of a brothel beside his house.[161] Writing about Calicut, Nicoli Conti observed, '[P]ublic women are everywhere to be had, residing in particular houses of their own in all parts of the cities who attract the men by sweet perfumes and ointment by their blandishments, beauty and youth for the Indians are much addicted to licentiousness'.[162] Abdur Razzaq, who visited Bijapur in the middle of the 15th century, intimated about the presence of brothels in the form of a bazaar in that city.[163] Badaoni informs that by the time of Akbar, their number had risen to such an extent that it was difficult to count them.[164] Their number continued to increase and by the end of 17th century, in the city of Lahore alone, 6,000 houses were occupied by the 'public' women.[165] During the time of later Mughals, it became a fashion to patronise a prostitute. The literary writings of the time make frequent references to prostitution, thus, showing the popularity this institution had gained in the society.[166]

The financial consideration was the major factor for women joining prostitution. In second half of the 17th century, some of the provincial Governors also forced a few of the unmarried ladies, both Hindus and Muslims, to join prostitution and live along with the other public women in areas earmarked for them.[167]

The society showed double standards in the treatment of prostitutes. On the one hand, the institution of public women was considered essential for social health but on the other hand, they were held in low esteem. Barani wrote that one Sayyid Nur-ud-din Mubarak Shah, a saint of the time of Iltutmish, considered prostitution necessary in order to save the modesty of pious women, but he wanted that such women should carry on their trade in a quiet and subdued manner.[168] Amir Khusrau, likewise, considered it essential for the diversion of youth and the soldiers.[169] But, himself being averse to them, he treated prostitute Bibi Tabha very shabbily. She was made to sit on an ass and was taken around the city to see whether anybody claimed her and when none came forward, he took her finally to the hakim for necessary punishment. He also showed his surprise as to why these ladies were not satisfied with one man and preferred to be the favourite of the masses.[170]

Once any lady joined this profession, she needed to be officially registered. After that all her family ties were broken and she was totally deprived of family affinity and love.[171] From the writings of the contemporary European travellers, it is noticed that the public stigma attached to visiting brothels gradually disappeared. The society developed a tolerance for the harlots and the profession of the prostitution remained no more a disgrace.[172] They got the patronage of the royalty and nobility all through in varying degrees. Accordingly, their status and recognition also oscillated up and down. Kaiqubad, for instance, was so much given to unrestrained pleasures and debauchery that following his example, the whole society suffered fall in moral values, resulting in an increase in demand of such women. While writing about this, Ferishta wrote:

> His own pursuits soon became the fashion at court, and in a short time licentiousness and vice prevailed to such an extent, that every shady grove was filled with women and parties of pleasure ... so that even the magistrates were seen drunk in public and music was heard in every house.[173]

Similarly, Qutb-ud-din Mubarak Shah had become so much a part of them that he often dressed like a female and went around the city in the company of harlots and even danced in the houses of the nobles.[174] They enjoyed the patronage of Emperors like Shah Jahan and those of later Mughals and also of their morally corrupt nobility.

It is of interest to note that except Aurangzeb, no Monarch ever thought of abolishing it altogether. Since public women were required to pay a fixed amount of money in the form of a tax, it was a source of revenue for them.[175] As per Ferishta, Ala-ud-din Khalji classified them into three categories and fixed their charges accordingly, ordering thereby that none should charge above the fixed rates. However, Amir Khusrau gives a contradictory view. According to him, he discouraged prostitution and, therefore, ordered all public women to get married within a fixed period. On this basis, K.S. Lal disapproves the classification in three categories.[176] However, from a thorough analysis vis a vis the situation that was then prevailing, it may be drawn that although Ala-ud-din Khalji was not in favour of prostitution, yet, till somebody was in the profession, he regulated their rates. This appears probable because, in spite of Ala-ud-din's strictness, their appeal to the public did not dwindle. Khusrau himself has narrated how Maulana Shams Asadi, a respectable religious leader, had been visiting such women regularly.[177]

Akbar, in order to check their rising popularity, secluded their habitation outside the capital that was called *Shaitanpura* (the 'Devils' Quarters). He also appointed state officials: a keeper, deputy and a secretary, for supervising the affairs of these quarters. It was required that whosoever wanted to visit the place or wanted to take any lady from there to his house had to register his name and other particulars with them. In case any well-known noble wanted to deflower a virgin, the prior permission was required to be taken from the emperor. He also privately enquired from the well-known prostitutes about the persons visiting them. He reprimanded and even punished such persons afterwards.[178]

Aurangzeb was the first Muslim monarch who thought of striking at the very root of the institution of prostitution. In order to abolish it, he ordered that the public women must either marry or leave his empire. He banned music, use and sale of wine and closed the public houses, the essential requirements for the profession of these ladies. But this order was also not very effective.[179] So, he issued another order and asked the censors to check this flesh trade.[180] These measures did seem to have an immediate impact. Manucci testified, 'This was the cause that the palaces and great enclosures where they dwelt went to ruin little by little; for some of them married and others went away or, at least concealed themselves'.[181]

But, in the long run, his efforts also proved abortive. In the later part of his reign (1690 A.D.), Ovington found a large number of prostitutes living in the city of Bombay.[182]

These public women were also responsible for the growing moral indecency and laxity in the society. In the early part of the period under study, they still appeared to have some norms of their profession. Once they had contract with somebody, they did not entertain another person under any pressure.[183] However, soon they were found indulging in unethical and objectionable practices. For instance, during the time of Iltutmish, Nizam-ud-din Sughra, who held the post of Shaikh-ul-Islam, conspired with a nautch girl named Gauhar to charge Shaikh Jalal-ud-din Tabrizi, a Sufi saint of repute, of having committed adultery with her. He promised to give her 500 coins for it. Luckily, the conspiracy failed.[184] Khusrau also describes the indecency of a dancing girl, who, in between her performance, attended the call of the nature in front of all present.[185] Further, writing during Jahangir's time, Withington mentioned that they openly offered themselves for sharing the bed.[186] The contemporary literature also depict their ill-practices. Describing about the prostitutes of Jaunpur, poet Vidyapati wrote in his *Kirtilata*, '*Chhanda*' 24 (a form of poetry writing) that they flocked the market and openly induced young damsels to join their trade. At another place ('*Chhanda*' 22), he writes that their shyness was unnatural and their youth was artificial. For the sake of money, they pretended love so as to covet other. They were greedy to better their fortunes. Deprived of husbands, the vermilion on their foreheads symbolised their ill repute. '*Chhanda*' 22 reads as follows:

Lajja kittim kapat tarunna
Dhan nimitte dahae prem,
Lobhe binaa saubhage Kaman
Binu svami sindur para parichaya apaman.[187]

Dancers and Singers

Another section of public women was that of dancers and singers. The writings of the contemporaries are replete with their references. Ibn Batuta mentioned about a separate market for singing girls in Daulatabad called Tarababad. Asad Beg, in his *Wikaya-i-Asad Beg*, confirmed about their establishments in the market in Bijapur during Akbar's reign. Della Valle describes about public performance of dance and music by Muslim women at Cambay. Amir Khusrau, Dargah Quli Khan, Terry and Manucci and many others have described their presence and activities.[188] The Muslim population kept alive their folk songs and dances that they usually displayed in festivals. On the eve of the coronation of Sher Shah, Sarwani reports of performance of Afghan dances that are construed to be Kathak dance of the Afghans.[189] Gradually, dancing and singing became an independent profession. These dancers were of different castes and with different names, such as *lalani*, *harakni*, *Kanjari* or *Kanchani* and *Domni*. They practised different kinds of music. They were commonly hired in feasts and festivals for regaling.[190]

The scope of the development of art of these ladies and also their material gains depended mainly on the patronage of the upper class. The contemporary authors show that female dancers and musicians were patronised.[191] There are many paintings of the time as well that depict this patronage, wherein the harem ladies are shown amusing themselves with music and dance.[192] The kings and the nobles maintained their own troupes of female dancers and musicians to add colour to occasions of enjoyment and mirth. Among the Mughals, the royal ladies also maintained their separate entertaining groups of Muslim dancing and singing girls.[193] Shah Jahan showed special favour towards the dancing girls called *kanchanis*. Bernier wrote that they were not the prostitutes seen in bazaar, but they belonged to a more private and respectable class, who attended the grand weddings of *omrahs* (nobility) and mansabdars (members of Imperial bureaucracy of Mughal empire, organised by Akbar in 1595–1996 A.D. for the purpose of singing and dancing. Most of these *kanchanis* were beautiful and well dressed and sang to perfection; and with their limbs being extremely supple, they danced with wonderful agility and were always correct with regard to time.[194] Manucci narrates that during Shah Jahan's reign, these *kanchanis* were under obligation to visit the court twice a week in order to give their scintillating performance and when they came, the Emperor Kept them in the palace for the whole night for amusement. Once, when Shah Jahan took one of them as concubine and nobles objected a woman of that rank being kept in the palace, the Emperor replied, '*Mithai nek har dukan kih baashad*'(Sweetmeats are good, whatever shop they may come from).[195] The dancing girls were also patronised by the princes and nobles. Bowery has written about their patronage by the nobles. It has already been discussed how Dara fell for dancing girl, Rana Dil, whom he subsequently took as wife. Bernier discusses about Shuja's liking for them.[196] Aurangzeb had a secret liking for them. This is revealed from the special names that he conferred on such ladies in the harem, the list of which has been provided by Manucci.[197] Aurangzeb's infatuation for a dancing girl Zainabadi is well known. He is reported to have agreed to have a cup of wine offered by her in order to test his love for her.[198]

The sway of these ladies reached its zenith during the reign of later Mughals. Lal Kanwar, a dancing girl turned wife of Emperor Jahandar Shah, and Hazrat Begam (Qudsia Begam), another dancing girl turned concubine of Emperor Muhammad Shah, are well known. So much was the influence of Lal Kanwar that the locality of her birth was named *Lal Kuan; Qila-i-Mubarak, Qila-i-Mualla* or *Qila-i-Shahjahanbad* came to be called *Lal-Qila*, her mosque as *Lal Masjid* and her burial place as *Lal Bangla*. Equally influential was Qudsia Begam.[199] The contemporary Dargah Quli Khan has identified 19 prominent women artists in dance and music of Emperor Muhammad Shah's time like Khushali Ram Jani, Behnai-Feel Sawar, Ad Begam, Chamani, Saras Roop, Nur Bai, Chakmak Dahni, Kali Ganga, Zeenat, Gulab, Ramzani, Rehman Bai, Panna Bai, Kamal Bai, Uma Bai, Panna and Tanu. Out of them, Nur Bai, Chamani, Chakmak, Kamal Bai and Panna were favourites of Muhammad Shah and enjoyed his patronage.[200] Except a few nobles like Murshid Quli Jafar Khan, Alivardi Khan and Safdar Jang, none could escape their evil influence.[201] Professionally, such ladies received a great boost but morally, they stooped to the lowest ebb.

Women and Morality

The Muslim women of the medieval times were subjected to all sorts of social restrictions and bondage with a view to preserve their chastity. There are numerous references in the works of contemporary poets and writers showing how the common Muslim women safeguarded their chastity. Amir Khusrau has narrated the story of a lady who was sought by a king. Finding herself helpless, she took out both her eyes with her fingers and sent them to the king. Moved at this and realising her determination, the king left her.[202] Manucci has narrated an anecdote wherein a man coveting a girl charged her with adultery. It was with great astuteness that she not only saved her modesty but also proved it so.[203]

The other side of the morality can be gauged from an anecdote of the Lodi period that has been narrated by different contemporary writers with some variation. It has been reported that a soldier's wife developed an affair with another man while her husband was away on an official assignment. The man started visiting her house frequently. One night, finding her crying child a hindrance in their amorous act, the woman strangulated him to death. She made the man dig out a grave for the child inside the house itself and when he was busy doing so, she hit him from the back and killed him also there and then. She buried both of them together over there. In the morning, she spread the story of her child having been taken away by wolf and also shed crocodile tears. When her husband returned, a neighbour narrated the true story to him. The husband, pretending that some treasure was buried by him inside the house, wanted to open the grave to know the truth. The lady became sceptical. She asked him to bring the digging instrument from inside the room and when he went in, she closed the door from outside and put the house on fire burning her husband also alive. The lady was ultimately given death penalty by the *qazi* for the triple murder.[204] Mushtaqi narrates another incident of the time of Khizr Khan wherein a woman killed her own son out of her rivalry for the second wife of her husband, who was very dear to him. After killing her son, she kept the blood-smeared dagger under the pillow of second wife in order to make her suspect of the murder. The man, however, was able to dig out the truth.[205]

The Muslim women were also found indulging in anti-social activities. Ibn Batuta narrated about the presence of enchantresses called *kaftars* in the Malabar area.[206] They indulged in gruesome activities of killing persons by a mere look. *Kaftar* literally means a hyena that digs up and devours. Hence, this metaphoric expression was used for such ladies. It was believed that if the chest of a person dying at their mere look was cut, one would find the heart missing. They believed that it was eaten up by the enchanter/enchantress. He also narrated an incident of a child killed by a *kaftar*. Although he did not specify the religion of these *kaftars*, his mentioning that Muslims also learnt this art, however, leads to the conjecture that some of those *kaftars* must be out of the Muslim community. The ladies were members of the gangs of dacoits also. They not only allured the customers by their beauty and tricks but even put the nooses around the necks of their preys themselves.[207]

The other sign of degradation was the habit of drinking among ladies. Amir Khusrau vehemently opposed drinking of wine by the ladies. He pleaded that drinking was the root cause of destruction and the breaking of the family bond.[208] This habit increased during the Mughal times. Aurangzeb counted names of only two persons: one of himself and other of his chief *Qazi* Abdul Wahab, who were teetotallers, although, interestingly, Wahab too was reported to be drinking in secret. He did not include the ladies in his list.[209] To check adultery, Ala-ud-din Khalji introduced harsh punishment of castration for the adulterer and death for the adulteress. As a result, Ibn Batuta reports that mother of Masud Khan, the brother of Muhammad bin Tughlaq, was stoned to death after her confession of adultery. She was daughter of Sultan Ala-ud-din Khalji.[210] Barani also pleaded for the Quranic death punishment for committing adultery with a married woman.[211] Notwithstanding, harsh punishments also could not check the malaise. The existence of sects like *Mulahidan* and *Ibahatiyan* during the sultanate period spoke volumes of the immorality that had crept into the society. They were probably the Karamarthians who were found in great numbers in western India during those days and were accused of practising *Ilhad* (heresy) and *Ibahat* (incest). The followers of these sects were allowed to have sex with any woman they got hold of in the darkness of the night when all lights were extinguished. Ala-ud-din persecuted them mercilessly. But, they emerged again and Firoz Tughlaq had to take severe action against them.[212]

During the Mughal period, with the moral values falling still further, the social evil of adultery spread unabated and the administrative efforts also could not contain it.[213] Jahangir, therefore, openly expressed his doubts about the fidelity of the Muslim women and the contemporary European travellers corroborated his view.[214]

General Social Attitude

A careful study of the developments reveals that the public behaviour towards women varied vastly, depending upon the particular situations they were placed in. Within the house, a woman was no more than a slave catering to the needs of all and bearing all sorts of treatments she was subjected to. Her fidelity still remained doubtful in the eyes of her husband.

The women were totally dependent on their menfolk and considered them their saviours. Men looked upon their women as the honour of the house and considered it their moral duty to safeguard them. It is understandable, in this context, that one of the reasons for Mahmud Shah bin Nasir Shah (1511–1531 A.D.), sultan of Malwa, for dismissing his Rajput minister Medini Rai was that the latter forcibly took away Muslim women and made them slaves and dancing girls. Ultimately, he had to seek pardon. He was ordered to free Muslim women and not to be cruel to them in future.[215] Similarly, Babur condemned Ghazi Khan of Milwat for becoming fugitive after leaving his womenfolk at the mercy of his enemy and the nobles of Humayun pleaded strict punishment for Kamran, who was notorious for defiling women. They wanted that a check should be put on this so as to ensure security to their women.[216] Even conversion of a Muslim lady was taken as an attack on the honour of the Muslims and was dealt with severely by the rulers. It is reported that during Jahangir's time, death punishment was given to a Hindu for taking a Muslim girl in marriage, although Hindu girls could be married by Muslim youths. Also, one of the reasons for Shah Jahan's action against Portuguese in 1629 A.D. was reported to be an incident wherein a Portuguese attacked a Mughal lady near Dacca whom he first baptised and then married.[217] There are instances where community as a whole rose against the disrespect shown to a single Muslim lady of their race. It is known that Mubarak Khan, a nephew of Sher Shah and Governor of Roh, fell for the beautiful daughter of one Alahdad Sambal and wanted to marry her. But her father declined the proposal under the excuse of difference in their social standards. He was of pure race and would not marry his daughter to Mubarak Khan, a son of a slave girl. In his frustration, the latter perpetrated atrocities on the Sambalis, pillaged their villages and took away the daughter of one Khairo, the Kotwal among the Sambalis, to his house. The Sambalis collectively turned to the Governor and asked him to return the girl or face the consequences. They declared, 'If you will turn your eye towards our women, we will kill you and in return for atoning your murder, Ser (Sher) Khan will slay some of the chiefs of the Sambalis to the utmost'. And they did kill him, although, in retaliation, the forces of Sher Shah slew most of their men.[218] There was a similar rising when Masud, minister regent (1673–1683 A.D.), betrothed Shahr Banu (Padishah Bibi), the sister of infant Sultan Adil Shah of Bijapur, to prince Azam in order to buy peace from the Mughals. It was only after promising that this clause would not be observed that Masud could pacify the uprising.[219] The honour of the women was such a sensitive matter and so sure was it to arouse the Muslim feelings that many of the opportunist kings frequently took the pretext of saving the honour of Muslim women so as to justify their attacks on others' territories or for other political moves. Puran Mal of Raisin, for instance, was a political challenge to Sher Shah. He attacked the territory and justified the attack on the plea that the Muslim ladies of Chanderi (Raisin was a part of it) had complained to the sultan against atrocities hurled on them by Puran Mal.[220] Similarly, noble Khawas Khan had supported the cause of Adil Shah against Islam Shah Sur. But when the latter became sultan, the former ran away and took shelter with the King of Kumaon. Sultan Islam Shah called him back from the shelter of the King of Kumaon under the pretext that he needed his help against Rana of Mewar who had carried away Muslim women, a pleading that was sure to work.[221] The author of *Tabaqat-i-Akbari* has narrated yet another incident wherein Sultan Mahmud Bin Sharqi attacked Nasir Khan, the ruler of Kalpi, one of the pretexts being that he had given Muslim women to Kafir.[222]

Attitude towards women was totally different when they were the relations of an enemy or an opponent or a rebel. The community and religious affinity relegated to the background then. All sorts of atrocities and insults were meted out to them. Innocent women were made to suffer for the wrongs of their men. Numerous such instances find mention in the writings of the contemporary historians. Ferishta and Ghulam Husain Salim (author of *Riyazu-s-Salatin*) narrate about Balban's capture, torture and slaughter of women and children of adherents of rebel noble Tughral of Lakhnauti whom he wanted to chastise; Nizam-ud-din Ahmad, author of *Tabaqat-i-Akbari*, describes Ala-ud-din Khalji's atrocities on women and children of rebels; Sirhindi informs as to how after murdering Sultan Qutb-ud-din Mubarak Shah, Khusrau Khan humiliated his women by marrying his widow himself and allowing the Hindus to carry away the remaining and how Muhammad bin Tughlaq tortured women and children of those victims whom he punished illegally or otherwise; Abul Fazl narrates about atrocities of Kamran on the women of Humayun's supporters and so on and so forth.[223] Even king like Sher Shah, who was considered to be having great concern for honour of ladies, was reported to be selling the wives and children of the rebel Zamindars after killing them.[224] The cruelties of the foreign Muslim invaders like Timur, Nadir Shah and Ahmad Shah Abdali are also vividly described by the historians who show how ruthless and cruel they were in torturing the public irrespective of religion, after their victory.[225] The helplessness of these ladies can be judged from the condition of Hazrat Begam. She was the maiden daughter of Emperor Muhammad Shah and had rejected the offer of marriage to Emperor Alamgir II. She was captured by Abdali and was forced to marry him. Abdali was 'of grand-fatherly age, whose two ears had been docked and nose was rotting from a leprous carbuncle'.[226]

Some of the rulers did display a positive attitude towards women. Humayun, for instance, had great respect for womankind and any immodesty or cruelty shown to them annoyed him. When he found that Rukayya Begam was subsisting on beef, he exclaimed in anger, 'O Kamran! was it the mode of your existence and did you feed the Asylum of Chastity on the flesh of cows! Could you not keep a few goats for her subsistence?'[227] Sher Shah was generally respectful to women. During the period when he managed the *jagir* of his father, he took strict action against the recalcitrant *Muqaddams* (the headman of a village (Muqaddams was responsible for collection of revenue and sole link between the government and the village) and as punishment, he used to take away their property and even women and children. However, while he distributed other confiscated property among his soldiers, he kept the family members under his careful custody and guard so that none misbehaved with them. Sarwani mentions that Sher Shah did not even allow his son, Jalal Khan, to misbehave with Mihr Sultan who refused to marry his daughter to him, in spite of the latter's desire.[228] His respectful return of the women of Humayun's camp is seen as a token of his highest regard for womanhood. In view of this, therefore, the incident like his selling the wives and children of the rebel Zamindars after the latter were killed by him, as reported by Qanungo and discussed above, could be an aberration and not the rule. Emperor Akbar was respectful to women, promulgated many orders in their favour, yet he could not rise above the sensuality of his age in his personal life. Alivardi Khan and one of the Sayyid brothers, Husain Ali Khan, are some other examples of such respectful persons. Alivardi had the rare distinction of having only one wife. He was respectful to the ladies of his enemies, like rebel Sham Sher Khan and of other Afghans.[229] There were kings like Bahlol Lodi, Jahangir and Shah Jahan who paid greatest regards to their favourite wives. Among the general public also, there were some examples of good behaviour towards women. Ovington has narrated the story of a Muslim porter who was employed in the English factory at Surat. He asked for leave and some money from his employer every Thursday so that he could go to his wife and show his love and concern for her by taking some gifts for her.[230] However, women, in general, were considered untrustworthy and synonymous with cowardice, inaction, incapability, helplessness, short-sightedness and instruments of sensuality. Mirza Nathan, for instance, observed that the women were 'not to be relied on like men; because even if women belong to a trustworthy and great family, yet they themselves do not belong to that class which characterise a trustworthy person'. The author of *Tarikh-i-Salim Shahi* compares a coward warrior running away from the battlefield to a woman; Sarwani while discussing about Lad Malika writes that she was incapable of ruling because she was a woman; Hamid-ud-din considers women second-rate; Aurangzeb equated women with short-sightedness; Abdul Hayy, author of *Maasir-ul-Umara*, decries women as having defective understanding and Manucci narrates about holy mendicants called *Sayyids* enticing ladies in the name of religion to satisfy their lust.[231] Above all, their greatest drawback was that they were 'females' and this cannot be explained in a better way than by the example of Razia who had to face all opposition, in spite of her capability and qualities of head and heart.

Notes

1. Amir Khusrau, *Hasht Bahisht*, ed. Maulana Sayyid Suleiman Ashraf (Aligarh: Aligarh Muslim University, 1918), 26–27; Amir Khusrau, *Matla-ul-Anwar* (Lucknow: Newal Kishore, 1302 A.H. [1884]), 223.

2. C. Colliver Rice, *Persian Women and Their Ways* (London: Seeley, Service & Co. 1923), 23–24.

3. *Atharvaveda*, Kand 6, *Sukt* 11, *Mantra* no. 3, trans. W.D. Whitney, *Atharvaveda Samhita* (Cambridge, Massachusetts, U.S.A.: Harvard University, 1905), 289; J. Tod, *Annals and Antiquities of Rajasthan*, vol. 1 (London: Smith Elder & Co., 1829), 636–639; Abul Fazl, *Ain-i-Akbari*, trans. H.S. Jarrett, vol. 3 (New Delhi: Crown Publications, 1988), 242.

4. Nur-ud-din Jahangir, *Tuzuk-i-Jahangiri*, trans. A. Rogers, ed. H. Beveridge, vol. 2 (Delhi: Munshiram Manoharlal, 1968), 181.

5. A.S. Beveridge, Introduction to *Humayun Nama, by* Gulbadan Begam (New Delhi: Idarah-i-Adabiyat-i-Delli, 1972), 9; Abul Fazl, *Akbar Nama*, trans. H. Beveridge, vol. 2 (Delhi: Ess Ess Publications, 1977), 510–511; Jahangir, *Tuzuk*, vol. 1: 1–2; Bikram Jit Hasrat, *Dara Shikuh, Life and Works* (New Delhi: Munshram Manoharlal, 1982), 1–2 (for Shah Jahan). See also Jafar Sharif, *Qanun-i-Islam*, trans. G.A. Herklots, ed. William Crooke (London: Oxford University Press, 1921), 17.

6. For first anecdote, see Ibn-i-Mohammad Sikander, *Mirat-i-Sikanderi*, in *Uttar Taimur Kaleen Bharat*, Part II, trans. S.A.A. Rizvi (Aligarh: Aligarh Muslim University, 1959), 371; also Rizkullah Mushtaqi, *Waqiat-i-Mushtaqi*, in *Uttar Taimur Kaleen Bharat*, Part II, trans. Rizvi (Aligarh: Aligarh Muslim University, 1958–1959), 564–565. Abul Fazl, *Akbar Nama*, vol. 3: 82–83; Blochmann, Notes to *Ain-i-Akbari*, by Abul Fazl, vol. 1: 375 (for Saif Khan).

7. *Aqiqah* literally means 'the hair of the new-born' and it referred to the shaving sacrifice usually observed on sixth or the seventh day. T.P. Hughes, *Dictionary of Islam*, (New Delhi: Rupa & Co., 1988), 50–51; James Hastings, ed., *Encyclopaedia of Religion and Ethics*, vol. 2 (New York, Charles Scribner's Sons, 1926), 659; Jafar Sharif, *Qanun-i-Islam*, 38, note 5. As per him, it was observed on 7th, 14th, 21st, 28th or 35th day after birth.

8. Niccolao Manucci, *Storia Do Mogor or Mogul India*, trans. William Irvine (New Delhi: Atlantic Publishers and Distributors, 1989), vol. 2: 320, vol. 3: 142–143 (for a rich man rejoicing on the birth of a son); Abul Fazl, *Akbar Nama*, vol. 2: 503; Khwaja Nizam-ud-din Ahmad, *Tabaqat-i-Akbari*, trans. B. De and Baini Prashad, vol. 2 (Calcutta: The Asiatic Society, 1973), 358 (rejoicing at Salim's birth); Mirza Nathan, *Baharistan-i-Ghaybi*, trans. M.I. Borah, vol. 2 (Guwahati: Government of Assam, 1936), 735–736 (celebrations of birth of Murad Bakhsh). There are many paintings depicting rejoicing at the birth of a prince. Refer P.N. Chopra, *Life and Letters Under the Mughals* (New Delhi: Ashajanak Publications, 1976), 197, notes 54–55; K.S. Lal, *The Mughal Harem* (New Delhi: Aditya Prakashan, 1988), pl.VI.

9. Abul Fazl, *Akbar Nama*, vol. 3: 816.

10. Tapan Raychaudhuri, *Bengal Under Akbar and Jahangir: An Introductory Study in Social History* (New Delhi: Munshiram Manoharlal, 1969), 14.

11. Mushtaqi, *Uttar Taimur*, Part I (1958), 100–101.
12. K.M. Ashraf, *Life and Conditions of the People of Hindustan*, 2nd ed. (New Delhi: Munshiram Manoharlal, 1970), 179, note 2.
13. Muhammad Kasim Hindu Shah Ferishta, *Tarikh-i-Ferishta*, trans. J. Briggs, vol. 2 (New Delhi: Atlantic Publishers & Distributors, 1989) 293, 295, 335–336. See also B.S. Chandrababu and Thilagavati, *Woman, Her History and Her Struggle for Emancipation* (Chennai: Bharathi Pusthakalayam, 2009), 181.
14. Ralph Fitch, in *Early Travels in India*, ed. William Foster (New Delhi: S. Chand & Co., 1968), 16–17; Edward Terry, in *Early Travels in India*, ed. William Foster (New Delhi: S. Chand & Co., 1968), 320–321; Nicholas Withington, in *Early Travels in India*, ed. William Foster (New Delhi: S. Chand & Co., 1968), 221; Robert Orme, *Historical Fragments of the Mogul Empire of the Morattoes, and of the English Concern in Indostan, from the year 1659*, ed. J.P. Guha, rpt. (New Delhi: Associated Publishing House, 1974), 301; Manucci, *Storia Do Mogor*, vol. 1: 201. Also see De Laet, *The Empire of the Great Mogol*, trans. and ann. J.S. Hoyland and S.N. Banerjee, vol. 1 (New Delhi: Idarah-i-Adabiyat-i-Delli, 1975), 31; J.F.G. Careri, *Indian Travels of Thevenot and Careri*, ed. S.N. Sen (New Delhi: National Archives of India, 1949), 248; Francois Pelsaert, *The Remonstrantie or Jahangir's India*, trans. W.H. Moreland and P. Geyl, rpt. (New Delhi: Idarah-i-Adabiyat-i-Delli, 1972), 84; M. De Thevenot, *Indian Travels of Thevenot and Careri*, ed. S.N. Sen (New Delhi: National Archives of India, 1949), 117; Abul Fazl, *Akbar Nama*, vol. 3: 791; Jafar Sharif, *Qanun-i-Islam*, 58; P.N.K. Bamzai, *A History of Kashmir* (Delhi: Metropolitan Book Co., 1962), 468.
15. Zahir-ud-din Babur, *Babur Nama*, trans. A.S. Beveridge, vol. 1 (New Delhi: Oriental Books Reprint Corp., 1970), 35; Beveridge, Appendix A to Gulbadan's *Humayun Nama*, 209 (for Aesha), 231–232 (for Gulchehra and Gulrang), 240 (for Hamida Banu), 214(for Bakshi Banu); Beveridge, Introduction to Gulbadan's *Humayun Nama*, 31 (for Gulbadan's marriage); also Gulbadan, *Humayun Nama*, 150–151 (for Hamida Banu); Mohammad Amir Qazwini, Muhammad Amin, *Badshah Nama*, Persian MS. (Patna: Buhar Collection), 30 (for Arjumand Banu).
16. Abdul Qadir Al Badaoni, *Muntakhabu-t-Tawarikh*, trans. W.H. Lowe, vol. 2 (New Delhi: Idarah-i-Adabiyat-i-Delli, 1973), 352 (for Salim); Abul Fazl, *Akbar Nama*, vol. 3: 791 (for Murad); J.N. Sarkar, *Studies in Aurangzib's Reign* (Calcutta: M.C. Sarkar & Sons, 1933), 1–2 (for Aurangzeb); K.R. Qanungo, *Dara Shukoh*, 2nd ed., vol. 1 (Calcutta: S.C. Sarkar, 1952), 13–14 (for Dara); Must'ad Khan, *Maasir-i-Alamgiri*, trans., ann. J.N. Sarkar (Calcutta: Royal Asiatic Society of Bengal, 1947), 31, 103, 40, 126 (for Muhammad Azim and Kam Baksh, respectively; J.N. Sarkar, *History of Aurangzib*, vol. 3 (New Delhi: New Orient Longman Ltd, 1972–1974), 44 (for Muhammad Sultan). See also Manucci, *Storia Do Mogor*, vol. 2: 324.
17. Terry, *Early Travels*, 321; Pelsaert, *The Remonstrantie*, 81; Manucci, *Storia Do Mogor*, vol. 3: 145; Francois Bernier, *Travels in the Mogul Empire, A.D. 1656–1668*, 2nd ed. (New Delhi: S. Chand & Co., 1968), 259.
18. Ferishta, *Tarikh-i-Ferishta*, vol. 2: 336 (for Adil Khan's daughter); Raychaudhuri, *Bengal Under*, 12, 230 (for practice in Bengal). Meer Hassan Ali, in *Observations of the Mussulmauns of India*, vol. 1 (New Delhi: Idarah-i-Adabiyat-i-Delli, 1973), 346–347, however, writes that in the cases where they were married at six or

seven, the couple was allowed to live in the same house so that they develop attachment for each other before they enter the actual married life.

19. Thevenot, *Indian Travels*, 117. See also J.S. Stavorinus, *Voyage to the East Indies (1768–1771)*, trans. Samuel Hull Wilcocke, vol. 1 (London: G. G. & J. Robinson, 1798), 440; Orme, *Historical Fragments*, 301 for similar views.
20. Abul Fazl, *Akbar Nama*, vol. 3: 791; Abul Fazl, *Ain-i-Akbari*, vol. 1: 213, note 1, 287; Badaoni, *Muntakhabu-t-Tawarikh*, vol. 2: 315, 349.
21. Abul Fazl, *Ain-i-Akbari*, vol. 1: 287–288; Badaoni, *Muntakhabu-t-Tawarikh*, vol. 2: 315, 349.
22. Badaoni, *Muntakhabu-t-Tawarikh*, vol. 2: 405.
23. Manucci, *Storia Do Mogor* (London: Murray, 1907), vol. 3: 55.
24. Gulbadan, *Humayun Nama*, 150, note 1 (on the authority of Jauhar).
25. J.N. Sarkar, *Fall of the Mughal Empire*, vol. 2 (Calcutta: M.C. Sarkar & Sons, 1966), 3.
26. Abbas Khan Sarwani, *Tarikh-i-Sher Shahi*, trans. B.P. Ambashthya (Patna: K.P. Jayaswal Research Institute, 1974), 205–206. See also K.R. Qanungo, *Sher Shah and His Times* (Bombay: Orient Longmans, 1965), 96–97, note 1.
27. Badaoni, *Muntakhabu-t-Tawarikh*, vol. 2: 405.
28. Shaikh Muhammad Kabir, 'Afsana-i-Badshahan', Photoprint of Microfilm copy (Patna: Patna University), fol. 39.
29. Ferishta, *Tarikh-i-Ferishta*, vol. 2: 238–239. See Amir Khusrau, *Dewal Rani Khizr Khan*, in *Khilji Kaleen Bharat*, trans. S.A.A. Rizvi (Aligarh: Aligarh Muslim University, 1917), 172 (for Khizr Khan's marriage).
30. Nizam-ud-din Ahmad, *Tabaqat-i-Akbari*, vol. 2: 599; Badaoni, *Muntakhabu-t-Tawarikh*, vol. 2: 352; Sujan Rai Bhandari, *Khulasat-ut-Tawarikh*, ed. Maulvi Zafar Hasan (New Delhi: G & Sons, 1918), 375–376.
31. Anonymous, *Iqbal Nama*, in *Iqbalnama by an Anonymous Contemporary Writer*, trans. S.H. Askari (Patna: Janki Prakashan, 1983), 4 (for Farrukhsiyar); Badaoni, *Muntakhabu-t-Tawarikh*, trans. Wolseley Haig, vol. 3: 99 (for dowry given by Kashmir Sultan); Bernier, *Mogul Empire*, 21, 22, note 1 (for prince Sultan Muhammad's dowry); Must'ad Khan, *Maasir-i-Alamgiri*, 73, 103, 129–130 (for dowries to Akbar, Azim and Kam Baksh).
32. Pelsaert, *The Remonstrantie*, 83; Harihar Das, *The Norris Embassy to Aurangzib (1699–1702)*, condensed and rearranged by S.C. Sarkar (Calcutta: K.L. Mukhopadhyay, 1959), 161; Manucci, *Storia Do Mogor*, vol. 3: 144–145.
33. Zia-ud-din Barani, *Tarikh-i-Firoz Shahi* (Calcutta: Bibliothica Indica, 1862), 117; also trans. S.A.A. Rizvi, in *Adi Turk Kaleen Bharat* (Aligarh: Aligarh Muslim University, 1956), 205.
34. Shams Siraj Afif, *Tarikh-i-Firoz Shahi*, ed. Maulvi Vilayat Husain (Calcutta: Bibliothica Indica, 1891), 180, 349–351; also R.C. Jauhri, *Firoz Tughluq* (Jalandhar: ABS Publications, 1990), 129. J.F. Richards, ed., *The Imperial Monetary System of Mughal India* (New Delhi: Oxford University Press, 1987), 139 (for *tanka*).
35. Mushtaqi, *Uttar Taimur*, Part II, 139.
36. Muhammad Hadi, *Tatimma-i-Waqiat-i-Jahangiri*, trans. H.M. Elliot and John Dowson, in *History of India as Told by Its Own Historians*, vol. VI (Allahabad: Kitab Mahal, 1964), 399; Mutamad Khan, *Iqbalnama-i-Jahangiri*, trans. Elliot and Dowson, in *History of India*, vol. VI (Allahabad: Kitab Mahal, 1964), 405.

37. Duarte Barbosa, *The Book of Duarte Barbosa*, trans. ed. and ann. M.L. Dames, vol. 1 (New Delhi: Asian Educational Services, 1989), 121 and note 2.
38. Abu-Umar-i-Usman Minhaj-ud-din Siraj, *Tabaqat-i-Nasiri*, trans. H.G. Raverty, vol. 1 (New Delhi: Oriental Books Reprint Corp., 1970), 650, note 4; Yahya Bin Ahmad Sirhindi, *Tarikh-i-Mubarak Shahi*, trans. K.K. Basu (Baroda: Abdullah Sirhindi Oriental Institute, 1932), 26 (he does not mention about her seeking divorce, but that she 'had been repudiated by him').
39. Badaoni, *Muntakhabu-t-Tawarikh*, vol. 3: 99.
40. Badaoni, *Muntakhabu-t-Tawarikh*, vol. 3: 59–60, 251.
41. Beveridge, Appendix A to Gulbadan's *Humayun Nama*, 209, 250–251, 230.
42. Samsam-ud-daula Shah Nawaz Khan and Abdul Hayy, *Maasir-ul-Umara*, trans. H. Beveridge, Part II, vol. 2 (Patna: Janki Prakashan, 1979), 819.
43. Hughes, *Dictionary of Islam*, 87. See also Chapter 1 for details.
44. Badaoni, *Muntakhabu-t-Tawarikh*, vol. 3: 147. Badaoni was a religious zealot and hence praised Shaikh Muin for such an attitude. For his concern for Shariat, see Mohibbul Hasan, ed., *Historians of Medieval India* (Meerut: Meenakshi Prakashan, 1968), 106–109.
45. Gulbadan, *Humayun Nama*, 130–131.
46. Beveridge, Appendix A to Gulbadan's *Humayun Nama*, 250.
47. J.M.S. Baljon, *Religion and Thought of Shah Wali Allah Dihlawi, 1703–1762 A.D.* (Leiden: E.J.Brill, 1986), 199.
48. F.W. Thomas, *Mutual Influence of Muhammadans and Hindus in India* (Cambridge: Deighton, Bell, 1892), 77; R. Burn, *Census of India (1901) Report*, XVI, 104.
49. A. Rashid, *Society and Culture in Medieval India 1206–1556 A.D.* (Calcutta: Firma K.L. Mukhopadhyay, 1969), 134.
50. Gulbadan, *Humayun Nama*, 113, 122, 129, 112; Beveridge, Appendix A to Gulbadan's *Humayun Nama*, 279; Abul Fazl, *Akbar Nama*, vol. 2: 569 (for Haj pilgrimages of these ladies).
51. Barani, *Tarikh*, 40–41 (for first reference). See Jahangir, *Tuzuk*, vol. 1: 172 (for second reference). For details about maintenance of widows, see Chapter 3.
52. Sirhindi, *Tarikh-i-Mubarak Shahi*.
53. Minhaj-ud-din Siraj, *Tabaqat-i-Nasiri*, trans. Raverty, vol. 1: 701; Ferishta, *Tarikh-i-Ferishta*, vol. 1: 133.
54. Mirza Muhammad Haider Dughlat, *Tarikh-i-Rashidi*, trans. N. Elias and E. Denison Ross (Patna: Academica, 1973), 251, note 3. Also Beveridge, Appendix A to Gulbadan's *Humayun Nama*, 291 (for Sultan Nigar Khanam); Manucci, *Storia Do Mogor*, vol. 1: 342–343 (for Rana Dil). 'Yanga' means 'aunt by marriage' or 'wife of an elder brother'.
55. Babur, *Babur Nama*, vol. 1: 18, vol. 2:704; Dughlat, *Tarikh-i-Rashidi*, 175, 239, 400 (he named the second husband as Hadi not Hada). See also Beveridge, Appendix A to Gulbadan's *Humayun Nama*, 250–251. He mentioned Mahdi as her first husband, then Shaibani and then Hada.
56. Abul Fazl, *Akbar Nama*, vol. 2: 197 and notes (for Bakshi Banu Begam), 526–527 (for Haji Begam).
57. Abul Fazl, *Akbar Nama*, vol. 2: 318, 364–365; Shah Nawaz Khan and Hayy, *Maasir*, Part I, vol. 2: 153.

58. Beveridge, Introduction to Gulbadan's *Humayun Nama*, 63; For other instances, Badaoni, *Muntakhabu-t-Tawarikh*, vol. 2: 59; Shah Nawaz Khan and Hayy, *Maasir*, Part II, vol. 2: 819.

59. Blochmann, Notes to *Ain-i-Akbari*, vol. 1, 321–323; Frederick Augustus, *The Emperor Akbar—A Contribution Towards the History of India in the 16th Century*, trans. A.S. Beveridge, vol. 2 (New Delhi: Atlantic Publishers and Distributors, 1989), 321.

60. Badaoni, *Muntakhabu-t-Tawarikh*, vol. 2: 367.

61. Anonymous, *Tarikh-i-Salim Shahi*, in *Memoirs of the Emperor Jahangir Written by Himself*, trans. David Price (New Delhi: Rare Books, 1904), 107–108; Beni Prasad, *History of Jahangir*, 3rd ed. (Allahabad: The Indian Press Ltd, 1940), 387–388. See Manucci, *Storia Do Mogor*, vol. 2: 118 (for Aurangzeb's permission).

62. Careri, *Indian Travels*, 249–250.

63. Manucci, *Storia Do Mogor*, vol. 1: 342–343.

64. Manucci, vol. 3: 145.

65. Simmi Jain, *Encyclopaedia of Indian Women Through the Ages: The Middle ages* (New Delhi: Kalpaz Publication, 2003), 111 (on the authority of an Urdu book, *Hindustani Mussalman Ek Nazar Men*, by Maulana Sayeed Abdul Hassan Ali Nadvi, 63).

66. Baljon, *Religion and Thought*, 199. See also Muhammad Ayub Qadri, *Majmua-i-Wasiya* (collection of Wills), Persian text (Hyderabad, Pakistan, 1964) point 7, 52; Urdu Trans., 82.

67. For details, see Chapter 4 of this book.

68. Ibn Batuta, *The Rehla of Ibn Batuta*, trans. Mahdi Husain (Baroda: Oriental Institute, 1953), 106, 122, 200, 208, 212–216.

69. Pelsaert, *The Remonstrantie*, 64; De Laet, *The Empire*, 90–91; also S.J. Monserrate, *The Commentary*, trans., ann. J.S. Hoyland and S.N. Banerjee (London: Oxford University Press, 1922), 202; Das, *Norris*, 267; Careri, *Indian Travels*, 247.

70. Barbosa, *The Book*, vol. 1:120.

71. J. Ovington, *India in the Seventeenth Century*, ed. J.P. Guha, vol. 1 (New Delhi: Associated Publishing House, 1976), 103.

72. Raychaudhuri, *Bengal Under*, 8–9, 231 (on the authority of Schouten, a European traveller). See also Barbosa, *The Book*, vol. 2:147–148 (about prevalent polygamy among Muslims of Bengal).

73. Badaoni, *Muntakhabu-t-Tawarikh*, vol. 2:211–212.

74. Blochmann, Notes to *Ain-i-Akbari*, by Abul Fazl, vol. 1:346 (for first explanation); Richard F. Burton, *Sind Revisited*, vol. 1 (London: Richard Bentley & Sons, 1877), 340 (for second explanation).

75. Abul Fazl, *Ain-i-Akbari*, vol. 1:288; Badaoni, *Muntakhabu-t-Tawarikh*, vol. 2: 367.

76. Nicoli Conti, *India in the Fifteenth Century*, ed. Richard Henry Major (London: Hak Society, 1857), 23; Terry, *Early Travels*, 320; Thevenot, *Indian Travels*, 117; Careri, *Indian Travels*, 248.

77. For details, see Chapter 4 of this book.

78. Khusrau, *Matla-ul-Anwar*, 117, 192; Das, *Norris*, 162; Stavorinus, *East Indies*, vol. 1: 440–441.

79. Barani, *Tarikh*, 340; Badaoni, *Muntakhabu-t-Tawarikh*, vol. 2: 192; Yusuf Mirak, *Mazhar-i-Shahjahani*, ed. Pir Husam-ud-din Rashidi (Hyderabad: Sindhi Adabi Board, n.d.), 21.

80. Khusrau, *Matla-ul-Anwar*, 198, 330.
81. Khusrau, *Matla-ul-Anwar*, 228; Khusrau, *Hasht Bahisht*, 27–30; Terry, *Early Travels*, 320.
82. Ferishta, *Tarikh-i-Ferishta*, vol. 1: 136.
83. Ibn Batuta, *Rehla*, 81.
84. Mushtaqi, *Uttar Taimur*, Part I, 115–117.
85. Beveridge, Introduction to Gulbadan's *Humayun Nama*, 65–66; Abul Fazl, *Akbar Nama*, vol. 2: 336; Augustus, *The Emperor*, vol. 1: 104.
86. Blochmann, Notes to *Ain-i-Akbari*, vol. 1, 389. See also Pelsaert, *The Remonstrantie*, 66; Manucci, *Storia Do Mogor*, vol. 2: 329, 435–436; Ovington, *Seventeenth Century*, vol. 1: 93–94.
87. Khusrau, *Hasht Bahisht*, 208–209.
88. Ibn Batuta, *Rehla*, 118.
89. Sirhindi, *Tarikh-i-Mubarak Shahi*, 234; Barani, *Tarikh*, 482–483, 506; Muhammad Bihamad Khani, *Tarikh-i-Muhammadi*, in *Tughlaq Kaleen Bharat*, Part I, trans. S.A.A. Rizvi (Aligarh: Aligarh Muslim University, 1956), 353–355.
90. Sirhindi, *Tarikh-i-Mubarak Shahi*, 234.
91. For details, see Chapter 5 of this book.
92. Nizam-ud-din Ahmad, *Tabaqat-i-Akbari*, trans. B. De and Baini Prashad, vol. 1: 190; Ferishta, *Tarikh-i-Ferishta*, vol. 1: 219. He named the sultan as 'Oomur' Khalji.
93. Nizam-ud-din Ahmad, *Tabaqat-i-Akbari*, in *Uttar Taimur*, Part II (Aligarh: History Department, Aligarh Muslim University, 1959), trans. Rizvi, 518; also trans. B. De and Baini Prashad, Part II, vol. 3 (Kolkata: Bibliothica Indica, 1939–1940), 656 (he represented the second lady as servant of the complainant). See Chapter 2, under the heading 'Women and Morality' for other examples.
94. Babur, *Babur Nama*, vol. 2: 477–478; Gulbadan, *Humayun Nama*, 108. Also see Rumer Godden, *Gulbadan-Portrait of a Rose Princess at Mughal Court* (London: MacMillan & Co., 1980), 39.
95. Dughlat, *Tarikh-i-Rashidi*, 176.
96. Babur, *Babur Nama*, vol. 1: 147; also Beveridge, Notes to Gulbadan's *Humayun Nama*, 272.
97. Gulbadan, *Humayun Nama*, 103–104, 112–113, and Beveridge's Notes, 256–258.
98. Gulbadan, *Humayun Nama*, 161, 178, 182, and Beveridge's Notes, 225–226.
99. Abul Fazl, *Akbar Nama*, vol. 3: 348, 547.
100. Nizam-ud-din Ahmad, *Tabaqat-i-Akbari*, trans. B. De and Baini Prashad, vol. 2: 237; Shah Nawaz Khan and Hayy, *Maasir*, Part II, vol. 2: 846.
101. Thomas Coryat, in *Early Travels in India*, ed. William Foster (New Delhi: S. Chand & Co., 1968), 278.
102. Inayatullah, *Takmila-i-Akbar Nama*, trans. Elliot and Dowson, in *History of India*, vol. VI (Allahabad: Kitab Mahal, 1964), 113; Augustus, *The Emperor*, vol. 2: 415.
103. Abul Fazl, *Akbar Nama*, vol. 3: 107–108, also 547; V.A. Smith, *Akbar: The Great Mogul, 1542–1605*, 3rd Indian Print (New Delhi: S. Chand & Co, 1966), 89, note 3; Badaoni, *Muntakhabu-t-Tawarikh*, vol. 2: 308.
104. Blochmann, *Notes to Ain-i-Akbari*, vol. 1: 343; Abul Fazl, *Akbar Nama*, vol. 2: 183, note 5, 230; Shah Nawaz Khan and Hayy, *Maasir*, vol. 1: 145, 384–385;

Badaoni, *Muntakhabu-t-Tawarikh*, vol. 2: 49, note 4; Augustus, *The Emperor*, vol. 1: 94.

105. Abdul Qadir Al Badaoni, *Nijat-ul-Rashid*, ed. Syed Moinul Haq (Lahore, 1972), 34; also Badaoni, *Muntakhabu-t-Tawarikh*, vol. 2: 87–88.

106. Jahangir, *Tuzuk*, vol. 1: 78, 84–85; Aurangzeb, *Rukkat-i-Alamgiri*, trans. J.H. Bilmoria (Delhi: Idarah-i-Adabiyat-i-Delli, 1972), 30, 173.

107. Jahangir, *Tuzuk*, vol. 1: 77–78, 81, 145.

108. William Hawkins, in *Early Travels in India*, ed. Foster, (New Delhi: Chand & Co., 1968), 118.

109. Jahangir, *Tuzuk*, vol. 1: 76. See also M.S. Randhawa, *Indian Miniature Painting* (New Delhi: Roli Books International, 1981), pl.4.

110. Jahangir, *Tuzuk*, vol. 1: 353.

111. Hamid-ud-din Khan, *Ahkam-i-Alamgiri*, in *Anecdotes of Aurangzib*, trans. J.N. Sarkar (Calcutta: M.C. Sarkar, 1949), 67.

112. Anonymous, *Tarikh-i-Ahmad-Shah*, trans. Elliot and Dowson, in *History of India*, vol. VIII (Allahabad: Kitab Mahal, 1964), 113–114; Sarkar, *Fall*, vol. 1: 209–210, 332–336.

113. For detail, see Chapter 5 of this book.

114. *Quran*, 16:90.

115. Gulbadan, *Humayun Nama*, 97–98.

116. Gulbadan, *Humayun Nama*, 89, 100–101, 103; Dughlat, *Tarikh-i-Rashidi*, 200; Abul Fazl, *Akbar Nama*, vol. 1: 230–233.

117. Beveridge, Introduction to Gulbadan's *Humayun Nama*, 20.

118. Gulbadan, *Humayun Nama*, 104, 110–111.

119. Gulbadan, *Humayun Nama*, 110, 130–131.

120. Jahangir, *Tuzuk*, vol. 2: 91, also, vol. 1: 36.

121. Sarkar, *Aurangzib*, vol. 1: 39–41. For their roles, see Chapters 5 and 6 of this book.

122. Hamid-ud-din Khan, *Ahkam-i-Alamgiri*, 97–98.

123. Thevenot, *Indian Travels*, 78–79. See Chapter 5 for other details.

124. Manucci, *Storia Do Mogor*, 2: 330–331.

125. Sarkar, *Fall*, vol. 1: 209–210.

126. S.M. Ikram, *Muslim Civilization in India* (London: Columbia University Press, 1964), 230.

127. For detailed study about Sati, see A.S. Altekar, *The Position of Women in Hindu Civilization* (New Delhi: Motilal Banarasidass, 1962), 115–142; V.N. Datta, *Sati* (New Delhi: Manohar Publications, 1988), 1–15; Tod, *Annals and Antiquities*, vol. 1: 266, 633–635, vol. 2: 461–462, 469, 497, 499, 623, 654, 745, 752. For *Jauhar*, see Tod, *Annals and Antiquities*, vol. 1: 265, 311, 594, 639–640, vol. 2: 251, 253–254, 763.

128. Amir Khusrau, *Nuh-Sipihr*, ed. M.W. Mirza, vol. 3 (Calcutta: Baptist Mission, 1948), 191–195; also trans. Elliot and Dowson, in *History of India*, vol. III, 564; see also Hughes, *Dictionary of Islam*, 47.

129. Ibn Batuta, *Rehla*, 109.

130. Jahangir, *Tuzuk*, vol. 2: 181.

131. Thevenot, *Indian Travels*, 120; Careri, *Indian Travels*, 249.

132. Aurangzeb, *Rukkat*, 74. From this, Tod (*Annals and Antiquities*, vol. 1, Chapter XI, 'Annals of Mewar', 378, note (a)) inferred that she desired to burn herself and showed that she was a Rajput. But J.N. Sarkar contradicted it since Hindu

queen, after been married to Muslim King, received Islamic burial. Therefore, as per him, Udaipuri meant to kill herself 'in passionate grief' on the death of Aurangzeb (*Aurangzib*, vol. 1: 35n.).

133. Sharafu-d-din Yazdi, *Zafar Nama*, trans. Elliot and Dowson, in *History of India*, vol. III (Allahabad: Kitab Mahal, 1964), 495.

134. Gulbadan, *Humayun Nama*, 143.

135. Nathan, *Baharistan-i-Ghaybi*, vol. 1: 141, 193, 440. See also vol. 2: 596, 599 in this regard.

136. Nathan, *Baharistan-i-Ghaybi*, vol. 2: 594–595.

137. Mohammad Yasin, *A Social History of Islamic India (1605–1748)* (Lucknow: The Upper India Publishing House, 1958), 90.

138. Maulana Muhammad Ali, *The Religion of Islam*, (New Delhi: S. Chand & Co., n.d.), 444–450; Hughes, *Dictionary of Islam*, 44–46.

139. Ibn Batuta, *Rehla*, 120–121.

140. Manucci, *Storia Do Mogor*, vol. 3: 145.

141. Afif, *Tarikh-i-Firoz Shahi*, 267–273; Ibn Batuta, *Rehla*, 63. Also see Jauhri, *Firoz Tughluq*, 126–128; Ashraf, *Life and Conditions*, 58–59; Irfan Habib, 'Non-agricultural Production and Urban Economy', in *The Cambridge Economic History of India*, ed. T. Raychaudhuri and Irfan Habib, vol. 1 (London: Cambridge University Press, 1982), 90–91.

142. Lal, *Harem*, 31; Sarkar, *Aurangzib*, vol. 1: 37.

143. Awfi, Mohammad, *Jawami-ul-Hikayat* (B.M.16, 862(II), Or.236 (II); Or.1734(III)), 105; Ibn Batuta, *Rehla*, 123, 150; Ashraf, *Life and Conditions*, 105; Or. 1734(III).); Habib, 'Non-agricultural', vol. 1: 92.

144. Barani, *Tarikh*, 322; Ibn Batuta, *Rehla*, 230; Ferishta, *Tarikh-i-Ferishta*, vol. 1: 207–208; Bernier, *Mogul Empire*, 134–136, 426; Abdul Karim, *Social History of Muslims in Bengal* (Dacca: Asiatic Society of Pakistan, 1959), 196.

145. Barani, *Tarikh*, 314; Shahbu-d-din Abdul Abbas Ahmad Umari, *Masaliku-L-Absar-Fi-mamaliku-L-Amsar*, in *Tughlaq Kaleen Bharat*, Part I (Aligarh: History Department, Aligarh Muslim University, 1956), trans. Rizvi, 325; Abu Al Abbas Qalqashandi, *Subh al Asha*, in *An Arab Account of India in the Fourteenth Century*, trans. Otto Spies (Stuttgart, 1936), 55–56. See also Ibn Batuta, *Rehla*, 123.

146. Babur, *Babur Nama*, vol. 2: 520. See also Habib, 'Non-agricultural', vol. 1: 92.

147. Sikander, *Mirat-i-Sikanderi*, 272; Gulbadan, *Humayun Nama*, 94–95. See also Ibn Batuta, *Rehla*, 63, 123; Barani, *Tarikh*, 322.

148. Abul Fazl, *Akbar Nama*, vol. 2: 246–247.

149. Abul Fazl, *Ain-i-Akbari*, vol. 1: 45 and Blochmann's Notes, 321–322; Jahangir, *Tuzuk*, vol. 1: 82, 87, 160; Sarkar, *Aurangzib*, vol. 1: 133.

150. Sarkar, *Fall*, vol. 2: 75–76; Ganda Singh, *Ahmad Shah Durrani* (Bombay: Asia Publishing House, 1959), 160, 169 (he called her Gunna Begam); William Irvine, 'Ahmad Shah Abdali and the Indian Wazir Imad-ul-Mulk (1756–57)', *Indian Antiquary*, 36, Feb., (1907): 46–49; H.R. Gupta, *Studies in Later Mughal History of the Panjab, 1707–1793* (Lahore, 1944), 127, 136.

151. Nizam-ud-din Ahmad, *Tabaqat-i-Akbari*, trans. B. De and Baini Prashad, Part II, vol. 3, 804; Ibn Batuta, *Rehla*, 63, 73, 122–123, 150; Gulbadan, *Humayun Nama*, 94–95.

152. Hamid-ud-din Khan, *Ahkam-i-Alamgiri*, 36–38.

153. Pelsaert, *The Remonstrantie*, 47; Bernier, *Mogul Empire*, 205; F.S. Manrique, *Travels of Fray Sebastien Manrique*, trans. Eckford Luard and S.J. Hosten, vol. 2 (London: Hak Society, 1927), 272. See Irfan Habib, *Agrarian System of Mughal India* (Bombay: Asia Publishing House, 1963), 323, note 25 (for the incident narrated).

154. Amir Khusrau, *Ijaz-i-Khusravi*, vol. 4 (Lucknow: Newal Kishore, 1876), 169–170, 334; Ashraf, *Life and Conditions*, 103–104 (on the authority of 'Fiqh-i-Firuz Shahi').

155. Minhaj-ud-din Siraj, *Tabaqat-i-Nasiri*, 630, 644.

156. Gulbadan, *Humayun Nama*, 112.

157. Qanungo, *Sher Shah*, 13.

158. Shah Nawaz Khan and Hayy, *Maasir*, vol. 1: 806 (he depicted her as mistress of Mir Khalil); Hamid-ud-din Khan, *Ahkam-i-Alamgiri*, 36–38 (he named the noble as Saif Khan); Manucci, *Storia Do Mogor*, vol. 1: 222. See also Sarkar, *Aurangzib*, vol. 1: 35–37.

159. Sarkar, *Aurangzib*, vol. 1: 34; Zahir-ud-din Faruki, *Aurangzeb and His Times* (Delhi: Idarah-i-Adabiyat-i-Delli, 1972), 545 (as per him, she was his wife not concubine).

160. Ferishta, *Tarikh-i-Ferishta*, vol. 1: 204–205.

161. K.A. Nizami, ed., *Politics and Society*, vol. 1 (New Delhi: People's Publishing House, 1974), 82–83.

162. Nicoli Conti, *Fifteenth Century*, 23.

163. Abdur Razzaq, *Matla-us-Sadain*, trans. Elliot and Dowson, in *History of India*, vol. IV (Allahabad: Kitab Mahal, 1964), 111–112.

164. Badaoni, *Muntakhabu-t-Tawarikh*, vol. 2: 311.

165. Manucci, *Storia Do Mogor*, vol. 2: 173.

166. Malik M. Jayasi, *Padmavat*, Muhammad (Chirgaon, Jhansi: Sahitya Sadan, Vikrami Sambat 2018), *Khand 2, Chhanda 38*, 44–45; Rahim, *Rahim Bilas*, ed. Brajratan Das (Allahabad: Ramnarayan Lal, 1948), *Doha 81*: 35; and Maya Shankar Dixit, ed., *Ratnavali* (Varanasi: Sahitya Sewa mandal, Vikrami Sambat 1995), *Doha 81*: 34. See also Lal, *Harem*, 198.

167. Thomas Bowrey, *A Geographical Account of Countries Round the Bay of Bengal*, ed. R.C. Temple (London: Hak Society, 1905), 206.

168. Zia-ud-din Barani, *Fatawa-i-Jahandari*, trans. Afsar Begam, in *The Political theory of the Delhi Sultanate*, by Mohammad Habib and Afsar Umar Salim Khan (Allahabad: Kitab Mahal, n.d.), 138.

169. Amir Khusrau, *Qiran-us-Sadain*, ed., Maulvi Mohammad Ismail and Syed Hasan Barani (Aligarh: Aligarh College Press, 1918), 107.

170. Khusrau, *Ijaz-i-Khusravi*, vol. 5: 151–152.

171. Umari, trans. I.H. Siddiqui and Qazi Mohammad Ahmad, *A Fourteen Century Account of India Under Sultan Mohd. Tughlaq* (Aligarh: Siddiqui Publishing House, 1971), 67.

172. Terry, *Early Travels*, 320; Thevenot, *Indian Travels*, 136; Stavorinus, *East Indies*, vol. 1: 409.

173. Ferishta, *Tarikh-i-Ferishta*, vol. 1: 152.

174. P. Thomas, *Indian Women Through the Ages* (New York: Asia Publishing House, 1964), 251; E. Thomas, *The Chronicles of the Pathan Kings of Delhi* (Delhi: Oriental Publishers, 1967), 139. Compare M. Mujeeb, *The Indian Muslims*

(London: George Allen & Urwin Ltd, 1967), 385, who writes, 'Most of the Courtesans had been in the palace and were or had been mistresses of dignitaries'.

175. Umari, trans. Siddiqui and Ahmad, 67; Abdur Razzaq, *Matla-us-Sadain*, 111–112; Manucci, *Storia Do Mogor*, vol. 1: 189; Bowrey, *A Geographical Account*, 206; Stavorinus, *East Indies*, vol. 1: 409–410.

176. Ferishta, *Tarikh-i-Ferishta*, vol. 1: 204–205; Amir Khusrau, *Khazain-ul-Futuh*, in *The Campaign of Ala-ud-din Khilji*, trans. Mohammad Habib (Bombay: D.B. Taraporewala sons & Co., 1931), 11; K.S. Lal, *History of the Khaljis* (Allahabad: The Indian Press, 1950), 264, note 15.

177. Khusrau, *Ijaz-i-Khusravi*, vol. 4: 206.

178. Badaoni, *Muntakhabu-t-Tawarikh*, vol. 2: 311–312.

179. Manucci, *Storia Do Mogor*, vol. 2: 3–6; Das, *Norris*, 149; Must'ad Khan, *Maasir-i-Alamgiri*, 45.

180. Ali Muhammad Khan, *Mirat-i-Ahmadi*, trans. M.F. Lokhandwala, 1st ed. (Baroda: Oriental Institute, 1965). 222, 250–251.

181. Manucci, *Storia Do Mogor*, vol. 2: 5.

182. Ovington, *Seventeenth Century*, vol. 1: 63, also editor's introduction, vi; Das, *Norris*, 149–150.

183. Khusrau, *Ijaz-i-Khusravi*, vol. 5:130; Umari, trans. Siddiqui and Ahmad, 67.

184. Jamali, Maulana Fadl-u-llah, *Siyar-u'l-Arifin* (Delhi: Ridwi Press, 1311 A.H.), 167–69. See also K.A. Nizami, *Some Aspects of Religion and Politics in India During the Thirteenth Century*, 2nd ed. (Delhi: Idarah-i-Adabiyat-i-Delli, 1974), 162–64.

185. Khusrau, *Ijaz-i-Khusravi*, vol. 5: 148–149.

186. Withington, *Early Travels*, 208–209.

187. Vidyapati, *Kirtilata* (Chirgaon, Jhansi: Sahitya Sadan, 1962), *Pallava* 2, *Chhanda* 24, *Doha* 138: 85, *Chhanda* 22, *Dohe* 132–133, 82–83.

188. Ibn Batuta, *Rehla*, 28, 171; Asad Beg, *Wikaya-i-Asad Beg*, trans. Elliot and Dowson, in *History of India*, vol. VI (Allahabad: Kitab Mahal, 1964), 164; Pietro Della Valle, in *European Travellers under the Mughals*, by M.A. Ansari (Delhi: Idarah-i-Adabiyat-i-Delli, 1975), 109. Khusrau, *Nuh-Sipihr*, 379–381, 383; Dargah Quli Khan, Introduction, in *Muraqqa-i-Delhi*, trans. Chander Shekhar and S.M. Chenoy (Delhi: Deputy Publication, 1989), xxxii; Terry, *Early Travels*, 310; Manucci, *Storia Do Mogor*, vol. 1:189. See also Ahmad Najma Perveen, Introduction and Historical Background, in *Hindustani Music* (Delhi: Manohar Publishers, 1984), 7, 9, 10.

189. Ashraf, *Life and Conditions*, 222, 245–246. Sarwani, *Tarikh-i-Sher Shahi*, trans. Ambashthya, 445, also trans. Imamuddin (Dacca, 1964), 104, note 2.

190. Abul Fazl, *Ain-i-Akbari*, vol. 3: 271–273; Peter Mundy, *The Travels of Peter Mundy in Europe and Asia*, ed. R.C. Temple, vol. II, second series no. XXXV. (London: Hak Society, 1914), 216; Pelsaert, *The Remonstrantie*, 83. *Kanchani* was originally called Kanjari. The new name was given to them by Akbar (Abul Fazl, *Ain-i-Akbari*, vol. 3: 272). It is derived from the word *kanchan*, that is, 'a dancing girl'. See also W. Crooke, *The Tribes and Castes of the North Western Provinces and Oudh*, vol. 4 (Calcutta: Office of the Superintendent of Govt. printing, 1896), 364, for the Kanchan caste.

191. Barani, *Tarikh*, 156–157; Khusrau, *Hasht Bahisht*, 34; Ibn Batuta, *Rehla*, 78–79; Sarwani, *Tarikh-i-Sher Shahi*, trans. Ambashthya, 723–724; Babur,

Babur Nama, vol. 2: 634; Nizam-ud-din Ahmad, *Tabaqat-i-Akbari*, trans. B. De and Baini Prashad, vol. 1: 73; Abul Fazl, *Ain-i-Akbari*, vol. 3: 272–273; Shiv Das Lakhnawi, *Shahnama-Munauwar Kalam*, trans. S.I I. Askari (Patna: Janki Prakashan, 1980), 122–123; Nicholas Downton, in *European Travellers Under the Mughals*, by MA Ansari (Delhi: Idarah-i-Adabiyat-i-Delli, 1975), 53–54; William Finch, in *Early Travels in India*, ed. Foster (New Delhi: Chand & Co., 1968), 183; Manrique, *Sebastien Manrique*, vol. 2: 161; Thevenot, *Indian Travels*, 33, 67; Stavorinus, *East Indies*, vol. 1: 437.

192. For paintings, see Ibn Batuta, *Rehla*, facing page 56; Lal, *Harem*, Pls 7, 8, 12, VI; Devee, Maharani Sunity, *The Beautiful Mughal Princesses* (Kolkata: Thacker & Spink, 1918), facing page 2 (showing a slave girl playing on violin while the queen is engrossed in this), also painting facing page 94; Percy Brown, *Indian Paintings under the Mughals* (London: Oxford University Press, 1924), pls. XXXI, XLVII, LVII, Fig. I; Rumer Godden, *Gulbadan-Portrait*, 47 (showing dance performance in *darbar*); Randhawa, *Indian Miniature*, Pl. 26 (Faizabad painting showing women amusing themselves with music and dance). See also Rashid, *Society and Culture*, 115–121; Ishwari Prasad, *A History of the Qaraunah Turks in India*, 1st ed., vol. 1 (Allahabad: Central Book Depot, 1974.), 309; J.M. Banerjee, *History of Firuz Shah Tughlaq* (Delhi: Munshiram Manoharlal Pvt. Ltd., 1967), 167; Hilde Bach, *Indian Love Paintings* (Varanasi: Lustre Press, 1985), Pl. 37 (showing late-night musical parties of Muhammad Shah's reign).

193. Manucci, *Storia Do Mogor*, vol. 2: 313–314.

194. Bernier, *Mogul Empire*, 273–274; Manucci, *Storia Do Mogor*, vol. 1: 189; Thevenot, *Indian Travels*, 71; Ovington, *Seventeenth Century*, vol. 1: 114.

195. Manucci, *Storia Do Mogor*, vol. 1: 189.

196. Manucci, *Storia Do Mogor*, vol. 1: 213 (for Rana Dil); Bernier, *Mogul Empire*, 7, 8 (Shuja's liking for dancing girls); Bowrey, *A Geographical Account*, 207 (patronage by the nobles).

197. Manucci, *Storia Do Mogor*, vol. 2: 312–313.

198. Shah Nawaz Khan and Hayy, *Maasir*, vol. 1, 806–807.

199. Carr Stephen, *Archaeology and Monumental Remains of Delhi* (Allahabad: Kitab Mahal, 1967), 216, 279–280 (for Lal Kanwar); Anonymous, *Tarikh-i-Ahmad Shah*, trans. Elliot and Dowson, in *History of India*, vol. VIII (Allahabad: Kitab Mahal, 1964), 113–114 (for Qudsia Begam). For details of their influence see Chapter 5.

200. Dargah Quli Khan, *Muraqqa*, 99, 100, 104–111, 115–125.

201. Ghulam Husain Salim, *Riyazu-s-Salatin*, trans. Abdus Salam (Delhi: Idarah-i-Adabiyat-i-Delli, 1975), 281 (for Murshid Quli Jafar Khan). Orme, *Historical Fragments*, 272; K.K. Datta, *Alivardi and His Times* (Calcutta: Calcutta University, 1939), 170 (for Alivardi Khan); A.L. Srivastava, *The First Two Nawabs of Awadh*, 2nd ed. (Agra, 1954), 241–242 (for Safdar Jang).

202. Khusrau, *Matla-ul-Anwar*, 231.

203. Manucci, *Storia Do Mogor*, vol. 1: 192–193. See also Anonymous, *Iqbal Nama*, trans. Askari, 7–9 for other examples of the time of Farrukhsiyar's reign.

204. Mushtaqi, *Uttar Taimur*, Part I, 179–180; Abdullah, *Tarikh-i-Daudi*, in *Uttar Taimur Kaleen Bharat*, trans. Rizvi, Part I (Aligarh: History Department, Aligarh Muslim University, 1958), 251–253; Ahmad Yadgar, *Tarikh-i-Shahi*, in *Uttar Taimur*, trans. Rizvi, Part I (Aligarh: History

Department, Aligarh Muslim University, 1958), 349–351. There is a little variation here and there in their narration. Besides, the first two writers considered the incident of the time of Bahlol Lodi, while as per the third, it was of the time of Ibrahim Lodi.

205. Mushtaqi, *Uttar Taimur*, Part I, 390–391.

206. Ibn Batuta, *Rehla*, 164–165, note 5. See also Mushtaqi, *Uttar Taimur*, Part II, 563–566 for another example of Muslim woman indulging in anti-social activity.

207. Mushtaqi, *Uttar Taimur*, Part I, 181–182; Thevenot, *Indian Travels*, 58. See also Manucci, *Storia Do Mogor*, vol. 1: 193–194 for another example.

208. Khusrau, *Matla-ul-Anwar*, 194, 226; *Nuh-Sipihr*, vol. 7: 379.

209. Manucci, *Storia Do Mogor*, vol. 2: 3, 139–140.

210. Barani, *Tarikh*, 295, 386; Khusrau, *Khazain-ul-Futuh*, 10–11; Ibn Batuta, *Rehla*, 85–86.

211. Barani, *Fatawa*, 59.

212. Khusrau, *Khazain-ul-Futuh*, 12; Firoz Shah Tughlaq, *Futuhat-i-Firoz Shahi*, ed. S.A. Rashid (Aligarh: Department of History, Aligarh Muslim University, 1954) 7–8; Barani, *Tarikh*, 336 (he only testified to the existence of the sect during the reign of Ala-ud-din Khalji but did not explain their activities). See also Jauhri, *Firoz Tughluq*, 143–144, nn. 27–28, 197–199 for detailed reading in this regard.

213. Thevenot, *Indian Travels*, 95. See also Badaoni, *Muntakhabu-t-Tawarikh*, vol. 2: 59; Salim, *Riyazu-s*, 284.

214. Jahangir, *Tuzuk*, vol. 1: 150; Thevenot, *Indian Travels*, 66; J. Ovington, *Seventeenth Century*, vol. 1: 93–94.

215. Nizam-ud-din Ahmad, *Tabaqat-i-Akbari*, trans. B. De and Baini Prashad, Part II, vol. 3: 596–598; Wolseley Haig, *The Cambridge History of India*, vol. 3 (Delhi: Concept Publishing Co., 1928), 368.

216. Babur, *Babur Nama*, vol. 2: 460–461(for Ghazi Khan's condemnation); Gulbadan, *Humayun Nama*, 200–201 (for Kamran incident).

217. Wolseley Haig, *The Cambridge History of India*, ed. Richard Burn, vol. 4 (London: Cambridge University Press, 1937), 181, 191; B.P. Saksena, *History of Shahjahan of Dihli* (Allahabad: Central Book Depot, 1958), 105–106 (for Shah Jahan's Portuguese attack).

218. Sarwani, *Tarikh-i-Sher Shahi*, trans. Ambashthya, 778–786.

219. Haig, *Cambridge History*, vol. 4: 274, 277.

220. Sarwani, *Tarikh-i-Sher Shahi*, trans. Ambashthya, 603–609; Qanungo, *Sher Shah*, 383–385.

221. Haig, *Cambridge History*, vol. 4: 59.

222. Nizam-ud-din Ahmad, *Tabaqat-i-Akbari*, trans. B. De and Baini Prashad, Part I, vol. 3: 454.

223. Salim, *Riyazu-s*, 83; Ferishta, *Tarikh-i-Ferishta*, vol. 1: 147–148 (for Balban's atrocities on Tughral); Nizam-ud-din Ahmad, *Tabaqat-i-Akbari*, trans. B. De and Baini Prashad, vol. 1: 157–158 (for Ala-ud-din Khalji's atrocities); Sirhindi, *Tarikh-i-Mubarak Shahi*, 86–87, 119 (for cruelty of Khusrau Khan and Muhammad Tughlaq, respectively); Abul Fazl, *Akbar Nama*, vol. 1: 509–510 (for Kamran's atrocities).

224. Qanungo, *Sher Shah*, 54.

225. Timur, *Malfuzat-i-Timuri*, trans. Elliot and Dowson, in *History of India*, vol. III (Allahabad: Kitab Mahal, 1964), 405, 425–428; Yazdi, *Zafar Nama* 503–504 (for cruelty of Timur); Gholam Hussein Khan, *Siyar-ul-Mutakherin*, trans. Nota Manus, *The History of Later Mughals Seir Mutakherin*, vol. 1 (Lahore: Oriental Publishers and Book Sellers, 1975), 316, also trans. J. Briggs, *The History of Mohamedan Power in India* (Delhi: Idarah-i-Adabiyat-i-Delli, 1973), 285; William Irvine, *Later Mughals*, vol. 2 (Calcutta: M. C. Sarkar & Sons, 1922), 367, 369 (for cruelty of Nadir Shah); Sarkar, *Fall*, vol. 2: 69–73, 83–84, 86–87, 89–90 (for atrocities of Ahmad Shah Abdali).

226. Sarkar, *Fall*, vol. 2: 89.

227. Ishwari Prasad, *Life and Times of Humayun* (Bombay: Orient Longmans, 1956), 371.

228. Qanungo, *Sher Shah*, 53. Sarwani, *Tarikh-i-Sher Shahi*, trans. Ambashthya, 254–255.

229. Salim, *Riyazu-s*, 358, note 2; Hussein Khan, *Siyar*, trans. Manus, vol. 2: 58–59; Orme, *Historical Fragments*, 272 (for Alivardi), and vol. 1: 122–124, also trans. Briggs, *Mohamedan Power*, 108–109 (for Husain Ali's respect for women).

230. Ovington, *Seventeenth Century*, vol. 1: 175.

231. Nathan, vol. 1: 344; Anonymous, *Tarikh-i-Salim Shahi*, trans. Price, 45; Sarwani, *Tarikh-i-Sher Shahi*, trans. Ambashthya, 202–203; Hamid-ud-din Khan, *Ahkam-i-Alamgiri*, 71; Aurangzeb, *Rukkat*, 72; Shah Nawaz Khan and Hayy, *Maasir*, Part II, vol. 2: 1078; Manucci, *Storia Do Mogor*, vol. 2: 9–11.

3

Economic Milieu

Theoretically, the Muslim women were bestowed with abundant economic rights and privileges. The Quran elaborated rules for the entitlements of a Muslim woman, to her maintenance and to *mahr*. It bestowed on her property rights through inheritance and through other means.

Right to Maintenance

Women were considered to be the honour of the family. As their movements were restricted by purdah and seclusion, it was not considered honourable for any family to allow them to go out for earning their livelihood. Writing about the index of social status of a family, a modern author opines that 'the ability to keep women in seclusion and uninvolved in economic activity outside the home is an important index of relative wealth, and ... of a family's worth, in an economic sense, but it also becomes indicative of their social worth, or their honour.'[1] It has been written in context of the present position of Muslim women but it was very much applicable on the family psychology of the medieval times. It was also provided in the Quran that both rich and poor considered it their duty to provide for the basic needs of their womenfolk. The women of the commoners, who had to undertake different economic activities or seek a job outside for their maintenance, were not given a respectable place in the society. The upper class ladies who remained confined within the four walls of their harem became their ideals and the symbol of social honour. Whosoever had sufficient resources for maintaining his family, his first concern was to stop ladies of the house from going out for a job. The rich people, who maintained large harems, would also make provision for them on priority. Irrespective of the size of the harem, they provided for all the inmates according to their own status. Also, each female in the harem was given an allowance according to her position. For instance, Sultan Ghias-ud-din of Malwa who had 15,000 ladies in his harem, Akbar who had 5,000 women in his seraglio and prince Shah Alam who had 2,000 women to support, all tried to maintain them in a dignified way. During sultanate period, there was an officer called *wakil-i-dar* who supervised payments, royal kitchen besides wine department and stables. The harem ladies approached him for various favours.[2] Abul Fazl describes the elaborate system having been worked out during the time of Akbar. Jahangir enhanced the allowances of all the *purdah nashin* ladies of the royal harem by 20–100 per cent, according to their condition and relationship, and of all the domestics by 20 per cent soon after his accession. Similarly, Manucci mentioned about separate allowances being provided to all royal queens, princesses and other inmates of royal household in Aurangzeb's time.[3]

As for the royal ladies, they were provided for according to their status in the harem and some of them were specially privileged. Mumtaz Mahal, for instance, enjoyed an annual allowance of ₹1 million.[4] Jahanara was given an annual allowance of ₹600,000 per annum by Shah Jahan initially, which reached to ₹1 million and then to ₹1.2 million per annum by 1666 A.D. and then again it was further enhanced to ₹1.7 million per annum by Aurangzeb.[5] Lal Kanwar had annual allowance of ₹20 million, besides jewels and clothes.[6]

The kings and nobility incurred huge expenses for the maintenance of their harems, which varied according to their own financial resources.[7] In a royal household establishment, the harem was the biggest department and also accounted for the heaviest expenditure. According to a modern estimation, the expenses on cash stipends to harem ladies of Akbar alone amounted to 35 million *dams*, besides 13.65 million *dams* on kitchen and more than 16.7 million *dams* on wardrobe annually, which amounted to 34.89 per cent (18.68+7.28+8.93) of the total harem expenditure. Similarly, Manucci described the expenses of Aurangzeb's harem as 'extraordinary' and that these never amounted to less than ₹10 million. This is in spite of the fact that Aurangzeb was considered to be a puritan king. The gifts to ladies on festivities further added to this figure.[8]

Many sultans were generous in providing for the livelihood of Muslim widows. Iltutmish introduced *iqta* (a small piece of land given to officers/nobles as revenue assignment in lieu of salary) system. In this system, the *iqtas* were generally given to the military men for a number of years or for the lifetime of the grantee who was expected to collect the revenue and after deducting from it the amount granted to him, he was to remit the balance to the central government. After the death of the *Muqti* (one who held charge of an *iqta*), in many cases, the widows continued to hold those lands, considering them as *inams* (present, gift) given to their husbands, thus having a good living. It was to curb such practices, realising that the system had outlived its utility, that Balban reduced and resumed many of them from which full or proper service was not forthcoming. However, he compensated them by providing allowances to the widows for their living.[9]

Muhammad bin Tughlaq had set up alms houses to help widows financially.[10] He was kind to the widow of Sultan Qutb-ud-din Mubarak Shah. He addressed her as sister and also placed her in the company of female members of his own household. Later on, he got her remarried to Ibn Qazi Misr. He also paid a visit to her every Friday.[11] Sultan Firoz Tughlaq conferred stipends upon widows for their maintenance.[12] If widows wanted to get remarried, the King's *Muhatasibs* (the censors of public morals in the *pargana*) recommended their cases to their guardians.[13] Sultan Sikander Lodi assigned the *jagir* of Kalpi, 120 horses and 15 elephants to Jalal Khan for comfort of Niamat Khatun, widow of Qutb Khan Lodi.[14] During the reign of the Mughals, efforts to help the widows continued and that has been confirmed by contemporaries of different times. Thus, there are references of maintenance of Humayun's and Akbar's widows; it is reported that after the death of Jahangir, Nur Jahan was given an allowance of ₹200,000 per annum for her maintenance; Lahori mentions about allowance of ₹1 million per annum given to Mumtaz Mahal by Shah Jahan. Further, Hamida Banu, the widow of Khalilullah Khan, *Subedar* (the governor of a suba) of Lahore, was provided with an annual stipend of ₹50,000 by Aurangzeb. The author of *Maasir-ul-Umara* also writes about fixing of allowances for maintenance of royal widows.[15] Jahangir established a fund for helping the widows. Aurangzeb maintained separate palaces known as *suhagpura* for royal widows for their upkeep and comfortable livings. The widows of Shah Jahan were kept there.[16] The royalty even provided for the maintenance of the enemy ladies. For instance, Babur bestowed a *pargana* worth ₹700,000 on the mother of Ibrahim Lodi.[17] These measures made widowhood less painful.

Jagirs and Inams for Maintenance

The bestowal of maintenance grant in the form of *jagirs* and *inams* was a common feature with the Mughals. Usually, out of the total allowance to the queens and princes, half was paid in cash from the royal treasury and the other half in the form of these *jagirs* or land rents. The collection from these land rents always yielded more than the amount in exchange for which they were granted.[18] Gulbadan narrates that Babur had assigned houses and lands to 96 *begams* and *khanams* and that soon after his accession, Humayun visited his mother, sisters and other ladies of his harem and confirmed their office, service, land and residence, as they held at that time.[19] Nur Jahan held so many *jagirs* spread all over the empire that on the basis of her rights, she could be conferred with the title equivalent to that of Commander of 30,000.[20] She held the *jagir* of Ramsar located about 20 miles south-east of Ajmer.[21] She was also bestowed with the *jagir* of Boda (Toda?), on the occasion of Khurram's Deccan victory in 1617 A.D., which had an annual revenue of ₹200,000.[22] Similarly, Haji Hur Parwar Khanam, Nur Jahan's maternal aunt (and also her sister-in-law since she was married to her brother Ibrahim Khan Fath Jang) who lived up to the middle of Aurangzeb's reign, held Kol Kalali as *altamgha*. *Altamgha* was a 'Grant in Seal', which was introduced by Jahangir. In this, grants were made under a particular form of seal. These grants, in contrast to other grants, were permanent and hence could not to be altered or resumed except by the emperor who could annul it at his will.[23] Jahanara Begam was the greatest beneficiary. She owned the villages of Achchol,[24] Farjahara,[25] Safapur,[26] Doraha,[27] Medina[28] and Panipat. From Panipat alone, she was getting an income of 10 million *dam*.[29] Such was her luxury that while Doraha was given to her for the maintenance of her gardens, the revenue of Surat, one of the biggest commercial centres of the time, was granted to her to meet out her betel expenses.[30] In the later Mughal period, Nawab Qudsia Begam, mother of Emperor Muhammad Shah, possessed full estate of her own including *jagirs* around Ujjain.[31]

Some of the kings showed concern for the maintenance of their female subjects of all classes. During the time of Firoz Tughlaq, in case of separation, the wife of a respectable person was entitled to a maintenance allowance that was estimated according to the standard diet taken by that class.[32] During the Mughal period, because of the escheat system, all belongings of a deceased noble would automatically become the property of the state. But as per the prevailing system, on the death of the noble, recovery was made from the assets of the deceased noble, whatever were his remaining dues to the treasury and the balance, as per the will of the emperor, were distributed among his heirs. The recovery could be more than due, but escheat of all assets of the deceased appears to have been rare. Thus, in practice, the emperors ordered to leave behind a lot for the widows and children of such nobles. It is reported by the author of *Maasir-ul-Umara* that Shah Jahan distributed ₹2 million out of the wealth of deceased Asaf Khan among his sons and daughters.[33]

Wazifa and Land Grants for Maintenance

One noteworthy contribution of the Mughal royalty was their patronage of the women who were without any means of livelihood. For the needy Muslim women, the help rendered by the kings like Firoz Shah Tughlaq and the royal ladies like Makhduma-i-Jahan, mother of Sultan Muhammad bin Tughlaq, Maham Begam, Nur Jahan and Mumtaz Mahal needs special mention. Because of this, many of the destitute women could maintain themselves.

They gave these destitute ladies *suyurghal* grants or donations of land as assistance for their livelihood. *Suyurghal* is a Chaghtai word and is translated by Arabic *madad-i-maash*, in Persian *madad-i-maash* or *madad-o-maash*. It means 'assistance of livelihood' and its equivalent is *milk* (property). It denoted 'lands given for benevolent purposes'. They were hereditary grants and hence differed from *jagir* or *tuyul* lands, which were given to *mansabdars* in lieu of salary for a specified period. Badaoni called such grants as *aymah* and also used the term, at times, in the sense of *aymah-daran*, that is, holders of grant lands.[34] This was a charitable grant given to needy, learned, religious or destitute men and women and was given in the form of land or subsistence allowance. The latter, paid in cash, was called *wazifa* and the lands bestowed were known as *milk* or *madad-i-maash*.[35]

Help in the form of *wazifa* (subsistence allowance) was given before the Mughals. About Sher Shah, Abbas Sarwani wrote, 'He gave money in cash as pension ... to those of its residents who in matter of their requirements had been incapacitated to earn their livelihood with their own hand, such as the blind, the old and the infirm, the widow, crippled and the sick....'[36]

However, the help in the form of *madad-i maash* seemed to be an innovation of Mughals. Abul Fazl's classification of the persons being covered for this grant did not contain any separate category of women grantees. Hence, all women falling under the four categories, namely needy, learned, religious or destitute, had the right of possession of such grants. It is further informed by Abul Fazl that the grant holders were habitual of encroaching on other's lands. Therefore, Akbar made a rule that in case of grantees holding more than 100 *bighas* (A traditional unit of measurement of area of a land in northern India), the excess of land above 100 *bighas*, which was not found specified in the *farmans* (official decree/a royal or govt. decree), was reduced to two-fifths, the remaining three-fifths being confiscated by the state. Only the Irani and Turani women were exempted from this rule, in whose case the order was that every excess of land above 100 *bighas* possessed by them should be enquired to see whether it was held correctly or not.[37] Yusuf Mirak mentioned about *Chakha-i-Musammati* grants whereby all the recipients were women.[38]

These were hereditary grants and differed from the *jagirs* that were conferred for a specified period. It appeared that during the time of Akbar and Jahangir, this inheritance was not well defined. As per a *farman* of renewal of the year 1575 A.D., the *madad-i-maash* grant given originally in 1559 A.D. was taken away by the state after the death of the initial recipient. His heirs had to approach the emperor afresh for its restoration that was done through this *farman*.[39] Thereafter, during the period when Mr Fathullah was the *Sadr* (dealing with religious and charity matters) (1585–1589 A.D.), another order was brought. As per this, if a co-sharer, wherein the shares were undefined, died, his share in such land was taken away by the state and was restored to his heirs only after they applied afresh.[40] The first regulation allowing the heirs to inherit directly a part of such grants was heard during the time of Shah Jahan when, as the order of fifth year of his reign, all grants of 30 *bighas* or less were to be wholly distributed among heirs on the death of the grantees. Out of grants larger than that, half was to be distributed among the heirs and the other half was resumed back by the state unless the heirs, by presenting themselves before the court, obtained *sanads* (a document certifying the grant of land or a perpetual stipend) for the same too. A new order was issued by him on his 18th year by which it was propounded that only in the case of the grant documents containing the word 'with his offspring' after the name of the grantee, half of the grant was to be allowed to the heirs. Otherwise, the whole of the grant was escheated. Aurangzeb lifted this condition and, in his third year, practically brought back the condition to that of Shah Jahan's order of the fifth year, with the difference that the limit of whole grant passing in inheritance was brought down from 30 to 20 *bighas*, above which half was resumed, as before, unless the heirs could manage this half too from the court.[41]

The women heirs were not only the co-sharers in such inheritance but their holdings also passed on to their heirs after their death. There is a *parwana* (royal order carried through the *Wazir* (minister, chief executive of the empire during Mughal period) of the tenth year of the reign of Alamgir I (1667 A.D.) according to which 20 *bighas* of land was settled in Shaikh Bhikham as *madad-i-maash* by Jahangir. After his death, the land passed on to Shaikh Habi-bullah and Musammat Salima Khatun. When both of them died, the land was given to their heirs, Inayatullah and Musammat Zainab.[42] In another *parwana* of the year 1676 A.D., the claim of Sayyid Muhammad Arif as heir of Bibi Shaha over the *madad-i-maash* land possessed by her during her life was confirmed.[43]

No uniform set of rules prevailed for the division among the heirs of the grantees. Usually, the heirs abided by the Muslim law of inheritance.[44] Aurangzeb, for the first time, laid down the code of inheritance for *madad-i-maash* lands in 1690 A.D. The Emperor declared such lands as *ariyat* (given on loan). He overlooked Shariat rules with regard to the following: (a) If a married daughter was a co-sharer with a son in the grant of their deceased father and she had property from her husband's side also, then she was debarred from inheritance. If the said daughter was a widow without any source of income and there were other female heirs also, then the son was responsible for their maintenance out of the income of the grant land. (b) If a daughter was the only child of the deceased and there were other agnatic heirs also, the daughter's succession to the whole grant was to be recognised in elimination of other heirs. (c) If a grantee died childless, it was wife's privilege to enjoy the grant during her lifetime and only after her death would it pass on to the heirs of her husband. In case there were no surviving relations of the husband, then it would pass on to the relatives of the wife. (d) If a mother, grandmother or some female Quranic heirs survived the grantee, whose maintenance was a charge on him, then the property was to pass on to them. A plain reading of these rules shows that these regulations were twisted, at times in favour of (as in [b] and [c] above) and at times against (as in [a] above) the ladies concerned. The main consideration seemed to be the extent of need of the different female heirs of the grantee.[45] Irrespective of these set rules, in the later Mughal period, they were not always followed. Thus, there is D. no. 44, which shows that *Qazi* Abdur Razzaq's only surviving heir was a daughter named Makhi (Bakhi) and the latter's only surviving heir, again, was a daughter named Man Bibi. But Malik Bhikari (Behari), a nephew (cousin) of Abdur Razzaq was considered a co-sharer with Man Bibi, being an agnatic heir, and thus point (b) of Alamgir's rules, as discussed above, got ignored.[46]

The granting of such lands to the needy women, both in individual and joint names, continued throughout the Mughal period. Under Jahangir, the policy was quite liberal because of the influence of Nur Jahan. It was ordained that all such land grants to the ladies should be made at the orders of Nur Jahan. Some available *farmans* of her time, where the grantees were ladies, do contain her reference, indicating thereby that the lands were granted at her behest.[47] Jahangir created a new post of *Sadr-un-nisa* to deal exclusively with the matters of land grants of ladies.[48] Only ladies could hold this post. Haji Kuka was the first incumbent of this post. Next was Dilaram, Nur Jahan's nurse and favourite servant, followed by Sati-un-nisa.[49] It was expected that the department of *Sadr* would hold good all grants made under her signatures. However, out of the documents available, only a few bear the seal of *Sadr-un-nisa*. Thus, Document no. 161 in *A calendar of Oriental Records* bore seal of Haji Kuka; Documents at Serial nos XV–XIX in *Mughal Farmans* show that they were issued through the *risala* (recommendation) of Haji Kuka and Document 31 in *Farman-i-Salatin* referred to at its back *Ismat Wa Iffat Dastgah Haji Kuka* (virtuous Haji Kuka). Perhaps it was a recommendation of this lady because of which a grant of 30 *bighas* was made to Adar Banu.[50]

There are many grant documents available that stand testimony to the generous grant of lands to destitute ladies during Jahangir's time. In 1616 A.D., Musammat Bibi Sandal and others were given 100 *bighas* of land as *madad-i-maash* that was further confirmed in 1618 A.D.[51] Musammat Zohra and others were bestowed with 200 *bighas* of such grants in 1618 A.D.[52] By an another *farman* in the same year, eight needy ladies of different families were jointly bestowed with 200 *bighas* of land, each having her specified share in the same.[53] Shah Jahan followed the policy of Jahangir. In 1642 A.D., 100 *bighas* of arable land was granted to Musammat Bibi Suhbat and others as *madad-i-maash*.[54] There is another *parwana* of 1643 A.D. by which 100 *bighas* of rent-free land worth cultivation in village Buhauddin Chak in *pargana* Chausa was given to Musammat Bibi Aulia.[55] We have still another document according to which 100 *bighas* of land, granted to Bibi Jiu and others, was consolidated in 1653 A.D. Still another document (Document no. 759 given by *Oriental Records*) shows grant of 210 *bighas* of cess-free land to Mst Bibi Shaha and others in *Pargana* Hisampur, *Sarkar* (a tax district, it was a revenue subdivision of the *suba* which comprised of a number of *parganas* [sub-districts]) Bahraich in 1641–1642 A.D.[56]

Aurangzeb continued bestowing such grants. In the year 1677 A.D., he gave 100 *bighas* of cultivable land to Musammat Zahra and others, each with a specified share.[57] Other document testified that 200 *bighas* of rent-free land, granted to Bibi Niamat and others, was brought under consolidation.[58] Another *document shows* 250 *bighas* of land in *pargana* Haveli of *sarkar* Bahraich given to Mst Hamirah and others as *madad-i-maash*.[59] Further, 'Aligarh Farmans' *(farmans* preserved in Aligarh Muslim University [AMU], Aligarh), nos 212, 213 and 220 show grant of 70 *bighas* of rent-free land at Kol to Mst Khatoon and 45 *biswas* (sub-unit of a *bigha*, each bigha may have 5–20 *biswa* in different regions) of land at the same place to Mst Maham.[60] There are many more such documents.[61]

During the later Mughal period, many such grants were conferred upon needy women. Bahadur Shah (I), during his second year of reign (1708 A.D.) granted village sultan in *pargana* Ander in the name of Musammat Fatima and others, heirs of Shaikh Abdul Hamid, and got it released in the same year.[62] Farrukhsiyar released 200 *bighas* of rent-free land to Bibi Aulia and 220 *bighas* of such land to Musammat Bibi Sahaba in the year 1716 A.D. and 1718 A.D., respectively.[63] Similarly, he granted 85 *bighas* at Kol to one Aisha and another 2 *bighas* at Jalali to Shah Bibi.[64] In the year 1729 A.D., Muhammad Shah bestowed grant of village Chak Wali as *madad-i-maash* on Musammat Hafiza and her sons.[65] We have documents at hand whereby Shah Alam II gave grant of village Bhatoria in *sarkar* Purnea to Musammat Peari Bai and 201 *bighas* of rent-free cultivable land in village Kojri in the district of Purnea to the widow of Muhammad Masoom.[66]

It was observed that at times, instead of land, a portion of the land revenue of a particular piece of land was bestowed as grant. We have two documents of the third year of the reign of Alamgir (II) whereby grant of 27,000 *dams* each was made from *pargana*s of Nizamuddinpur and Gadh Chaund in exchange of daily allowances to Musammats Khair-un-nisa and Amin-ul-Fatima as *madad-i-maash*.[67] There are two other documents of the sixth year of his reign that stipulated the release of the grant of 130,490 *dams* in *pargana* Kasmar as gift to Saiyada Karim-un-nisa and 37,000 *dams* from *pargana* Saraisa, *sarkar* Hajipur, *suba* (province, it was the largest unit of provincial administration, headed by a *subedar* [governor]) Bihar to Musammat Mehr-un-nisa.[68]

Many release orders were issued by these emperors from time to time. Whenever there was a delay in implementation of their *farmans* making such grants, *parwanas* followed for enforcing them. A study of the available documents revealed that while some of them were issued soon after the issue of the *farman*, there were others that were released after a gap of many years. In some other cases, the *farman* was issued by one emperor and release order was passed by another. There is *parwana* dated 10 January 1643 A.D. of Shah Jahan's reign for the release of 100 *bighas* of rent-free cultivable land in village Bahuddin Chak to Musammat Bibi Aulia in accordance with the *farman* issued three years earlier, in 1640 A.D.[69] Another *parwana* of the 20th year of Aurangzeb's reign (13 July 1677 A.D.) was for the release of 40 *bighas* of rent-free land to Noor Bibi in accordance with the *farman* issued 12 years earlier in the 8th year of the Emperor's reign.[70] For the *farman* of Alamgir II for grant of 27,000 *dams* each in the names of Khair-un-nisa and Amin-ul-Fatima, the release orders were passed by Emperor Shah Alam II in 1765 A.D.[71]

The women grantees were not free from such corrupt practices as they were generally associated with men grantees, lamented Abul Fazl. They not only encroached upon the neighbouring lands but also changed their own lands, at times, with some more fertile piece in some other area.[72] The practice of annual verification and scrutiny was followed when the land grant of a deceased was to pass on to his/her successors. The grant was confirmed or renewed accordingly.[73] In case of any disorder, it was reduced or confiscated. Aurangzeb reduced, at his own will, a grant from 150 to 100 *bighas* of Musammat Shahi and six other ladies at the time of its renewal in 1666 A.D. and also revised the share of each co-sharer accordingly.[74] Sometimes, on an application, the old grants merged with the *khalsa* (the category of land which belonged to the Emperor directly and was under the direct supervision and control of the government) land were again revived in favour of the ladies after proper verification.[75]

The verification required the personal presence of the grantee. During the reign of Jahangir, exemption from verification and personal presence was made.[76] Yusuf Mirak wrote that some zamindars of Sind acquired *madad-i-maash* land by buying *musammati farmans*.[77] Lahori also confirmed people getting grants without being presented. He also narrated as to how one of the complaints against Musawi Khan, a *Sadr* during the time of Jahangir, was that he made grants without bringing the grantee before the emperor's presence. It is because of this that he was removed from office during the time of Shah Jahan.[78] Later on, the scrutiny of all such cases, including those of women, became more and more strict. By the time of Aurangzeb, it was only after an on-the-spot enquiry or/and the production of any reliable evidence that a renewal and confirmation of a previous grant and the exemption from annual verification were given to women grantees. They had to prove that they had no means of livelihood. For instance, Bibi Jan and others, the heirs of Sayyid Ahmad and others, produced not only reliable witnesses but also a certificate from the previous *Sadr* to the effect that they had no means of livelihood and that they were already in possession of the land. It was only after this that the renewal of this grant of 2220 *bighas* of land was granted to the applicants in 1662 A.D.[79] Musammat Bibi Hafiza and others, heirs of late Muhammad Omar and Sayyid Ibrahim and others, produced not only the reliable witnesses but an on-the-spot enquiry was also made for ascertaining their genuineness and financial conditions before their application for renewal of previous grant of 420 *bighas* of land was accepted in 1695 A.D.[80]

At times, personal presence of women grantees was also pressed upon. However, for old ladies and those in purdah, representation through *vakil* (advocate/lawyer) was allowed. There is an interesting case in this regard. Musammats Kasban, Rabiah and Khayrun had received 100 *bighas* of land in *pargana* Sahali from Jahangir. They did not come personally to the court for the confirmation in 1651 A.D. (Document 7). But when they required such confirmation again, just three years later (Document 5), and again during the third year of Alamgir's reign, they had to personally present themselves in the court (Document 16). After 20 years, during 23rd year of Alamgir's reign, they were too old to be personally present. Hence, a *vakil* was sent on their behalf for such verification (Document 18).[81]

Madad-i-maash grants were non-proprietary in nature since they could not be sold or transferred except through inheritance. There is a judgement to that effect of the time of Aurangzeb (1666 A.D.). The hereditary share of Bibi Lajyat out of the *madad-i-maash* grant of her father Sayyid Muhammad was usurped by one Sayyid Usman on the plea that the former had transferred the ownership of the land to him along with other property. On this, the order was issued that since such grant was not alienable, the land had to be restored to Bibi Lajyat,[82] but the rule was not strictly followed. Before the passing of this judgement and even thereafter, such lands were subjected to partition and transfer. In a partition deed dated 1629 A.D., Sayyid Afzal divided his *madad-i-maash* land measuring 75 *bighas* in five equal parts, two portions out of which were given to Musammat Ghammu and one portion jointly to Bibi Man and Bibi Shah.[83] In another deed of the year 1679 A.D., 115 *bighas* of rent-free land of Sayyid Afzal was divided into five equal parts, out of which one portion was transferred jointly to Bibi Man and Bibi Khumar and two portions to Bibi Chaheti.[84] In the 18th century, due to the weakening of the Mughal empire, the legal position of the unalienability could not be enforced and such grants came to be freely sold. There are two documents, pertaining to the years 1763 and 1764 A.D., showing exchange of zamindari rights in plots of land received as *aima* for residential purpose. Although no lady was involved in these cases, but they showed that such lands were alienated in later period.[85]

Apparently, such legal security of maintenance created an impression that Muslim women were privileged. Later historical developments reveal as to how heavily they had to pay for such a privilege. Since a man was considered superior to a woman because he provided for the latter's necessities of life, an element of subordination among women was evident and inherent.

The *madad-i-maash* grants brought only some relief to a few destitute women of the lower strata. Because of the prevalent corruption and the checks on their free movements, they had to face many odds. For instance, it was stipulated with regard to these grants that half should be comprised of tilled land and the other half of cultivable land. But this rule was rarely followed, particularly with regard to women, as evident from the documents available. In the beginning, major portion (three-fourths) of the grants comprised of fallow lands.[86] But in the later period, most of the grants made to them comprised of barren lands.[87] These lands were exempted from government demands and taxes, yet the *zamindars* and *jagirdars* did not lag behind in extracting money from them in different forms, like charging of *muqarrari* and land revenue, under threat. For instance, there is a document that shows charging of a fixed amount known as *muqarrari-i-aymah*. This document mentioned about the charge (*sir bigha*) of ₹244 and 6 *annas* at the rate of 8 *annas* (a unit of currency) per *bigha* from one Birlas Begam on her land measuring 476 *bighas* and 1 *biswa* in 1647 A.D. (increased to 900 *bighas* in 1649 A.D.). This *muqarrari* was later on exempted by Shah Jahan in two instalments, first ₹56 and subsequently the remaining amount of ₹188 and 6 *annas* in 1649 A.D.[88] Still another document shows payment of *muqarrari* by one Mst Sajidah having land grant of 250 *bighas*. She could get rid of this forced *muqarrari* only after getting written exemption from Alamgir I in 1695 A.D.[89] Yusuf Mirak, who himself belonged to the *aymah* (grantee) class also confirmed it. He had narrated some cases wherein such grantee women sought redress from the appropriate authorities. He reported the extortion of money by the revenue officials from the *madad-i-maash* lands in Sind. When the matter was brought to the notice of Jahangir, the rights of the complainants on their lands were duly confirmed.[90] Similarly, during the governorship of Ahmad Beg Khan in Sind, his brother, Mirza Yusuf, fixed exorbitant land revenue on all the *Musammat*i and also on some of the *Muzakkarati* grants. Once he did not give any respite even at the time of natural calamity during the rabi crop. The matter was reported to Shah Jahan. On his orders, due consideration was shown and whatever was collected during the rabi crop was returned.[91] Such cases of complaints for redress were only a few, as it was difficult for women to visit the court for lodging complaints.

Mahr as an Economic Right

In Islam, marriage was a contract and the *mahr* was the price of it, and hence a prerequisite before the consent of the girl was taken for entering into a wedlock. If the husband died without paying it, then, legally, the wife's claim took precedence over his other heirs.[92] Its payment might, however, be prompt or deferred for a later date. In

India, it was mostly the deferred promise that met the condition of law of Muslim marriages, although instances of prompt payment of *mahr* were also available. Ibn Batuta narrates about prompt payment of *mahr* in the marriage of two sons of Khudavandzada, whom he accompanied, to the two daughters of the Wazir Khwaja Jahan.[93] There are examples of Mughal times as well. Gulbadan has written that when Humayun got married to Hamida Banu, he 'gave the mir (Mir Abul-baqa) two lacs of ready money for the dower'. Mir Abul-baqa conducted the marriage ceremonies. Similarly, another contemporary work describing about Jahangir-Nur Jahan marriage reported about dower of 8 million *asharfis* (gold coins) of five *methkals* (a measurement of weight, used for weighing gold) (equivalent to ₹72 million), the sum Nur Jahan 'requested as indispensable for the purchase of jewels' and hence it was given by Jahangir without any grumbling.[94] As for deferred dower, observing about Mohammadans of Cambay, Barbosa wrote, 'They can divorce themselves whenever they wish on paying to the wife certain moneys which they promise her at the time of marriage, if they changed their minds after a certain time'.[95] Manucci wrote, 'He (*mulla*) makes them husband and wife on condition that if there is any divorce the bridegroom will have to pay the bride so many millions'.[96] In such *mahr*, the point that remained to be seen was whether anything substantial passed to the lady or not, in the event of divorce or death of the husband. There are a few documents of the Mughal period wherein the widows were granted a share in family properties and holdings in lieu of their *mahr* deferred partly or fully. According to a *tamlik-nama* (deed of transfer) of 1625 A.D., Musammat Bibi Sappo had a share in a plot of land in village Sama-ud-Dinpura that she inherited from her husband as part of the dower debt.[97] In another case, even the *zamindaris* (villages) were received by the women in payment of the *mahr*.[98] In view of these examples, Rafat Bilgrami dismissed the erstwhile belief that *mahr* was mere 'matrimonial ritual' and a symbol of 'bridegroom's status' and not an amount that anybody expected to be paid.[99]

A scrutiny of the cases quoted by Bilgrami reveals that these were the cases of the widows who seemed to have been given share in property out of sympathy. They have not elaborated the method of evaluating and working the family property and the share of women in this. If she happened to be a joint holder of the family property along with other members of the family, her individual rights were subjected to so many restrictions. In such a case, she did not have any right to alienate her share separately. Management of the joint property always remained with the menfolk, who took all decisions about it including the selling of the joint property. Regarding *mahr* on divorce, it appears to have been honoured more in breach than following. The contemporary European travellers like Barbosa and Manucci have not discussed any instance of dower having been paid to any lady at the time of divorce or otherwise. Pelsaert has given a full description of the ceremonies of a Muslim marriage, but he has not mentioned *mahr* at all. According to him, 'The ceremony consists merely in the registration in the kazi's book, showing that such and such a person has acknowledged taking such and such a woman as his wife'.[100] The conspicuous absence of the mention of *mahr* of Lad Malika on her marriage with Sher Shah Suri by a Muslim author like Abbas Sarwani, particularly when he has given great details of her presents to him is not without significance.[101]

In the beginning of the medieval period, the amount of dower fixed was small, and so it was easy to pay. But with the passage of time, the amount of dower increased beyond the paying capacity of the husband in the later period. Abul Fazl has written, 'His majesty disapproves of high dowries; for as they are rarely ever paid, they are mere sham; but he admits that the fixing of high dowries is a preventive against rash divorces'.[102] Aurangzeb tried to abolish the demand and payment of extravagant sums as dower that as per him had become customary in those days, but his efforts could not make much headway.[103] Consequently, high amounts of *mahr* announced at the time of marriages became mere promises.

The royalty and nobility did not pay much attention to the directives of the Quran and broke the tenets in different matters including *mahr* and marriage rules. The Quran gave power to the woman to forgo her *mahr* and this was considered a very pious act. In the face of such provisions, it was not difficult for authoritative husbands to get a remittance of the *mahr* amount from their voiceless and suppressed wives. Under such circumstances, the best course for the ladies was not to press their claim of *mahr*. Doing so, they not only protected their maintenance by their husbands but also became pious in the eyes of the religion. There was yet another method to get rid of the wives and still avoid the payment of *mahr*. A man could torture his wife to such an extent that the latter would be forced to initiate a divorce even at the cost of losing her right of *mahr*.[104] The promise of high marriage portion, therefore, could only give some mental solace to the ladies.

The *mahr* varied from lady to lady, depending on latter's appeal and the social worth. For instance, while Jahanzib Banu, daughter of Dara and a pet of Jahanara, was promised a marriage portion of ₹600,000 on marrying prince Azam, Zubdat-un-nisa, Aurangzeb's daughter, got ₹400,000 while marrying Sipihr Shukoh, Dara's son. Shahr Banu, the princess of Bijapur, but a war captive, was promised only 500 dirhams while marrying prince Azam.[105] Similarly, Salima Banu Begam got marriage portion of ₹500,000 at the time of marrying prince Muhammad Akbar; daughter of Murad Bakhsh got dower of ₹200,000 while marrying Khwaja Yaqub; *mahr* of ₹100,000 for Sakina Banu while marrying prince Murad; *mahr* of ₹500,000 for the bride of Dara; mahr of ₹400,000 for bride of Shuja; *mahr* of 100,000 gold coins fixed for marriage of Ajit Singh's daughter with Farrukhsiyar, which, according to author of *Shahnama*, however, was ₹500 million; *mahr* of ₹5 million fixed for marriage of Farrukhsiyar's daughter with Emperor Muhammad Shah in 1721 A.D. and *mahr* of ₹200,000 for Sahia at the time of her marriage with prince Bidar Bakht.[106]

Thus, *mahr*, which was supposed to be paid to the women, in prompt or deferred way, lost its practical significance and it failed to bring the desired financial support to women and deterrence to men against rash divorces.

Property Rights

Muslim women enjoyed definite inheritance rights. The Quranic rules of property division were very complex. It recognised several classes of heirs, and claims of some of them had a priority even to the total exclusion of others. These rights came into force only after the death of the person whose property was to be divided and not before that. It was in their position as wife of the man or mother or daughter of the deceased person that, theoretically, women could never be excluded from inheritance. A number of instances revealed that women, both of upper and middle classes, inherited property in the form of houses, lands and *zamindaris*. During the time of Firoz Shah Tughlaq, the practice was that when an amir died, his position was taken by his son, son-in-law, slaves and near relations in the order of succession and when none of them existed, only then his wife was taken as his successor. She was not given the post but only the grants attached to the post.[107] It has also been reported by the author of *Mirat-i-Sikanderi* that Sultan Mahmud Begrah of Gujarat had ordained that when any of his amirs or soldiers died fighting or otherwise, then his *jagir* should be bequeathed to his son(s) and in case he had no son, then half of it should go to his daughter(s) and in case he had no daughter also, then it should be distributed among his relatives. It is interesting to note that once when a person pointed out about the son of an amir not being worthy of holding a *jagir*, the sultan retorted that the *jagir* would make him worthy of that.[108] During the reign of Sultan Muzaffar II of Gujarat (1511–1526 A.D.), the Quranic principles of inheritance were reported to be followed regarding *aima* grants and a woman got half the share of that of a man.[109]

During the Mughal period, women inherited a share in the family property or in the property of the husband. From some of the documents at hand, it has been brought out that in some communities and families of the *suba* of Awadh, such inheritance by women was a set practice. Thus, some documents show daughters of Sandnagar families of *qasba* (town) of Sandila inheriting their share; their daughters-in-law were also given a share in the property of their deceased husbands, while other document shows wife inheriting from her husband.[110] There are 'Bilgram Documents' that depict recognition to women's property rights in Sayyid family of *Qasba* of Bilgram and also the wife inheriting land from her husband; these documents pertain to years 1734 and 1732 A.D, respectively.[111] Further, there are documents showing Shaikh families of *Qasba* of Bilgram recognising women's property rights.[112] But, it is not clear from these documents whether the women received the legal share or not. The will of Hamida Banu, mother of Akbar, stipulated that her large treasure should be divided among her male descendants.[113] Similarly, after the death of Mumtaz Mahal, half of the property left by her, comprising more than ₹10 million, was inherited by Begam Sahib (Jahanara) and the other half was divided among her other children including daughters.[114]

The Shariat law of inheritance was not followed while determining women's share. It was subjected to adjustments because of the personal influence of the ladies, as happened in the case of Jahanara, or because of the local customs. However, the monarch had the overriding power. He had unlimited authority to take away any property and to distribute it in any way he liked. There was, for instance, a noble named Mian Muhammad, son of the sister of Sultan Bahlol, who held *jagirs* under Bahlol, Sikander and Ibrahim

Lodi and amassed great wealth. He had a daughter, Fath Malika besides a son named Mian Niamu from a slave girl, whom he had acknowledged as his son. When he died during the reign of Ibrahim Lodi, the sultan ignored the inheritance of his son and daughter. After taking possession of his resources, he declared Shaikh Mustafa, husband of Fath Malika, as his successor and bestowed majority of his property on him, except some *pargana*s that were given as *jagir* to Niamu.[115] Although, indirectly, majority of the wealth came to the possession of Fath Malika, daughter of the deceased, but the sultan did not allow it to happen in natural course according to the Shariat law. Similarly, after the death of Itimad-ud-daulah, his daughter Nur Jahan was given all his property and establishments in spite of her having other brothers and sisters.[116] Muslim women often did not receive their share unless there were no close male relatives or the parents were very wealthy. Levy writes:

> In most lands of Islam, it is the exception rather than the rule for daughters to inherit, inspite of Koranic prescription. Accounts of the customary laws prevalent amongst the communities of Muslim India shows that where there are sons or sons' sons, female children and often both parents too, are excluded from succession to property, particularly if it consists of land or other immovable possessions.[117]

They were not in a position to assert for their rights also. They could not afford to affront their fathers or brothers on whom they depended for their maintenance in the event of their widowhood or divorce.

There have been some cases where women moved to the courts for their property rights. In one case, Musammat Banu, wife of Jahan and also of Fattu, filed a suit against Abdul Halim Chaudhary in 1656 A.D. for appropriating her *sattari (zamindari)* dues from village Karna Chaura, which she had inherited from her husbands. The *qazi*, however, decided the matter against her on the evidence that her husbands had relinquished their rights on the property in favour of Chaudhary during their lifetimes.[118] In another case, a widow Musammat Maham filed a petition against her stepson, Buddan (Buddha) from another wife, in 1666 A.D. for not releasing half share in her husband's property that the latter had given to her during his lifetime. The matter was decided in favour of the lady.[119] But such instances were only a few. In most of the cases, an illiterate *purdah nashin* Muslim woman could hardly take to such recourse. Sometimes, exploiting the weakness of sisters, the brothers appropriated more productive parts of land for themselves, leaving the less fertile portion for their sisters.[120] In view of such instances, Orme observed, 'No property in lands admits of disputes concerning them. The slavery to which the rights of parent and husband subjects the female ... abolishes at once all suits of dowries, divorce, jointures settlements....'[121]

Notwithstanding the above, the women did enjoy full ownership rights that entailed independent holding of the property, its control and management and the right to alienate it. They held properties independent of all males including their husbands. Thus, one document shows Sharifa Banu and Zahida Banu holding village Diwanpur as *Jagir* in lieu of their salaries in 1679 A.D.[122] Besides, they also found their properties through bequeathal, gift mortgage and transfer. To give some instances for bequeathal, there are documents no. 44, 39 and 54 in 'Bilgram Documents', first one showing a family of Bilgram bestowing its entire property wherein women were also co-sharers; second one depicting bequeathal of property by a lady on her grandson and the third showing the widow of Nawab Rashid Khan bequeathing whole or her property during Aurangzeb's time.[123] As for gifts, document no. 42 in 'Bilgram Documents' shows gift of family land, in which women also were co-sharers, to Abdul Wahab during Akbar's time and another document no. 1241 in *Oriental Records* depicts gift of village Antura Buzurg by Bibi Achhi in favour of Nur Muhammad, her adopted son, in 1732 A.D.[124] A document in 'Aligarh Farmans' shows property transfer by mortgage.[125] Further, to show property transfers, there is a *tamlik-nama* of 1625 A.D. on behalf of Mst Bibi Sappo, voluntarily transferring all her rights in a plot of land to Abdul Halim. There is another document, *Dastak* (summons), informing about Mst Lodhiyan having transferred half of the village Sikandarpur to her grandson, Muhammad Qaim.[126]

There were numerous cases of land ownership by a lady individually or jointly with other co-owners and sale of land by them. Musammat Shaubha Nau, for instance, sold her land comprising of one-third of village Debidaspur in 1681 A.D.[127] Various other documents show: one document shows Bibi Ujyali selling her share in residential plot, which she held jointly; others show Bibi Haibat selling the house inherited by her from mother, one half to Abdul Hamid in 1626 A.D. and other half to Muhammad Jafar and Muhammad Sharif in 1643 A.D. Yet another document records wife of Mian Omar selling land measuring 2 *bighas* and 5 *biswas* to Mian

Saiduddin in 1634 A.D.; another shows Bibi Shah Jahan selling her land for ₹4 and five *tankas* in 1645 A.D.; still another document shows Bibi Rakhi, Sukhi and Saba selling their respective lands through the representation of husband, a *vakil* and son, respectively, and another one depicts Muhammad Mahmud and Bibi Baghi, joint owners selling 4 *biswas* of land in *mauza* (a type of administrative district corresponding to a specific land area within which there may be one or more settlements) Kahjari. There are many more cases of such joint sale.[128] It is interesting to note that during those days, before a transfer of property actually took place by whatever way, three things were generally verified, namely the source from where the property was acquired (purchase, inheritance or in case of women even *mahr*), whether it was in possession and use of the owner at the time of transfer and the ownership duly witnessed to the effect that he/she was the real owner. Clearly, the women who sold their properties during this period were the legal owners of such properties. In these property transactions, some Muslim women even signed the documents of their own.[129]

Gifts also added to the immovable properties of the ladies. Lakhnawi, author of *Shahnama*, has mentioned about gift of a part of deceased Hazrat Begam's property to Mihr-un-nisa alias Mihr Parwar Begam. He depicted Hazrat Begam as the daughter of Aurangzeb.[130] On certain occasions, some women got such gifts from the state. One such lady was Musammat Nija, a prostitute, who was bestowed with a grant of 900 *bighas* of rent-free land as gift through a *sanad* of the reign of Aurangzeb (1662 A.D.).[131] Sometimes, in order to safeguard the shares of the females in the property from being encroached upon by some male members, some families singled out their female members and gifted properties to them by writing *tamlik-nama* (bestowal deed).[132]

Women and Family Economy

Being confined within the house, the foremost economic activity of Muslim women, except those of higher strata, remained the household work like cooking, weaving, sewing, spinning and fetching water. In fact, home was considered the right place for women and the contemporaries vehemently propounded women's engagement in the domestic activities alone.[133] Even though house management entailed a constant hard labour, still it was not given any importance because it could not be measured in terms of tangible economic gains.

The women belonging to the agricultural and labour class were always a helping hand to their menfolk in their economic activities like agriculture, animal husbandry, spinning, weaving and tailoring. They were equal partners in supplementing their economic resources. For their products, village was the ready market. They supplied their goods and services on customary basis and took, in return, a share in the agricultural produce.[134] In the cities, the artisans supplied articles to meet the luxury needs of the royalty, nobility and the well-to-do. According to Orme, in the coast of Coromandel and in the province of Bengal, it was difficult to find a village where every man, woman and child were not engaged in making a piece of cloth. He recorded how at Coromandel coast and at Dacca in Bengal (which supplied a major part of fine linen and silk for the king and his seraglio), the women of these artisans did all the primary work up to weaving with expertise. About the silk industry, he wrote:

> The women wind off the raw silk from the pod of the worm. A single pod of raw silk is divided into twenty different degrees of fineness; and so exquisite is the feeling of these women, that whilst the thread is running through their fingers so swiftly that their eye can be of no assistance, they will break it off exactly as the assortments change, at once from the first to the twentieth, from the nineteenth to the second.[135]

Similarly, about the acrobatics of the jugglers, English ambassador Norris has narrated how the female members of the family also displayed accuracy, fineness and perfection in giving their shows. He recorded his appreciation for items like the woman sitting on top of five earthen pots placed on the head of her man; or a woman climbing to the top of a stick about a yard and a half high placed on the head of the man and performing different types of risky tricks or a girl of 10 years climbing to the top of a rod measuring 26 yards and performing her gymnastic tricks over there.[136] It was because of this close economic association of lower class Muslim women with their menfolk that they remained free from a practice like purdah and did not suffer seclusion.

Service

Muslim women of the economically backward class were engaged in varied jobs for financial gains. Some of the women of the higher class also took up these jobs after they were captured in the wars. These workers were mainly of two types, namely those who worked for wages and those who followed their independent professions for earning their living.

For the women who worked for wages, the houses of the economically well off and the harems of the royalty and nobility were the main places of their employment. Besides being a good help in household activities, they did all sorts of jobs for the rich ladies. Within the seraglio of Sultan Ghias-ud-din of Malwa, there were two corps of amazons of 500 each, one of Abyssinian origin and the other of Turkish slave girls who flanked the throne from two sides in public audiences. From among the 15,000 ladies in his harem, there were women trained in different trades and they were organised in different departments. There were lady musicians, dancers, lady teachers, goldsmiths, blacksmiths, shoemakers, weavers, potters, tailors, makers of bows, arrows and quivers, carpenters, wrestlers and jugglers.[137] Many ladies were working in the administration also. They performed duties as *Hakima* (looked after the internal management of the harem during the sultanate period), *Mahaldars* (the highest female official, who was overall incharge of the harem), *Darogas* (incharge of the general administration who also controlled the maid servants and the dancing girls) and *Tahwildars* (cash keeper) or as one among the hundreds of workers and slaves posted under them. They worked as guards of the harems. There was universal employment of dancing and singing girls to rejoice the masters and mistresses.[138] There were also lady mimics to amuse the aristocratic and well-to-do class. It is corroborated by a painting showing women mimics in front of Lucknow Nawab.[139]

The ladies were paid according to their ranks. Sultan Ghias-ud-din made payment of fixed salaries to his lady employees of the harem. He paid daily two *seers* (s`er) a unit of measurement) of grain and two copper *tankas* to each individual working therein. Ferishta informs that 'the king himself regulated with nicety the pay and allowances of all....' Similarly, Razia provided for salary and land grants to her companions in harem. Further, Abbas Ahmad Umari informs that Sultan Muhammad bin Tughlaq gave to each of his slaves a monthly ration of two *mans* (a unit of measurement) of wheat and rice and three *seers* of meat together with other necessaries. Besides, each one was paid 10 *tankas* per month and 4 suits of clothes every year.[140] Abul Fazl wrote that in the 19th year of Akbar's reign, the ladies were divided into two categories. The first category was of high-ranking ladies known as *mahin bano*. They received between ₹1028 and ₹1610 per month. The other female inmates were in second category, which was further divided into two grades, Grade I with monthly stipend of ₹20–51 and Grade II with ₹2–40. These payments were not made at random. If a woman employee wanted anything within the limits of her salary, she applied to one of the *tahwildars* of the seraglio. The latter, a lady officer, then, sent the memorandum to the accounts officer who, after checking, sent it to the general treasury, where the payment was made in cash.[141] By the time of Aurangzeb, these salaries had been revised upwards. According to Manucci, the matrons, superintendents of music and their women players received, generally, between ₹300 and ₹500 per month while the other slaves and servants received between ₹50 and ₹200. As compared to the other official of the empire, these harem employees were more regularly paid and did not face so much inconvenience as others would face.[142] All these ladies were paid in ready money.[143]

The salaries were greatly supplemented by the daily awards and presents they received from their lavish masters and mistresses. The quantity of such bounties depended on the status of their employer and the extent of pleasure and satisfaction the employer derived from their services.[144] Many of the ladies working in the royal harem made a lot of extra money through gratification or otherwise. Once, when the assets of a maid were confiscated for committing the crime of kissing a eunuch, these amounted to ₹100,000 and 60,000 in cash and jewellery on evaluation.[145] Similarly, out of the vast accumulations made by Aqa Aqayan, the favourite maid of Jahangir, who served him for 33 years, she built a garden, a *sarai* (inn) and her tomb.[146]

Outside the harem, the women were engaged in important jobs, particularly in the work of spying for the royalty. Sultan Muhammad bin Tughlaq had infiltrated slave girls in the house of the amirs who passed all information about them to the sultan. He engaged female sweepers who had free access to the houses of the nobles for sanitation. With the connivance of the slave girls cum spies already present there, they gathered secret information and passed it on to the king.[147] Women spies were actively engaged within the Mughal harems also. A lady named Aqa-i-Sarvkad was in the harem of Babur, Humayun and Akbar. She worked as spy against Abdur Rahim Khan-Khana and other amirs of the time.[148]

The second category was that of the self-employed women. Many of them adopted the profession of midwifery. They worked within their own circles that were well demarcated. A lady in this job would get a definite number of households in inheritance from her mother-in-law. In fact, the profession had become so popular that in due course, a separate exclusive caste of ladies was found practising it and they were having their special uniform too. They could be recognised by the 'tufts of silk on their shoes or slippers, all others wearing plain'.[149] There were women who made bracelets (*churigars*).[150] Others made veils and scarfs out of muslin.[151] Still, others earned money by unknitting woollen and silken fabrics after their colours got faded.[152] The job of wet nurse was also very popular, who were paid 10 *tankas* for suckling a child during the time of Amir Khusrau.[153] There were many who worked as domestic slaves. Being attached to the households, they did not require to be paid any wages. However, the employer had to ensure their maintenance.[154]

Commercial Activities

The women of the lower classes were found running shops wherein they sold different merchandise. For instance, Chamoo, a common woman, had a shop in Delhi where she sold opium.[155] Sultan Ghias-ud-din of Malwa had a women's market within his seraglio where all vendors were women.[156] At times, royal ladies, following the austere behaviour of their king involved themselves in some sort of selling and earned their living. The royal women of Firoz Shah Bahmani's time (1397–1422 A.D.) supported them by selling the garments embroidered by them.[157] Badaoni referred to a woman running a wine shop during Akbar's reign.[158] Jahangir's mother, Mariyam-Zamani sent shiploads of commodities for sale to outside countries. The contemporaries confirm that she also had her own ships and junk. Jourdain called her ship 'Rahimi', although at times, he called it 'Beheme'.[159] Finch has recorded that once in 1610 A.D., her agents were out to buy indigo from the Bayana market in order to send it for sale to Mocha (Moka). Meanwhile, Finch gave bid against her agents and bought whole of indigo. This annoyed her and she complained to the emperor. As a result, Hawkins (Finch worked under him) fell into disfavour and had to be called back by the East India Company.[160]

Nur Jahan maintained a number of ships and traded in foreign lands, particularly in indigo and embroidered cloth, and made huge profits.[161] The volume of her trade was so much that she hired other highland ships also for the purpose. It is known that in 1622 A.D., the English seized many Indian ships returning from Mocha (Moka). Out of them, the goods loaded in one of them belonged to Nur Jahan.[162] Her shipmen paid customs to Portuguese who controlled the Arabian sea. She granted tax rebates to the English. There are two official documents of the time of Jahangir that show *hukum* (order) of Nur Jahan of 13 June 1627 that made it incumbent upon the officials of her *jagir*s between Akbarabad and Surat to obey Jahangir's *farman* of 1624 A.D. This *farman* exempted the English from *zakat* (road tolls) and other cess once they paid usual customs at Surat or Bharoach. She forbade levying *zakat* and other unauthorised cess on the English.[163] She also managed favourable *farmans*, conferring concessions on them, and preferred engaging English ships to those of Portuguese for sending her goods.[164]

Nur Jahan had active participation in internal trade. Through the river Jamuna, articles manufactured in Agra were sent to other parts of the country. Pelsaert, while writing about Agra, mentioned about collection of duties by officers of Nur Jahan Begam before the merchandise was sent across the river. De Laet, while describing Sikandra, wrote, 'Hither are brought all kinds of merchandise from Purob, Bengala, Purbet and Bouten(Bhutan); these pay dues to the queen before they are taken across the river'.[165]

Jahanara Begam had a number of ships through which she carried on trade. Her most well-known ship was called 'Sahibi', after her popular title *Begam Sahib*, and was used by her both for trade and Haj pilgrims. She also had another ship named 'Gunjawar', which was presented to her by Shah Jahan and which too operated from Surat.[166] She had friendly relations with both the Dutch and the English, with the help of whom she extended her commercial activities and earned huge profits.[167]

Income from Gifts and Presents

Gifts and presents in cash, jewellery or other movable assets received at different occasions contributed a lot to the resources of the royal ladies. They received these gifts from their male or female relations, the nobility, the public and even from the foreigners. But, among all of them, the king remained the greatest donor. Every sultan gave away something to somebody for any excuse almost every day. Ladies, invariably, enjoyed his bounty. These royal gifts were magnificent both in quality and in value. Muhammad bin Tughlaq was known for his lavish gifts.[168]

The Mughal emperors surpassed the sultans who preceded them. Not only the gifts they gave were of fabulous amounts but they also added many more occasions for the distribution of regular gifts, like the garden parties or weighing ceremonies of the emperors, etc. Babur's gifts to his lady relations, all other ladies of the harem and also to the ladies of his kinsmen and officers after his victory in the battle of Panipat are well known. To each begam, he gave one gold plate full of jewels, two small mother-of-pearl trays full of *asharfis*, two trays of *shahrukhis* (silver tanka [coin]) and all sorts of gifts in nines—that is four trays and one plate, besides a dancing girl or girls.[169] In the mystic feast about which Gulbadan has given a vivid account, Humayun distributed gifts of *asharfis* and *shahrukhis* to the begams present on the occasion.[170] Akbar, with all the grandeur of his empire, continued this practice on all occasions of mirth and gaiety.[171] The occasion of such gifts increased more and more during the time of his successors. Jahangir's *Memoirs* make frequent references to such gifts and presents on different occasions. At the time of his marriage with the daughter of Jagat Singh, Jahangir presented ₹80,000 to his bride as part of her *sachaq*. Similarly, it is informed that Jahangir presented a necklace of pearl containing 40 beads, each bead costing ₹40,000, to Nur Jahan at the time of his marriage with her.[172] On the occasion of marriage of Khurram in 1612 A.D., presents were made to mothers, begams and female servants.[173] Similarly, in recognition of the invention of a new *itr* (perfume) named *itr-i-Jahangiri* in 1614 A.D., a string of pearls was gifted by Jahangir to Esmat Banu Begam, his mother-in-law.[174] Khurram presented ₹200,000 to Nur Jahan and 60,000 each to other mothers and begams at the time of celebrating his Deccan victory in 1617 A.D.[175] Shah Jahan spent ₹16 million in his coronation. Out of this, only 3 million were gifted to the nobles, the rest were spent on presents to the members of his family. Mumtaz Mahal alone got a gift of 200,000 *asharfis* and ₹600,000 (silver), besides an annual allowance of ₹1 million; Jahanara Begam was given 100,000 *asharfis* and ₹400,000, besides an annual allowance of ₹600,000 and Roshanara and Surayya Begam were to share an amount of ₹350,000 with Murad and Lutfullah.[176] During the *Nauroz* festival that followed immediately after his coronation, besides other costly gifts, he distributed an amount of ₹2.5 million among his sons and daughters except Jahanara who was separately given an amount of ₹2.5 million and ornaments.[177] During the marriage of prince Murad Bakhsh with Sakina Banu in 1642 A.D., the latter was given jewels and ornaments worth ₹100,000 and cash gift of ₹40,000, besides costly dresses and other articles as part of her *sachaq*.[178] Once, when his aunt Shukr-un-nisa Begam came from Akbarabad to felicitate him on his victory at Balkh, he showered his magnanimity on her by giving her a *lal* (precious stone) worth ₹40,000, besides cash of ₹100,000 as present.[179]

Aurangzeb, notwithstanding his austerity, was also zealous in bestowing presents on the royal ladies. Contemporary authorities have given a number of instances of such gifts bestowed on different occasions. At the time of his second coronation in 1659 A.D., he awarded ₹500,000 to Padshah Begam (Roshanara) in recognition of her services to him. Of his four daughters, he gave ₹400,000 to Zeb-un-nisa, ₹200,000 to Zinat-un-nisa, ₹160,000 to Badr-un-nisa and ₹150,000 to Zabat-un-nisa. The royal maids were also rewarded.[180] Must'ad Khan's book *Maasir-i-Alamgiri* contains repeated references of gifts to royal ladies during Aurangzeb's time. To narrate a few, on the eve of Id in 1666 A.D., he gave 100,000 gold coins along with enhancement in annual pension to Begam Sahib (Jahanara) and ₹100,000 each to Pur Hunar Banu Begam and Gauharara Begam, daughters of Shah Jahan; on the eve of Muhammad Azam's marriage with Jahanzib Banu Begam (daughter of Dara Shukoh), the latter was given ₹160,000 as *sachaq*, presents of one elephant worth ₹15,000 to Begam Sahib (Jahanara) and two elephants to Jahanzib Banu were given on the occasion of marriage of Azam in 1669 A.D. In 1617 A.D., on the eve of Id, Pur Hunar Banu Begam and Gauharara Begam were presented with 5,000 *mohars* (gold coin weighing 169 grains [10.95 grams]) each and Getiara and Iffatara Begams, the daughters of Muhammad Azam, were presented with ornaments worth ₹8,000–10,000 each on the occasion of their visit to the court.[181] It is also reported that on the recovery of Jahanara from her burns in 1644 A.D., Aurangzeb gave her jewels worth ₹1 million. Further, Aurangzeb is said to have given gift worth ₹200,000 to Sahia, bride of prince Bidar Bakht.[182]

During the later Mughal period, the depleted treasury could not afford lavish gifts. Yet, Lal Kanwar received huge gifts. On the occasion of marriage of Emperor Muhammad Shah with Badshah Begam, valuable presents were made to his mother Qudsia Hazrat Begam.[183]

Besides the generosity of the kings, these ladies received presents from the foreign entrepreneurs, nobles and the public as well. Mughal ladies like Nur Jahan, Jahanara and their lady employees got frequent presents from the foreign entrepreneurs. Hawkins presented jewels to Shukr-un-nisa Begam and Nur Jahan, Jahangir's sister and wife, respectively.[184] Similarly, Robert Coryat, another Englishman, gave a ruby-studded gold whistle to Jahangir at the time of his departure in 1611 A.D. from Agra which the Emperor 'gave to one of his great women' (in all probability to Nur Jahan).[185] Thomas Roe also presented Nur Jahan many things, chief among them being an English coach, a mirror chest and many toys.[186] Jahanara Begam received presents from the Dutch who sought her favour to settle their problems.[187] The English gave her numerous gifts in the form of perfumed oils, broad and embroidered cloth, mirror and cabinets.[188] Gifting, in fact, had become such an accepted norm that while giving the guidelines for the establishment of French factories in the Mughal empire and realising the weight that Roshanara could carry with Aurangzeb, Bernier wrote on 10 March 1668 A.D. from Surat that 'Roshan Ara Begum is so much in favour that it would perhaps be better to give her a few presents'. However, he suggested, at the same time, to be cautious while doing so.[189]

When Jahangir visited his mother's apartment along with the nobles, the latter offered gifts to the queen mother.[190] Similarly, when Itimad-ud-daulah threw a royal entertainment in honour of Jahangir in 1619 A.D., he offered gifts worth ₹100,000 in jewelled ornaments and clothes to the begams and other ladies of Jahangir's harem.[191] These different sources brought fabulous amounts in possession of the royal ladies. The individuals, however, had wealth varying according to their economic and political involvement, their closeness to the king and also according to the period to which they belonged. There is no doubt that such women, in general, were wealthy.

To sum up, the maintenance of Muslim women of the upper strata was well cared for during the period. The state provided for them in the form of *jagirs*, retention of *iqtas, suyurghal* grants, cash *wazifa*, grants of villages and right of collection of land revenue. Many women of the lower strata also got benefitted by the generosity of the royalty and nobility in the form of *Suyurghal* grants and other acts of piety and charity aimed at helping the women. The *mahr*, her Quranic right, was, paid only in the early years when the *mahr* amount used to be low. With the increase in the amount, it came to be reduced to be a mere promise. Some of them inherited property, enjoyed ownership rights and even went to courts to defend them. But the *purdah-nashin* ladies were handicapped, as all property transactions remained mainly the handiwork of their men. The upper strata Muslim ladies of Mughal time were engaged in lucrative trade while the common Muslim women undertook different occupations outside as salaried employees, slave girls or independent professionals. The ladies of agricultural and labour class provided a helping hand in their family bread-earning activities. Muslim women, of both upper and lower classes, got a lot of money through gifts and gratification from different sources. On the whole, the ladies of the Mughal period were richer than their counterparts in the sultanate period.

Notes

1. Jeffery Patricia, *Frogs in a Well, Indian Women in Purdah* (New Delhi: Vikas Publishing House, 1979), 25.
2. Satish Chandra, *Medieval India: From Sultanat to the Mughals-Delhi Sultanat (1206–1526), Part*-I (New Delhi: Har-Anand Publications Ltd, 2006), 139.
3. Abul Fazl, *Ain-i-Akbari*, vol. 1 (New Delhi: Crown Publications, 1988), 40–41, 51–53, 55 (for Akbar's arrangements); Nur-ud-din Jahangir, *Tuzuk-i-Jahangiri*, vol. 1 (New Delhi: Munshiram Manoharlal, 1968), 10 (Jahangir's increase of allowances); Niccolao Manucci, *Storia Do Mogor or Mogul India*, trans. William Irvine, vol. 2 (New Delhi: Atlantic Publishers and Distributors, 1989), 310, 350–351 (for allowances during Aurangzeb's time).
4. Abdul Hamid Lahori, *Badshah Nama*, ed. K.A. Ahmad and Abdal Rahim, Part I, vol. 1 (Calcutta: Bibliothica Indica, 1867), 96.
5. Must'ad Khan, *Maasir-i-Alamgiri*, trans., ann. J.N. Sarkar (Kolkata: Royal Asiatic Society of Bengal, 1947), 36; B.P. Saksena, *History of Shahjahan of Dihli* (Allahabad: Central Book Depot, 1958),63–64.Latif, by mistake, has written her allowance at ₹6 million per annum during Shah Jahan's time (S.M. Latif, *Lahore, Its History, Architectural Remains and Antiquities* (Lahore: New Imperial Press, 1892), 58).

6. Wolseley Haig, *The Cambridge History of India*, ed. Richard Burn, vol. 4 (London: Cambridge University Press, 1937), 326; William Irvine, *Later Mughals*, vol. 1 (Kolkata: M.C. Sarkar & Sons, 1922), 194.

7. Shireen Moosvi, *The Economy of the Mughal Empire* (Delhi: Oxford University Press, 1987), 248; Manucci, *Storia Do Mogor*, vol. 2: 315–316.

8. Moosvi, *The Economy*, 248–277. Dam was a copper paise/coin (J.F. Richards, ed., *The Imperial Monetary System of Mughal India* (Delhi: Oxford University Press, 1987), 20, 173).

9. R.P. Tripathi, *Some Aspect of Muslim Administration* (Allahabad: Central Book Depot, 1966), 244–246, 249–250. See also K.A. Nizami, *Some Aspects of Religion and Politics in India During the Thirteenth Century*, 2nd ed. (New Delhi: Idarah-i-Adabiyat-i-Delli, 1974), 128–131; Irfan Habib, 'Agrarian Economy', in *The Cambridge Economic History of India*, vol. 1 (London: Cambridge University Press, 1982), 68–75 (particularly 68, 74, 75).

10. N.N. Law, *Promotion of Learning in India During Muhammedan Rule* (Delhi: Idarah-i-Adabiyat-i-Delli, 1973), 45.

11. Ibn Batuta, *The Rehla of Ibn Batuta*, trans. Mahdi Husain (Baroda: Oriental Institute, 1953), 140.

12. S. Moin-ul-Haq, *Barani's History of the Tughlugs* (Karachi: Pakistan Historical Society, 1959), 98.

13. Zia-ud-din Barani, *Fatawa-i-Jahandari*, trans. Afsar Begam, in *The Political Theory of the Delhi Sultanate*, by Mohammad Habib and Dr Afsar (Allahabad, n.d.), 6.

14. Abdullah, *Tarikh-i-Daudi*, in *Uttar Taimur Kaleen Bharat*, Part I, trans. S.A.A. Rizvi, 279; Niamatullah, *Tarikh-i-Khan Jahani wa Makhzan-i-Afghana*, in *Niamtullah's History of the Afghans*, trans. N.B. Roy (Calcutta: Shantiniketan, 1958), 89; Abdul Qadir Al Badaoni, *Muntakhabu-t-Tawarikh*, trans. S.A. Ranking, vol. 1 (New Delhi: Idarah-i-Adabiyat-i-Delli, 1973), 423, note 2.

15. Abul Fazl, *Akbar Nama*, vol. 3 (New Delhi: Ess Ess Publications, 1977), 107 (for Humanyun's widow); William Finch, in *Early Travels in India*, ed. William Foster (New Delhi: Chand & Co., 1968), 186 (for Akbar's widows). Samsam ud-daulah Shah Nawaz Khan and Abdul Hayy, *Maasir-ul-Umara*, Part II, vol. 2 (Patna: Janki Prakashan, 1979), 1078; Latif, *Lahore*, 58 (for allowance of Nur Jahan. But according to Blochmann, Elphinstone, by mistake, mentioned it as ₹200,000 per annum (Notes to *Ain-i-Akbari*, by Abul Fazl, vol. 1 (New Delhi: Crown Publications, 1988), 574, note 3); Lahori, *Badshah Nama*, Part I, vol. 1: 96 (for allowance of Mumtaz Mahal; Must'ad Khan, *Maasir-i-Alamgiri*, 23 (for allowance of Hamida Banu, the widow of Khalilullah Khan). See also Shah Nawaz Khan and Hayy, *Maasir*, vol. 2: 525 (for fixing of allowances for their maintenance).

16. Anonymous, *Tarikh-i-Salim Shahi*, in *Memoirs of the Emperor Jahangir Written by Himself*, trans. David Price (New Delhi: Rare Books, 1904), 106 (for Jahangir's widow fund). Manucci, *Storia Do Mogor*, vol. 2: 118 and footnote 133, 286 (for Aurangzeb's arrangements).

17. Zahir-ud-din Babur, *Babur Nama or Memoirs of Babur*, trans. A.S. Beveridge, vol 2, rpt. (New Delhi: Oriental Books Reprint Corpn, 1970), 478.

18. Manucci, *Storia Do Mogor*, vol. 2: 350–351.

19. Gulbadan Begam, *Humayun Nama*, trans. A.S. Beveridge (New Delhi: Idarah-i-Adabiyat-i-Delli, 1972), 97 (for Babur), 110 (for Humayun).

128 The Status of Muslim Women in Medieval India

20. Mutamad Khan, *Iqbalnama-i-Jahangiri*, trans. Elliot and Dowson, *History of India*, vol. VI (Allahabad: Kitab Mahal, 1964), 405; Muhammad Hadi, *Tatimma-i-Waqiat-i-Jahangiri*, trans. H.M. Elliot and John Dowson, *History of India as Told by Its Own Historians*, vol. VI (Allahabad: Kitab Mahal, 1964), 398–399; Beni Prasad, *History of Jahangir*, 3rd ed. (Allahabad: The Indian Press Ltd., 1940), 166.
21. Jahangir, *Tuzuk*, vol. 1: 342; Blochmann, Notes to *Ain-i-Akbari*, vol. 1: 574.
22. Jahangir, *Tuzuk*, vol. 1: 380 and footnote 1. He referred to it as Boda that might have been mistaken for Toda. The footnote clarifies that there was a place called Bodah in *Sarkar* Marosor in Malwa, but its revenue was only ₹250,000 of *dams*. 'The two I.O. MSS. and Debi Prasad's Hindi version have Toda. Toda was in Ajmer and its revenue in Akbar's time was 1.5 lacs of rupees'. See Abul Fazl, *Ain-i-Akbari*, vol. 1: 294, for reference of Toda.
23. Blochmann, Notes to *Ain-i-Akbari*, vol. 1: 575. For *Altamgha*, see W.H. Moreland, *The Agrarian System of Moslem India*. (Delhi: Oriental Books Reprint Corpn., 1968), 127, 270.
24. Lahori, *Badshah Nama*, Part II, vol. 1: 51, also Part I, vol. 2: 206; Muhammad Amin Qazwini, *Badshah Nama*, Transcription, Part III (Aligarh: Aligarh Muslim University), fol. 626. The village is named as Shahbabad by Lahori and Begamabad by Qazwini.
25. Lahori, *Badshah Nama*, Part II, vol. 2: 582.
26. Lahori, *Badshah Nama*, Part II, vol. 1: 27.
27. Aurangzeb, *Rukkat-i-Alamgiri*, trans. J.H. Bilmoria (New Delhi: Idarah-i-Adabiyat-i-Delli, 1972), 77.
28. Shah Nawaz Khan and Hayy, *Maasir*, Part II, vol. 2: 701 and footnote 1.
29. Muhammad Salih Kambo, *Amal-i-Saleh*, ed. G. Yazdani, vol. 3 (Calcutta: Asiatic Society, 1939), 109 (given to her at the start of the 23rd year of Shah Jahan's reign).
30. Mirza Muhammad Kazim, *Alamgir Namah* (Calcutta: Bibliothica Indica, 1865–1873), 134–135; Manucci, *Storia Do Mogor*, vol. 1: 63, 208.
31. Zahir-ud-din Malik, *The Reign of Muhammad Shah* (New York: Asia Publishing House, 1977), 294, 322.
32. K.M. Ashraf, *Life and Conditions of the People of Hindustan* (New Delhi: Munshi Ram Manoharlal, 1970), 219, note 7 (on the authority of 'Fiqh-i-Firuz Shahi'). William Hawkins, in *Early Travels in India*, ed. William Foster (New Delhi: Chand & Co., 1968), 112; J.B. Tavernier, *Travels in India by Jean Baptiste Tavernier*, trans. V. Ball, ed. William Crooke, vol. 1 (New Delhi: Oriental Books Reprint Corpn., 1977), 15; Tapan Raychaudhuri, 'The State and the Economy: The Mughal Empire', in *The Cambridge Economic History of India*, vol. 1 (London: Cambridge University Press, 1982), 183 (for prevailing system).
33. Shah Nawaz Khan and Hayy, *Maasir*, vol. 1: 293.
34. Blochmann, Notes to *Ain-i-Akbari* vol. 1: 280 (for details about *Suyurghal*); Badaoni, *Muntakhabu-t-Tawarikh*, vol. 2: 207, 261. See also K.K. Datta, ed., *Introduction*, in *Some Mughal Farmans, Sanads, Parwanahs etc. 1578-1802* (Patna: State Central Records Office, 1962), iii, iv.
35. Abul Fazl, *Ain-i-Akbari*, vol 1: 278.
36. Sarwani, *Tarikh-i-Sher Shahi*, trans. B.P. Ambashthya (Patna: K.P. Jayaswal Research Institute, 1974), 770.
37. Abul Fazl, *Ain-i-Akbari*, vol. 1: 279–280; Badaoni, *Muntakhabu-t-Tawarikh*, vol. 2: 261, 282 The narration of Abul Fazl makes it very clear that these grants were held by all, but special exemption from Akbar's rule was given to only to *Irani*

and *Turani* women, who belonged to the ruling class. This rule was applicable only to grantees having more than 100 *bighas*. Only the women of *Irani* and *Turani* origin were granted such big chunks of land and the rest of the lower strata Hindustani Muslim women received only smaller chunks. It was probably because of this that Abul Fazl incorporated the names of *Irani* and *Turani* women only while mentioning this special privilege. The author, therefore, tends to differ from learned modern writers like Rekha Mishra (*Women in Mughal India* (Allahabad: Munshiram Manohar Lal, 1967), 136, note. 7) and Rafat Bilgrami ('Women Grantees in the Mughal Empire', *Quarterly Journal of Pakistan Historical Society* XXXVI, Part III (July 1988): 207), who tend to draw from this that only *Irani* and *Turani* women held these grants during Akbar's time.

38. Yusuf Mirak, *Mazhar-i-Shahjahani*, ed. Pir Husam-ud-din Rashidi (Hyderabad: Sindhi Adabi Board, n.d.), 158. These grants held by men were known as *Muzakkarati*.

39. K.P. Srivastava, ed., *Mughal Farmans 1540 A.D. to 1706 A.D.*, vol. 1 (Lucknow: U.P. State Archives, 1974), 5–6.

40. Abul Fazl, *Ain-i-Akbari*, vol. 1: 280.

41. Irfan Habib, *Agrarian System of Mughal India 1556–1707* (Mumbai: Asia Publishing House, 1963), 305–306; Abdur Rashid Shaikh, 'Suyurghal Lands Under the Mughals', in *Essays presented to Sir Jadunath Sarkar*, ed. H.R. Gupta (Chandigarh: Punjab University, 1958), 313–322.

42. Datta, ed., *Some Mughal Farmans*, Pw. no. 503: 110–111.

43. Oriental Records, *A Calendar of Oriental Records*, ed. B.P. Saxsena, vol. 3 (Allahabad: Government Central Record Office, 1959), D. no. 1201: 16–17, also D. no. 1202: 2–3; (1956), vol. 2: D. nos. 44, 55: 88–90, 44–45 resp.; (1955), vol. 1: D. no. 44: 19–21 for other example.

44. Bilgrami, 'Women Grantees', 210 (mentioned about two *farmans* of the times of Shah Jahan and Aurangzeb, respectively, whereby the property division had been made as per Shariat).

45. Srivastava, ed., *Mughal Farmans*, vol. 1: Sr. no. XLII: 70–71.

46. *Oriental Records* vol. 1: D. no. 44: 19 and vol. 2: 88–90.

47. Srivastava, ed., *Mughal Farmans*, vol. 1: Sr. nos. XV, XVI, XVIII, XIX: 24–26, 28–31. She has been referred to as '*Nawab Mahd Uliya*' in all these documents.

48. Blochmann in Notes to *Ain-i-Akbari*, vol. 1: 574 named this post as *Sadr-i-anas* while Bilgrami, ('Women Grantees', 207), called it *Sadr-i-inath*. In *Maasir-ul-Umara*, Dilaram has been referred to as *Sadr-i-Anath* (Shah Nawaz Khan and Hayy, *Maasir*, Part II, vol. 2: 1077–1078) while Sati-un-nisa (of the time of Shah Jahan) and Fatima Begam (of the time of Aurangzeb) as *Sadr-un-nisa* (Shah Nawaz Khan and Hayy, *Maasir*, vol. 1: 295, 355). Sarkar named it as *Sadr* or 'Superintendent of the harem' (J.N. Sarkar, *Studies in Aurangzib's Reign* (Kolkata: M.C. Sarkar & Sons, 1933), 24).

49. Hadi, *Tatimma-i-Waqiat-i-Jahangiri*, 398; Anonymous, *Intikhab-i-Jahangir Shahi*, trans. H.M. Elliot and John Dowson, vol. VI, 447; Shah Nawaz Khan and Hayy, *Maasir*, vol. 1: 260–261, also Part II, vol. 2: 1077–1078.

50. *Oriental Records*, vol. 2: D. no. 161: 34; Srivastava, ed., *Mughal Farmans*, vol. 1: Sr. nos. XV–XIX: 24–31; *Farman-i-Salatin*, ed. Bashir-ud-din Ahmad) (Delhi, 1926), D. 31.

51. *Oriental Records*, vol. 2: D. nos. 161, 162: 34–35; also D. no. 163: 33–34 for another such grant in 1614 A.D.

52. *Oriental Records*, vol. 1: D. no. 750: 86.

53. Srivastava, ed., *Mughal Farmans*, vol. 1: Sr. no. XIX: 30–31. See also Sr. no. XV–XVIII: 24–29 for other grants.

54. *Oriental Records*, vol. 2: D. no. 156: 59, also D. nos. 158, 159, 160: 36–38 of the years 1649 and 1651 A.D. for other examples.

55. Datta, ed., *Some Mughal Farmans*, Sr. no. 289: 70.

56. *Oriental Records*, vol. 3: D. no. 874: 26, also vol. 1: D. no. 759: 80.

57. Srivastava, ed., *Mughal Farmans*, vol. 1: Sr. no. XL: 66–67.

58. *Oriental Records*, vol. 3: D. no. 881: 28–29.

59. *Oriental Records*, vol. 2: D. no. 165: 46.

60. 'Aligarh Farmans', University Collection, History Department (Aligarh: Azad Library, Aligarh Muslim University), Sr. nos. 212, 213, 220.

61. Datta, ed., *Some Mughal Farmans*, Sr. nos. 77, 79, 82, 90, 373: 17, 18, 19, 85.

62. Datta, ed., *Some Mughal Farmans*, Sr. no. 82: 34.

63. Datta, ed., *Some Mughal Farmans*, Sr. nos. 311, 310: 73–74 resp.; see also Sr. no. 84: 18.

64. 'Aligarh Farmans', (Aligarh: Azad Library, Aligarh Muslim university), Sr. nos. 195, 196, also Fr. nos. 176, 198, 201, 205, 207, 209, 216, 221, 223–225, 238, 246, 255 in this regard.

65. Datta, ed., *Some Mughal Farmans*, Sr. no. 484: 107; also Sr. no. 246: 63.

66. Datta, ed., *Some Mughal Farmans*, Sr. nos. 345, 343: 79–80 resp.

67. Datta, ed., *Some Mughal Farmans*, Sr. nos. 545, 546: 118–119.

68. Datta, ed., *Some Mughal Farmans*, Sr. nos. 126, 424: 42, 95.

69. Datta, ed., *Some Mughal Farmans*, Sr. no. 289: 70.

70. Datta, ed., *Some Mughal Farmans*, Sr. no. 77: 33.

71. Datta, ed., *Some Mughal Farmans*, Sr. no. 548: 119. For other release orders, see Sr. nos. 296, 328: 71, 76.

72. For details, see Abul Fazl, *Ain-i-Akbari*, vol. 1: 279–280 and Blochmann's Notes, 281–282; Badaoni, *Muntakhabu-t-Tawarikh*, vol. 2: 261, 282, 379.

73. Srivastava, ed., *Mughal Farmans*, vol. 1: Sr. no. XXX: 48–49; Datta, ed., *Some Mughal Farmans*, Sr. nos. 102, 105: 37, 110; 'Firangi Mahal Documents', Transcript (Aligarh: History Department Library, Aligarh Muslim University), Sr. nos. 7, 5, 16, 18 (for examples of confirmation of grants of women). See also Srivastava, ed., *Mughal Farmans*, vol. 1: Sr. no. XXXVIII: 62–63; Datta, ed., *Some Mughal Farmans*, Sr. nos. 241, 246–248, 496: 62, 63; *Oriental Records*, vol. 2: D. no. 169, 166: 41–42, 47 resp. (for cases or renewal of grants of women pertaining to years 1662 and 1695 A.D. resp.).

74. Srivastava, ed., *Mughal Farmans*, vol. 1: Sr. no. XXVIII: 62–63. See also *Oriental Records*, vol. 3: D. no. 789: 14 (for reduction of grant of Jauhar Jahan from 200 to 190 *bighas* at renewal by Shah Jahan in 1629 A.D.).

75. Datta, ed., *Some Mughal Farmans*, Sr. nos. 81 (1631 A.D.), 399 (1661 A.D.), 379 (1718 A.D.), 17–18, 399, 379 resp.

76. Srivastava, ed., *Mughal Farmans*, vol. 1: Sr. nos. XV, XVI, XVIII, XIX: 24–26, 28–29.

77. Mirak, *Mazhar-i-Shahjahani*, 191.

78. Lahori, *Badshah Nama*, vol. 2: 365–366 (for people getting grants without being presented) and 165–166 (about Musawi Khan); Shah Nawaz Khan and Hayy, *Maasir*, Part I, vol. 2: 327(for Musawi's dismissal from service).

79. *Oriental Records*, vol. 2: D. no. 169: 41–42.
80. *Oriental Records*, vol. 2: D. no. 166: 47; also vol. 3: D. nos. 815-1, 2, 1228, 816-1, 2: 19, 4–5, 20 resp. for other references. (They pertained to years 1691, 1697 and 1704 A.D. resp.).
81. 'Firangi Mahal Documents', nos. 7, 5, 16, 18. The documents were calendared by Iqbal Husain, *Proceedings of Indian History Congress*, Aligarh, 1975 (available in Research Library, Department of History, Aligarh Muslim University). Also see *Oriental Records*, vol. 3: D. nos. 815-1, 2, 1189: 19, 69 (for representation through *vakil*).
82. *Oriental Records*, vol. 3: D. no. 1189: 69.
83. *Oriental Records*, vol. 3: D. no. 895: 52.
84. *Oriental Records*, vol. 3: D. no. 1210: 54.
85. *Oriental Records*, vol. 2: D. nos. 457, 439: 1–3; see also Muzaffar Alam, *The Crisis of Empire in Mughal North India; Awadh and the Punjab (1707–1748)* (Delhi: Oxford University Press, 1986), 223 and nn. 62–65.
86. *Oriental Records*, vol. 2: D. nos. 161, 162: 34–35; Srivastava, ed., *Mughal Farmans*, vol. 1: Sr. nos. XV, XVI, XVIII: 24, 25, 28. All these documents pertain to Jahangir's time.
87. *Oriental Records*, 2: D. no. 163: 33 (Jahangir's time); D. nos. 158–160, 156: 36–38, 59 (Shah Jahan's time); Datta, ed., *Some Mughal Farmans*, Sr. nos. 77, 79, 98, 296: 17, 19, 71 (Aurangzeb's time), Sr. no. 246: 63 (Muhammad Shah's time).
88. *Oriental Records*, vol. 1: D. no. 5: 34–35; vol. 2: 35–36 (for charging a fixed amount known as *muqarrari-i-aymah*. This document mentioned about the charge (*sir bigha*) of ₹244 and 6 *annas* at the rate of 8 *annas* per *bigha* from one Birlas Begam on her land measuring 476 *bighas* and 1 *biswa in 1647 A.D.* (increased to 900 *bighas in 1649 A.D.*). This *muqarrari* was later on exempted by Shah Jahan in two instalments, first ₹56 and subsequently the remaining amount of ₹188 and 6 *annas* in 1649 A.D.
89. Datta, ed., *Some Mughal Farmans*, Sr. no. 78: 17.
90. Mirak, *Mazhar-i-Shahjahani*, 146–147.
91. Mirak, *Mazhar-i-Shahjahani*, 158–161.
92. M.M. Siddiqi, *Women in Islam* (New Delhi: New Taj Office, 1991), 48.
93. Ibn Batuta, *Rehla*, 81–82.
94. Gulbadan, *Humayun Nama*, 151; Anonymous, *Tarikh-i-Salim Shahi*, 46.
95. Duarte Barbosa, *The Book of Duarte Barbosa*, trans., ed. and ann. Mansal Longworth Dames, vol. 1 (New Delhi: Asian Educational Services, 1989), 121.
96. Manucci, *Storia Do Mogor*, vol. 3: 144.
97. *Oriental Records*, vol. 2: D. no. 326, 11.
98. 'Shamsabad and Bilhaur Documents', Transcript no. 104 (Aligarh: History Department, Aligarh Muslim University), 70.
99. Rafat Bilgrami, 'Property Rights of Muslim Women in Mughal India' (paper presented at proceedings of Indian History Congress, 48th session, Goa, 1987, 261–270). For erstwhile belief about *mahr*, see T.P. Hughes, *Dictionary of Islam* (New Delhi: Rupa & Co., 1988), 91; Gregory C. Kozlowski, 'Muslim Women and the Control of Property in Northern India', *The Indian Economic and Social History Review* 24, Issue 2 (1987): 163–164.
100. Francisco Pelsaert, *The Remonstrantie or Jahangir's India*, trans. W.H. Moreland and P. Geyl, rpt. (New Delhi: Idarah-i-Adabiyat-i-Delli, 1972), 83.

101. Sarwani, *Tarikh-i-Sher Shahi*, trans. B.P. Ambashthya, 205–206.

102. Abul Fazl, *Ain-i-Akbari*, vol. 1: 288.

103. S.H. Hodivala, 'The Dirham-i-Sharai', *Journal of Asiatic Society of Bengal*, New Series13 (1917): 47–48.

104. The practice has remained prevalent even in modern times. See A.A.A. Fyzee, *Outlines of Muhammadan Law*, 3rd ed. (London: Oxford University Press, 1964), 335–336; Indian Council of Social Science Research, *Status of Women in India* (New Delhi: Indian Council of Social Science Research, 1975), 15. Refer also to the discussions on divorce in Chapter 2.

105. Must'ad Khan, *Maasir-i-Alamgiri*, 49, 77, 129.

106. Must'ad Khan, *Maasir-i-Alamgiri*, 73, 103 (for Salima Banu Begam daughter of Murad Bakhsh); Lahori, *Badshah Nama*, vol. 2: 305 (for Sakina Banu); Saksena, *History of Shahjahan*, 312 (for Dara and Shuja); Irvine, *Later Mughals*, vol. 1: 304, Shiv Das Lakhnawi, *Shahnama Munawwar_Kalam*, trans. Syed Hasan Askari (Patna: Janki Prakashan, 1980), 6, note 21 of 158 (for *mahr* of Ajit Singh's daughter; Irvine, *Later Mughals*, vol. 2: 124 (for *mahr* of Farrukhsiyar's daughter; Ishwar Dass Nagar, *Futuhat-i-Alamgiri*, trans., ed. Tasneem Ahmad (New Delhi: Idarah-i-Adabiyat-i-Delli, 1978), 179 (for Sahia).

107. Firoz Shah Tughlaq, *Futuhat-i-Firoz_Shahi*, ed. S.A. Rashid (Aligarh, 1954), Rules 25, 26, 18; Shams Siraj Afif, *Tarikh-i-Firoz_Shahi*, ed. Maulvi Vilayat Husain (Kolkata: Bibliothica Indica, 1891), 96–97.

108. Ibn-i-Mohammad Sikander, *Mirat-i-Sikanderi*, in *Uttar Taimur Kaleen Bharat*, Part II, trans. S.A.A. Rizvi (Aligarh: Aligarh Muslim University, 1959), 301–302.

109. Sikander, *Mirat-i-Sikanderi*, Part II, trans. S.A.A. Rizvi, 375–376. These grants were given to men of piety and learning.

110. *Oriental Records*, vol. 2: D. nos. 452, 325, 366, 459, 471, 415:79, 75, 79–80, 82, 15, 84 resp., also D. nos. 319, 322, 429, 467, 460, 408: 60, 61, 61–62, 65–66, 69, 73 resp. (for other references), also *Oriental Records*, vol. 3: D. no. 1241: 55 (for wife inheriting).

111. 'Bilgram Documents', Transcript no. 89 (Aligarh: History Department, Aligarh Muslim University), Sr. nos. 46, 78 (women's property rights), D. no. 46 (wife inheritance).

112. 'Sharaif-i-Usmani Documents', Transcript No. 82 (Aligarh: History Department Library, Aligarh Muslim University), Sr. nos. 157–159 (for Shaikh families of Qasba of Bilgram).

113. V.A. Smith, *Akbar: The Great Mogul (1542–1605)*, 3rd Indian Print (New Delhi, 1966), 229–230.

114. Shah Nawaz Khan and Hayy, *Maasir*, vol. 1: 295.

115. Sarwani, *Tarikh-i-Sher Shahi*, trans. B.P. Ambashthya, 250–251.

116. Jahangir, *Tuzuk*, vol. 2: 228; also Blochmann, Notes to *Ain-i-Akbari*, vol. 1: 574, 576 (for Nur Jahan's *Jagirs* and pedigree table of Itimad-ud-daulah).

117. R. Levy, *The Social Structure of Islam* (London: Cambridge University Press, 1957), 245–246. See also Fyzee, *Muhammadan Law*, 335–336; V.R. Bevan and L. Jones, *Women in Islam: A Manual with Social Reference to Conditions in India* (Lucknow: The Lucknow Publishing House, 1941), 242–244; Z. Eglar, *A Punjabi Village in Pakistan* (New York: Columbia University Press, 1960), 45, 186–199.

118. *Oriental Records*, vol. 2: D. no. 359: 15–16, vol. 1: D. no. 44: 19–21 and vol. 2: 88–89 for other reference; 'Shamsabad and Bilhaur', 47; 'Bilgram Documents', nos. 1, 42, 49.

119. *Oriental Records*, vol. 1: D. no. 47: 3 and vol. 2: 17–18.

120. 'Shamsabad and Bilhaur', D. no. 48: 63.

121. Robert Orme, *Historical Fragments of the Mogul Empire of the Morattoes, and of the English Concerns in Indostan, from the Year 1659*, ed. J.P. Guha, rpt. (New Delhi: Associated Publishing House, 1974), 281. See also Pushpa Suri, *Social Conditions in Eighteenth Century Northern India* (Delhi: University of Delhi, 1977), 237.

122. *Oriental Records*, vol. 3: D. no. 1211: 65; also 'Bilgram Documents', nos. 31, 34.

123. 'Bilgram Documents', nos. 37, 77(about family of Bilgram), no. 44 (for bequeathal on grandson); 'Shamsabad and Bilhaur', no. 39: 54 (for widow of Nawab Rashid Khan).

124. 'Bilgram Documents', note 42 (for Abdul Wahab); *Oriental Records*, vol. 3: D. no. 1241: 55 (for Bibi Achhi).

125. 'Aligarh Farmans', no. 52.

126. *Oriental Records*, vol. 2: D. no. 326: 11 (*tamlik-nama* of 1625 A.D.); also *Oriental Records*, vol. 3: D. no. 1191: 58 (*Dastak* about Mst. Lodhiyan).

127. *Oriental Records*, vol. 3: D. no. 1216: 35–36.

128. *Oriental Records*, vol. 2: D. no. 452: 79 (for Bibi Ujyali), vol. 2: D. nos 322, 344: 61, 62 (for Bibi Haibat), vol. 2: D. no. 429, 61–62 (for wife of Mian Omar), vol. 2: D. no. 464: 62 (for Bibi Shah Jahan); 'Aligarh *Farmans*', nos. 2, 22 and 49, 57 (for Bibi Rakhi, Sukhi and Saba); *Oriental Records*, vol. 2: D.no. 319, 60 (for Muhammad Mahmud and Bibi Baghi). For other cases of joint sales, see *Oriental Records*, D. nos. 290 (1710 A.D.), 467 (1712 A.D.), 458 (1746 A.D.), 470 (1747 A.D.), 460 (1753 A.D.), 349 (1765 A.D.): 65, 65–66, 77, 77–78, 69, 78, respectively.

129. *Oriental Records*, D. no. 319: 60 (1579 A.D.); 458: 77 (1746 A.D.).

130. Lakhnawi, *Shahnama*, 129. She must be Zinat-un-nisa Begam who died in May, 1721 A.D. All the other daughters of Aurangzeb died during his life time (J.N. Sarkar, *History of Aurangzib*, 1st Imp., vol. 1 (New Delhi: New Orient Longman Ltd., 1972–1974), 37–39).

131. Datta, ed., *Some Mughal Farmans*, Sr. no. 309: 73.

132. 'Shamsabad and Bilhaur', no. 70, 92 (late seventeenth century); 'Bilgram Documents', nos. 31, 34.

133. Khwaja Abdul Malik Isami, *Futuh-us-Salatin*, ed. A. Mahdi Husain (Agra: Educational Press, 1938), 129; Amir Khusrau, *Matla-ul-Anwar* (Lucknow, 1884), 255, Amir Khusrau, *Hasht Bahisht*, ed. Maulana Sayyid Suleiman Ashraf (Aligarh: Aligarh Muslim University, 1918), 28–29; Hamid Qalander, *Khair-ul-Majalis*, ed. K.A. Nizami (Aligarh: Aligarh Muslim University, n.d.), 93.

134. Irfan Habib, 'Non-agricultural Production and Urban Economy', in *The Cambridge Economic History of India*, Part I, eds T. Raychaudhuri and Irfan Habib. (London: Cambridge University Press, 1982). 279; Orme, *Historical Fragments*, 303 (for women's contribution in agricultural processes).

135. Orme, *Historical Fragments*, 263, 265. Also, Neera Desai and Krishnaraj Maithreyi, *Women and Society in India* (Delhi: Ajanta Publications, 1987), 53; K.K. Datta, *Alivardi and His Times* (Calcutta: Calcutta University, 1939), 249.

136. Harihar Das, *The Norris Embassy to Aurangzib (1699-1702)*, Condensed and rearranged by S.C. Sarkar, 1st ed. (Kolkata: K. L. Mukhopadhyay, 1959), 166–167. See also Ashraf, *Life and Conditions*, 248 (for rope tricks shown by juggler women).

137. Muhammad Kasim Hindu Shah Ferishta, *Tarikh-i-Ferishta alias Gulshan-i-Ibrahimi*, in *History of Rise of the Mahomedan Power in India*, trans. J. Briggs, rpt., vol. 4 (New Delhi: Atlantic Publishers & Distributors, 1989), 143; Ulugh Khani Abdullah Mohammad Bin Umar Al Makki Al Asafi, *Zafar-ul-Waleh be Muzaffar Wa Aaleh*, in *Uttar Taimur Kaleen Bharat*, Part II (Aligarh: History Department, Aligarh Muslim University, 1959), trans. Rizvi, 162–163 (gives the total no of Harem ladies as 12,000); Abdul Baqi Nahavandi, *Maasir-i-Rahimi*, ed. S.M. Hidayat Husain, vol. 1 (Calcutta: Asiatic Society of Bengal, 1924), 145; Wolseley Haig, *The Cambridge History of India*, vol. 3 (New Delhi: Concept Publishing Co., 1928), 362.

138. See Chapters 4 and 2.

139. M.S. Randhawa, *Indian Miniature Painting* (New Delhi: Roli Books International, 1981), Pl. 29.

140. Ferishta, *Tarikh-i-Ferishta*, vol. 2: 227–228, vol. 4: 143; Haig, *Cambridge History*, vol. 3: 362 (for Ghias-ud-din); Jamila BrijBhushan, *Sultan Raziya, Her Life and Times* (New Delhi: Manohar Publications, 1990), 29 (for Razia); Shahbu-d-din Abdul Abbas Ahmad Umari, *Masaliku-L-Absar-Fi-mamaliku-L-Amsar*, in *Tughlaq Kaleen*, Part I, trans. Rizvi, 316 (for Muhammad Tughlaq).

141. Abul Fazl, *Ain-i-Akbari*, vol. 1: 46. See also Abul Fazl, *Akbar Nama*, vol. 3: 105.

142. Manucci, *Storia Do Mogor*, vol. 2: 308, 315, 366.

143. Manucci, *Storia Do Mogor*, vol. 2: 351.

144. Abul Fazl, *Ain-i-Akbari*, vol. 1: 46; Manucci, *Storia Do Mogor*, vol. 2: 308, 310.

145. M.A. Ansari, *Social Life of the Mughal Emperors 1526–1707* (New Delhi: Shanti Prakashan, 1974), 71, note 57.

146. Jahangir, *Tuzuk*, vol. 2: 110–111.

147. Ibn Batuta, *Rehla*, 105.

148. Bayazid Biyat, *Tazkirah-i-Humayun-wa-Akbar*, ed. M.H. Husain (Calcutta: Bibliothica. Indica, 1941), 290. See also A.L. Srivastava, *The First Two Nawabs of Awadh*, 2nd ed. (Agra, 1954), 203 (for Wazir Safdar Jang infiltrating eight women spies in royal seraglio to keep a watch on queen mother Udham Bai).

149. Thomas Roe and John Fryer, *Travels in India in the Seventeenth Century* (London: Trubner & Co., 1873), 281; S.S. Gupta, ed., *Women in Indian Folklore* (Calcutta: Indian Publications, 1969), 267n.

150. Shah Nawaz Khan and Hayy, *Maasir*, vol. 1: 532.

151. J.B. Tavernier, *Travels in India by Jean Baptiste Tavernier*, trans. V. Ball, ed. William Crooke, vol. 1 (New Delhi: Oriental Books Reprint Corpn, 1977), 42.

152. P.N. Chopra, *Some Aspects of Society and Culture During the Mughal Age, 1526–1707* (Agra: Educational Publishers, 1976), 122.

153. Amir Khusrau, *Ijaz-i-Khusravi*, vol. 2 (Lucknow, 1875–1876), 152. See also Shibnarayan Kabiraj, 'Hindu and Muslim Women in Folk Customs, Rites and Traditions', in *Women in Indian Folklore*, ed. S.S. Gupta (Calcutta: Indian Publication, 1969), 271.

154. Qalander, *Khair-ul-Majalis*, 138.

155. Khusrau, *Matla-ul-Anwar*, 57–58.

156. Abdullah Mohammad Bin Umar Al Makki Al Asafi, *Zafar-ul-Waleh*, in *Uttar Taimur Kaleen Bharat*, Part II, trans. Rizvi, 163.

157. K.A.N. Sastri, *A History of South India*, 4th ed. (New Delhi: Oxford University Press, 1976), 246.

158. Badaoni, *Muntakhabu-t-Tawarikh*, vol. 2: 311.

159. William Foster, ed., *Letters Received by the East India Company from its Servants in the East*, vol. 2 (London, 1897), 213 (for her owning a Junk. Junk was a warship of Chinese make with bow and stern shaped alike); John Jourdain, *The Journal of John Jourdain (1608–17)*, ed. William Foster (London: Hak Society, 1905), 155–156, 186, 191, 209.

160. Finch, The Early Travels, 123, 129; Jourdain, *The Journal*, 155–156.

161. D. Pant, *Commercial Policy of the Mughals*, 1st ed., rpt. (New Delhi: Idarah-i-Adabiyat-i-Delli, 1978), 109.

162. R.K. Mukerjee, *The Economic History of India* (Allahabad: Kitab Mahal, 1967), 83.

163. Hasan Farhat, 'Two Official Documents of Jahangir's Reign, Relating to the English East India Company' (Proceedings of Indian History Congress, 46th session, Amritsar, 1985, 334).

164. Roe and Fryer, *Travels in India*, 144; Pant, *Commercial Policy*, 165 (for preference for English ships).

165. Pelsaert, *The Remonstrantie*, 4; De Laet, *The Empire of the Great Mogol*, trans., ann. J.S. Hoyland and S.N. Banerjee, rpt. (New Delhi: Idarah-i-Adabiyat-i-Delli, 1975), 41, note 54.

166. Pant, *Commercial Policy*, 211; see also Shireen Moosvi, 'Mughal Shipping at Surat in the First Half of 17th Century' (Proceedings of Indian History Congress, 51st Session, Calcutta, 1990, 309, 312–313 and 311 (for Gunjawar).

167. William Foster, ed., *The English Factories in India* (Oxford: The Clarendon Press, 1906–1927), (1642–1645), 148; (1646–1650), 219–220; (1651–1654), 11, 50, 112.

168. Zia-ud-din Barani, *Tarikh-i-Firoz Shahi* (Kolkata: Bibliothica Indica, 1862), 460–462; Muhammad Bihamad Khani, *Tarikh-i-Muhammadi*, in *Tughlaq Kaleen Bharat*, Part I, trans. S.A.A. Rizvi (Aligarh: Aligarh Muslim University, 1956), 353–254; Umari, *Masaliku*, in *Tughlaq Kaleen Bharat*, Part I, trans. Rizvi, 322. See also Ibn Batuta, *Rehla*, 80, 122.

169. Gulbadan, *Humayun Nama*, 95–96; also Khwaja Nizam-ud-din Ahmad, *Tabaqat-i-Akbari*, trans. B. De and Baini Prashad, vol. 2 (Kolkata: The Asiatic Society, 1973), 25. *Shahrukhi* was a coin of silver of one *misqual* weight (about 4.6 grams). It was commonly in use during the time of Babur and Humayun. Its minting in India was stopped in 964 A.H. (Richards, *The Imperial Monetary*, 14).

170. Gulbadan, *Humayun Nama*, 125; Nizam-ud-din Ahmad, *Tabaqat-i-Akbari*, trans. B. De and Baini Prasad, vol. 2: 365.

171. Nizam-ud-din Ahmad, *Tabaqat-i-Akbari*, trans. B. De and Baini Prashad, vol. 2: 559–560 (for Akbar's gifts to Hamida Banu, Gulbadan Begam and others on the occasion of *Nauroz* festival).

172. Jahangir, *Tuzuk*, vol. 1: 144;Anonymous, *Tarikh-i-Salim Shahi*, 40 (for 40 beads necklace). *Sachaq* were pre-marriage presents given to the would-be bride by the would-be bridegroom.

173. Jahangir, *Tuzuk*, vol. 1: 224–225.

174. Jahangir, *Tuzuk*, vol. 1: 270–271.
175. Jahangir, *Tuzuk*, vol. 1: 401.
176. Lahori, *Badshah Nama*, Part I, vol. 1: 96–97; R.P. Tripathi, *Rise and Fall of the Mughal Empire* (Allahabad: Central Book Depot, 1987), 420.
177. Lahori, *Badshah Nama*, Part I, vol. 1: 191–192; Muhammad Hashim Khafi Khan, *Muntakhab-al-Lubab*, Part I, ed. Maulvi Kabir-ud-din Ahmad (Calcutta: Bibliothica Indica, 1869), 400 (who, however, stated that ₹200,000 were given to Jahanara and ₹500,000 were distributed among other royal children).
178. Lahori, *Badshah Nama*, vol. 2: 305; also M. Quamruddin, *Life and Times of Prince Murad Baksh* (Calcutta: Author himself, Syed Amir Ali Avenue, 1974), 49.
179. Khafi Khan, *Muntakhab-al-Lubab*, Part I, 646.
180. Khafi Khan, *Muntakhab-al-Lubab*, Part II, 77; Must'ad Khan, *Maasir-i-Alamgiri*, 13–14; Sarkar, *Aurangzib*, vol. 2: 385; Kazim, *Alamgir Namah*, 368.
181. Must'ad Khan, *Maasir-i-Alamgiri*, 36, 47 and 49, 67, 306 (gifts at second coronation, on the occasion of marriage of Azam, on the eve of *Id* in 1617 A.D. to Getiara and Iffatara Begams on the occasion of their visit to the court, respectively).
182. Sarkar, *Aurangzib*, vol. 1: 41 (on the recovery of Jahanara from her burns). Also Nagar, *Futuhat-i-Alamgiri*, 179 (for gift to Sahia).
183. Irvine, *Later Mughals*, vol. 2: 125.
184. Hawkins, *Early Travels*, 94, note 3.
185. Hawkins, *Early Travels*, 67, note 1.
186. Thomas Roe, *The Embassy of Sir Thomas Roe to the Court of the Great Mughal*, ed. William Foster, vol. 2 (London: Hak Society, 1899), 324, 384–386, 427, 458.
187. William Foster, ed., *English Factories*, (1651–154), 11, 50, 112; (1646–1650), 219–220.
188. William Foster, ed., *English Factories*, (1646–1650), 304; also *Journal of Asiatic Society of Bengal*, 1911, 453–455 (for Persian letters of Jahanara to Raja Budh Parkash of Sirmur, showing receipt of gifts sent for seeking her favour).
189. Anirudha Ray, 'Last Memoir of Francois Bernier from Surat: March 10, 1668' (Proceedings of Indian History Congress, 42nd session, Magadh University, Bodhgaya, (1981), 241–257, esp. 246).
190. De Laet, *The Empire*, 101.
191. Jahangir, *Tuzuk*, vol. 2: 80.

4

The Harem and Purdah

The Harem

The term 'harem' denoted the segregated place of residence of ladies within a house and included its female inmates. Harem consisted of wives, concubines, mothers, sisters, daughters and other female relatives, female slaves, the eunuchs and the attendants.[1] According to a modern writer, the term 'harem' itself evoked an image of a highly fortified place 'for carrying out one man's sexual fantasies, with hundreds of women of all shapes and sizes, colours and ethnic groups at his beck and call'. This image was contrary to the actual meaning of this sacred word that denoted 'a place of worship, the sanctum sanctorum, where the committing of any sin is forbidden (*haram*)'. Thus, conceptually, it is a place of restraint, rather than of sexual excesses.[2] The pivot of the harem was the sultan, the emperor or the noble who maintained it. The seraglio existed for them and the whole life within the seraglio revolved around them. Thus, with the sultan or the emperor as centre of power, the maintenance of the royal household also became of prime importance.

In the pre-Mughal period, a large harem was a status symbol and the number depended on the fantasy of the harem holder. The size denoted the dignity and the status of the ruler. It was to maintain this 'singularity of status, pride, aloofness', wrote Barani, that these Sultans of Delhi, like the Sassanid Kings of Iran, had the desire to build lofty palaces and to maintain harems with large establishments of domestics and attendants.[3] Qazi Mughis-ud-din advised Sultan Ala-ud-din Khalji to increase the expenses of his harem tenfold with the set purpose that a big and splendid harem would generate awe and resultant respect for the King in the minds of the people.[4] Imitating kings, some of the wazirs also had huge harems. Khan Jahan Maqbul, the wazir of Firoz Shah Tughlaq, had 2,000 women in his harem including the beauties, not only from within the country but also from Rum (it was a medieval Turko-Persian Sunni Muslim State in Anatolia [Asia Minor]) and China.[5] The provincial kings like Feroz Shah Bahmani and Ghias-ud-din of Malwa also maintained large harems. Mushtaqi mentions about Ghias-ud-din having remarked once that he had thousands of women in his harem and yet he was dissatisfied for not having found a lady of his imagination and how, thereafter, one of the persons present then stealthily fetched a beautiful girl and presented her to the king for his harem. However, subsequently, on the complaint of the parents when the facts came to light, the sultan repented and ordered his servants not to seek and produce any woman to him thereafter.[6]

The harems of Babur and Humayun were small in size, not exceeding more than 200 members each.[7] With the coming of Akbar, the practice of large seraglio was re-established. His own harem contained more than 5,000 women.[8] Jahangir had 300 wives besides other inmates in his harem.[9] The harem of Shah Alam had 2,000 women.[10] Akbar's policy of seeking peace and strengthening relations by matrimonial alliances, which was also followed by his successors, was a major factor.[11] Each campaign, generally, brought in as its consequence a girl of the vanquished ruler in marriage tie with the emperor or the prince. The entourage of these ladies and also of Rajput princesses, who joined Mughal harems, added to the number of the harem inmates.

Accommodation

To accommodate such large establishment, many palaces were built from time to time. These palaces invariably had separate female apartments.[12] Dwelling was provided to all inmates of the harem. Separate, spacious and splendid houses were the privilege of a selected few. The serving class lived in humble dwellings of mud and bamboo with thatched roofs, the ladies of lower rank in verandas and dormitories, more important queens in magnificent rooms and only some special women in exclusive palaces. Some of the exclusive mahals of the time were Jodha Bai Palace at Fatehpur Sikri for Akbar's queens and Mariyam's palace at the same place, Khas-Mahal of Jahanara in Shah Jahan Fort, separate dwellings of Shahzada Khanam, Rochia

(Ruqqaiya) Sultan Begam and Gulziar (Gulzar) Begam in Agra and mahal of Shah Begam.[13]

When the Mughal emperors were on the move, a part of their seraglio also moved along with them. Mini palaces were built at different places for the moving harem. Akbar built many women's apartments at every 8 kos (ancient measurement of distance) from Agra to Ajmer, each of which accommodated 16 ladies with servants.[14] These royal journeys, consequently, led to scattering of the inmates of harem that lessened the pressure of habitation at one place. Houses of the nobles and the rich were divided into two distinct parts: *Diwan Khana* or the men's quarters and the *Zanan-Khana* or the ladies' apartments.[15] The women's apartments were in the centre and one had to pass through two or three big courts and a few gardens before reaching there.[16] Sufficient provision of water, air, gardens were made within these palaces.[17] These houses were scattered in every direction, generally away from the royal harem, to avoid court intrigues.

Internal Administration

To maintain and control such a multitude of women, a system of internal administration was required. This organisational arrangement was all the more important because of the sensitivity towards women.

The first concern of the administration was the security of the seraglio. During the sultanate, the security of the harem from outside was entrusted to the eunuchs called *Khwajah Sara*.[18] They were in such a demand that their supply was met by importing them from the neighbouring countries. Purchase of eunuchs in markets continued throughout the Muslim period. Some modern authorities hold that since Prophet had prohibited human castration, their demand was met by imports only.[19] However, the facts speak otherwise. The contemporary authorities show that for ensuring their supply, castration seemed to be a common practice, both during the sultanate and Mughal period. Barbosa and Abul Fazl mentioned about this being commonly practised in Bengal, particularly in Sylhet. Jahangir informed that in Sylhet, it became a custom with the people to castrate a few of their sons and give them to the Governor in lieu of their revenue demands. This practice was followed in other provinces also, so much so that the emperor passed orders to check it. The practice, however, continued even thereafter and Aurangzeb brought injunctions against it. But the practice continued even thereafter.[20]

These eunuchs worked as messengers and were a link between the harem and the outside world. They also served the sultan in his private chambers. Therefore, their selection was made with great care and only really capable and dependable eunuchs were assigned this task. As a second line of internal defence, in the inner pavilions and halls situated outside the female apartments, there was another guard called *Sara-purdah-daran-i-khas*, headed by some reliable noble who was entitled *Purdahdar-i-Khas*.[21] Barani informs about an officer called *Uhdahdar-i-darha* or the officer of the gates whose duty was to ensure the proper closure of the gates and ensure their supervision at night. He further recorded that when the sultans moved out for hunts, processions or otherwise, there was another pocket of infantry, comprised mainly of slaves, who defended the royal entourage.[22] There were other officials named *Mufrads* who performed the guard duty.[23] All this team guarded the Seraglio so zealously that it became almost impregnable. It is known that once rebel Ikat Khan, the nephew of Ala-ud-din Khalji, tried to enter the Sultan's harem, but Malik Dinar, who was incharge of the security, stood like a rock on his way and did not allow him to enter the harem, insisting that till he brought the head of the Sultan, he would not be permitted to do so.[24] Similarly, relying on the tight security of the harem, Prince Mubarak Khan, son of Ala-ud-din Khalji, fearing an attack from Malik Naib, took refuge in the female apartment and came out only after the murder of the latter.[25]

A *Hakima* or Governess was appointed to look after the internal management of the harem during the sultanate period. She herself belonged to a noble family. The wife of Nizam-ud-din held this post during the time of Kaiqubad.[26] The *Hakima* was assisted by many minor women officials, who not only performed the guard duty or maintained the records of the income and expenditure of the harem but were also engaged in performing varied other duties within the seraglio.[27]

Some of the sultans took keen interest in the management of their harems to make the living therein more harmonious and comfortable. In order to avoid any confusion or irregularity, Feroz Shah Bahmani (1397-1422 A.D.) framed rules that were to be strictly observed by the inmates of the harem. He allowed maximum three attendants to a lady who were always of the same nation and spoke the same language as that of the mistress. He divided his attention to them so equally that each lady fancied herself to be the most loved by the King. He liked his ladies to be away from the gaze of the strangers, and therefore harem rules were observed strictly.[28] For the convenience of his ladies, Sultan Ghias-ud-din of Malwa established a separate market within his harem in which all the necessary items of requirement were made available. In fact, organisation wise, his harem was a 'kingdom in miniature'.

Babur and Humayun could not do anything worthwhile. Khwandamir wrote that Humayun made the gradation of the ranks of his officials by distribution of arrows. There were total 12 orders or arrows, the 12th and 11th arrows belonged to the King and his relations, respectively. In this ranking, sixth arrow was awarded to the harems and to the well-behaved female attendants, fifth to young maid servants, fourth to treasurers and stewards, second to the menial servants and first to the palace guards, camel drivers and the like.[29] With the coming of Akbar, great improvement took place. According to Abul Fazl, the imperial harem and household were 'in the best order'.[30]

The nobles, rajput guards, *ahadis* and other troops were posted at the outermost cordon of the security of the seraglio.[31] This practice of appointing Rajput contingents originated with Akbar and continued till the beginning of 18th century. Rajputs were considered to be devoted towards their duties. During Aurangzeb's reign, when the Marathas attacked Jahan Banu Begam's camp, these Rajputs defended her devoutly and as a reward for this, the Begam gave her pearl necklace to their commander Anurudh Singh.[32] Next to the Rajput guards, on the outer fringe, were placed eunuchs. These eunuchs were organised in a hierarchical order. A number of them were under a senior eunuch called *Nazir* who was under a chief *Nazir* with the title Itimad Khan or Aitbar Khan.[33]

Within the harem, this hierarchy of eunuchs was of great importance. The chief *Nazir* was highly respected by the king. He was not only incharge of all the palace expenditure on linen, precious stones, jewellery, but also of everything that went into or came out of the palace.[34] *Nazir*s were the persons of great confidence. One Aitbar Khan accompanied Akbar's mother and other Begams from Kabul to Hindustan in 1558 A.D.[35] Another eunuch entitled Itimad Khan escorted the daughter of Miran Mubarak Shah, King of Khandesh

(1555–1566 A.D.), to the harem of Akbar.[36] Each queen, princess or other lady of the royalty had a *Nazir* incharge of her property, lands and income.[37] During the period of the later Mughals also, this office was conferred only on dependable eunuchs. They were made incharge of *Gulalpara* (incense and perfume department) and also the steward of the household.[38]

All the major officials, slaves and servants were obliged to submit a report of their activities to the *Nazir*. The eunuchs under them not only worked as messengers but also as guards at the palace gate. Everybody, including doctors and unknown ladies, were put to thorough investigations and search before he/she was allowed to go inside the harem. All items were also scrutinised thoroughly to check smuggling of intoxicants or other objectionable articles. As a part of vigilance, they also closed all the gates of the palace at sunset by bolting them from outside and torches were kept burning the whole night.[39] In spite of such tight security, there were incidents of surreptitious entrance of menfolk inside the harem. Jahanara and Roshanara were reported to have managed smuggling of men to their respective rooms. Manucci writes about Roshanara keeping nine youths in secret.[40]

Inside the harem, sober and active women were posted as armed guards known as *Urdu Begis*. The most reliable were placed near the royal apartments. Abyssinian, Tartar, Turki, Uzbeg, Kashmiri and *Pathani* women were generally posted on such duties. They were tough and good at use of lance, arrow and sword.[41] Their cadre was constantly replenished through imports. Aurangzeb, for instance, was reported to have purchased Uzbeg and Tartar women from the Balkh envoys who visited him in 1661–1662 A.D. and put them on such duties.[42] So strong were these ladies that Aurangzeb did not come to meet Shah Jahan during the war of succession lest he would get killed by these Tartar ladies.[43] Similarly, in 1719 A.D. when Farrukhsiyar took shelter in his harem for fear of his opponents, these Abyssinian and Turkish women were determined to fight in order to check their entrance to the harem.[44] Even when the royal seraglio was on the move or in camps, these women guards, along with the eunuchs, performed their duties zealously and anybody who tried to come too near the royal procession or tent had to face their wrath.[45]

For the general administration within the harem, there were all women officials who were divided into three sections—the high (*Mahin Banu*), the middle (*Paristaran-i-hudur*) and the low (*Paristar or Bandis*). The first two grades consisted of superior staff while the third one consisted of the menial servants and slaves. The highest female official, who was overall incharge of the harem, was *Mahaldar*. She was the chief supervisor of the harem. Hamid-ud-din Khan, the author of *Ahkam-i-Alamgiri*, narrated two incidents bringing forth the importance of these ladies in contemporary harem life. Hamida Banu, *Mahaldar* of the harem of prince Muhammad Muazzam, spied for Emperor Aurangzeb. She wrote her confidential notes in a memorandum book. The Emperor had ordered her that she or her deputy Sharf-un-nisa should be personally present whenever the prince wanted to see her pen case and memorandum book. The prince made it a practice to take them in his private chamber where his ladies also used to be present. As per etiquettes, the *Mahaldar* could not go inside. So, she reported the matter to the Emperor and sought his fresh instructions. Aurangzeb once again ordered her not to leave these things with the prince. In another incident, *Mahaldar* Nur-un-nisa had a tussle with prince Muhammad Azam, because the latter expelled her from his assembly. When reported, Emperor Aurangzeb supported the *Mahaldar* and believing the complaint of Bahroz Khan, the *Nazir* of the prince, that the prince had misbehaved with Nur-un-nisa, he asked the prince to beg pardon of her and fined him ₹50,000.[46]

Under *Mahaldar*, there were *Darogas* or matrons A group of menial staff formed a section and each *Daroga* or matron or superintendent was incharge of a section or a group of sections of the subordinates. Manucci referred to them as matrons while the incharge of sections of the dancers and singers was referred to as superintendents. He has also given list of the names of some important matrons and superintendents of Aurangzeb's time.[47] They were appointed by the Emperor himself on the basis of merit and trustworthiness of the lady. Since it was considered to be a prestigious post, many ladies of high families and nobles (like the mother of Nur Jahan, whom Jahangir mentioned as matron [*kad-banu*]) were also appointed for this post.[48] They read out the reports of *Waqia Nawis* and *Khufia Nawis* to the king. The officials outside also received through them the orders of the emperor issued from within the harem. They worked as spies for their masters. At times, some educated matrons also worked as tutors to the princesses. Sati-un-nisa was one of them who tutored Jahanara.[49] Other lady officials were *Tahwildar*, incharge of the accounts, and *Waqia Nawis* and *Khufia Nawis*, who kept all the details about the harem. There were female storekeepers, also called *Ashraf*, who took charge of supplies and accounts and put forth estimates of expenditure for the next year.[50]

The harems of the nobles were equally well guarded. They also kept eunuchs and Bengali slaves for the safety of their wives and to ensure that they were not exposed to any other male. If any eunuch failed in his duty, he was severely punished.[51]

Thus, the harems segregated the women from the outside world. Manucci was not far from the truth when he likened harem to virtual 'prison for the ladies'.[52]

Titles and Epithets

Many ladies were given high titles by the kings to show their reverence and to satisfy their ego. Shah Turkan was entitled as *Khudawandah-i-Jahan*.[53] The title of *Malika-i-Jahan* was bestowed on the wives of Jalal-ud-din Khalji,[54] Husain Shah Sharqi[55] and the mothers of Sultan Nasir-ud-din Mahmud Shah[56] and Muhammad Shah Bahmani I.[57] The mother of Muhammad bin Tughlaq was adorned with the title *Makhduma-i-Jahan*.[58] One of the wives of Ala-ud-din Shah Bahmani II (1435–1557 A.D.) was given the title of *Perichehra* (fairy face).[59]

Akbar's mother was given the title of *Mariyam Makani* (The Mary of both the Worlds or Dwelling with Mary).[60] Jahangir's mother enjoyed the title of *Mariyam-Zamani* (The Mary of the Universe).[61] Shah Jahan's mother was entitled *Bilqis-Makani* (The Lady of Pure Abode).[62] Jahangir's favourite wife Mehr-un-nisa received the title of *Nur Mahal* (The Light of Palace) in 1611 A.D. that was, later on, replaced by the title *Nur Jahan* (The Light of the World).[63] The title of *Shah Begam* was given to Man Bai, the Rajput wife of Jahangir and to Roshanara *Begam*, the sister of Aurangzeb.[64] The title of *Padshah Mahal* was given to Saliha Banu Begam, a wife of Jahangir.[65] Zinat-un-nisa, the second daughter of Aurangzeb, was entitled *Padshah Begam*.[66] Shah Jahan's wife Arjumand-Banu Begam enjoyed the title of *Malika-i-Jahan* and was popularly known as *Mumtaz Mahal* (exalted one of the palace), a title bestowed on her by Shah Jahan on his accession.[67] Jahanara Begam enjoyed the title of *Begam Sahib*. She was also given the titles of *Padshah Begam, Nawab Qudsia* and *Sahibat-uz-Zamani*, the last title was bestowed on her death.[68] Aurangzeb's wife Dilras Banu was entitled *Rabia-ud-daurani* and his another wife, Rahmat-un-nisa, was entitled *Nawab Bai*.[69] In the later period, Lal Kanwar was conferred with the title of *Imtiaz Mahal* (the chosen of the palace).[70] Muhammad Shah's mother was entitled *Hazrat Begam* (the exalted lady) or *Nawab Qudsia* or *Qudsia Begam* or *'the Fatima of the age'* or *'the Mariam of the time'*.[71] His chief wife Badshah Begam was having the title of *Malika-uz-Zamani* (queen of the world).[72] His another wife Udham Bai, the mother of his son and successor Ahmad Shah, was given the titles of *Bai-Jiu Sahiba, Nawab Qudsia, Sahiba-uz-Zamani, Sahibjiu Sahiba, Hazrat* and *Qibla-i-Alam*. She also received title of *Mumtaz Mahal* after the accession of her son.[73]

A subtle difference in status was implied in the use of different terms for the ladies. During the sultanate period, the epithets of *Khatun* and *Bibi* were generally found, such as Nusrat Khatun (famous singer of Jalal-ud-din Khalji's reign), Shams Khatun (chief queen of Bahlol Lodi), Bibi Ambha (Hindu wife of Sultan Bahlol Lodi), Bibi Mattu (wife of Islam Khan Lodi of Bahlol's time), Bibi Bai (wife of Islam Shah Suri). The Mughals used the epithets of *Begam, Khanam* and *Mahal* with the names of the royal ladies, sometimes even for new born princesses of royal blood. Begam was most frequently used. Manucci gives the list of names of these ladies during Aurangzeb's time.[74] *'Aghacha'* or *'Agha'* denoted a slightly inferior origin and status, irrespective of the fact that she was legally married to the Emperor and was his love. Babur's Afghan wife never had an epithet of 'Begam'; she has been mentioned by Babur and also by Gulbadan as Afghani Aghacha. Also, while talking of his brothers and sisters, Babur mentioned the mother of Yadgar Sultan Begam as Agha Sutan, she being a mistress.[75] At times, the nature of job and the consequent status were also depicted by such words. During Aurangzeb's time, the names of the matrons of the kingdom ended with *Banu* and those of dancers with *Bai*.[76] In the later Mughal period, since many of the ladies rose from their ranks even to become queens, we find these epithets used even with the names of queens and their relations. They also assumed the epithet of *Mahal*. Aurangzeb's secondary wives were Nawab Bai and Aurangabadi Mahal, and his concubine was known as Udaipuri Mahal. Similarly, Emperor Ahmad Shah's mother was known as Udham Bai, his favourite wife as Inayetpuri Bai and his daughter, Muhammadi Begam, as Dilafroz Banu.[77] Paradoxically, in those degrading times, the title of *Begam* and *Khanam* came to be attached with the names of the dancers. The lady accompanists of Nur Bai, the famous dancer of Muhammad Shah's time, were addressed as *Begam* or *Khanam*.[78]

Pomp and Magnificence

Cut off from the general society, the majority of the inmates of the harems passed their lives in extravagant festivities, meaningless intrigues, vocal jealousies and showy vanity that affected the status of women adversely. These ladies spent their time by enjoying the pleasure of possessing and spending money. They lived a life of luxury, pomp and magnificence. Everything related to them, -their persons, houses, food, dresses, mannerism and habits, -smacked of luxury and licentiousness.

Toilets and Adornments

With the aim of remaining attractive for their master, the king or the noble, the ladies of royalty and nobility spent a major portion of their time and money in toilets and personal adornments. Muslims adopted 16 constituents of Hindu women's toilet. Amir Khusrau, Malik Muhammad Jayasi and Abul Fazl referred to them. Manucci gave a vivid and true-to-life description of the beautification of these ladies.[79] Everything fine, gilded, silvered, jewelled, precious-stone studded and scented attracted their attention. Their clothes were embroidered with gold threads and laces and so were their shoes gilded and studded with jewels and covered with silver and golden flowers. Muhammad bin Tughlaq kept 4,000 manufacturers of golden tissues, weaving gold brocades that were worn by the ladies of the royalty and were also gifted by them to amirs or their wives.[80] According to Manucci, the shoes of the wife of Khalilullah Khan (*Subedar* of Lahore) were worth ₹3 million on account of the precious stones studded in them.[81] This extravagance was visible even in the headgear worn by some of the Mughal ladies with special permission of the king. It was a sheet of cloth studded with gold pieces or a turban with an aigrette having pearls and precious stones all around.[82] Such brocading and gilding were also found in the attires of those ladies who served the upper class and worked for their amusement. Barani described dresses of slave girls embroidered with gold thread. Similarly, Afif mentioned about gold- and silver-brocaded dresses of the dancing girls, costing even up to 40,000 *tankas*.[83]

The cloth of their attires was so finely woven that one could see through it. This is reflected in the paintings of Mughal harem also.[84] Their shawls were so thin that they could be passed through a small finger ring and so were their dresses too. Tavernier mentioned about a kind of muslin named *Sironj* that was totally transparent. It was manufactured exclusively for the use of Mughal seraglio in the summers. When Aurangzeb reprimanded his daughter for wearing scanty dresses, the princess replied that she was wearing seven garments made of muslin known as *Ab-i-ravan*.[85] In spite of their being so expensive and exquisite, these dainties would put them on only once after which they gave them away to their servants.[86]

The ladies were fond of a variety of costly ornaments. The list of ornaments given by Abul Fazl and the detailed discussion of Manucci and other European travellers show that these ladies were laden with ornaments from head to toe.[87] Manucci narrated that each princess owned six to eight sets of jewels alone, besides other sets. They vied with one another to possess a costlier item. Nur Jahan, for example, wore a necklace containing 40 beads, each bead costing ₹40,000. This necklace was presented to her by Shah Jahan. She had another string of pearl and rubies, each ruby costing ₹10,000 and each pearl was worth ₹1,000.[88]

Similar was their fascination for perfumes. Their hair had scented oil. They also used costly *itr* (scent) extracted from flowers and other sources for their bodies and dresses. Abul Fazl gives a detailed account about the scents of Akbar's time and informs that the consumption of these scents was so much that Akbar even opened a special department for it under the name *Khushbu Khana* with Shaikh Mansur as its incharge.[89] During the time of Jahangir, the experts worked hard to invent 'exciting perfumes and efficacious preserves'.[90] Esmat Banu Begam, mother of Nur Jahan, invented an essence from rose water named *Jahangiri Itr*. About Esmat Banu's scent, Jahangir wrote, 'There is no other scent of equal excellence to it. It restores hearts that have gone and brings back withered souls'.[91]

They used all sorts of make-ups for body decoration. Besides floral adornments, the frequent use of soap, *ghasul* (a liquid soap), *opatnah* (mixture of butter, flour, some colour and scented oil), pounded sandalwood, hair dyes, *kazal*, *missia* (a sort of black powder for blackening between the teeth), *anjan* (antimony) for darkening their eye lashes, *mehndi* for colouring their feet, hands and nails, betel leaf for reddening their lips besides making different hairstyles find repeated mention in the contemporary writings, literature and paintings. Jayasi, for instance, in his *Padmavat*, mentions about use of beauty aids. Similarly, there is a painting of later Mughal period showing the lady colouring her feet.[92]

Interior Decoration

The interior decoration of their apartments was another example
of their pomposity. These houses were decorated with exotic carpets, splendid paintings, valuable porcelain vases and flower pots,
grand mirrors, gold-, silver- and stone-studded pillars and ceilings.
An example of this splendour, still existing, is Shah Jahan's Delhi
Fort. The *Diwan-i-Khas* attached with the royal apartment and
used by the emperor mainly for recreation with royal ladies was
resplendent with gilded decorations and ceiling and pillars studded with gold, silver and precious stones. There was an inscription
in one of the walls, 'if there is a paradise on earth, it is this, it is
this, it is this'—a couplet that matched the lifestyle of these harem
inmates. The residential portion of this was equally magnificent
with its gilt domes, hanging balconies, inlaid colourful and gilded
carvings, marble-paved floors, ornamental fountains and beautiful
paintings. Even the very names of the buildings like *Hira Mahal,
Moti Mahal* and *Rang Mahal* and of canals like *Nahr-i-Bahisht*
(stream of Paradise) sounded affluent and 'breathed the very spirit of
romance'.[93] A recent excavation done by Aligarh Muslim University
under professor R.C. Gaur at Fatehpur Sikri near the *Samosa Mahal*
revealed harem buildings that were internally decorated with 'dado
paintings in black, flanked by red lines', another room with only
paintings and still another with mural paintings. The water chan-
nels had shallow pools at regular intervals; the ornamental gardens
were divided into six parts, with walkways made of rubble stones
and 'the whole have been knitted into one single harmonious whole
with an octagonal tank'.[94]

The interiors of the apartments of the ladies of nobility were
equally glittering. They might not be having as big establishments
as those of the kings, nevertheless, they did not lag behind in
extensive use of gold and silver and costly decorations of carpeting,
curtains, wall paintings, exquisite flower pots and vases, comfortable
mattresses and the like. Their bedsteads and other furniture, wrote
Pelsaert, were 'lavishly ornamented with gold or silver'.[95] Sultan
Firoz Tughlaq's order against the use of ornamented, silver- and
gold-plated ewers and goblets, cups and other articles of use in the
houses, shows that such articles were in common use during the
sultanate period as well.

Khushroz

The Mughals introduced a peculiar celebration named *Khushroz* (joyful days), wherein a fair cum bazaar was arranged within the precincts of the palace, exclusively for the amusement and enjoyment of harem ladies alone. It began with Humayun; Akbar modified and institutionalised it and Shah Jahan made it most elaborate. During these days, a special market known as *Meena Bazar* (fancy fair) was held. No male, except the emperors and princes, was permitted to enter this bazar; buying and selling took place in this fair. Abul Fazl writes, 'His Majesty gives to such days the name of *Khushroz*, or the joyful day, as they are a source of much enjoyment.'[96] It was organised at different intervals. Thus, according to Abul Fazl, the festivity was held once in a month; but as per Badaoni and Mundy, it was celebrated every year on New Year's day. Bernier mentions that initially the celebration was sometimes during some festivals, but with Shah Jahan, it took place on every festival. According to Manucci and Coryat, however, it was organised once in a year.[97] As for the days of celebrations, Manucci mentions eight days, Thevenot five days and Tod nine days at a stretch.[98] In this fair, beautiful ladies of all classes, high and low, rich and poor, put their stalls of different items. Their purchasers were the king, the princes, the begams, the princesses and other distinguished ladies of the seraglio. The way the emperor haggled with these beautiful ladies for each penny created a lot of fun and frolic. The gaiety enhanced further during the time of Shah Jahan, who specifically appointed dancing and singing girls known as *kanchanis* for this occasion. Their main duty was to entertain the king, the begams and other ladies by singing and dancing the whole night. Therefore, Bernier called it a 'whimsical kind of fair'.[99]

Abul Fazl tried, and understandably so, to attach a sublime motive to Akbar behind arrangement of this fair when he wrote,

> His majesty uses such days to select any articles which he wishes to buy or to fix the price of things and thus add to his knowledge. The secrets of the empire, the character of the people, the good and bad qualities of each office and workshop, will then appear.

But this seems to be defence of a court poet. Otherwise, many other contemporaries held the sensuality of these kings behind the genesis of this fair. Badaoni wrote, 'And the important affairs of those who were outside the haram, and marriage contracts and betrothals of sons and daughters were transacted in those assemblies' Tod was more vocal when he penned, 'The ingenuous Abul Fazl thus softens down the unhallowed purpose of this day ... there is not a shadow of doubt that many of the noblest were dishonoured on the Noroza.' Manucci was equally candid to write that it was Shah Jahan's constant 'search for women to serve his pleasure' that this function was organised and that for the ladies who sold goods in those stalls, 'the best piece of goods she could produce was her own body'. Considering the debauchery of the age and the narration of the contemporary, it is clear that for the kings, this bazaar served as the best opportunity to satisfy their carnal desires.[100] The ambitious ladies, therefore, made it a point that their young daughters accompanied them to the fair with the hope that they might be selected by the king to be fit for being in his harem. Tod narrated that when the eyes of Emperor Akbar fell on the wife of Rai Singh in one of such fairs, she returned to her house only after her chastity was despoiled. Wife of Prithviraj Singh, younger brother of Rai Singh, could save her chastity with great difficulty.[101]

Fairs and Festivals

The public celebrations of the most popular festival was that of *Nauroz* (the Persian New Year day) that brought pompous enjoyments for many days. This celebration was borrowed from Persia. It marked the start of spring and was held on 20th or 21st of March or first *Farwardin*, the first month of the Persian year. As against the *Khushroz*, *Nauroz* was mainly a court function, the ladies' participation in it was incidental. Father Monserrate, describing the *Nauroz* festival of March 1582, wrote, 'Women were allowed to visit the palace and see its magnificent appointments'. Similarly, Badaoni wrote:

> And in order to abolish the stall of the glory of our religion, he ordered the stalls of the *nouroz* to be thrown open from time to time for the amusements of the Begums and people of the *harem*, and the wives of high and low, and on such occasions distributed gold.[102]

Unlike Persians, who celebrated it for 12 days, the contemporary authorities give varied number of days of this celebration. Thus, according to Sijzi, author of *Fawa'id-u'l-Fu'ad*, the celebration was for four days; Gulbadan wrote about it being celebrated for 17 days; according to Hawkins and De Laet, it was for 18 days; *Ain-i-Akbari* and *Tuzuk-i-Jahangiri* mention this celebration for 19 days; according to Monserrate, Manrique and Thevenot, it was for 9 days and for Manucci, six to nine days. Nizami, taking support from Sijzi, opines that the celebration was for four days.[103]

The queens and the princesses witnessed this from separate enclosures. They celebrated it among themselves also inside the harem. For this, the ladies of the nobility of the court were required to attend the royal harem. They brought presents for the royal ladies and in return, received robes of honour. They remained within the seraglio till the celebrations lasted. They were entertained by dancing and singing girls. Ultimately, they departed with presents known as *khichri* (mixture of gold and silver coins and precious stones).[104] Even the religious festivals like *Shab-i-barat* and *Id* had less of serenity and more of pomp and grandeur in their celebrations by the royal harem. While state banquets, rejoicings and exchange of gifts marked the Id celebrations, the celebration of *Shab-i-barat* was conspicuous by the extensive fire work. *Tuzak-i-Jahangiri* narrates about a grand feast organised by Nur Jahan on one such occasion.[105] The Hindu festivals like *Dussehra*, *Diwali*, *Raksha Bandhan*, *Holi*, *Janamashtami* and *Shivratri* were also celebrated within the Mahal under the influence of Rajput inmates.[106]

Recreation

Enjoying more freedom as compared to that of their counterparts in the sultanate period, the Mughal ladies whiled away their time in outdoor recreations like sightseeing, picnics, boating, garden parties and even hunting. Numerous such accounts find place in the narration of the contemporaries. For example, Gulbadan mentions about Babur's excursion with harem ladies to Dholpur and also about their pleasure trips with Humayun. *Akbar Nama* describes about outings of Mughal ladies to gardens with Akbar; *Tuzuk-i-Jahangiri* accounts for their sojourn to Kabul with Jahangir and merriment at *Shaharara Bagh* and Jahangir going along with ladies in a boat to *Nur-afshan* garden. Bernier writes about Aurangzeb's journey to Kashmir and Lahore with Roshanara and other ladies. Humayun, in fact, is credited with the introduction of river picnics.[107] During his stopover in Gujarat, Jahangir was entertained for some days by one of his queens named Khair-un-nisa Begam in the garden of her father. There was a sumptuous feasting. The King was presented with jewels, pieces of richest fabric, horses of highest value, all valuing not less than ₹400,000. The King, in return, gave her a chaplet of pearl valuing ₹500,000.[108] Shah Jahan laid out many gardens—*Anguri Bagh* in Agra Fort, *Shalimar Bagh* at Lahore and another at Badli Sarai—for the enjoyment of the harem ladies.[109] They went along with the Emperor on his hunting trips also. Nur Jahan herself was a very good shot. She killed many tigers on different occasions. Her husband gave her costly gifts at her success in hunting.[110]

Another amusement of these ladies was to lighten large torches made of wax or oil at night. As per Manucci's estimation, the expenses on this amounted to more than ₹150,000.[111] People used to illuminate the bazars (*Ain-bandi*) to mark the days of festivity. The practice was made more extensive by Maham Begam, mother of Humayun. At her initiative, the King's palace, the houses of the nobles and also the residences of the soldiers were illuminated. After this, such illuminations became common in India.[112]

Mode of Travel

Purdah and inaccessibility were the yardstick of their respectability. Hence, these ladies, generally, travelled by veiled palanquins and covered wagons. There were other modes called *dolas* or *hindolas, palkis* and *dolis* that have been extensively mentioned by the contemporary European travellers. Palanquins were covered litters carried on shoulders by six or eight men. They were used for long distances. *Hindolas* and *dolas* were like palanquins and were used for short distances.[113] Ibn Batuta described the *dolas* of ladies as having the shape of a cot, knitted with silken threads, covered by bent stick and overhung with silken curtains.[114]

It is revealed from the writings of the contemporary European travellers that the Mughals introduced new modes, besides the old ones, for the travel of their ladies. They were *chaudol* (like *takht-i-ravan* or field throne for a woman to sit, carried on men's shoulders), *khajwah* (capacious litters suspended between two camels or elephants wherein two ladies could sit on each side), *Pitambar* (an elephant litter), *hauda* (used for elephant ride) *mikdembers* (a type of *hauda*), *amaris* (a covered *hauda* or litter) and special wheeled carriages that suited their showy behaviour. There was another carriage with wheels that was pulled by female attendants. It carried the princesses inside the houses of the nobles after they alighted from the palanquins at their gates. Nur Jahan, in her exquisite style, used an English coach that was presented to her by Sir Thomas Roe. After Jahangir, the use of coaches seemed to have become out of fashion. A number of camels, elephants and horses were maintained by the emperors for this purpose.[115] The striking feature with regard to all these modes of travel was their scintillating decoration with gold, jewels, precious stones and looking-glass carvings, gold or silk nets, velvet cushions, embroidered tapestries, beautiful fringes and tassels and so on and so forth. The animals were decked with bells, rich trappings and multicoloured mantles that brought out vividly the grand living style of these ladies.[116]

A royal lady moved in a grand group, surrounded by eunuchs, female guards, prominent nobles on elephant, horse or camel backs or on foot, making frantic efforts to guard her from any intruder, to clear the way by shouting, pushing and jostling people and also by getting water sprinkled in front to lay the dust. Describing Roshanara's journey to Kashmir along with Aurangzeb in 1664 A.D., Bernier wrote:

> Stretch imagination to its utmost limits, and you can conceive no exhibition more grand and imposing than when Rauchenara Begum, mounted on a stupendous *Pegu* elephant and seated in a *Mikdember*, blazing with gold and azure ... followed by five or six other elephants ... nearly as resplendent as her own, and filled with ladies attached to her household ... (then) chief eunuchs, richly adorned and finely mounted, a troop of female servants, Tartars and Kachmerys, fantastically attired and riding handsome pad horses ... several eunuchs on horseback, accompanied by a multitude of Pagys ... for ... clearing the road ... followed by... fifteen or sixteen females of quality ... with a grandeur of appearance, equipage and retinue more or less proportionate to their rank.... There is something very impressive of state and royalty in the march.[117]

Manucci's elaboration of Jahanara's going to court is equally high sounding: with 'much cavalry and infantry and many eunuchs'; with sprinkling of water on the roads; with her *palki* decked with rich cloth or net of gold, sometimes ornamented with precious stones; with eunuchs driving away flies with the help of peacock feathers having handle adorned with gold and silver and shouting for clearing the way and so on.[118] Such were the etiquettes of the time that if any nobleman happened to pass that way, he stood with hands crossed out of respect. In case the princess wanted to honour him, then she sent pan to him wrapped in gold brocade bag.[119] The wives of the nobles imitated the ladies of royalty.

Unsatiety and Reaction

In spite of all luxuries and resources at their command, the harem women were an unsatiated lot. According to Pelsaert, 'These wretched women wear indeed, the most expensive clothes, eat the daintiest food, and enjoy all worldly pleasures except one, and for that one they grieve, saying they would willingly give everything in exchange for a beggar's poverty'.[120]

Many references, reflecting such unsatiety, are found in the writings of contemporary chroniclers of the Mughal period. There are many examples that show that many of these ladies maintained only an outward docility while they were always on the lookout to satisfy their natural desire. Manucci was the physician of the royal harem. He has narrated about a Dil-jo, a female servant of Shah Alam's harem, suffering from a strange disease that got cured after she got married to a male slave on his recommendation. After that he found many other fellow maid servants pretending to be ill and imploring him to suggest the same remedy.[121] He mentioned about harem ladies getting the vicarious satisfaction by his mere touch. When he extended his hand behind the curtain to feel their pulse for diagnosis, they pressed and kissed it and even softly bit it. At times, they applied it to their breasts too.[122] Coryat, writing at the time of Jahangir, mentioned about the checks being imposed on entry of virile objects inside the harem for fear of their 'unnatural abuse'. Writing 50 years hence, Manucci corroborated the same being followed in the Mughal harem and so did Ovington who wrote, 'His (Aurangzeb) women are all closely guarded, not visible to any, whose virile parts were cut off smooth, to prevent the least temptation from the sex....'[123]

There are references of secret love affairs of these ladies when messages were sent through slave girls. Manucci mentions about his own love affair with the widowed daughter of Dindar Khan and also about secret love affair of daughter of Chief *qazi* who, unknowingly, even solemnised her marriage.[124] The contemporary travellers also mentioned about smuggling of men inside the harem as referred to earlier.[125] Although the authenticity of many of such scandals cannot be tested since they were based on hearsays, nonetheless, the very fact that they became the talk of the public does indicates the sexual unsatiety of these ladies. Ghasiti Begam, the daughter of Alivardi Khan (Nawab of Bengal), was notorious for her sensual pursuits. Her husband Newazish Mahmud Khan was given to feminine joy. Hence, Ghasiti Begam was always ready to listen to petition of any good-looking man. It was believed that she used to send invitations and messages, and a 'stout, handsome man was not always safe in the streets'.[126] They freaked out, at times, under some pretext. In one of the anecdote of the time of Aurangzeb narrated by Manucci, 12 nobles went to Dilkush garden in Delhi for flirting. One of them was caught red-handed because the woman he was teasing turned out to be his wife. Interestingly, the lady herself was an adulteress and had gone there with the same motive. Ovington has also reported a similar incident and has given justification for their behaviour. He writes:

> And all the women of fashion in India are close penned in by their jealous husbands, who forbid them the very sight of all strangers. However, the watch is neither so careful, nor their modesty so blameless, but that they sometimes will look abroad for variety, as well as their roving husbands do.[127]

References also appear of these ladies having unnatural relations with eunuchs or the prevalence of lesbianism. Mandelslo observed:

> They (women) have also a great kindness for the Eunuchs in whose custody they are, to engage them to afford their more liberty in their restraint, which they brook so ill, that in those parts a man would think polygamy should rather be permitted to women then (than) the men.[128]

Another narration gives two incidents of amorous affairs with eunuchs during Jahangir's reign.[129] The description of Javed Khan as gallant of Qudsia Begam, mother of Emperor Ahmad Shah, and Mughlani Begam's objectionable relations with eunuchs and others reflect unsatiety of these ladies.[130] There are paintings of Jahangir's time showing paintings of lesbianism.[131]

Jahanara was even scandalised of having incestuous connection with Shah Jahan.[132] In the later Mughal period, *Khanazads* and

Salatins provided good substitutes for these ladies to gratify their desires. *Khanazads* were men like foster brothers who were born and brought up within the harem. *Salatins* were the descendants of the former emperors, going back to the time of Shah Jahan, and were, thus, distant relations of the king. Since many of them were married to princesses, they were confined within the palace so as to check the possibility of their being used by ambitious nobles. Because of their familiarity, these *Khanazads* and *Salatins* were an easy excess for the harem ladies. Manucci mentioned about Jahanara–Dulera affair, the latter was a *Khanzad*.[133]

Maslow, the renowned human behavioural scientist of the 20th century, writes about 'Hierarchy of Needs'. His theory propounds that the social need, which entails the desire for social recognition, comes only after the fulfilment of first basic and then security needs. Sex, the basic need, remained unfulfilled for these ladies. Thus, deprived of the basic need, they neither craved for having a social recognition for themselves nor did they try to achieve one.

Drinks and other intoxicants provided a good diversion to the craving hearts of these harem ladies. The ladies of the sultanate period were also not free from these vices, but they became more pronounced during the Mughal period. Writing about the time of Jahangir, Pelsaert observed: 'In the cool of the evening, they (the noble ladies) drink a great deal of win, for the women learn the habit quickly from their husbands, and drinking has become very fashionable in the last few years'.[134]

The addiction became worse and the ladies called for these intoxicants stealthily. Manucci wrote that during the time of Aurangzeb, the eunuchs had tough time in checking intoxicants like wine, opium, bhang, nutmegs and drugs being smuggled inside the harem. He also informed about the excessive drinking of Udaipuri Mahal and Jahanara. Jahanara virtually had to be lifted to her bed after drinks. In order to replenish her quota, she not only distilled wine herself but also imported it from Persia, Kabul and Kashmir.[135] In the later Mughal period, Lal Kanwar's losing senses because of excessive drinking is well known.[136] There are numerous paintings of the time that also throw ample light on their drinking habit and other addictions.[137]

The enjoyment of material pleasures in the most magnificent and lustrous way became the only aim of the life of most of the harem ladies. Pelsaert summed up their life in the following manner: 'Their Mahal are adorned internally with lascivious sensuality, wanton and reckless festivity, superfluous pomp, inflated pride and ornamental daintiness'.[138]

Equally revealing is Manucci's description who observed:

> Thus the women, being shut up with this closeness and constantly watched, and having neither liberty nor occupation, think of nothing ... but malice and lewdness.... If they have any other thought, it is to regale themselves with quantities of delicious stews; to adorn themselves magnificently, either with clothes or jewelry, pearls etc., to perfume their bodies with odours and essences of every kind ... to enjoy the pleasure of the comedy and the dance, to listen to tales and stories of love, to recline upon beds of flowers, to walk about in gardens, to listen to the murmur of the running waters, to hear singing, and other similar pastimes.[139]

In short, with all this glamour, lethargy and relaxation, they pined to bring the heaven down to the earth. But destined to be only *hurris* for the enjoyment of the kings, princes and the nobles, they themselves remained a starved lot and at times, they even stooped too low for the satisfaction of their basic desire. Amidst such a lifestyle of self-conceit and petty pursuits, barring a few exceptions, they remained the objects of sensual pleasure of the harem owners.

Neglected Life

In the whole set-up of harem system, the society did not seem to have ever felt that women too could have an emotional world of their own, an urge to be free and a yearning to be exclusive claimant of their master's love. Their sentimentality seemed to have been buried so deep under the layers of social apathy and negation that women of the harem themselves appeared to have accepted the subordination they were subjected to, as their fait accompli.

A life of luxury and pomp without any worthwhile capability cannot provide, to anybody, a permanent social status. The life of the harem ladies provided a testimony to this. It is also well known how the harem of the last sultanate King, Ibrahim Lodi, became a part of war booty distribution spree undertaken by Babur. These ladies were still lucky since they found Mughals as the successor to their masters, and hence got a secure place to live in, although most of them became dancing or slave girls. But the ladies of the later Mughal period had neither any capability to fend for themselves nor any powerful king to look forward to for a safe habitat. They could not maintain their superficial awe in the society because of the declining power and the diminishing resources of their masters.[140] The plunder by the invaders like Nadir Shah and Ahmad Shah Abdali and reckless squander of royal treasury by the then king and his harem inmates brought the resources to almost a total depletion.[141] It was clear that it would not be possible to keep a large number of women and eunuchs confined, hungry and naked, within the harem enclosures for long. At the fall of Abdullah, one of the Sayyid brothers in 1720 A.D., as soon as the news of the his captivity reached Delhi, his large harem was in dismay and barring a few, a majority of the ladies made best of the opportunity. They seized whatever they could and disguising themselves under the cover of veils and sheets ran away before the royal guards arrived.[142] Such incidents of the ladies coming out of the harem continued even after that. In 1757 A.D., during the reign of Alamgir II (1754–1759 A.D.), when the kitchen did not run for three days, the princesses, unable to bear the starvation, rushed out of the palace to the city in total disregard of purdah. Luckily, the fort gates were closed, and hence they remained in men's quarters for a day and a night. It was with great persuasion that they could be prevailed upon to return to their quarters.[143] Since these ladies had not learnt any skill or developed any vocation to fall back upon in rainy days, they could not earn a decent living for themselves. They did not stand a chance of a decent marriage either. The only way left for them was to change the course of history and instead of dancing girls and prostitutes visiting the royal palaces, it was now the turn of the royal ladies who, out of their sheer helplessness, joined the profession of dance and prostitution. The eunuchs took to dancing and singing as *bhands* (families engaged in folk entertainment as their hereditary profession) at the same time. Thus, the vast harems of the royalty and nobility got lost in the crowd. This explains the preponderance of *bhands*, pimps, procurers and prostitutes in Delhi and other cities of northern India after the decline of Mughal power.[144]

Purdah in Practice

Development

In the medieval Indian society, purdah was common with the Muslim ladies. Strict purdah originated with Amir Timur, when he conquered

India and entered in this country with his army and womenfolk. He made the proclamation, 'As they were now in the land of idolatry and amongst a strange people, the women of their families should be strictly concealed from the view of stranger'.[145] Purdah, thus, became common among the Muslim ladies, although it was not as rigid with the Hindu women. A girl started observing seclusion near her puberty and generally, continued to adhere to it till her death. Although the tenets of the Quran allowed her to dispense with it after she passed the childbearing age, but by that time, she got so much used to it that she felt more comfortable living in seclusion than out of it.

The Muslim men were very zealous in guarding their women from public gaze and considered it a dishonour if they were exposed unveiled. Monserrate, mentioning about harem ladies of Akbar's time, wrote that they 'are kept rigorously secluded from the sight of men'.[146] Similarly, Manucci, writing during the time of Shah Jahan and Aurangzeb, recorded, '[T]he Mahomedans are very touchy in the matter of allowing their women to be seen, or even touched by hand....'[147] At other place, he writes that amongst them, 'it was a great dishonour for a family when a wife is compelled to uncover herself'. He also refers to an incident concerning this wherein a soldier was travelling in a cart along with his wife and daughter, when the tax collectors tried to check his cart by force. The soldier became so furious that he chopped off the head of that tax collector and also wounded many of his attendants. Thereafter, feeling dishonoured, as his wife and daughter had been seen by the tax collectors, he killed both the ladies too.[148] Similarly, Amir Khan, a noble, felt dishonoured when his wife could not observe purdah in an effort to save her life by jumping from the back of an elephant she was riding, who had run amuck, and decided to divorce her. It was at the intervention of Shah Jahan, who rebuked him and forbade him from doing so.[149] They were so much protective of their women that they would not allow their wives to talk even to their relatives except in their presence. Consequently, all Muslim ladies, except those belonging to peasant or inferior servants, followed purdah strictly.

Two factors were mainly responsible for this. Firstly, since the royalty and nobility religiously practised it to maintain their exclusiveness, it came to be regarded as a symbol of respectability. It percolated down but only to the extent the lower classes were able to afford it. Secondly, the threat of invaders and also the sensual laxity and outrages perpetrated by the Muslim royalty and nobility of the sultanate and the Mughal periods had instilled a sense of insecurity among the Muslim subjects and also among the Hindus. Consequently, they relegated their women meekly behind the purdah so as to save them from the lustful eyes of these masters.[150] The more was the slackening of the morals, the stricter became the rules of women seclusion. A majority of the Muslim population of India were Hindu converts. These neo-Muslims were more zealous in following the tenets of the 'Faith' embraced than those to whom it came as a matter of course. Such persons enforced the purdah norms most assiduously upon their womenfolk.

There was a direct nexus between the rules of Muslim marriage and purdah. The Quran has prescribed the list of prohibited relations with whom one cannot enter into a matrimonial alliance. Such persons are called *mahrams* (forbidden). Purdah from such persons was only a matter of routine and not strictly enforced. All others, that is, those with whom matrimonial alliance can be established are called *na-mahrams*. Purdah was strictly propounded from such persons. The contemporary society tried to compensate itself for the weakening moral values of the menfolk by overemphasising the chastity and morality of a girl. Purdah was taken as the safest instrument to avoid contact with the *na-mahrams*. Under the conditions, the menfolk not only refrained from giving social freedom to their women but also abstained from marrying the ladies who enjoyed such liberties.[151]

Observance of Purdah

From the beginning, the royal and aristocratic classes, with the exception of the Turkish women and a few others, were more rigid in adhering to the rules of purdah. Not only the walls of the harem became higher and stronger with the passage of time, the restrictions imposed also increased successively. So strict was their seclusion that even when they fell ill, the attending doctors were not allowed to touch and feel their pulse. Therefore, for their examination, a handkerchief was first wrapped all over the body of the patient, this cloth was then dipped into a jar of water and it was through its smell that they were required to diagnose the disease and prescribe the medicine.[152] Later on, some selected physicians like Bernier and Manucci were allowed to feel the pulse of the harem ladies. But such special privilege was given to them only after an established familiarity and a long testing. They were also subjected to surprise checks. Manucci narrated that once when he stretched his hand inside the curtain to feel the pulse of a lady-patient, it turned out to be the hand of Shah Alam himself.[153] Nonetheless, these physicians were not permitted to see the ladies. Whenever their services were required inside the harem, their heads were covered by the thick shawl hanging down to their waist or feet and were led in and brought out like blind men by the eunuchs.[154] The ladies also were such touch-me-nots that if they were to show some ailing part of their body to the doctor, they would see to it that he could see only that part. Even the old mother of Shah Alam, who needed to be operated upon for gout twice a year, would put her arm out from the curtain, only uncovering two fingers wide of the affected part and the rest of it would be carefully covered with cloth.[155]

The whole outer world was inaccessible for these ladies. If ever they moved out, it was in covered *palkis* and *dolas* surrounded on all sides by alert guards. So much so that if they were to travel on elephants, they would ride them inside a tent pitched near the palace gate. Even the mahouts of the elephants covered their heads so that they could not see the royal ladies while they rode the animals. On the elephant-backs, they sat inside covered *haudas*.[156] Their slave girls were also made to move in covered conveyances. The slave girls of Tatar Khan, a noble of Sultan Firoz Shah Tughlaq, were reportedly carried in locked conveyances lest the eyes of *na-mahrams* would fall on them.[157]

Purdah, in-fact, had come to be regarded as a symbol of honour. The worst punishment they could think of for their enemies was to parade their womenfolk unveiled and best honour they could extend to a person was by asking their harem ladies to unveil themselves before him. Describing about a custom prevalent in Malabar coast, Ovington wrote that the husbands, 'even the prime nobility' offered their wives to the guests as a mark of welcome to them and refusing the offer was considered as an 'affront'. That is why the women there gained the name of 'Malabar Quills'.[158]

The stress on observance of purdah differed during different periods. Muhammad bin Tughlaq, for example, was so scrupulous in this regard that when he entered his harem, he was careful that his eyes did not fall on a *na-mahram*.[159]

It is, however, interesting to note that contrary to Indian conditions, there was no complete seclusion of Turkish ladies from the outside world. Annette Beveridge wrote, 'It appears probable that there was no complete seclusion of Turki women from the outside world as came to be the rule in Hindustan. The ladies may have veiled themselves but they received visitors more freely....' She noted how the senior nobles and officers of Babur regaled harem ladies in Kabul with interesting stories about India.[160] According to Gulbadan, the ladies of royal harem of Humayun mixed freely with their friends and visitors, went out dressed like males at time, enjoyed picnics and music with their mates, played polo and so on. She has described numerous such occasions.[161] Manrique recorded that he dined with the Wazir Asaf Khan and met the Emperor and many members of the imperial family and in the feast, many unveiled ladies of rank took their seats at the table.[162] In *Meena Bazar*, all ladies appeared without purdah following the principle, as narrated by the author of *Qanun-i-Islam*, that 'women need not be veiled before the king or a bridegroom, both known as Shah'.[163]

There are, at least, two clear examples, those of Razia[164] and Nur Jahan[165], when a lady came out of the covering of the burqa and discharged the administrative responsibilities like their male counterparts. Nur Jahan even came to the balcony for *Jharokha-Darshan* (a daily practice of public audience by the king at the balcony). Rajput queens in the Mughal harems did not observe purdah on many occasions.[166] Similarly, the Kashmiri women guards of the palace were, generally, found without purdah.[167] The lively paintings of Maham Anaga in *Akbar-Nama*, with her impressive facial contours and white and yellow robes, clearly indicates that it could not be the work of imagination but of someone who had observed her closely.[168] In the later Mughal period, Mughlani Begam looked after administration of Panjab without observing any purdah.[169] On the contrary, there are examples like that of Chand Bibi who, in spite of her active political career, supported a veil.[170] Similarly, Zeb-un-nisa helped Aurangzeb in administration and court discussions and yet appeared in purdah.[171] Taj Mahal, the chief queen of Emperor Muhammad Shah, was so strict in her observance of purdah that she would not take a male child in her lap and would cover her face even before a boy of 4. Even when she was on her death bed, she permitted no doctor to feel her pulse.[172] As a general rule, since the harem was inhabited by women only, no purdah was needed within the harem except when persons like physicians, goldsmiths, jewellers, artisans and masons visited the seraglio on asking. But, in the latter half of 17th century and after, when *Khanazads, Salatins* and other *na-mahram* relatives also started staying within the palace, the contact among them was discouraged by the observance of purdah within the harem also. Ovington, writing during Aurangzeb's time, mentioned that the emperor's women were closely guarded and were not visible to anybody except the emperor and the eunuchs.[173] In the later Mughal period, because of moral laxity, political disorder and financial constraints, the purdah norms for the ladies of royalty and nobility also got slackened. When prince Jahan Shah made a surprise attack on his brother, Emperor Jahandar Shah, the Emperor could escape, hidden under a sheet and being carried as if he were a woman; his lady Lal Kanwar fled with the crowd without any veil.[174]

Among the Muslims, in general, purdah was a common practice. The contemporary writers like Isami and Amir Khusrau vehemently advocated total seclusion of women so that they were free from all types of suspicions and allegations regarding their chastity. Khusrau, in his metaphoric expression, compared a free woman with a bitch in his *Hasht Bahisht*. Similarly, stressing the importance of *dupatta* (an upper covering like a scarf) in his another poem *Matla-ul-Anwar*, he likened it to the crown of a sultan. He considered an unveiled face just like an uncovered food open for cats and dogs to smear.[175]

Firoz Tughlaq enforced purdah on his subjects for the first time and forbade the Muslim women from visiting the tombs of the saints, considering this practice as un-Islamic.[176] Sultan Sikander Lodi continued these restrictions.[177] Akbar made the rule still harder. According to Badaoni, he ordained:

> And if a young woman were found running about the lanes and bazars of the town, and while so doing either did not veil herself, or allowed herself to become unveiled, ... she was to go to the quarter of the prostitutes, and take up the profession.[178]

It was directed that a woman should live within the four walls of her house, keep herself covered with *chadar* (a sheet—it referred to the traditional garment of Muslim women, consisting of a long, usually black or drab coloured cloth or veil, that enveloped the body from head to foot and covered entire or some part of the face). They were to use covered *amari* while on journey and travel only under the supervision of a man.[179]

Numerous references of observance of purdah are found in the writings of the contemporary foreign travellers. Barbosa wrote that the Mohammadans of his time (he visited Bengal and Cambay) kept their women carefully guarded.[180] Thereafter, a number of them—Monserrate of the time of Akbar, Terry and Della Valle of the time of Jahangir, De Laet of the time of Shah Jahan, Manucci of the time of Shah Jahan and Aurangzeb, Ovington, Thevenot, Careri, Fryer and Marshall of the time of Aurangzeb and Hamilton of the period of Aurangzeb and beyond (1666–1732 A.D.)—confirmed this view.[181] Many of them described categorically that purdah had come to stay as a symbol of decency, status and modesty and only women of easy virtues or of the poor families were seen out moving without veils. Terry, for instance, wrote, 'The Mahometan women, except they bee dishonest or poor, come not abroad'. Similar reporting has been done by De Laet, Careri and Ovington.[182] The practice prevailed not only in the Delhi Empire but also within the territories of other Muslim states of India. For instance, there are references of purdah being observed in Kashmir except in lower classes and of the Muslim ladies of Bijapur going out with their faces covered (on the authority of Varthema (1505 A.D.).[183] To maintain the sanctity of purdah, elephants were not allowed to pass by the houses, where ladies lived.[184] In another anecdote of the time of the *Nizamat* (civil administration) of Nawab Jafar Khan, an English factory chief wanted to construct two- and three-storeyed buildings near Hugli. Since high buildings endangered the privacy of the women of nearby houses, there was great opposition to this from the Muslim population. As a result, the Nawab had to issue orders to stop the construction.[185]

The women of the lower strata were comparatively freer from the restrictions of this seclusion. The women of agricultural and working classes lent a helping hand to their husbands in outdoor activities as well. Such women could not afford and so did not support elaborate burqa. For them, covering of their head and a part of their face with their *dupatta* or other head dress, when they passed a stranger, was sufficient. There are abundant references to the common sight of women water carriers walking along the street without purdah. Ovington's description of their ornaments and adornment suggest that they must be moving without purdah.[186]

Impact

Purdah as an institution and in the form it was adopted by the Muslim society did a great harm to the Mohammadan women and their standing in the society.[187] The conservatives might support its observance as a part of the social need of the time. But the very fact that it curtailed woman's freedom of growth and advancement and made her subservient to the will of man was a great blow to her independent status in the society. It segregated the whole gamut of social life into two exclusive spheres: outdoor and indoor. The male-dominant society closed the gates of outer world of action and challenges for the woman and confined her within the four walls of the house. The closed and dingy atmosphere within was not conducive for her physical and mental growth. Not only her health suffered but her mental development also became circumscribed. She had to satisfy herself with the roles of a serving mother, docile wife and tolerant daughter-in-law. Her very birth was unwanted and she was subjected to neglect in the society. She was denied the enlightenment of education and the upliftment of her personality. Thus, groping in the darkness of *zanana* with equally ignorant inmates and having been denied the company of men or the exposure to a wider horizon, superstitions, taboos and prejudices became a part of her life. In the long run, her development was obstructed and she became totally dependent on man for meeting even her basic needs.

The rigours of purdah were a little less stringent for the ladies of the higher strata. They had the facility of private coaching and exclusive entertainment. They were, however, deprived of the knowledge of the outside world and the experience of a mixed society.[188]

With the observance of purdah, Muslim women were destined to a virtual life of prisoners, suffering from feeble health, dulled senses, ignorance and prejudices.

Notes

1. Shahbu-d-din Abdul Abbas Ahmad Umari, *Masaliku-L-Absar-Fi-mamaliku-L-Amsar*, in *Tughlaq Kaleen Bharat*, Part I, trans. Rizvi, 314; K.M. Ashraf, *Life and Conditions of the People of Hindustan*, 2nd ed. (New Delhi: Munshiram Manoharlal, 1970), 55, 171; M.T. Houtsma et al., *Encyclopaedia of Islam*, vol. 2 (London: Leyden, 1938), 268.
2. Harbans Mukhia, *The Mughals of India* (Oxford: Blackwell Publishing Ltd., 2004), 113.
3. Zia-ud-din Barani, *Fatawa-i-Jahandari*, trans. Afsar Begam, in *The Political theory of the Delhi Sultanate* by Mohammad Habib and Afsar Begam (Allahabad, n.d.), 40.
4. Zia-ud-din Barani, *Tarikh-i-Firoz Shahi* (Kolkata: Bibliothica Indica, 1862), 294.

5. Shams Siraj Afif, *Tarikh-i-Firoz Shahi*, ed. Maulvi Vilayat Husain (Kolkata: Bibliothica Indica, 1891), 400.

6. Muhammad Kasim Hindu Shah Ferishta, *Tarikh-i-Ferishta*, trans. J. Briggs (New Delhi: Atlantic Publishers & Distributors, 1989), vol. 2: 227–228; vol. 4: 143; Rizkullah Mushtaqi, *Waqiat-i-Mushtaqi*, in *Uttar Taimur Kaleen Bharat*, Part II, trans. Rizvi (Aligarh: Aligarh Muslim University, 1958–1959), 134–136, 138. Khwaja Nizam-ud-din Ahmad, in *Tabaqat-i-Akbari*, Part II, trans. B. De and Baini Prashad, vol. 3 (Kolkata: Bibliothica Indica, 1939–1940), 549–550 has also narrated the same anecdote. Also see Abdullah Mohammad Bin Umar Al Makki Al Asafi Ulugh Khani, *Zafar-ul-Waleh*, in *Uttar Taimur Kaleen Bharat*, Part II, trans. Rizvi, 162.

7. K.S. Lal, *The Mughal Harem* (New Delhi: Aditya Prakashan, 1988), 19–20.

8. Abul Fazl, *Ain-i-Akbari*, vol. 1 (New Delhi: Crown Publications, 1988), 46; also V.A. Smith, *Akbar: The Great Mogul (1542–1605)*, 3rd Indian Print (New Delhi, 1966), 260–261. See also Ralph Fitch, in *Early Travels in India*, ed. William Foster (New Delhi: S. Chand & Co., 1968), 17 (for Akbar's 800 concubines).

9. William Hawkins, in *Early Travels in India*, ed. William Foster (New Delhi: Chand & Co., 1968), 101; also John Jourdain, *The Journal of John Jourdain (1608–17)*, ed. William Foster (London: Hak Society, 1905), 165; Edward Terry, in *Early Travels in India*, ed. William Foster (New Delhi: S. Chand & Co., 1968), 406; Beni Prasad, *History of Jahangir*, 3rd ed. (Allahabad: The Indian Press Ltd, 1940), 26.

10. Niccolao Manucci, *Storia Do Mogor or Mogul India*, trans. William Irvine, vol. 2 (New Delhi: Atlantic Publishers and Distributors, 1989), 320.

11. Abul Fazl, *Ain-i-Akbari*, vol. 1: 45; Abul Fazl, *Akbar Nama*, trans. H. Beveridge, vol. 2 (New Delhi: Ess Ess Publications, 1977), 351–352, 518–319.

12. Afif, *Tarikh-i-Firoz Shahi*, 100–101; Ashraf, *Life and Conditions*, 204.

13. Wolseley Haig, *The Cambridge History of India*, ed. Richard Burn, vol. 4 (London: Cambridge University Press, 1937), 542 (Jodha Bai palace and Mariyam's palace); Haig, *Cambridge History*, vol. 4: 561; Samsam ud-daulah Shah Nawaz Khan and Abdul Hayy, *Maasir-ul-Umara*, Part I (Patna: Janki Prakashan, 1979), 268; Francois Bernier, *Travels in the Mogul Empire, A.D. 1656–1668*, 2nd ed. (New Delhi: S. Chand & Co., 1968), 267–268 (for *Khas-Mahal* of Jahanara); Francisco Pelsaert, *The Remonstrantie or Jahangir's India*, trans. W.H. Moreland and P. Geyl, rpt. (New Delhi: Idarah-i-Adabiyat-i-Delli, 1972), 2–3; De Laet, *The Empire of the Great Mogol*, trans., ann. J.S. Hoyland and S.N. Banerjee, rpt. (New Delhi: Idarah-i-Adabiyat-i-Delli, 1975), 37–39 and note 50 (for Shahzada Khanam, Rochia Sultan and Gulziar Begams); William Finch, in *Early Travels in India*, ed. William Foster (New Delhi: Chand & Co., 1968), 164 (for Shah Begam).

14. De Laet, *The Empire*, 44; Finch, *Early Travels*, 149.

15. Pelsaert, *The Remonstrantie*, 67–68; Finch, *Early Travels*, 151.

16. J.B. Tavernier, *Travels in India by Jean Baptiste Tavernier*, trans. V. Ball, ed. William Crooke, vol. 1 (New Delhi: Oriental Books Reprint Corpn., 1977), 313.

17. Pelsaert, *The Remonstrantie*, 1, 64, 66; Finch, *Early Travels*, 164–166, 182, 185; Bernier, *Mogul Empire*, 247–248.

18. Barani, *Tarikh*, 375, 506. See also Jamia BrijBhushan, *Sultan Raziya, Her Life and Times* (New Delhi: Manohar Publications, 1990), 27 (for harem being guarded by eunuchs during Razia's time)

19. I.H. Qureshi, *The Administration of the Sultanate of Delhi*, 5th revised ed. (New Delhi: Oriental Books Reprint Corpn., 1971), 63–64.

20. Duarte Barbosa, *The Book of Duarte Barbosa*, trans., ed. and ann. Mansal Longworth Dames, vol. 2 (New Delhi: Asian Educational Services, 1989), 147, note 1; Abul Fazl, *Ain-i-Akbari*, trans. Jarrett, vol. 2: 136; Nur-ud-din Jahangir, *Tuzuk-i-Jahangiri*, vol. 1 (New Delhi: Munshiram Manoharlal, 1968), 150–151, 168; Ali Muhammad Khan, *Mirat-i-Ahmadi*, trans. M.F. Lokhandwala, 1st ed. (Baroda: Oriental Institute, 1965), 251; Manucci, *Storia Do Mogor*, vol. 2: 72; Bernier, *Mogul Empire*, 135; Must'ad Khan, *Maasir-i-Alamgiri*, trans., ann. J.N. Sarkar (Kolkata: Royal Asiatic Society of Bengal, 1947), 48; J.N. Sarkar, *History of Aurangzib*, 1st Imp., vol. 3 (New Delhi: New Orient Longman Ltd., 1972–1974), 61 (for Aurangzeb's injunction). See also Lal, *Harem*, 26.

21. Afif, *Tarikh-i-Firoz Shahi*, 279; Abul-Fadl Baihaqi, *Tarikh-i-Baihaqi*, ed. W.H. Morley (Kolkata: Bibliothica Indica, 1862), 817; also Ibn Batuta, *The Rehla of Ibn Batuta*, trans. Mahdi Husain (Baroda: Oriental Institute, 1953), 80 (he called them *Amir-i-Pardahdaria*).

22. Barani, *Tarikh*, 406, 273.

23. Amir Khusrau, *Qiran-us-Sadain*, ed. Maulvi Mohammad Ismail (Aligarh, 1918), 140.

24. K.S. Lal, *History of the Khaljis* (Allahabad: The Indian Press, 1950), 104–105.

25. Yahya Bin Ahmad Sirhindi, *Tarikh-i-Mubarak Shahi*, trans. K.K. Basu (Baroda: Abdullah Sirhindi Oriental Institute, 1932), 81.

26. Barani, *Tarikh*, 134.

27. Abdul Halim, *History of the Lodi Sultans of Delhi and Agra*, rpt. (Delhi: Idarah-i-Adabiyat-i-Delli, 1974), 229.

28. Ferishta, *Tarikh-i-Ferishta*, vol. 2: 228.

29. Khwandamir, *Humayun-Nama*, trans. Elliot and Dowson, in *History of India*, vol. V, 123; see also trans. Baini Prashad, as *Qanun-i-Humayuni of Khwandamir* (Calcutta: Royal Asiatic Society of Bengal, 1940), 31–32, nn. 1–3. (His translation with regard to sixth and fifth rankings is different from that of Elliot and Dowson. It runs: 'The sixth was assigned to the heads of clans and the good tempered Uzbegs and the fifth was given to young volunteers'. He considers the translation of fifth order as 'young maid servants' as an incorrect translation).

30. Abul Fazl, *Ain-i-Akbari*, vol. 1: 45.

31. Abul Fazl, *Ain-i-Akbari*, vol. 1: 47; Bernier, *Mogul Empire*, 258.

32. M.A. Ansari, *Social Life of the Mughal Emperors 1526–1707* (New Delhi: Shanti Prakashan, 1974), 71.

33. Abul Fazl, *Ain-i-Akbari*, vol. 1: 46–47; Peter Mundy, *The Travels of Peter Mundy in Europe and Asia*, ed. R.C. Temple, vol. II, second series no. XXXV (London: Hak Society, 1914), 201; Manucci, *Storia Do Mogor*, vol. 2: 326–327.

34. Manucci, *Storia Do Mogor*, vol. 2: 328.

35. Abul Fazl, *Ain-i-Akbari*, vol. 1: 442.

36. Abul Fazl, *Akbar Nama*, vol. 2: 351–352.

37. Manucci, *Storia Do Mogor*, vol. 2: 328.

38. Gholam Hussein Khan, *Siyar-ul-Mutakherin*, in *The History of Later Mughals Seir Mutakherin*, trans. Nota Manus, vol. 1 (Lahore: Oriental Publishers and Book Sellers, 1975), 146–147, also trans. J. Briggs, *The History of Mohamedan Power in India* (New Delhi: Idarah-i-Adabiyat-i-Delli, 1973), 131.

39. Manucci, *Storia Do Mogor*, vol. 2: 328.

40. Bernier, *Mogul Empire*, 12–14, 132; Tavernier, *Travels in India*, vol. 1: 300; Manucci, *Storia Do Mogor*, vol. 2: 31–32, also 177. But Manucci's information is discredited by J.N. Sarkar (*Aurangzib*, vol. 3: 39).

41. Abul Fazl, *Ain-i-Akbari*, vol. 1: 46–47; Manucci, *Storia Do Mogor*, vol. 2: 309, 328; Lal, *Harem*, 56.

42. Manucci, *Storia Do Mogor*, vol. 2: 38.

43. Bernier, *Mogul Empire*, 65.

44. Muhammad Hashim Khafi Khan, *Muntakhab-al-Lubab*, Part II, ed. Maulvi Kabir-ud-din Ahmad (Kolkata: Bibliothica Indica, 1869), 814–816.

45. Bernier, *Mogul Empire*, 372–374; Manucci, *Storia Do Mogor*, vol. 2: 437.

46. Hamid-ud-din Khan, *Ahkam-i-Alamgiri*, in *Anecdotes of Aurangzib*, trans. J.N. Sarkar (Kolkata: M.C. Sarkar, 1949), 58–59, 64–65, see also 63, 73. During Jahangir's time, Dilaram, who had nursed Nur Jahan during her childhood, was holding this post and before that Haji Kuka held this post (Anonymous, *Intikhab-i-Jahangir Shahi*, trans. Elliot and Dowson, in *History of India*, vol. VI, 447). Sati-un-Nisa held this post in Shah Jahan's time (J.N. Sarkar, *Studies in Aurangzib's Reign* (Kolkata: M.C. Sarkar & Sons, 1933), 24; Soma Mukherjee, *Royal Mughal Ladies and Their Contributions* (New Delhi: Gyan Publishing House), 37.

47. Abul Fazl, *Ain-i-Akbari*, vol. 1: 46; Manucci, *Storia Do Mogor*, vol. 2: 308, 311–312.

48. Jahangir, *Tuzuk*, vol. 2: 216; also Abul Fazl, *Ain-i-Akbari*, vol. 1: 45–46.

49. Manucci, *Storia Do Mogor*, vol. 2: 308–309, 311; Sarkar, *Studies*, 21–26.

50. Ashraf, *Life and Conditions*, 57; also Abul Fazl, *Ain-i-Akbari*, vol. 1: 46.

51. Pelsaert, *The Remonstrantie*, 65.

52. Manucci, *Storia Do Mogor*, vol. 2: 326.

53. Abu-Umar-i-Usman Minhaj-ud-din Siraj, *Tabaqat-i-Nasiri*, trans. H.G. Raverty, vol. 1 (New Delhi: Oriental Books Reprint Corp., 1970), 630, note 3.

54. Barani, *Tarikh*, 221.

55. Ferishta, *Tarikh-i-Ferishta*, vol. 4: 218.

56. Minhaj-ud-din Siraj, *Tabaqat-i-Nasiri*, trans. H.G. Raverty, vol. 1: 676.

57. Ferishta, *Tarikh-i-Ferishta*, vol. 2: 185.

58. Barani, *Tarikh*, 483; Ibn Batuta, *Rehla*, 118.

59. Ferishta, *Tarikh-i-Ferishta*, vol. 2: 262.

60. Abul Fazl, *Akbar Nama*, vol. 3: 1222–1223; A.S. Beveridge, Introduction to *Humayun Nama*, by Gulbadan Begam (New Delhi: Idarah-i-Adabiyat-i-Delli, 1972), 83, note 2.

61. Jahangir, *Tuzuk*, vol. 1: 76. Pelsaert (*The Remonstrantie*, 3) seems to have written it as '*Maryam Makani*' by mistake.

62. Muhammad Amin Qazwini, *Badshah Nama*, Aligarh Transcript, Part I (Aligarh: Aligarh Muslim University), f. 49a.

63. Jahangir, *Tuzuk*, vol. 1: 319; Mutamad Khan, *Iqbalnama-i-Jahangiri*, trans. Elliot and Dowson, vol. VI, 405; Muhammad Hadi, *Tatimma-i-Waqiat-i-Jahangiri*, trans. H.M. Elliot and John Dowson, *History of India as Told by Its Own Historians*, vol. VI (Allahabad: Kitab Mahal, 1964), 398.

64. Jahangir, *Tuzuk*, vol. 1: 56; Mirza Muhammad Kazim, *Alamgir Namah* (Kolkata: Bibliothica Indica, 1865–1873), 368; Tavernier, *Travels in India*, vol. 1: 299–300.

65. Jahangir, *Tuzuk*, vol. 2: 86n.; Shah Nawaz Khan and Hayy, *Maasir*, Part II, vol. 2: 926; Blochmann, Notes to *Ain-i-Akbari*, vol. 1: 401.

66. Hamid-ud-din, *Ahkam-i-Alamgiri*, 64; Shah Nawaz Khan and Hayy, *Maasir*, Part II, vol. 2: 646; William Irvine, *Later Mughals*, vol. 1 (Kolkata: M.C. Sarkar & Sons, 1922), 2.

67. Abdul Hamid Lahori, *Badshah Nama*, ed. K.A. Ahmad and Abdal Rahim, Part I, vol. 1 (Kolkata: Bibliothica Indica, 1867), 92, 96.

68. Manucci, *Storia Do Mogor*, vol. 2: 118, 175; Tavernier, *Travels in India*, vol. 1: 299; S.M. Latif, *Lahore, Its History, Architectural Remains and Antiquities* (Lahore, 1892), 58 (for *Padshah [Badshah] Begam*); Ishwar Dass Nagar, *Futuhat-i-Alamgiri*, trans., ed. Tasneem Ahmad (Delhi: Idarah-i-Adabiyat-i-Delli, 1978), 93, 137; Syed, A.J., *Aurangzeb in Muntakhab-al Lubab* (Mumbai, 1977), 26, 100 (for *Qudsia [Qudsi] Begam*). Must'ad Khan *Maasir-i-Alamgiri*, 131 (for *Sahibat-uz-Zamani*). See also Sarkar, *Aurangzib*, vol. 3: 37–38.

69. Sarkar, *Aurangzib*, vol. 1: 33–34; Nagar, *Futuhat-i-Alamgiri*, 93 (for *Nawab Bai*).

70. Nur-ud-din Faruqi, 'Jahandar Nama', Rotograph (Aligarh: Aligarh Muslim University), f. 37a; Irvine, *Later Mughals*, vol. 1: 193.

71. Mirza Muhammad Bakhsh Ashub, 'Tarikh-i-Shahadat-i-Farrukhsiyar-wa-Julus-i-Muhammad Shahi Badshah', Rotograph, vol. 1 (Aligarh: History Department, Aligarh Muslim University), f. 27b; Irvine, *Later Mughals*, vol. 2: 125 (for *Hazrat Begam*); Lakhnawi, *Shahnama Munawwar Kalam*, trans. Syed Hasan Askari (Patna: Janki Prakashan, 1980), 120; Irvine, *Later Mughals*, vol. 2: 264; Zahir-ud-din Malik, *The Reign of Muhammad Shah* (New York: Asia Publishing House, 1977), 56–58 (for Qudsia *Begam*). Hussein Khan, *Siyar*, trans. Manus, vol. 1: 146, note 130 (called her '*Navvab Cadeffiah*').

72. Ashub, Tarikh-i-Shahadat, vol. 1: f. 20b; Irvine, *Later Mughals*, vol. 2: 124.

73. J.N. Sarkar, *Fall of the Mughal Empire*, vol. 1 (Kolkata: M.C. Sarkar & Sons, 1966), 210; also Carr Stephen, *Archaeology and Monumental Remains of Delhi* (Allahabad: Kitab Mahal, 1967), 274 (for *Qudsia Begam*). See also Malik, *Muhammad Shah*, 407, note 1 (for title of Mumtaz Mahal).

74. Manucci, *Storia Do Mogor*, vol. 2: 310–311.

75. Zahir-ud-din Babur, *Babur Nama or Memoirs of Babur*, trans. A.S. Beveridge, vol 1., rpt. (New Delhi: Oriental Books Reprint Corpn., 1970), 723; Beveridge, Appendix A to Gulbadan's *Humayun Nama*, 294 & 261, 204, 205 (for Yadgar Sultan Begam, Afghani Aghacha and Agha Sultan Aghacha, resp.).

76. Manucci, *Storia Do Mogor*, vol. 2: 312–313. A list of their names has also been given by him.

77. Sarkar, *Fall*, vol. 1: 334; see also Sarkar, *Aurangzib*, vol. 1: 33–34 (for Aurangzeb's wives).

78. Dargah Quli Khan, *Muraqqa-i-Delhi*, trans. Chander Shekhar and S.M. Chenoy (New Delhi: Deputy Publication, 1989), 111.

79. Malik M. Jayasi, *Padmavat* (Chirgaon, Jhansi: Sahitya Sadan, Vikrami Sambat 2018), *Khand* 27, *Doha* 296–300: 346–351; Amir Khusrau, *Hasht Bahisht*, ed. Maulana Sayyid Suleiman Ashraf (Aligarh: Aligarh Muslim University, 1918), 31 (referred to *Hapth-wa-nuh*); Abul Fazl, *Ain-i-Akbari*, vol. 3: 342–343; Manucci, *Storia Do Mogor*, vol. 2: 316–318.

80. Umari, *Masaliku*, trans. Rizvi, 316, also see trans. Elliot and Dowson, in *History of India*, vol. 3 (Allahabad: Kitab Mahal, 1964), 578 (he gave the number as 500 instead of 4,000).

81. Manucci, *Storia Do Mogor*, vol. 1: 186–187. See also Bhushan, *Bhushan Granthavali*, ed. Rajnarayan Sharma (Allahabad: Hindi Bhavan, 1950), Kavitt 5–6 (for costly shoes of the royal ladies).

82. Manucci, *Storia Do Mogor*, vol. 2: 318; Abdul Aziz, *Arms and Jewellery of the Indian Mughals* (Lahore, 1947), 212–213.

83. Barani, *Tarikh*, 157; Afif, *Tarikh-i-Firoz Shahi*, 363. See also Thomas Roe and John Fryer, *Travels in India in the Seventeenth Century* (London: Trubner & Co., 1873), 384; Manucci, *Storia Do Mogor*, vol. 2: 318.

84. Lal, *Harem*, Pls. I, III, IV, V, 2, 8.

85. Tavernier, *Travels in India*, vol. 1: 47, note 1.

86. Manucci, *Storia Do Mogor*, vol. 2: 318; Bernier, *Mogul Empire*, 259.

87. Abul Fazl, *Ain-i-Akbari*, vol. 3: 343–345, 434; Manucci, *Storia Do Mogor*, vol. 2: 316–318. See also J. Ovington, *India in the Seventeenth Century*, ed. J.P. Guha, vol. 1 (New Delhi: Associated Publishing House, 1976), 320; Terry, *Early Travels*, 323; J.F.G. Careri, *Indian Travels of Thevenot and Careri*, ed. S.N. Sen (New Delhi: National Archives of India, 1949), 248; M. De Thevenot, *Indian Travels of Thevenot and Careri*, ed. S.N. Sen (New Delhi: National Archives of India, 1949), 53.

88. Manucci, *Storia Do Mogor*, vol. 2: 317; Anonymous, *Tarikh-i-Salim Shahi*, in *Memoirs of the Emperor Jahangir Written by Himself*, trans. David Price (New Delhi: Rare Books, 1904), 46; Jahangir, *Tuzuk*, vol. 2: 74 (for second necklace), resp.

89. Abul Fazl, *Ain-i-Akbari*, vol. 1: 78–81. See also Nizam-ud-din Ahmad, *Tabaqat-i-Akbari*, trans. B. De and Baini Prashad, vol. 2: 494; Manucci, *Storia Do Mogor*, vol. 2: 318.

90. Pelsaert, *The Remonstrantie*, 65.

91. Jahangir, *Tuzuk*, vol. 1: 270–271. See also Manucci, *Storia Do Mogor*, vol. 1: 158–159.

92. Abul Fazl, *Ain-i-Akbari*, vol. 3: 342–343, also vol. 1: 79–80; Manucci, *Storia Do Mogor*, vol. 2: 318; Jayasi, *Padmavat, Khand* 41, *Doha* 47: 603 (*missia* referred to as *masi*). See also Pratapditya Pal, *Court Paintings of India* (New Delhi: Navin Kumar for Kumar Gallery, 1983), Fig. M 67; Lal, *Harem*, Pl. 14.

93. Haig, *Cambridge History*, vol. 4: 556–558; Bernier, *Mogul Empire*, 256–258. The Persian text of the couplet is:

> *Agar Firdaus bar rue zamin Ast,*
> *Hamin ast hamin ast wa hamin ast.*

94. Lal, *Harem*, 40.

95. Pelsaert, *The Remonstrantie*, 67; also Bernier, *Mogul Empire*, 247–248.

96. Gulbadan Begam, *Humayun Nama*, 126; Abul Fazl, *Ain-i-Akbari*, vol. 1: 286–287; Khwandamir, trans. Baini Prashad, 138–139; Thomas Coryat, in *Early Travels in India*, ed. William Foster (New Delhi: S. Chand & Co., 1968), 278; Mundy, *The Travels*, vol. 2: 238; Manucci, *Storia Do Mogor*, vol. 1: 188; Bernier, *Mogul Empire*, 272–273; Thevenot, *Indian Travels*, 70–71.

97. Abul Fazl, *Ain-i-Akbari*, vol. 1: 286 (once in a month). Abdul Qadir Al Badaoni, *Muntakhabu-t-Tawarikh*, trans. S.A. Ranking, vol. 2 (New Delhi: Idarah-i-Adabiyat-i-Delli, 1973), 350; Mundy, *The Travels*, vol. 2: 238 (every year on New Year's day). Bernier, *Mogul Empire*, 272–273 (initially sometimes during festivals but with Shah Jahan, on every festival). Manucci, *Storia Do Mogor*, vol. 1: 188; Coryat, Early Travels, 278 (once in a year).

98. Manucci, *Storia Do Mogor*, vol. 1: 188 (for eight days); Thevenot, *Indian Travels*, 71 (for five days); J. Tod, *Annals and Antiquities of Rajasthan*, vol. 1 (London: Smith Elder & Co., 1829), 344 (for nine days).

99. Thevenot, *Indian Travels*, 71; Bernier, *Mogul Empire*, 273–274.

100. Abul Fazl, *Ain-i-Akbari*, vol. 1: 287; Badaoni, *Muntakhabu-t-Tawarikh*, vol. 2: 350; Tod, *Annals and Antiquities*, vol. 1: 344–345; Manucci, *Storia Do Mogor*, vol. 1: 188. See also; Bernier, *Mogul Empire*, 272–273; Bishan Bahadur, 'Akbar as Depicted by Prominent contemporary Hindu Poets' (Proceedings of India History Congress, 45th session, Annamalainagar, 1984, 461–463).

101. Tod, *Annals and Antiquities*, vol. 1: 345–346. These incidents were, however, discredited by A.L. Srivastava, *Studies in Indian History* (Agra: Shiva Lal Agarwala, 1974), 135–36.

102. Khwaja Nizam-ud-din Ahmad, *Tabaqat-i-Akbari*, trans. B. De and Baini Prashad, vol. 2 (Kolkata: The Asiatic Society, 1973), 556; Badaoni, *Muntakhabu-t-Tawarikh*, vol. 2: 350; Abul Fazl, *Ain-i-Akbari*, vol. 1: 276–277; S.J. Monserrate, *The Commentary*, trans., ann. J.S. Hoyland and S.N. Banerjee (London: Oxford University Press, 1922), 175–176.

103. Amir Hasan Sijzi, ed., *Fawa'id-u'l-Fu'ad* (Lucknow: Newal Kishore, 1302 A.H./1884 A.D.), 127; Gulbadan, Begam, *Humayun Nama*, 179; Hawkins, *Early Travels*, 117; De Laet, *The Empire*, 100; Abul Fazl, *Ain-i-Akbari*, vol. 1: 286; Jahangir, *Tuzuk*, vol. 1: 48–49; Monserrate, *The Commentary*, 174–175; F.S. Manrique, *Travels of Fray Sebastien Manrique*, trans. Eckford Luard and S.J. Hosten, vol. 2 (London: Hak Society, 1927), 192; Thevenot, *Indian Travels*, 71; Manucci, *Storia Do Mogor*, vol. 2: 322; K.A. Nizami, *Some Aspects of Religion and Politics in India During the Thirteenth Century*, 2nd ed. (New Delhi: Idarah-i-Adabiyat-i-Delli, 1974), 94, note 3.

104. Manucci, *Storia Do Mogor*, vol. 2: 322–323; Nizam-ud-din Ahmad, *Tabaqat-i-Akbari*, trans. B. De and Baini Prashad, vol. 2: 559–60; also Monserrate, *The Commentary*, 175–176; Thevenot, *Indian Travels*, 70–71.

105. Babur, *Babur Nama*, vol. 1: 235–236; Abul Fazl, *Akbar Nama*, vol. 3: 109; Jahangir, *Tuzuk*, vol. 1: 45–46; Manucci, *Storia Do Mogor*, vol. 2: 325–326 (all for celebration of Id). Jahangir, *Tuzuk*, vol. 1: 385–386 (for celebrations of *Shab-i-Barat*), also vol. 1: 22, 94 (for Nur Jahan arranging grand feast on the occasion of *Shab-i-Barat*).

106. Abul Fazl, *Ain-i-Akbari*, vol. 1: 210; Jahangir, *Tuzuk*, vol. 1: 252, 226, 246, 361 and vol. 2: 176.

107. Gulbadan Begam, *Humayun Nama*, 104, 190–191; Abul Fazl, *Akbar Nama*, vol. 3: 543, 889; Jahangir, *Tuzuk*, vol. 1: 106–107, also 384–386 and vol. 2: 199; Bernier, *Mogul Empire*, 350–351, 361 resp. See also Ashraf, *Life and Conditions*, 232 (for river picnics).

108. Anonymous, *Tarikh-i-Salim Shahi*, 202–204.

109. Lahori, *Badshah Nama*, Part II, vol. 1: 240–241; Latif, *Lahore*, 140–141, n. (for *Shalimar Bagh*).

110. Jahangir, *Tuzuk*, vol. 1: 129–130, 203–204, 348, 375, also vol. 2: 73–74. Also, Chittraman Kayath, 'Chahar Gulshan' (Aligarh: Azad Library, Aligarh Muslim University), fol. 156; Mulla Kami Shirazi, 'Fateh Nama-i-Nur Jahan Begam' (Aligarh: History Department, Aligarh Muslim University), fols 31–32.

111. Manucci, *Storia Do Mogor*, vol. 2: 318.

112. Gulbadan Begam, *Humayun Nama*, 113, note 3.

113. Ibn Batuta, *Rehla*, 79; Must'ad Khan, *Maasir-i-Alamgiri*, 103; Mundy, *The Travels*, vol. 2: 188, 189, 191; Bernier, *Mogul Empire*, 372 (for *palki* and *doli*). Thevenot, *Indian Travels*, 76; Ovington, *Seventeenth Century*, vol. 1: 113; Pietro Della Valle, *Travels of Pietro Della Valle in India*, trans. G. Havers, ed. Edward Grey, vol. I (London: Hakluyt Society, 1892), 31; Tavernier, *Travels in India*, vol. 1: 313 (for palanquins). Manucci, *Storia Do Mogor*, vol. 2: 330–331 (for covered seats with peeping windows having netting of gold); Sarkar, *Fall*, vol.I: 334 (for covered wagons).

114. Ibn Batuta, *Rehla*, 122 and note 1.

115. Mundy, *The Travels*, vol. 2: 190–191 (for *khajwah*, *chandoli [chaudols]* and *amari*); Bernier, *Mogul Empire*, 371–373 (for *chaudol, Amari, Chandol, khajwah* and *mikdember*); Monserrate, *The Commentary*, 79 (for *hauda*); Tavernier, *Travels in India*, vol. 1: 313 (for special wheeled carriage); Della Valle, trans. G. Havers, ed. Edward Grey, vol.1: 62 (for elephants with covered litters); Manucci, *Storia Do Mogor*, vol. 2: 66–67 (for *pitambar*). Must'ad Khan, *Maasir-i-Alamgiri*, 103 (for *chaudol*). Abdul Qadir Al Badaoni, *Nijat-ul-Rashid*, ed. Syed Moinul Haq (Lahore, 1972), 460; Careri, *Indian Travels*, 227, 370, note 77 (for *amaris*). Thomas Roe, *The Embassy of Sir Thomas Roe to the Court of the Great Mughal*, ed. William Foster, vol. 2 (London: Hak Society, 1899), 324 (for Nur Jahan's coach).

116. Bernier, *Mogul Empire*, 371–372; Tavernier, *Travels in India*, vol. 1: 313; Manucci, *Storia Do Mogor*, vol. 2: 66–67.

117. Bernier, *Mogul Empire*, 372–373; Manucci, *Storia Do Mogor*, vol. 2: 66–67.

118. Manucci, *Storia Do Mogor*, vol. 1: 212; also Monserrate, *The Commentary*, 79 (for general description).

119. Manucci, *Storia Do Mogor*, vol. 1: 212.

120. Pelsaert, *The Remonstrantie*, 66.

121. Manucci, *Storia Do Mogor*, vol. 2: 372.

122. Manucci, *Storia Do Mogor*, vol. 2: 329.

123. Coryat, *Early Travels*, 278–279; Manucci, *Storia Do Mogor*, vol. 2: 329. Ovington, *Seventeenth Century*, vol. 1: 92–93.

124. Manucci, *Storia Do Mogor*, vol. 2: 200–201, 176, respectively.

125. Refer to reference no. 40 of this Chapter.

126. Hussein Khan, *Siyar*, trans. Manus, vol. 1: 422, note 23.

127. Manucci, *Storia Do Mogor*, vol. 2: 435–436. See also Ovington, *Seventeenth Century*, vol. 1: 93–94.

128. J.A. De Mandelslo, *The Voyage and Travels of J. Albert de Mandelslo... into the East Indies*, trans. John Davies (London: Printed for John Starkey, and Thomas Basset, 1669), 64. Also Pelsaert, *The Remonstrantie*, 66; Manucci, *Storia Do Mogor*, vol. 2: 74.

129. H.M. Elliot and John Dowson, 'Institutes of Jahangir', in *History of India as Told by its Own Historians*, vol. 7 (Allahabad: Kitab Mahal, 1964), Appendix: 505.
130. Anonymous, *Tarikh-i-Ahmad Shah*, trans. Elliot and Dowson, in *History of India*, vol. VIII (Calcutta: Royal Asiatic Society of Bengal, 1940), 113–114 (for Javed Khan and Qudsia Begam); Ganda Singh, *Ahmad Shah Durrani* (Mumbai: Asia Publishing House, 1959), 142; H.R. Gupta, *Studies in Later Mughal History of the Panjab* (Lahore, 1944), 122, 141, 154; Sarkar, *Fall*, vol. 2: 35–37 (for Mughlani Begam).
131. Hilde Bach, *Indian Love Paintings* (Varanasi: Lustre Press, 1985), pls. 33, 34.
132. Bernier tops in scandalising this affair (Bernier, *Mogul Empire*, 11). Manucci termed Bernier's statement totally wrong, considering it to have been founded on the talk of low people (Manucci, *Storia Do Mogor*, vol. 1: 208–209). So is the view of Catrou who considered it 'a popular rumour which never had any other foundation than in the malice of the courtiers' (Bernier, *Mogul Empire*, 11, note 1). Tavernier (*Travels in India*, vol. 1: 275) also made reference of the prevailing suspicion of her having improper relation with her father, though he did not give his own view. But, his translator V. Ball (vol. 1: 276, f.n. 1) considers it a mere court gossip, B.P. Saksena (*History of Shahjahan of Dihli* (Allahabad: Central Book Depot, 1958), 338–342) is also of the same view. Richard Temple also regarded it 'scandalous gossip' ('Shahjahan and Jahan Ara', *Indian Antiquary* XLIV (1915): 111–112). But V.A. Smith, relying on the evidence of De Laet and Thomas Herbert, held, 'Although it may be reasonably regarded as improbable, it cannot be dismissed summarily as incredible' ('Joannes De Laet on India and Shahjahan', *Indian Antiquary*, XLIII (1914): 240–244).
133. Manucci, *Storia Do Mogor*, vol. 1: 210; Lal, *Harem*, 181, 199.
134. Pelsaert, *The Remonstrantie*, 65.
135. Manucci, *Storia Do Mogor*, vol. 2: 328, 99–100 (for Udaipuri) and vol. 1: 211(for Jahanara).
136. Khafi Khan, *Muntakhab-al-Lubab*, Part II, 690.
137. Herman Goetz, *Art and Architecture of Bikaner State* (London: Oxford University Press, 1950), 174–175; Lal, *Harem*, Pl. 8; M.S. Randhawa, *Indian Miniature Painting* (New Delhi: Roli Books International, 1981), Pls. 26, 28 (showing women smoking *hookah*).
138. Pelsaert, *The Remonstrantie*, 64.
139. Manucci, *Storia Do Mogor*, vol. 2: 329.
140. Anonymous, *Tarikh-i-Alamgir Sani*, trans. Elliot and Dowson, in *History of India*, vol. VIII (Allahabad: Kitab Mahal, 1964), 142; Sarkar, *Fall*, vol. 2: 149, 174–175; Percival Spear, *Twilight of the Mughals* (London: Cambridge University Press, 1951), 28, 60–61; Lal, *Harem*, 195–197.
141. Jourdain, The Journal, 164–165; Hawkins, *Early Travels*, 104; Bernier, *Mogul Empire*, 222; Manucci, *Storia Do Mogor*, vol. 2: 315–316; Shireen Moosvi, 'Expenditure on the Imperial Household', in *The Economy of the Mughal Empire* (New Delhi: Oxford University Press, 1987), Chapter 2: particularly 248–268 (all for huge Harem expenses). L. Lockhart, *Nadir Shah* (London: Luzac & Co., 1938), 152, note 5; Anand Ram Mukhlis, *Tazkira*, trans. Elliot and Dowson, in *History of India*, vol. VIII (Allahabad: Kitab Mahal, 1964), 88–90; Sarkar, *Fall*, vol. 1: 3; Irvine, *Later Mughals*, vol. 2: 371–373; Haig, *Cambridge History*, vol. 4: 362–363 (for loot of Nadir Shah). For Abdali's plunder, see Sarkar, *Fall*, vol. 2: 89–91.

142. Khafi Khan, *Muntakhab-al-Lubab*, Part II, 933–934.
143. Sarkar, *Fall*, vol. 2: 26.
144. Lal, *Harem*, 198.
145. Meer Hassan Ali, *Observations of the Mussulmauns of India*, vol. 1, rpt. (New Delhi: Idarah-i-Adabiyat-i-Delli, 1973), 322–323. See also Lal, *Harem*, 198.
146. Monserrate, *The Commentary*, 203.
147. Manucci, *Storia Do Mogor*, vol. 2: 195.
148. Manucci, *Storia Do Mogor*, vol. 2 (London: Murray, 1907), 175.
149. Shah Nawaz Khan and Hayy, *Maasir*, vol. 1: 251–252.
150. Meer Hassan Ali, *Observations*, vol. 1: 317–318.
151. Ashraf, *Life and Conditions*, 175.
152. John Marshall, *John Marshall in India*, ed. Shafaat Ahmad Khan (London: Oxford University Press, 1927), 327–328.
153. Manucci, *Storia Do Mogor*, vol. 2: 373.
154. Manucci, *Storia Do Mogor*, vol. 2: 328–329, 333; Bernier, *Mogul Empire*, 267.
155. Manucci, *Storia Do Mogor*, vol. 2: 331.
156. Manucci, *Storia Do Mogor*, vol. 2: 311.
157. Afif, *Tarikh-i-Firoz Shahi*, 393–394.
158. Nizam-ud-din Ahmad, *Tabaqat-i-Akbari*, trans. B. De and Baini Prashad, Part II, vol. 3: 804; Ulugh Khani, *Zafar-ul-Waleh*, in *Uttar Taimur*, Part II, trans. Rizvi, 445–446; Jahangir, *Tuzuk*, vol. 1: 351. See Ovington, *Seventeenth Century*, vol. 1: 94 (for 'Malabar Quills'). See also P. Thomas, *Indian Women Through the Ages* (New York: Asia Publishing House, 1964), 252.
159. Barani, *Tarikh*, 506; Ulugh Khani, *Zafar-ul-Waleh*, in *Uttar Taimur*, Part II, trans. Rizvi, 445–446.
160. Beveridge, Introduction to Gulbadan's *Humayun Nama*, 7.
161. Beveridge, Introduction to Gulbadan's *Humayun Nama*, 120–121. See also Introduction, 8, 95–96, 97, 101–102, 113.
162. Manrique, *Travels of Fray*, 52. Also see H.G. Keene, *History of Hindustan* (New Delhi: Idarah-i-Adabiyat-i-Delli, 1972), 199.
163. Jafar Sharif, *Qanun-i-Islam*, in Islam in India, ed. William Crooke, rpt. (London: Oxford University Press, 1921), 80.
164. Minhaj-ud-din Siraj, *Tabaqat-i-Nasiri*, trans. H.G. Raverty, vol. 1: 638, 643; Ferishta, *Tarikh-i-Ferishta*, vol. 1: 121; Anonymous, 'Tarikh-i-Haqqi', Persian Ms. No. 89, Cat. No. 537 (Bankipur, Patna: The Khuda Baksh Oriental Public Library), fol. 8a. Razia broke the purdah norms in the later part of her career. Sirhindi, however, mentioned about her coming out 'with veils on' (Sirhindi, *Tarikh-i-Mubarak Shahi*, 25). See also Royal Asiatic Society of Bengal, *Introducing India*, Part I (Calcutta: Royal Asiatic Society of Bengal, 1947), Article No. 9, 92; B.S. Chandrababu, and Thilgavathi, *Woman: Her History and Her Struggle for Emancipation* (Chennai: Bharathi Pusthakalayam, 2009), 180 (they mention that Razia came out without Purdah, but with her face covered up to lips).
165. Beni Prasad, *History of Jahangir*, 159.
166. Tod, *Annals and Antiquities*, vol. 2: 355.
167. Manucci, *Storia Do Mogor*, vol. 2: 328.
168. Geeti Sen, *Paintings from the Akbar Nama* (New Delhi: Roli Books, 1984), Pls. 16–18.
169. Sarkar, *Fall*, vol. 2: 42.

170. Ferishta, *Tarikh-i-Ferishta*, vol. 2: 168.

171. Zeb-un-Nisa, *Diwan-i-Makhfi*, in *The Diwan of Zeb-un-Nissa*, Introduction, trans. Magan Lal and Jessie Duncan (London: Westbrook, 1913), 11.

172. Zahir-ud-din Azfari, *Waqia-i-Azfari*, trans. A. Satter (Madras: Oriental Research Institute, Madras University, 1937), 26.

173. Lal, *Harem*, 115; Ovington, *Seventeenth Century*, vol. 1: 92.

174. Hussein Khan, *Siyar*, trans. Manus, vol. 1: 31–32, also trans. Briggs, 28.

175. Amir Khusrau, *Hasht Bahisht*, 27, 29; Amir Khusrau, *Matla-ul-Anwar* (Lucknow, 1884), 224, 226; Khwaja Abdul Malik Isami, *Futuh-us-Salatin*, ed. A. Mahdi Husain (Agra: Educational Press, 1938), 130.

176. Firoz Shah Tughlaq, *Futuhat-i-Firoz Shahi*, ed. S.A. Rashid (Aligarh, 1954), Rule 10, 8–9. Also Afif, *Tarikh-i-Firoz Shahi*, 373–374; Nizam-ud-din Ahmad, *Tabaqat-i-Akbari*, trans. B. De and Baini Prashad, vol. 1: 259–260.

177. Ferishta, *Tarikh-i-Ferishta*, vol. 1: 343.

178. Badaoni, *Muntakhabu-t-Tawarikh*, vol. 2: 405.

179. Badaoni, *Nijat*, 460.

180. Barbosa, *The Book*, vol. 2: 147, also vol. 1: 121.

181. Terry, *Early Travels*, 309; De Laet, *The Empire*, 81; Manucci, *Storia Do Mogor*, vol. 1: 61; Ovington, *Seventeenth Century*, vol. 1: 93; Thevenot, *Indian Travels*, 53; Careri, *Indian Travels*, 248; John Fryer, *A New Account of the East Indies and Persia (1672–81)*, ed. W. Crooke, vol. 2, second series no. XX (London: Hak Society, 1912), 117–118; Marshall, *Marshall in India*, 328; Alexander Hamilton, *Account of the East Indies*, vol. 1 (Edinburg: John Mosman, one of His Majesty's Printers, and sold at the King's printing house in Craig's Closs, MDCCXXVII (1927), 163.

182. Terry, *Early Travels*, 309; De Laet, *The Empire*, 81; Careri, *Indian Travels*, 248; Ovington, *Seventeenth Century*, vol. 1: 93.

183. P.N.K. Bamzai, *A History of Kashmir* (New Delhi: Metropolitan Book Co., 1962), 467 (for purdah in Kashmir); K.A.N. Sastri, *A History of South India*, 4th ed. (New Delhi: Oxford University Press, 1976), 316 (for purdah in Bijapur).

184. Mirza Nathan, *Baharistan-i-Ghaybi*, trans. M.I. Borah, vol. 2 (Guwahati: Government of Assam, 1936), 523.

185. Ghulam Husain Salim, *Riyazu-s-Salatin*, trans. Abdus Salam (New Delhi: Idarah-i-Adabiyat-i-Delli, 1975), 31–32.

186. Barani, *Tarikh*, 56; Ain-ul-Mulk Abdullah Multani, *Insha-i-Mahru*, ed. S.A. Rashid (Lahore: Idarah-Yi-Tahqiqat-i-Pakistan, Danishgah-Yi-Punjab, 1965), Letter No. 94, 179; Ovington, *Seventeenth Century*, vol. 1: 142. See also K.S. Lal, *Early Muslims in India* (New Delhi: Books & Books, 1984), 149.

187. Mazhar-ul-Haq Khan, *Social Pathology of the Muslim Society* (New Delhi: Amar Prakashan, 1978), 19, 34.

188. Thomas, *Indian Women*, 252.

5

Political Platform

Prophet Mohammad had exhorted his wife Ayisha at the time of his death that women should not interfere in public affairs, yet she was instrumental in opposing Hazrat Ali's election to the Caliphate. Since then, Muslim women have taken part in politics whenever opportunities appeared, despite disapproval and criticism from moralists, zealots and other vested interests. Muslim women in India were no exception. Their role in the politics of Delhi Sultanate and Mughal Empire has been a well-researched subject in various monographs dealing with various rulers and dynasties. A concise account is presented here for a complete understanding of the status of Muslim women.

An Overview

The Turks brought along with them the Persian–Arabic heritage and gradually assimilated the indigenous Indian traditions. They allowed women's participation in politics and accepted their right to sovereignty, drawing inspiration from the Iranian tradition where two daughters of Khusrau Parvez—Puran Dukht and Arjumand Dukht—ascended the throne of Persia, one after the other in the 7th century.[1] The Afghans also allowed their ladies to have some say in political affairs. The Mughals permitted their ladies to enjoy political clout without a right to sovereignty. Thus, it is reported that once Shah Begam of Badakhshan wrote to Babur that she being a woman could not attain sovereignty while her grandson, Mirza Khan, could hold it.[2]

Muslim women in India influenced the politics of their respective times in three ways: (a) actively participating in political activities as a sovereign; (b) working as regents of minor kings or incapacitated monarchs and (c) operating behind the scene as political manipulators. The different wives of the ruler promoted their own children in anticipation of the inevitable war of succession on the death of the ruler because of the lack of rule of primogeniture in Islamic civilisation.

It will not be out of place to mention that different lineage groups jockeyed for power and influence from time to time. The impact of Muslim women, however, varied from time to time according to their personality, family connections, political situation and the character of the sultan or emperor. The nature of this impact on the state also varied from time to time according to the motive and insight of the lady at the helm of affairs. At one time, by virtue of their intelligence, diplomacy and tact, they strengthened the empire but, at the other, by their intrigues and selfishness, they created more problems and weakened the fabric of the political life. Right from the rule of Turks till the reign of Aurangzeb, the ladies of high birth, royalty and nobility participated in the political arena. In the post-Aurangzeb period, instead of queens, princesses or ladies of high birth, concubines and dancing girls of low origin became prominent in the power politics. Being upstarts, they tried to grasp both power and pelf through their nefarious designs and intrigues, without any concern for the prestige of the state. They exploited the sensual laxity of the then emperors to make a place for themselves in the political arena.

The Sultanate Period

The earliest instance of a lady interfering in political activities in the sultanate period was that of Shah Turkan.[3] She was the wife of Iltutmish and mother of Rukn-ud-din Firoz. From a Turkish slave maid, she rose to the status of chief queen of Sultan Iltutmish.[4] She wanted her son Rukn-ud-din to succeed while Iltutmish had nominated Razia as heir apparent. She won over a section of nobility and with its support, she manipulated her son's succession.

Rukn-ud-din Firoz was totally incompetent. Shah Turkan concentrated all political authority in her hands and issued royal commands. She utilised her authority for settling her personal scores and exterminating her son's opponents. She tortured the inmates of the harem and executed some of them. She got Qutb-ud-din, another son of Iltutmish, blinded and ultimately killed. She conspired to eliminate Razia. Her reckless behaviour antagonised the nobles and provincial Governors. They rose in revolt and ultimately, she was overthrown. Rukn-un-din, in all probability, was also put to death.[5]

Razia[6] succeeded Rukn-ud-din Firoz. Her accession heralded a new epoch in the history of Muslim women in India and established woman's right to sovereign power. Her administrative qualities were visible even during the reign of her father. Since the late sultan noticed in her indications of sovereignty and high spirit, in spite of her being a daughter, he groomed her to be his successor.[7] He made all efforts to give her proper training in administration. He allowed her to exercise authority in the affairs of the state. When he left Delhi for an expedition to Gwalior in 1231 A.D., she was left behind to manage the affairs at Delhi that she did with perfection. Therefore, when the sultan returned from the Gwalior conquest, he directed Taj-ul-Mulk Mahmud, the *Mushrif-i-Mumalik* (secretary of state), to draw a decree naming her as his heir apparent.[8]

Theoretically and constitutionally, the Turks were not opposed to Razia's nomination and nor did any Muslim jurist question its legality.[9] However, they were men of the 'Man's' age and did not like a lady to rule them. They represented against this nomination to the sultan. The sultan silenced them explaining the incapability of his sons and the competence of Razia: 'After my death, it will be seen that not one of them will be found to be more worthy of the heir-apparentship, than she, my daughter'.[10] After the sultan's death, they sidetracked her and raised Rukn-ud-din to throne. When Rukn-ud-din's indolence and Shah Turkan's reign of terror annoyed the nobles, she rose to the occasion and sought their support. It is said that she addressed the army from the Jama Masjid at Daulat Khan, reminded them of her father's good reign and his 'Will', promised to relieve them of the oppressive regime and resolved to abdicate if she failed to keep her promise. They lent support and elevated her to the throne.[11]

Her work as a sovereign is too well known to need mention. However, her attempt to organise a group loyal to her only proved her undoing. Malik Hindu Khan, a slave of Iltutmish and of Indian origin, continued to be her treasurer besides being incharge of the fort of Ucch.[12] She appointed Jamal-ud-din Yaqut, an Abyssinian slave, to the high post of *Amir-i-Akhur* (the master of the imperial stables). Isami, followed by Sirhindi, Nizam-ud-din Ahmad, Ferishta and Badaoni charged Razia of too much intimacy with Yaqut and considered it an important factor leading to her fall.[13] Minhaj, with all praise for her qualities of head and heart, lamented, '...but, as she did not attain the destiny, in her creation, of being computed among men, of what advantage were all these excellent qualifications unto her'.[14]

Another lady participating in court politics was the wife of Malik Nizam-ud-din, a noble during the reign of Kaiqubad. She was the daughter of Fakhr-ud-din, the Kotwal of Delhi. She gained a complete hold on the administration of the royal harem and came to be regarded as queen mother of the sultan. Simultaneously, she also furthered the cause of her father and husband in the administration.[15]

Malika-i-Jahan, the wife of Jalal-ud-din, the mother of Rukn-ud-din Ibrahim and the mother-in-law of Ala-ud-din Khalji, played politics in the capacity of these three relations. During her husband's reign, she had complete sway over the administration. So much so that when once the King wished to be entitled *Al Mujahid Fi Sabilulah* (The fighter in the path of the almighty) and thought that the proposal should come from the nobles, he sought her help. Malika-i-Jahan had such influence upon the nobility that she manoeuvred them to sponsor the proposal. However, the sultan changed his mind and declined to accept the same.[16] She could sense Ala-ud-din's plans and constantly warned her husband. Her influence embittered the relations between them.[17] She goaded her daughter to have a nagging attitude towards him.[18] After Jalal-ud-din's death in 1296 A.D., sultan's eldest son, Arkali Khan, a reputed soldier, could be the best choice as his successor. He was at Multan. The queen neither waited for him nor did she consult any of the nobles and declared her infant son Rukn-ud-din Ibrahim as the next sultan with herself as regent. She tried to win over the amirs by lavish gifts. However, her machinations failed and Ala-ud-din routed her. She fled to Multan. She realised her mistake and even sought Arkali's pardon.[19]

Ala-ud-din Khalji's despotism left little room for women's role in politics. Amir Khusrau recorded that his attack on Gujarat was partly due to the solicitation of Kamla Devi.[20] His chief queen Mahru intrigued for her brother Alp Khan. She managed the marriage of his two daughters to her two sons, prince Khizr Khan and prince Shadi Khan.[21] When Ala-ud-din fell ill, she conspired with her brother for securing the throne for her son Khizr Khan. Her plan misfired and consequently, Khizr Khan was imprisoned, blinded and then killed.[22] Mahru was also imprisoned.

Among the Tughlaqs, the reign of Muhammad bin Tughlaq is important for ladies' participation in court politics. It is surprising that none of his wives is mentioned in the historical chronicles. The very fact of his marriage is shrouded in mystery. From a passing reference of Afif, it appears that he did marry in early part of his father's reign.[23] But no details about this are recorded. The contemporary authorities mention the role played by his mother and sister. While the mother's role provided sublimity to women's participation, the sister, once again, drew it back to the narrow circles of selfish intrigues.

Makhduma-i-Jahan's direct interference in contemporary politics does not find a mention in the historical accounts. But Sultan Muhammad bin Tughlaq, her son, had immense regard for her political acumen and she had 'behind the curtain' influence on the policies of the sultan. Her counsel was an important factor for granting clemency by the sultan to the rebel nobles like Ain-ul-Mulk, Ali Shah Kar, Hushang and Nusrat Khan.[24] Besides, she participated in day-to-day court life, received envoys (like Ibn Batuta) and royal guests and exchanged gifts with them.[25]

Khudavandzada, a sister of the sultan appeared on the political scene after the death of Muhammad bin Tughlaq. She raised the claim of her son Dawar Malik for succession, but the impending danger of Mongol invasion silenced her. Firoz Shah Tughlaq succeeded with the help of the nobles. He tried to keep her in good humour and got his coronation done through her. He visited her every Friday and discussed the issues of importance with her. In spite of this magnanimity shown towards her, the lady hatched a conspiracy to kill him. Luckily, the conspiracy was exposed and the sultan escaped. She was imprisoned, her vast wealth was confiscated and her husband, Khusrau Malik, was banished.[26]

Among the Lodis, the ladies played varied political roles. While Bibi Mattu held the command in the war field, Shams Khatun was an instigator and Bibi Ambha was involved in the succession politics.

Bibi Mattu, wife of Islam Khan Lodi, showed her heroism and leadership during the time of Bahlol Lodi in 1452 A.D. Bahlol was away to Sirhind and there were only a few males in the fort of Delhi. Mahmud Sharqi of Jaunpur besieged the fort. Unnerved, Bibi

Mattu rose to save the fort. She made the ladies to dress like men and take positions on the rampart of the fort. She gave guidance for each and every detail and then ordered beating of the drum, giving the semblance of victory for her forces. All this led Mahmud to raise the siege.[27] In another incident of 1517, Sultan Sikander Lodi deprived Prince Jalal Khan Lodi, son of Mahmud Khan Lodi, of the governorship of Kalpi. It was at the intervention of Bibi Mattu, who was wet nurse of Prince Jalal Khan, that the prince was restored the governorship, besides getting a robe of honour, horses and elephants.[28]

Shams Khatun was the chief queen of Bahlol Lodi. Her brother, Qutb Khan, was imprisoned while Bahlol Lodi was fighting against Mahmud Shah Sharqi of Jaunpur in 1457 A.D. Meanwhile, Mahmud died and was succeeded by Muhammad Shah Sharqi. A peace was signed between the latter and Bahlol. But when Bahlol was still on his way back, he received a letter from Shams Khatun asking him not to relax till her brother was freed. Her message was sufficient for the sultan to retrace his steps and re-attack Jaunpur with greater force.[29]

Bibi Ambha,[30] another wife of Sultan Bahlol Lodi, was daughter of a Hindu goldsmith. After the death of Bahlol in 1489 A.D., among the hordes of contenders for the throne, she pressed the claim of her son Nizam Khan (Ferishta names him Sikander Khan). It seems that Bibi Ambha was competing on account of weak lineage as compared to descent of other claimants. Isa Khan, nephew of Bahlol and one of the contenders of throne, rebuked the lady telling her that a goldsmith's son was not worthy of the throne. She won over the nobles and raised her son, Nizam Khan, to the throne under the title Sultan Sikander Lodi.[31]

Ibrahim Lodi's mother played a negative role by poisoning Babur to avenge the death of her son.[32]

As for the contemporary smaller Muslim kingdoms, there are some other politically active ladies. In Bihar, Dudu Bibi worked as a regent to her son in his minority from 1529.[33] In the conflict between Lodis and Sharqis, two harem ladies played significant role. One was Bibi Raji, the daughter of Sultan Mubarak Shah Sayyid. She was married to Mahmud Sharqi, the then crown prince of Jaunpur, as part of the peace treaty following a war between Mubarak Shah and Ibrahim Sharqi in 1427 A.D. When Mahmud Sharqi became the sultan of Jaunpur subsequently (1440–1457 A.D.), Bibi Raji instigated her husband to march against Bahlol Lodi to avenge the defeat of her father and even threatened him that if he did not do so, she would herself lead the army. This resulted in Mahmud's attack on Delhi (battle of Narela in 1452 A.D.). Again in 1456 A.D., when Bahlol Lodi marched upon Samsabad to eject its Sharqi governor and in the ensuing battle, Qutb Khan Lodi, his Commander-in-chief and brother-in-law (brother of Shams Khatun) was imprisoned, it was Bibi Raji, who kept Qutb Khan at Jaunpur in her safe custody for seven months, guarded him against the murderous conspiracy of Muhammad Shah, the succeeding king and as a reconciliation, and ultimately released him in 1458 A.D. After the death of Mahmud Sharqi in 1457, she became the de facto ruler of Jaunpur and remained so till her death in 1477. She immediately declared her eldest son Bikkhan Khan as the next king under the title Muhammad Shah and signed a treaty with Bahlol on mutual terms of restoring each other's possessions, although the truce was short-lived because of the role of Shams Khatun, as narrated above. However, when she found Muhammad Sharqi unworthy of the throne and indulging in conspiracies, she secretly conspired and enthroned Prince Husain with the title of Husain Shah in 1458. Muhammad was pursued and ultimately killed. In the same year, to fill the chasm between Sharqis and Lodis, she signed a fresh treaty with Bahlol on status quo basis and released Qutb Khan Lodi from her confinement. Her authority is considered to be even more than that of Nur Jahan by a modern writer, who opines: 'Such was her love of power that she may be compared with Catherine de Medici of France minus her foibles, or more properly she may be termed the Indian Irene'.[34]

This peace, however, proved short-lived because of the negative role of *Malika-i-Jahan* Bibi Khunza, wife of King Husain Shah. At her instigation, her husband attacked Bahlol. But the latter, with diplomacy, cleverly turned the tide in his favour and even imprisoned Bibi Khunza. Although she was respectfully restored to her husband by Bahlol, yet, she again goaded her husband to avenge her captivity. This led Husain Shah to violate the treaty and again march against Delhi, resulting in his repeated defeats. Jaunpur was conquered by Bahlol's forces in 1483 and in spite of many efforts by Husain to regain it, he could not succeed. The Sharqi kingdom was finally usurped by Sikander Lodi. Bibi Khunza, thus, became instrumental for the defeats and misfortune of her husband and, ultimately, the end of Sharqi rule.[35]

In Malwa, Rani Khurshid, the chief queen of Sultan Ghias-ud-din, played her role by plunging Malwa in a fratricidal war (1499–1500), like Nur Jahan, which finally resulted in her confinement, imprisonment of the sultan and perhaps in his poisoning by the heir apparent, Prince Nasir-ud-din. As against him, she favoured the throne for her younger son, prince Shuj'at Khan. She, therefore, poisoned the ears of the sultan against Prince Nasir-ud-din and also indulged in petty machinations.[36]

In Deccan, in the kingdom of Bahmani, when Nizam Shah (1461–1463 A.D.), son of Humayun Shah, ascended the throne, he was in his eighth year. It was his mother Makhduma-i-Jahan (also had the title of Malika-i-Jahan) who as his regent was incharge of the administration and she 'directed all her energies in furnishing the bed of equity and justice'. She supported the veil, yet her two ministers, Khwajah Jahan and Malik-ut-tujjar Gawan, ran the administration with her consultation. At that point of time, Sultan Mahmud Khalji of Malwa advanced to attack Bahmani Empire but was defeated at the hands of the latter. However, Malika-i-Jahan was informed of the treachery and deceit of Khawajah Jahan, who was the leader of the centre of the army. She immediately assigned the defence of the fort of Bidar to Mallu Khan and proceeded to Firuzabad along with Nizam Shah and from there she sought the help of Sultan Mahmud of Gujarat.[37]

Still another lady, Malika-i-Jahan, the mother of Sultan Shihab-ud-din Mahmud Shah (1482–1518 A.D.), son and successor of Sultan Muhammad Shah III, was the regent of the kingdom on behalf of her young son of 12 years. The Bahmani rule was then involved in a factional fight between the Turkish and Deccani amirs. Yet, Malika-i-Jahan held the reign of the government and even the wazirs like Nizam-ul-Mulk and Imad-ul-Mulk consulted her for running the affairs of the kingdom.[38]

The Mughal Period

During Babur's time, three generations of ladies—his maternal grandmother, mother and wives—were actively involved in politics. Babur was only 11 years of age when his father died. Surrounded from all sides by enemies and rivals, it was through the wisdom and far-sightedness of his grandmother, Ehsan Daulat Begam, that he steered clear of the rough political weather. Babur himself wrote, 'Few amongst women, will have been my grandmother's equal for judgement and counsel. She was very wise and far-sighted and most affairs of mine were carried through under her advice'.[39] Acting as the real head of affairs, she managed the administrative complexities with all tact and sagacity. She also foiled the conspiracy of Hasan to dethrone Babur.[40]

Babur's mother, Qutlugh Nigar Khanam, always shared her son's political vicissitudes and wanderings, advising him in need and supporting him in adversity. Babur wrote, 'She was with me on most of my guerilla expeditions and throne-less time.... Few of her sex excelled her in sense and sagacity'.[41]

Babur's Shia wife, Maham Begam, stood by him through all odds.[42] It was at her instance that Mir Khalifa's conspiracy fizzled out.[43] After Babur's death, she continued taking active part in contemporary politics till her death.[44] In order to win over Yusufzai tribe,[45] Babur married Bibi Mubarika of this tribe in 1519 A.D. She helped him in ending the bitterness with Yusufzais.[46]

Humayun's wives took active interest in the affairs of the state. Bega Begam's brother-in-law, Zahid Beg, was favoured when he was appointed Governor of Bengal which the latter declined. Humayun wanted to punish him but she interceded, though in vain, to seek the Emperor's pardon for him.[47] Hamida Banu kept him informed about the political developments during his illness. She even accompanied him in the battlefield. There is a portrait depicting Hamida on the horseback, accompanying Humayun in the battlefield. This pertains to the period 1546, when Humayun was engaged in his struggle for Kabul.[48] She also interceded to save her recalcitrant brother, Khwaja Muazzam.

Mahchuchak Begam, another wife of Humayun, was active at Kabul. Humayun had appointed Muhammad Hakim, her three-year-old son, as the nominal Governor of Kabul under the regency of Munim Khan. This arrangement was irksome for the lady and she contrived to free her son from the control of the regent. Munim Khan left for the court in 1561, leaving behind Ghani Khan, his son, as regent helped by Abul Fath Beg. The new regent was weak. Mahchuchak conspired with other three nobles, namely Fath Beg, his father Fazl Beg and Wali Atgah. Once, when Ghani Khan was temporarily absent from the town, she got the gates of the city closed for him with the help of these three nobles. Thereafter, she got Fath Beg and Fazl Beg exterminated. About the third counsel, Wali Atgah, it was rumoured that he had a love affair with Mahchuchak. So, Akbar sent Munim Khan with a force to set things right. But the royal forces were routed at the hands of this lady and Munim had to flee for life. She, then, put all those, who were suspected of infidelity, to death. Wali Atgah was one of them. Haider Qasim became her new advisor to whom, it is learnt, she got married later on.[49] Meanwhile, Abul Ma'ali, a rebel, being pursued by the imperial forces, took refuge at Kabul. Impressed by his affirmations of faithfulness, she married her daughter to him. But the latter proved treacherous. He murdered both Mahchuchak and Haider Qasim and usurped all authority. Thus, he 'fixed a term to the sanguinary deeds of this terrible woman'.[50]

Khanzada Begam, a sister of Babur, was divorced by her first husband, Shaibani Khan, for her favouring Babur in disputed matters.[51] During Humayun's time, she was made the principal lady of the palace after Maham's death in 1532–1533 A.D. Her help was frequently sought by Humayun and his brothers. In a tussle over Qandhar between Hindal and Kamran, Emperor Humayun engaged her to bring about the reconciliation between the two. Later on in 1545 A.D., when Humayun's forces had besieged Qandhar and Askari was holding the fort, Kamran sent a secret message through this lady that he should hold on till his arrival. When the fall of the fort became imminent, Askari sent her to Humayun to negotiate peace and plead a mild treatment for him. She, however, did not succeed in her mission. She pleaded with Humayun, but, before the matter could be solved, she fell ill and died in September 1545.[52]

Dildar Aghacha Begam, mother of Hindal, tried to dissuade him from disloyalty towards Humayun.[53]

In the early part of Akbar's reign, Maham Anaga and other ladies endeavoured to control and run the administration. It is a matter of controversy as to what extent was Akbar under the tutelage of Maham Anaga. One group comprising of V.A. Smith, Augustus and Haig considered Akbar totally under their control. V.A. Smith wrote, 'Akbar shook off the tutelage of Bairam only to bring him under the "monstrous regiment" of unscrupulous women'. But Tripathi, S. R. Sharma, A.L. Srivastava, Ishwari Prasad and Rekha Mishra did not agree to this. All these authorities, pro and against, however, agreed that their influence remained only up to 1562 A.D., except V.A. Smith and Haig, who extended it up to 1564 A.D.[54] The historical developments show that her influence was only for the initial years of Akbar's reign when he was still trying to establish himself and have his hold. Her role in the fall of Bairam Khan is also controversial. Badaoni, Nizam-ud-din Ahmad, followed by modern writers, Haig and Augustus, held 'harem-party' responsible for this while Abul Fazl followed by modern writers, Tripathi, A.L Srivastava and Elphinstone, opined that Khan-Khana's own actions concerned Akbar personally and paved the way for his dismissal. Since different happenings do not have their impact in isolation, the third view of author of *Maasir-ul-Umara* appears to be most balanced and convincing which holds that Maham Anaga and party were mainly responsible for perverting Akbar's feelings towards him, although Bairam's high-handedness gave the final blow.[55] When Akbar went out of Agra for hunting, Maham Anaga and party managed to bring the Emperor to Delhi under the pretext of illness of his mother. At Delhi, they complained about the authoritative power of Bairam Khan and that Akbar would not get real power in his hand till he remained in authority. Maham Anaga and Shahab-ud-din even offered to proceed to Mecca.[56] Akbar, already dissatisfied with Bairam Khan, utilised the opportunity and dismissed him.

In the state of confusion that prevailed after Bairam Khan, Maham Anaga along with Shahab-ud-din Ahmad Khan started functioning like a de facto Prime Minister. But overambitious as Maham was, she wanted to make Shahab-ud-din merely her tool. This arrangement failed and she, therefore, got Shahab-ud-din removed and brought Bahadur Khan Uzbek in his place. This arrangement also did not click because of her over-assertiveness. So, she won over Bahadur Khan's supporters and thereafter not only got him removed as Prime Minister but also sent him to Etawah. Munim Khan joined her as Prime Minister in September 1560 A.D. He found it difficult to run the administration without Maham's help. Akbar appointed Shams-ud-din Atka Khan, his foster father, to succeed Munim Khan in November 1561 A.D. Since he did not toe Maham's line, he was murdered by Adham Khan, Maham's son.

Furthering the cause of her son, Adham Khan, Maham Anaga managed for him to head an army against Baz Bahadur of Malwa so that he received an opportunity of acquiring wealth and glory. Simultaneously, she sent Pir Muhammad along with him as his counsellor and thus, very tactfully, removed 'an inconvenient rival from court'. Adham Khan defeated Baz Bahadur in 1561 A.D. All his treasures and the harem fell into Adham Khan's hands. After the victory, he sent only a few elephants to the Emperor and kept back the rest of the treasure and also the beauties with him. This enraged Akbar and he personally marched towards Malwa. Maham Anaga, as a shrewd politician, sent a message to her son, forewarning him about the Emperor's march, and headed towards Malwa along with the royal seraglio. But Akbar reached earlier and took Adham by surprise. Adham Khan submitted but it was only after the arrival of Maham Anaga and at her intercession that, ultimately, the Emperor pardoned him. Adham Khan presented whole of the war booty to Akbar but again kept back two of the beauties of Baz Bahadur's harem for himself. When this was discovered, Maham, with all brutality, got those girls killed. This crime was detected but Akbar ignored it.[57] Immediately after returning from Malwa, Akbar recalled Adham Khan. Later on, when he murdered the Prime Minister Atka Khan, the Emperor did not leave him and imparted the severest punishment of being thrown from the palace parapet till death. Akbar himself broke the news of his death to ailing Maham Anaga. She simply murmured, 'You did well' and not being able to bear the shock, she died just 40 days after the death of her son.[58]

Hamida Banu Begam, Akbar's mother, also took interest in politics. She was a party to Maham Anaga in bringing about the downfall of Bairam Khan. Salima Sultan Begam mediated between Akbar and Salim (Jahangir). On Salim's rebellion at Allahabad, she along with Hamida Banu and Gulbadan Begam brought rapprochement.[59] It is noteworthy that Akbar's Rajput wives have not been mentioned for having played any active political role.

In the very first year of Jahangir's reign, his eldest son Khusro revolted. His mother Shah Begam (Man Bai), Jahangir's favourite queen, tried to restrain Khusro, assuring him Jahangir's kindness and affection. Failing in her attempt, she committed suicide, hoping that 'her fate would bring her undutiful son to contrition'. Khusro's revolt was suppressed. At the intercession of his stepmothers, sisters and Mahabat Khan, Jahangir pardoned him and allowed audience in the *darbar*.[60] Khusro's supporter, Mirza Aziz Koka, was also pardoned at the instance of Salima Sultan Begam and other princesses of Akbar's harem.[61]

Beni Prasad wrote, 'No incident in the reign of Jahangir has attracted such attention as his marriage with Nur Jahan. For full fifteen years that celebrated lady stood forth as the most striking and most powerful personality in the Mughal Empire'. Good or bad, her influence was discernibly felt in every sphere. She sat on *jharokha* for receiving homage of the public, which otherwise was the prerogative of the emperor; her name was inscribed in the coinage; the royal seal on *farmans* bore her signatures and all administration was run by her. She was almost the de facto ruler, with the exception that *Khutaba* was not read in her name to make her a sovereign. Mutmad Khan, the author of *Iqbalnama-i-Jahangiri*, aptly described:

> At last her authority reached such a pass that the king was such only in name. Repeatedly he gave out that he has bestowed the sovereignty on Nur Jahan Begam and would say 'I require nothing beyond a *sir* of wine and half a *sir* of meat'.[62]

The salutary impact of Nur Jahan improved the health of the Emperor and made him more serene in his public behaviour.[63] With her qualities of wisdom, drive, hard work, presence of mind, resourcefulness, bravery and leadership, she proved herself to be an able administrator and a capable commander of her army.[64] Her aesthetic taste and philanthropic pursuits brought splendour and benevolence.[65] Later on, when her parents died and Jahangir's health failed, the scene changed dramatically. Her desire to remain at the helm of affairs, even after Jahangir died, led to well-known revolts of prince Khurram and Mahabat Khan. 'The issue was perfectly clear', wrote Beni Prasad, 'Nur Jahan must either soon retire from public life or supersede Shah Jahan by a more pliable instrument'. [66] Out of the other three sons of Jahangir, Khusro was already dead and Parvez was a spent force. Shahryar, a lad of 16 and *nashudani* (good for nothing), was Nur Jahan's choice. She got her daughter, Ladli Begam, married to him. She also got the fiefdom of Dholpur bestowed on him as against Khurram's asking for it.[67] With the intention of sending Khurram out of India, she obtained Jahangir's order, appointing him for Qandhar campaign. Khurram put many conditions and was declared a rebel. After three years of miserable life, Khurram's rebellion ended in utter failure. Nur Jahan forced him to surrender the forts of Rohtas and Asirgarh and send his two sons, Dara and Aurangzeb, as hostages. He was left with Balaghat only.

Mahabat Khan could have been another challenge to Nur Jahan. He was an officer who had opposed her sway over Jahangir and, with his usual frankness, had impressed upon the Emperor to free himself from the petticoat bondage.[68] She was apprehensive of Mahabat Khan joining hands with Parvez. Both had worked together in quelling Shah Jahan's revolt. Nur Jahan asked Mahabat Khan to send war booty collected during Shah Jahan's revolt. Her designs were evident to Mahabat Khan and he rose in revolt. It was a novel rebellion wherein, without harming the Emperor, he just imprisoned him and separated him from the company of Nur Jahan. Nur Jahan was able to free the Emperor tactfully and Mahabat's rebellion failed.

On Jahangir's death at Lahore, Nur Jahan called a meeting of the nobles. Asaf Khan, who was supporting the cause of his son-in-law Shah Jahan, did not allow it to be held. Nur Jahan managed to send a message to Shahryar to collect army and come to Lahore. Asaf Khan, on the contrary, declared Dawar Bakhsh, son of Khusro, a makeshift Emperor till Khurram came from the South. He sent an army against Shahryar. Shahryar was defeated and blinded. After the arrival of Shah Jahan, Dawar Bakhsh was removed and Shah Jahan ascended the throne. Nur Jahan retired from the politics.[69] So complete was her political eclipse that according to the records of *English Factories*, within a few months of her husband's death, all rupees bearing her stamp were called in and 'were not to be uttered' at Agra.[70]

During Shah Jahan's time, his wife Mumtaz was the centre of attraction. She became the chief lady of the harem and was frequently consulted by her loving husband in the matters of the state.[71] She was entrusted with royal seal to be put on the state documents after they were finally drafted.[72] Saif Khan, her brother-in-law, was removed from the Governorship of Gujarat and was ordered to be arrested because of his dubious conduct during the Emperor's march from Gujarat to Delhi. It was at the intercession of Mumtaz that Shah Jahan ordered Sher Khan, the new Governor, to not inflict any injury on him.[73] During this march, Shah Jahan had looted the rich Hindu merchants of Ahmedabad. The officials continued the looting even after Shah Jahan's departure. It was at the interference of Mumtaz and her sister that the Emperor forbade the plunder.[74] The trouble with the Portuguese was initiated at her instance, as they had carried away two of her slave girls.[75] The persecution of the Portuguese was the outcome.

After the death of Mumtaz Mahal, Shah Jahan's eldest daughter, Jahanara Begam, popularly known as Begam Sahib, took over the role of the principal lady. Bernier wrote, '...her ascendancy in the court of the Mogol should have been nearly unlimited; that she should always have regulated the humours of her father, and exercised a powerful influence on the most weighty concerns'.[76]

As such, she was the most respected lady of the court. In the administrative sphere, her hold was so pervading that all matters passed through her. The Governor of Thatta was to be punished for his tyranny and extortion. Since he gratified the Emperor, Jahanara and others with presents, the punishment was forgiven. He was rewarded with the Governorship of Allahabad.[77] Similarly, Prithi Chand, the King of Kashmir, took the help of Jahanara to please Shah Jahan.[78] Aurangzeb, the then Viceroy of Deccan, attacked Qutb-ul-Mulk, the ruler of Golkunda in 1656 A.D. for non-payment of arrears of tribute. When the prince was about to annex it, the Emperor asked him to call off the siege after realising the indemnity. Jahanara, in connivance with Dara, was responsible for this.[79]

Several letters written to or by Jahanara showed the recommendations made by or to her in favour of a specific person for a specific appointment. These are available in the form of manuscripts 'Adab-i-Alamgiri' and 'Rukkat-i-Alamgiri' in Aligarh Muslim University library. Both these collections contain documents that showed Aurangzeb having recommended the case of Murtaza Quli Khan for appointment and Jahanara recommending Muhammad Nabi to open a *karkhana* (a factory) in Burhanpur and Machlipattam.[80] Further, 'Rukkat-i-Alamgiri' contains other set of documents depicting Aurangzeb requesting Jahanara to help him in getting back the fort of Asirgarh, which was handed over to Murad after being taken away from him; or Jahanara recommending Aurangzeb to appoint Mir Nasir in place of Multafit Khan that Aurangzeb promised to do and Jahanara having written to Aurangzeb about the claims of Aatish Khan to which Aurangzeb replied that her wish would be carried through.[81] Similarly, author of *Maasir-ul-Umara* recorded Jahanara recommending Zahid Khan Koka for promotion to one of the princes.[82] The records of *English Factories* testified as to how foreigners in India sought her favour to promote their interests. Dutch traders frequently approached her through her *Diwans* (incharge of revenue administration of a province during the Mughal times) and maids to get her *nishans* (royal edict issued by one of the emperor's kin) so as to facilitate the recovery of their debts. The records of the *English Factories* for the years 1646–1659 mentioned how Hakikat Khan assured the Dutch to procure a *nishan* from Jahanara for helping them to recover their debt from Chattarsal; the records of 1651–1654 narrate about David's visit to Jahanara, to pay respect to her, immediately after landing in India and records of 1655–1660 inform as to how with the help of her *nishan*, Dutch could recover their insurance money.[83]

She supported the cause of Dara in the war of succession. She tried to persuade her brothers to avoid the battle and proposed a partition of the empire. She also tried to arrange a meeting between Aurangzeb and Shah Jahan. After her failure, she joined Shah Jahan in confinement.[84] She entreated the captive Shah Jahan thrice to forgive Aurangzeb and succeeded ultimately to get a formal pardon for him.[85] Aurangzeb held her in great esteem. He restored her all powers and made her head of the harem.[86] Sipihr Shukoh and Izid Bakhsh, sons of Dara and Murad, respectively, were released at her instance and rewarded with suitable *mansabs*.[87] She counselled Aurangzeb against re-imposing *jazia*.[88] She remained effective till her death in 1681 A.D. Aurangzeb deeply mourned her death and ordered her name to be entered in all official papers in future as *Sahibat-uz-Zamani* or 'the mistress of the age'.[89]

Some of Shah Jahan's mistresses also exercised influence on contemporary politics. Farzana Begam, wife of Jafar Khan, was one of them. Manucci narrated that in order to get her, Shah Jahan wanted to eliminate her husband. But it was at her asking that not only did the Emperor shelve this idea but he also sent her husband as the Governor of Bihar. Similarly, when Khalilullah Khan was punished for teasing a *kanchani*, it was at her recommendation that Shah Jahan pardoned him.[90]

Aurangzeb's favourite sister, Roshanara, helped him during the war of succession and handed him over all the gold and silver she possessed.[91] Bernier recorded that while arranging a meeting between Aurangzeb and Shah Jahan, Jahanara had conspired to arrest the former with the help of Tartar women. It was Roshanara's spying that Aurangzeb came to know of this conspiracy and he did not visit Shah Jahan. Similarly, working for the cause of Aurangzeb, she demanded capital punishment for Dara after his arrest.[92] After his accession, Aurangzeb kept the seal of the empire (*Mohar-i-Ozak*) under her care. The signet with which it had to be impressed was, however, kept back by him to ensure that the princess did not make use of the instrument to promote any sinister design.[93] According to Bernier, she fell from favour during Aurangzeb's illness in 1662, because she misused the royal seal in her possession as she wrote letters to Governors and Generals, seeking support for Sultan Azam, Aurangzeb's nine-year-old son, in the event of Emperor's death. This enraged Aurangzeb and led to her eclipse. Travernier, however, was of the opinion that the smuggling of a young man by the princess into her compartment for 15–20 days was the reason for their strained relations.[94]

Aurangzeb's daughter, Zeb-un-nisa, was adept in politics. She frequently attended the court and helped her father.[95] Her correspondence with Aurangzeb shows her administrative participation like making appointments, disbursing salaries, dismissing and promoting officials. Aurangzeb's 'Rukkat' manuscript at Aligarh Muslim University records many such references. As per one folio, Aurangzeb wrote to her, suggesting a particular name for a particular post, adding, however, that the final choice lay with her. Another folio showed that she asked Aurangzeb for disbursement of the pay of some official to which Aurangzeb informed that he had sent necessary instructions to the clerk concerned. Aurangzeb also wrote to her that if Hakim Abdulla was not dependable, then he should be replaced by Kokazada after being promoted.[96] It also records that at her asking, Muhammad Ibrahim, the paymaster, was raised to the post of *Seh-Hazari* with a title of *Mirza Khani* and a present of ₹2,000.[97] Shah Nawaz khan, her maternal grandfather, was released at her intervention.[98] It was for her love for Shivaji that she planned his escapement from Aurangzeb's captivity by hiding in a fruit basket. This invited for her wrath of her father and might have become one of the reasons for her imprisonment.[99] Her secret correspondence with her rebel brother, Muhammad Akbar, brought about her fall in 1681. She was deprived of her property and annual pension of ₹400,000 and imprisoned in the fort of Salimgarh, where she remained till her death in 1702 A.D.[100]

Zinat-un-nisa played a reconciliatory role in the family. She secured interview with the Emperor for erring princes, Kam Bakhsh and Azam.[101] She was entrusted with the task of looking after the Maratha captives, Yesu Bai, widow of Shambhaji and her son Shahu. She developed a soft corner for them and helped in their release from the Mughal control.[102] She managed her father's household in Deccan for quarter of a century till her death.[103]

Among Aurangzeb's wives, Udaipuri Mahal managed pardon many a time for Kam Bakhsh.[104] His another wife, Nawab Bai, got her two sons, Muhammad Sultan and Muazzam, pardoned. When Muhammad Sultan was imprisoned for his rebellion, his mother managed his release and a *mansab* of 8,000 + 2,000 for him from the Emperor.[105] During the expedition against Rana of

Chittor, the Rajputs instigated Muazzam to rebel, but Nawab Bai dissuaded him. However, at other occasions, she could not check her sons from rebellious inclinations. Muazzam was even arrested for this.[106]

Jahandar Shah's mistress, Lal Kanwar, played a significant political role. Her worthless relatives and friends were raised to dignity with *mansabs*, titles and presents. Her brother, Khoshal Khan, received a *mansab* of 7,000 and her uncle, Niamat Khan, of 5,000. Khoshal Khan also coveted the Viceroyalty of Akbarabad to which the Emperor agreed. However, such usurpations were highly resented to by the nobles and Zulfiqar Khan very sarcastically brought it to the notice of the Emperor. He delayed the preparation of the *farman* in this regard and asked for a bribe of 5,000 guitars and 7,000 trimbels. The matter was reported to Lal Kanwar, who conveyed her resentment to the Emperor. The latter called for the explanation of the Wazir and wanted to know the reason for such a demand. To this, the Wazir replied that since the high positions had already been occupied by the dancers and singers, he wanted these musical instruments to be distributed among the dispossessed Governors and Generals to learn them so that they could fill the vacancies created by the dancers and singers, in order to earn their living. Khoshal Khan could not get the *subedari* nor could the Emperor punish the wazir.[107]

Many of the lowly placed acquaintances of Lal Kanwar were highly favoured. Zahra or Zohra, a vegetable seller, rode an elephant magnificently, decorated and surrounded all around by her people, who were equally insolent and insulting to the passers-by. In one of her journeys, when Chin Qulich Khan (afterwards Nizam-ul-Mulk), the ex-commander-in-chief, happened to pass her way, without any provocation, she called him 'the son of a blind man' and then complained against him to Lal Kanwar. It was his good luck that at the behest of the Wazir, the matter was ultimately dropped. Her ascend, thus, had a negative impact on the king and the administration. Haig aptly sums it up, '...the crown was stripped of dignity and prestige in the public eye and the entire tone of society and administration was vulgarized'.[108]

Farrukhsiyar's daughter, Malika Zamani, managed the support of Husain Ali Khan, one of the Sayyid brothers, with the help of other harem ladies.[109] Thereafter, his mother, titled *Sahiba-i-Nishwan*, fully ensured his favour through her negotiations.[110] With the help of Sayyid brothers, Farrukhsiyar ultimately succeeded to the throne of Delhi.

During the reign of Muhammad Shah, his mother, Qudsia Begam (Fakhr-un-nisa), was instrumental in getting the throne for her son and also in the downfall of Sayyid brothers.[111]

Another woman was Rahim-un-nisa, the daughter of a *dervesh* (one who was treading a Sufi Muslim ascetic path) and popularly known as Koki Jiu. She came into prominence after the fall of Sayyid brothers and the death of Amin Khan, the Wazir. She became a confidant of the Emperor and was entrusted with the royal seal, with the authority to imprint it on the state documents. Her four brothers were raised to high ranks; their total income from *jagirs* amounted to ₹2.5 million. The Emperor was so much under her influence that he regretted having not been able to make her wazir because of her being a female.[112] She was a corrupt woman and accepted gratifications. Muhammad Khan Bangash promised her ₹100,000 on his being appointed to the government of Malwa.[113] She formed a clique with Roshan-ud-daulah Zafar Khan, the *Bakshi* (incharge of army organisation in the *suba*), eunuch Khwaja Khidmatgar, a close companion of the Emperor and Abdul Ghafur, a *dervesh* who became popular in the harem through his art of magic. This group collected a lot of money as *peshkash* (offer/allurement to get one's work done).[114] Nizam-ul-Mulk, the Wazir, was an eye sore for them and was forced to withdraw from the scene and leave for Deccan.[115] Her influence lasted till 1732 A.D.

During the reign of Ahmad Shah, his mother, Udham Bai (Nawab Qudsia), had great political sway. Her brother, Man Khan, a male dancer, was raised to a *mansab* of 6,000 along with a title of *Mutaqad-ud-daulah* because of her influence. Eunuch Javed Khan, her gallant, became all powerful in administration by her backing. After the murder of Javed Khan, Ahmad Shah left administration to her, himself relegating to pleasures. She became a de facto administrator, transacting all the state business. She was actively involved in the factional court rivalries of the time and made infructuous conspiracy with Turani group, headed by Intizam-ud-daulah, to kill the then Wazir, Safdar Jang. The conspiracy failed because it was leaked out to the Wazir by Malika-uz-Zamani, the other widow of Muhammad Shah.[116]

Away from the Delhi politics, in the far-flung provinces of the Mughal Empire, some ladies showed interest in the political activities of their husbands and relations. In Bengal, after the death of the Governor Murshid Quli Jafar Khan, there was a tussle for Governorship between his son-in-law, Shuja-ud-din Muhammad Khan, and latter's son, Serferaz Khan. It was through the mediation of the widow of Murshid Quli Jafar Khan that Serferaz Khan agreed to submit in favour of his father.[117] Thereafter, Alivardi Khan, the then Deputy Governor of Bihar, having an eye on the Governorship of Bengal, tried to create dissensions between Serferaz Khan and his stepbrother Taqi Khan. Although the Governor could bring reconciliation between his sons, yet being angry with Taqi Khan for his behaviour, he forbade him from coming to see and salute him. It was at the intercession of Zinat-un-nisa Begam, mother of Serferaz Khan, that the matters were settled between them.[118] When Alivardi Khan was given the Deputy Governorship of Azimabad, she, on her own, conferred on him not only rich *Khilat* (an honorific robe—it denotes ceremony of awarding the honorific robe) but also the government of Bihar from her side.[119]

Nafisa Begam, uterine sister of Serferaz Khan, was responsible for furthering the cause of her son, Murad Ali Khan. It was at her asking that her son was married to the daughter of Serferaz Khan, the Governor of Bengal after Shuja-ud-din, and was gradually raised from the post of Superintendent of the *Nawarah* (war vessels) to the Deputy Governor of Jahangirnagar (Dacca).[120] She was so important that when Alivardi Khan became the Governor of Bengal after killing her brother Serferaz (who had succeeded his father as Governor of Bengal), he went to her for begging pardon.[121]

Durdanah Begam, another sister of Serferaz Khan, was a great instigator. She was married to Murshid Quli Khan, the Governor of Orissa. Alivardi Khan, after getting the *Nizamat* of Bengal, attacked Orissa. Murshid Quli Khan wanted to patch up but Durdanah Begam wanted to avenge the death of her brother and insisted on her husband to fight, which, ultimately, led to his rout.[122]

Alivardi Khan's wife, Nawab Begam Sahib, moved along with her husband on an elephant in the battlefield and counselled him even in critical moments.[123] During the battle with Marathas under Raghoji Bhosla, she played the role of a supreme political officer. The Begam sent a political mission to Raghoji's camp for a peace treaty.[124]

Ghasiti Begam, daughter of Alivardi Khan, was also active politically. After Alivardi, Siraj-ud-daulah, the son of his youngest daughter, Amna Begam, and also his heir apparent, succeeded him.

Ghasiti Begam opposed his succession and appointed Mir Nazar Ali as Commander of her vanguard and Nawab Bairam Khan as General of her army. But, on the persuasion of her mother and noble Jagat Set, she changed her hostile attitude. Nevertheless, the Nawab imprisoned her, demolished her house and looted her treasure. Incensed at this, she secretly joined hands with the enemies of Siraj-ud-daulah, like Mir Jafar Khan. Mir Jafar became the Nawab after killing Siraj-ud-daulah and soon after, he once again captured Ghasiti Begam, her sister Amna Begam (mother of Siraj-ud-daulah) and her other relations. Both the sisters were thrown overboard in the river.[125]

The above survey proves that politics was the privilege and pastime of the women belonging to royalty and nobility and some dancing girls or concubines in their close contact in later Mughal period. The common women, at large, had no role in the political sphere.

Notes

1. A.B.M. Habibullah, 'Sultanah Raziah', *Indian Historical Quarterly* XVI No.1 (March 1940): 753.
2. Mirza Muhammad Haider Dughlat, *Tarikh-i-Rashidi*, trans. N. Elias and E. Denison Ross (Patna: Academica, 1973), 203.
3. M. Aziz Ahmad (*Political History and Institutions of the Early Turkish Empire of Delhi* (New Delhi: Oriental Books Reprint Corpn, 1972) has named her Turkan Khatun at one place (p. 191) and Shah Turkan at other (p. 188). K.A. Nizami (*Some Aspects of Religion and Politics in India During the Thirteenth Century*, 2nd ed. (New Delhi: Idarah-i-Adabiyat-i-Delli, 1974)) also named her Turkan Khatun at one place (136) and Shah Turkan at other (135). As per him, both names are of the same lady (Nizami, *Religion and Politics*, 2nd ed., Index, 419). But as per Abu-Umar-i-Usman Minhaj-ud-din Siraj (*Tabaqat-i-Nasiri*, trans. H.G. Raverty, vol. 1 (New Delhi: Oriental Books Reprint Corp., 1970), 638), Turkan Khatun was the name of Razia's mother and not of this lady.
4. Minhaj-ud-din Siraj, *Tabaqat-i-Nasiri*, trans. Raverty, vol. 1: 630, 631, note 4. He depicted her as 'head' of the Sultan's harem while at page 638, he referred Razia's mother as 'greatest' of the ladies. In the original text, the word used for Shah Turkan is '*Mahtar*' at p. 181 and that for Razia's mother is '*Bujurgtar*' at p. 185. Since the status for both could not be the same, it appears that Shah Turkan was his first concubine in point of time and age while Razia's mother was his chief wife. See also Khwaja Abdul Malik Isami, *Futuh-us-Salatin*, ed. A. Mahdi Husain (Agra: Educational Press, 1938), 128. Also, S.B.P. Nigam, *Nobility Under the Sultans of Delhi, A.D. 1206–1398* (Delhi: Munshram Manohar Lal, 1968), 28 (supports Raverty's view); M. Aziz Ahmad, *Political History*, 188 (depicts Shah Turkan as his 'Chief Wife'). Thus, both these modern authors support Raverty's view.

5. Minhaj-ud-din Siraj, *Tabaqat-i-Nasiri*, trans. Raverty, vol. 1: 631–636; Yahya Bin Ahmad Sirhindi, *Tarikh-i-Mubarak Shahi*, trans. K.K. Basu (Baroda: Abdullah Sirhindi Oriental Institute, 1932), 21–23; Muhammad Kasim Hindu Shah Ferishta, *Tarikh-i-Ferishta*, trans. J. Briggs, vol. 1 (New Delhi: Atlantic Publishers & Distributors, 1989), 120–121; Khwaja Nizam-ud-din Ahmad, *Tabaqat-i-Akbari*, trans. B. De and Baini Prashad, vol. 1 (Kolkata: The Asiatic Society, 1973), 72–74; Abdul Qadir Al Badaoni, *Muntakhabu-t-Tawarikh*, trans. S.A. Ranking, vol. 1 (New Delhi: Idarah-i-Adabiyat-i-Delli, 1973), 97–98. Strangely, Isami totally overlooked her fair and foul activities.

6. Raverty, in his translation of *Tabaqat-i -Nasiri*, converts Razia into Raziyyat by contending that Raziyyat has a meaning while Razia does not have. But, it is not necessary that a name should have a meaning. Since she is famous in history as Razia, the same has been used in this study.

7. Minhaj-ud-din Siraj, *Tabaqat-i-Nasiri*, trans. Raverty, vol. 1: 638. It is said that he even struck a coin in Razia's name to lend her popularity among the masses (A.B.M. Habibullah, *The Foundation of Muslim Rule in India* (Allahabad: Central Book Depot, 1961), 114). Nelson Wright (*Coins and Metallurgy of the Sultans of Delhi* (Delhi: Published for Govt. of India by Manager of Publications, 1936), 40, note 161A) opined that Razia, as Queen, herself issued it and dated it 1237 A.D.

8. Minhaj-ud-din Siraj, *Tabaqat-i-Nasiri*, trans. Raverty, vol. 1: 638; Nizam-ud-din Ahmad, *Tabaqat-i-Akbari*, trans. B. De and Baini Prashad, vol. 1: 74; Isami, *Futuh*, 126; Ferishta, *Tarikh-i-Ferishta*, vol. 1: 121. It is opined by some authors that he later on cancelled Razia's nomination and opted for Rukn-ud-din Firoz (Yusuf Ali, *Medieval India, Social and Economic Conditions* (London: Oxford University Press, 1932), 76). This view is not supported by any of the contemporary authorities.

9. It was only 400 years later that Shaikh Abdul Haqq expressed his surprise at the conduct of jurists and Shaikhs in giving this tacit approval to Razia's succession to throne. Nizami, *Religion and Politics*, 172; A. Schimmel, *Islam in the Indian Subcontinent* (Leiden: E. J. Brill, 1980), 12.

10. Minhaj-ud-din Siraj, *Tabaqat-i-Nasiri*, trans. Raverty, vol. 1: 638–639, note 4; also Nizam-ud-din Ahmad, *Tabaqat-i-Akbari*, trans. B. De and Baini Prashad, vol. 1: 74–75; Isami, *Futuh*, 126.

11. Ibn Batuta, *The Rehla of Ibn Batuta*, trans. Mahdi Husain (Baroda: Oriental Institute, 1953), 34, nn. 2–4, 99, 104; Isami, *Futuh*, 126–127; Minhaj-ud-din Siraj, *Tabaqat-i-Nasiri*, trans. Raverty, vol. 1: 636; also Nizami, *Religion and Politics*, 136. As per Isami, she addressed the people and it was a people's rising. *Tabqat-i-Nasiri* did not narrate about her having addressed to the people but indicated about people's rising. Nizami also considered it so, basing his view on these authorities. As per Ibn Batuta, she addressed the *annas* who after listening to her agreed to appoint her as their ruler. The word *annas* literally means 'mankind'. This signified army or soldiers and not the people in general. This meaning is supported by the word *asakar* which means 'armies' and is used in the very next line: 'When Rukn-ud-din was killed the armies (*asakar*) agreed unanimously to appoint his sister Raziya as ruler'. *Asakar* is the plural of *askar*, the Arabic form of the Persian word *lashkar* meaning 'army'. This is a convincing view since the concept of people's rising for the political upheaval was unknown during those days. It must be the rising of the soldiers and *amirs*.

In fact, Minhaj's description in very next para in the same page also points at this wherein he described how the soldiers and the *amirs* dethroned the King and Shah Turkan thereafter.

12. Minhaj-ud-din Siraj, *Tabaqat-i-Nasiri*, trans. Raverty, vol. 2: 745–746. Imad-ud-din Raihan possibly was another officer of Indian origin (M. Aziz Ahmad, *Political History*, 200, note 1).

13. Isami, *Futuh*, 130–131; Sirhindi, *Tarikh-i-Mubarak Shahi*, 25; Nizam-ud-din Ahmad, *Tabaqat-i-Akbari*, trans. B. De and Baini Prashad, vol. 1: 76–77 and also 76, note 3; Ferishta, *Tarikh-i-Ferishta*, vol. 1:122–123; Badaoni, *Muntakhabu-t-Tawarikh*, vol. 1: 120–121.

14. Minhaj-ud-din Siraj, *Tabaqat-i-Nasiri*, trans. Raverty, vol. 1: 638, also trans. Elliot and Dowson, in *History of India*, vol. II, 332, whose translation is more clear: 'but she was not born of the right sex, and so in the estimation of men all these virtues were worthless'.

15. Zia-ud-din Barani, *Tarikh-i-Firoz Shahi* (Kolkata: Bibliothica Indica, 1862), 134; Ferishta, *Tarikh-i-Ferishta*, vol. 1: 154.

16. Barani, *Tarikh*, 196–197; Nizam-ud-din Ahmad, *Tabaqat-i-Akbari*, trans. B. De and Baini Prashad, vol. 1: 139–140.

17. Ferishta, *Tarikh-i-Ferishta*, vol. 1: 171–172.

18. K.S. Lal, *History of the Khaljis* (Allahabad: The Indian Press, 1950), 42–43; also Ibn Batuta, *Rehla*, 40. Abdullah Mohammad Bin Umar Al Makki Al Asafi Ulugh Khani, however, considered that Ala-ud-din's secret love for Mahru marred his domestic peace. Ala-ud-din married her later on (*Zafar-ul-Waleh*, in *Khalji Kaleen Bharat*, trans. Rizvi, 230).

19. Barani, *Tarikh*, 238–239; also Nizam-ud-din Ahmad, *Tabaqat-i-Akbari*, trans. B. De and Baini Prashad, vol. 1: 152; Ferishta, *Tarikh-i-Ferishta*, vol. 1: 182; Amir Khusrau, *Khazain-ul-Futuh*, in *The Campaign of Ala-ud-din Khilji*, trans. Mohammad Habib (Mumbai: D.B. Taraporewala sons & Co., 1931), 38.

20. Amir Khusrau, *Dewal Rani Khizr Khan*, in *Khalji Kaleen Bharat*, trans. S.A.A. Rizvi, 173; Lal, *Khaljis*, 297–298.

21. Khusrau, *Dewal Rani*, trans. Rizvi, 173; also M. Wahid Mirza, *The Life and Works of Amir Khusrau* (Delhi: Idarah-i-Adabiyat-i-Delli, 1974), 119; Wolseley Haig, *The Cambridge History of India*, vol. 3 (New Delhi: Concept Publishing Co., 1928), 118–119 (narrates about marriage of Shadi Khan with daughter of Alps Khan).

22. Ibn Batuta, *Rehla*, 42–43. He named her Mahhaq instead of Mahru. See also Barani, *Tarikh*, 367–368 (he, however, wrote that Ala-ud-din himself had declared Khizr Khan as his heir apparent).

23. Shams Siraj Afif, *Tarikh-i-Firoz Shahi*, ed. Maulvi Vilayat Husain (Kolkata: Bibliothica Indica, 1891), 49, 54.

24. Haig, *Cambridge History*, vol. 3: 160.

25. Ishwari Prasad, *A History of the Qaraunah Turks in India*, 1st ed., vol. 1 (Allahabad: Central Book Depot, 1974), 310; see also Ferishta, *Tarikh-i-Ferishta*, vol. 2: 286–287, 294–295, 303–304; K.A.N. Sastri, *A History of South India*, 4th ed. (Delhi: Oxford University Press, 1976), 253–254.

26. Afif, *Tarikh-i-Firoz Shahi*, 45–46, 100–104; also R.C. Jauhri, *Firoz Tughluq* (Jalandhar: ABS Publications, 1990), 10, 15, 38–39.

27. Abdullah, *Tarikh-i-Daudi*, in *Uttar Taimur Kaleen Bharat*, Part I, trans. S.A.A. Rizvi, 246–247; Ahmad Yadgar, *Tarikh-i-Shahi*, in *Uttar Taimur*, trans. Rizvi, Part I, 311; Rizkullah Mushtaqi, *Waqiat-i-Mushtaqi*, in *Uttar Taimur Kaleen Bharat*, Part I, trans. Rizvi (Aligarh: Aligarh Muslim University, 1958–1959), 95–96 (he called her Bibi Mastu); also Abdul Halim, *History of the Lodi Sultans of Delhi and Agra*, rpt. (New Delhi: Idarah-i-Adabiyat-i-Delli, 1974), 21 (he depicted her as widow of Sultan Shah Lodi and mother-in-law of Bahlol Lodi).

28. S.A. Halim, 'Harem Influence in the 15th Century Politics of India', *Muslim University Journal* II (October, 1938): 49–52.

29. Niamatullah, *Tarikh-i-Khan Jahani wa Makhzan-i-Afghana*, in *Niamtullah's History of the Afghans*, trans. N.B. Roy (Kolkata: Shantiniketan, 1958), 38; Nizam-ud-din Ahmad, *Tabaqat-i-Akbari*, trans. B. De and Baini Prashad, vol. 1: 342–343; Ferishta, *Tarikh-i-Ferishta*, vol. 1: 323–324; Abdullah, *Tarikh-i-Daudi*, 249; Halim, *Lodi Sultans*, 27; Halim, 'Harem Influence', 54–55.

30. Niamatullah, Introduction, xxiv; Ferishta, *Tarikh-i-Ferishta*, vol. 1: 328–329 (named her Bibi Zeina). Haig (*Cambridge History*, vol. 3: 235) named her Ziba; Yadgar (*Tarikh-i-Shahi*, 315) called her Hema; Halim (*Lodi Sultans*, 58) called her Bibi Sonari.

31. Niamatullah, Introduction, xxiv; Halim, *Lodi Sultans*, 59; K.S. Lal, *Twilight of the Sultanate* (Bombay: Asia Publishing House, 1963), 163.

32. Zahir-ud-din Babur, *Babur Nama or Memoirs of Babur*, trans. A.S. Beveridge, vol 2., rpt. (New Delhi: Oriental Books Reprint Corpn., 1970), 541–543.

33. Sarwani, *Tarikh-i-Sher Shahi*, trans. B.P. Ambashthya (Patna: K.P. Jayaswal Research Institute, 1974), 108; A.S. Beveridge, Appendix A, in Gulbadan's *Humayun Nama* (New Delhi: Idarah-i-Adabiyat-i-Delli, 1972), 226

34. Halim, 'Harem Influence', 52–54. See also Yogeshwar Tewari, 'Influence of Harem on Politics in the Sultanate Period', in *Region in Indian History*, ed. Mahendra Pratapa and S.Z.H. Jafri (New Delhi: Anamika Publishers & Distributors (P)Ltd., 1908), 135.

35. Nizam-ud-din Ahmad, *Tabaqat-i -Akbari*, trans. B. De and Baini Prashad, Part I, vol. 3: 460–463; Halim, 'Harem Influence', 57–58. Also, Yogeshwar Tewari, 'Influence of Harem', 135.

36. Nizam-ud-din Ahmad, *Tabaqat-i-Akbari*, trans. B. De and Baini Prashad, Part II, vol. 3: 554–562, 566; Halim, 'Harem Influence', 58–60.

37. Nizam-ud-din Ahmad, *Tabaqat-i-Akbari*, trans. B. De and Baini Prashad, Part I, vol. 3: 86.

38. Nizam-ud-din Ahmad, *Tabaqat-i-Akbari*, trans. B. De and Baini Prashad, Part I, vol. 3: 87–89 and note 1 to 89; Part II, vol. 3: 534–535 and note 2 to 534.

39. Nizam-ud-din Ahmad, *Tabaqat-i-Akbari*, trans. B. De and Baini Prashad, Part I, vol. 3: 112.

40. Babur, *Babur Nama*, vol. 1: 43.

41. R. Williams, *An Empire Builder of the Sixteenth Century* (London: Longman, 1918), 34–36.

42. Babur, *Babur Nama*, vol. 1: 21.

43. Babur, *Babur Nama*, vol. 1: 358.

44. Ishwari Prasad, *The Life and Times of Humayun*, rpt. (Mumbai: Orient Longmans, 1956), 33–34, 36, 38; also Williams, *An Empire Builder*, 171–172.

45. S.K. Banerji, *Humayun Badshah* (Lucknow: Maxwell Company, 1941), 2, 314.

46. This was one of the most ferocious among the nomadic clans of the time. They inhabited the mountainous region, north of Kabul river and stretched west from the Indus. They created a lot of problems for Babur (Frederick Augustus, *The Emperor Akbar—A Contribution Towards the History of India in the 16th Century*, trans. A.S. Beveridge, vol. 2 (New Delhi: Atlantic Publishers and Distributors, 1989), 167, 171).

47. Babur, *Babur Nama*, vol. 1: 375; S.K. Banerji, *Humayun Badshah*, vol. 2 (Lucknow: Maxwell Company, 1941), 321–322.

48. Prasad, *Humayun*, 123 and note 2; Abul Fazl, *Akbar Nama*, trans. H. Beveridge, vol. 1 (New Delhi: Ess Ess Publications, 1977), 341.

49. Prasad, *Humayun*, 257. See also Rumer Godden, *Gulbadan-Portrait of a Rose Princess at Mughal Court* (London: MacMillan & Co., 1980), 87 (for Hamida portrait).

50. Beveridge, Introduction to Gulbadan's *Humayun Nama*, 63.

51. Augustus, *The Emperor Akbar*, vol. 1: 101–102; Abul Fazl, *Akbar Nama*, vol. 2: 288–293, 317–319; Samsam ud-daulah Shah Nawaz Khan and Abdul Hayy, *Maasir-ul-Umara*, vol. 1 (Patna: Janki Prakashan, 1979), 134–139; also V.A. Smith, *Akbar: The Great Mogul (1542–1605)*, 3rd Indian Print (New Delhi, 1966), 46–47; Wolseley Haig, *The Cambridge History of India*, ed. Richard Burn, vol. 4 (London: Cambridge University Press, 1937), 85.

52. Beveridge, Appendix A, in Gulbadan's *Humayun Nama*, 251.

53. Gulbadan, *Humayun Nama*, 160–161; also Prasad, *Humayun*, 216. See also Soma Mukherjee, *Royal Mughal Ladies and their Contributions* (New Delhi: Gyan Publishing House, 2001), 121.

54. Abul Fazl, *Akbar Nama*, vol. 1: 338–339; Prasad, *Humayun*, 129.

55. Augustus, *The Emperor Akbar*, vol. 1: 84, 94; Haig, *Cambridge History*, vol. 4: 79–84; Smith, *Akbar*, 35, 48, R.P. Tripathi, *Rise and Fall of the Mughal Empire* (Allahabad: Central Book Depot, 1987), 183; S.R. Sharma, *Mughal Empire in India*, rpt. (Agra: Stoddard Press, 1971), 119; A.L. Srivastava, *Akbar the Great*, vol. 1 (Agra: Shiva Lal Agarwala, 1962), 71–72; Ishwari Prasad, *A Short History of Muslim Rule in India*, 1st ed. (Allahabad: The Indian Press Ltd., 1939), 343–344; Rekha Mishra, *Women in Mughal India* (Allahabad: Munshiram Manohar Lal, 1967), 29.

56. Nizam-ud-din Ahmad, *Tabqat-i-.Akbari*, trans. B. De and Baini Prashad, vol. 2: 237–238; Badaoni, *Muntakhabu-t-Tawarikh*, vol. 2: 30–31; Augustus, *The Emperor Akbar*, vol.1: 78–84; Haig, *Cambridge History*, vol. 4: 78–79; Abul Fazl, *Akbar Nama*, vol. 2: 141, 161–167; Tripathi, *Rise and Fall*, 178–183; Srivastava, *Akbar*, vol. 1: 40–42); M.S. Elphinstone, *The History of India*, rpt. (Allahabad: Kitab Mahal, 1966), 431–433; Shah Nawaz Khan and Hayy, *Maasir*, vol. 1: 372–373.

57. Nizam-ud-din Ahmad, *Tabaqat-i-Akbari*, trans. B. De and Baini Prashad, vol. 2: 237–238; Ferishta, *Tarikh-i-Ferishta*, vol. 2: 119; Shah Nawaz Khan and Hayy, *Maasir*, Part 2, vol. 2: 846; Haig, *Cambridge History*, vol. 4: 77; Smith, *Akbar*, 32–33; Augustus, *The Emperor Akbar*, vol. 1: 82–83.

58. Abul Fazl, *Akbar Nama*, vol. 2: 214, 218–221; Shah Nawaz Khan and Hayy, *Maasir*, vol. 1: 146;Augustus, *The Emperor Akbar*, vol. 1: 90–94; Haig, *Cambridge History*, vol. 4: 79–81; Smith, *Akbar*, 36–38.

59. Abul Fazl, *Akbar Nama* vol. 2: 235, 268–275; Shah Nawaz Khan and Hayy, *Maasir*, vol. 1: 147–148; Haig, *Cambridge History*, vol. 4: 81. Also Mohammad Yasin, *A Social History of Islamic India (1605–1748)* (Lucknow: The Upper India Publishing House, 1958), 128. He opined, 'Maham's failure to rise above the weakness of a mother made her unworthy of rule'.

60. Abul Fazl, *Akbar Nama*, vol. 3: 1222–1223, 1228, 1230.

61. Nur-ud-din Jahangir, *Tuzuk-i-Jahangiri*, vol. 1 (New Delhi: Munshiram Manoharlal, 1968), 55–56, 252; also Jahangir, *Wakiat-i-Jahangiri*, trans. Elliot and Dowson, vol. VI (Allahabad: Kitab Mahal, 1964), 294–295, 336–337.

62. Shah Nawaz Khan and Hayy, *Maasir*, vol. 1: 328; Abul Fazl, *Ain-i-Akbari*, vol. 1 (New Delhi: Crown Publications, 1988), 345.

63. Beni Prasad, *History of Jahangir*, 3rd ed. (Allahabad: The Indian Press Ltd, 1940), 147. See also Francisco Pelsaert, *The Remonstrantie or Jahangir's India*, trans. W.H. Moreland and P. Geyl, rpt. (New Delhi: Idarah-i-Adabiyat-i-Delli, 1972), 50, 51, 53; Pietro Della Valle, *Travels of Pietro Della Valle in India*, trans. G. Havers, ed. Edward Grey (London: Hakluyt Society, 1892), 54; Edward Terry, in *Early Travels in India*, ed. William Foster (New Delhi: S. Chand & Co., 1968), 329; Anonymous, *Intikhab-i-Jahangir Shahi*, trans. Elliot and Dowson, vol. VI, 451; Mutamad Khan, *Iqbalnama-i-Jahangiri*, trans. Elliot and Dowson, vol. VI, 405. See also Anonymous, *Tarikh-i-Salim Shahi*, in *Memoirs of the Emperor Jahangir Written by Himself*, trans. David Price (New Delhi: Rare Books, 1904), 46–47 (wherein Jahangir has written, 'the whole concern of my household, whether gold or jewels, is under her sole and entire management' and that she is 'the inseparable companion of all my cares').

64. Stanley Lanepoole, *Mediaeval India Under the Mohammedan Rule (A.D. 712–1764)*, (Delhi: Seema Publication, 1980), 298.

65. Mutamad Khan, *Iqbalnama-i-Jahangiri*, 405; Beni Prasad, *History of Jahangir*, 159. See also S.A. Tirmizi, *Edicts of the Mughal Harem* (Delhi: Idarah-i-Adabiyat-i-Delli, 1979), 20–53 (for Nur Jahan's extent of influence in administration).

66. See also Chapter 6 for details.

67. Beni Prasad, *History of Jahangir*, 274. See also R.P. Khosla, *Mughal Kingship and Nobility* (Allahabad: The Indian Press, 1934), 100–104 (for a detailed account of Nur Jahan's role in the fratricidal war that followed Jahangir's death).

68. Jahangir, *Tuzuk*, vol. 2: 235; Ghulam Husain Salim, *Riyazu-s-Salatin*, trans. Abdus Salam (New Delhi: Idarah-i-Adabiyat-i-Delli, 1975), 181; William Foster, ed., *The English Factories in India (1622–23)* (Oxford, 1906–1927), 99; Haig, *Cambridge History*, vol. 4: 171; Beni Prasad, *History of Jahangir*, 300.

69. Anonymous, *Intikhab-i-Jahangir Shahi*, trans. Elliot and Dowson, vol. VI, 451–452; Beni Prasad, *History of Jahangir*, 338–339; Khosla, *Mughal Kingship*, 262–264.

70. Mutamad Khan, *Iqbalnama-i-Jahangiri*, 435–438; Shah Nawaz Khan and Hayy, *Maasir*, vol. 1: 289–292; Beni Prasad, *History of Jahangir*, 368, 370–373; Haig, *Cambridge History*, vol. 4: 183–184; B.P. Saksena, *History of Shahjahan of Dihli* (Allahabad: Central Book Depot, 1958), 56-62.

71. Foster, ed., *English Factories* (1624–1629), 241.

72. J.N., Chowdhuri, 'Mumtaz Mahall', *Islamic Culture* XI (July 1937): 377. J.N. Sarkar, *Studies in Aurangzib's Reign* (Kolkata: M.C. Sarkar & Sons, 1933), 9; G. Yazdani, 'Jahanara', *Journal of Punjab Historical Society* II (1912): 153.

73. Muhammad Hashim Khafi Khan, *Muntakhab-al-Lubab*, ed. Maulvi Kabir-ud-din Ahmad, vol. 1 (Kolkata: Bibliothica Indica, 1869), 393; Muhammad Amin Qazwini, *Badshah Nama*, Aligarh Transcript, Part II (Aligarh: Aligarh Muslim University), fols 227, 277; Shah Nawaz Khan and Hayy, *Maasir*, Part II, vol. 2: 689–691; Foster, ed., *English Factories* (1624–1629), 206; also Saksena, *History of Shahjahan*, 61; M.S. Commissariat, *A History of Gujrat*, vol. 2 (Bombay: Orient Longmans, 1957), 107–108. Saif Khan was married to Malika Banu, real sister of Mumtaz Mahal.

74. Foster, ed., *English Factories* (1624–1629), 189, 191.

75. Niccolao Manucci, *Storia Do Mogor or Mogul India*, trans. William Irvine, vol. 1 (New Delhi: Atlantic Publishers and Distributors, 1989), 176; Saksena, *History of Shahjahan*, 106–107, note 10.

76. Francois Bernier, *Travels in the Mogul Empire, A.D. 1656–1668*, 2nd ed. (New Delhi: S. Chand & Co., 1968), 11; Manucci, *Storia Do Mogor*, vol. 1: 208; J.B. Tavernier, *Travels in India by Jean Baptiste Tavernier*, trans. V. Ball, ed. William Crooke, vol. 1 (New Delhi: Oriental Books Reprint Corpn., 1977), 15.

77. Tavernier, *Travels in India*, vol. 1: 14–15.

78. K.R. Qanungo, *Dara Shukoh*, vol. 1 (Calcutta, 1952), 136–137.

79. J.N. Sarkar, *History of Aurangzib*, 1st Imp., vol. 1 (New Delhi: New Orient Longman Ltd., 1972–1974), 130–131, 208; also Bernier, *Mogul Empire*, 20–21; Qanungo, *Dara*, vol. 1: 137–138; Tripathi, *Rise and Fall*, 468–472 (he considers their impact only partly true. Shah Jahan himself did not want to entangle his forces in a prolonged fight).

80. Aurangzeb, 'Rukkat-i-Alamgiri', Lytton Collection (Aligarh: Aligarh Muslim University), fols 200a and 200b; Aurangzeb, 'Adab-i-Alamgiri', Abdus Salam Collection (Aligarh: Aligarh Muslim University), fols. 197a, 197b, 200a, 200b.

81. Aurangzeb, 'Rukkat-i-Alamgiri', fols. 200b and 201b, 198b, 199a, resp.

82. Shah Nawaz Khan and Hayy, *Maasir*, Part II, vol. 2: 1021–1022.

83. Foster, ed. (*English Factories* (1646–1659), 219–220) mentioned how one Hakikat Khan assured the Dutch to procure a *nishan* from Jahanara for helping them to recover their debt from Chattarsal); (1651–1654), 50 (about David's visit to Jahanara to pay respect to her immediately after landing in India); (1655–1660), 15, 73–74 (how with the help of her *nishan*, Dutch could recover their insurance money).

84. Aqil Khan Razi, *Waqiat-i-Alamgiri*, ed. Maulvi Haji Zafar Hasan (Delhi: Aligarh Historical Institute, 1946), 16–17, 28; Ishwar Dass Nagar, *Futuhat-i-Alamgiri*, trans., ed. Tasneem Ahmad (New Delhi: Idarah-i-Adabiyat-i-Delli, 1978), 36–37; Tavernier, *Travels in India*, vol. 1: 299; Sarkar, *Aurangzib*, vol. 2: 258, 264; Bernier, *Mogul Empire*, 61, 64.

85. Khafi Khan, *Muntakhab-al-Lubab*, Part 2, 188; Sarkar, *Aurangzib*, vol. 3: 36.

86. Tavernier, *Travels in India*, vol. 1: 299; Manucci, *Storia Do Mogor*, vol. 2: 117–118; Sarkar, *Aurangzib*, vol. 3: 37.

87. Nagar, *Futuhat-i-Alamgiri*, 93–94.

88. Manucci, *Storia Do Mogor*, vol. 3: 274–276.

89. Sarkar, *Aurangzib*, vol. 3: 38.

90. Manucci, *Storia Do Mogor*, vol. 1: 186, 189, respectively.

91. Tavernier, *Travels in India*, vol. 1: 299.

92. Bernier, *Mogul Empire*, 61, 65, 100, respectively.

93. Bernier, *Mogul Empire*, 125; Khosla, *Mughal Kingship*, 44.

94. Bernier, *Mogul Empire*, 123; Manucci, *Storia Do Mogor*, vol. 2: 49–51, 54–55; Tavernier, *Travels in India*, vol. 1: 300. See also Sarkar, *Aurangzib*, vol. 3: 38.
95. Zeb-un-Nisa, *Diwan-i-Makhfi*, in *The Diwan of Zeb-un-Nissa*, Introduction, trans. Magan Lal and Jessie Duncan (London: Westbrook, 1913), 11.
96. Aurangzeb, 'Rukkat-i-Alamgiri', fols. 313a, 133b.
97. Aurangzeb, *Rukkat*, 160, note 1.
98. Hamid-ud-din Khan, *Ahkam-i-Alamgiri*, in *Anecdotes of Aurangzib*, trans. J.N. Sarkar (Kolkata: M.C. Sarkar, 1949), 43.
99. Zeb-un-Nisa, *Diwan-i-Makhfi*, trans. Magan Lal and Jessie Duncan, Introduction, 17; Maharani Sunity Devee, *The Beautiful Mogul Princesses* (Calcutta: Thacker & Spink, 1918), 74–78; Soma Mukherjee, *Royal Mughal Ladies*, 156.
100. Must'ad Khan, *Maasir-i-Alamgiri*, trans., ann. J.N. Sarkar (Kolkata: Royal Asiatic Society of Bengal, 1947), 126; Nagar, *Futuhat-i-Alamgiri*, 182; Sarkar, *Aurangzib*, vol. 3: 35; Sarkar, *Studies*, 87–88.
101. Must'ad Khan, *Maasir-i-Alamgiri*, 217; Sarkar, *Aurangzib*, vol. 5: 73; Hamid-ud-din, *Ahkam-i-Alamgiri*, 64–65.
102. G.S. Sardesai, *New History of the Marathas*, vol. 1 (Bombay: Phoenix, 1946), 350, 355.
103. Sarkar, *Aurangzib*, vol. 1: 38; Haig, *Cambridge History*, vol. 4: 302.
104. Sarkar, *Aurangzib*, vol. 1: 35; Manucci, *Storia Do Mogor*, vol. 2: 296, 438.
105. Nagar, *Futuhat-i-Alamgiri*, 93.
106. Khafi Khan, *Muntakhab-al-Lubab*, Part 2, 264; Must'ad Khan, *Maasir-i-Alamgiri*, 63, 178–179 (for Muazzam), 17, 74 (for Muhammad Sultan); also Sarkar, *Aurangzib*, vol. 1: 34.
107. Gholam Hussein Khan, *Siyar-ul-Mutakherin*, in *The History of Later Mughals Seir Mutakherin*, trans. Nota Manus, vol. 1 (Lahore: Oriental Publishers and Book Sellers, 1975), 36–37, also trans. J. Briggs, *The History of Mohamedan Power in India* (New Delhi: Idarah-i-Adabiyat-i-Delli, 1973), 31–32; Nur-ud-din Faruqi, 'Jahandar Nama', Rotograph (Aligarh: Aligarh Muslim University), ff. 37a, 37b (Niamat Khan depicted as brother of Lal Kanwar and pining for Governorship of Multan); Khafi Khan, *Muntakhab-al-Lubab*, Part 2, 689–690 (held Khoshal Khan's *mansab* as 5,000 + 3,000. His narration too differed a little bit. As per him, Zulfiqar Khan explained to the Emperor that he wanted the bribe of guitar players and drawing masters (*ustad-i-nakkashi*) in order to make the nobles to learn their art and be fit for high offices which the Emperor had started bestowing on such persons). See also William Irvine, *Later Mughals*, vol. 1 (Kolkata: M.C. Sarkar & Sons, 1922), 193–194; Satish Chandra, *Parties and Politics at the Mughal Court* (New Delhi: People's Publishing House, 1979), 72.
108. Hussein Khan, *Siyar*, trans. Manus, vol. 1: 37–39, also trans. Briggs, 32–34; Irvine, *Later Mughals*, vol. 1: 194–195. See also Haig, *Cambridge History*, vol. 4: 326.
109. Hussein Khan, *Siyar*, trans. Manus, vol. 1: 42–43, also trans. Briggs, 35–37.
110. Hussein Khan, *Siyar*, trans. Manus, vol. 1: 47, also trans. Briggs, 41; Satish Chandra, *Parties and Politics*, 91–92; Irvine, *Later Mughals*, vol. 1: 206; Shah Nawaz Khan and Hayy, *Maasir*, vol. 1: 710.
111. Zahir-ud-din Malik, *A Mughal Statesman of the Eighteenth Century* (Bombay: Asia Publishing House, 1973), 57–59, also 407, note 1 (for her name as Fakhr-un-nisa); Irvine, *Later Mughals*, vol. 2: 3–4, 57, 60–61; Satish Chandra, *Parties and Politics*, 157.

112. Shah Nawaz Khan and Hayy, *Maasir*, Part II, vol. 2: 606; Irvine, *Later Mughals*, vol. 2: 265; Satish Chandra, *Parties and Politics*, 171; Malik, *A Mughal Statesman*, 54.

113. Irvine, *Later Mughals*, vol. 2: 265; also Malik, *A Mughal Statesman*, 54 (it is narrated that she 'revelled in all the license of sovereign power, exceeded the bond of public and private virtue... and extracted money from all sources for the Emperor').

114. Khafi Khan, *Muntakhab-al-Lubab*, Part 2, 940, 951; Hussein Khan, *Siyar*, trans. Manus, vol. 1: 244, also trans. Briggs, 223; Shah Nawaz Khan and Hayy, *Maasir*, Part II, vol. 2: 606. See also Irvine, *Later Mughals*, vol. 2: 131, 265–266; Malik, *A Mughal Statesman*, 49–50; Satish Chandra, *Parties and Politics*, 213 (as per him, Khwaja Khidmatgar was averse to bribery, hence, he fell from the group).

115. Khafi Khan, *Muntakhab-al-Lubab*, Part II, 946–947; Irvine, *Later Mughals*, vol. 2: 131–133; Satish Chandra, *Parties and Politics*, 174; Malik, *A Mughal Statesman*, 19–20, 49.

116. J.N. Sarkar, *Fall of the Mughal Empire*, vol. 1 (Kolkata: M.C. Sarkar & Sons, 1966), 209–212, 286–287; A.L. Srivastava, *The First Two Nawabs of Awadh*, 2nd ed. (Agra, 1954), 208–213.

117. Salim, *Riyazu-s*, 288; C. Stewart, *The History of Bengal* (Delhi: Orient Publishers, 1971), 414; J.N. Sarkar, ed., *History of Bengal* (Patna: Academica Asiatica, 1973), 422–423. Jafar Khan died in 1727 A.D./1139 A.H. (Karam Ali, *Muzaffarnamah*, trans. J.N. Sarkar [Calcutta: Asiatic Society, 1952], 13). But Stewart (*History of Bengal*, 413) gave this date as 1725 A.D.

118. Salim, *Riyazu-s*, 297–298. As per the author of *Siyar-ul-Mutakherin*, the name of mother of Serferaz Khan was Zinat-un-nisa and she was the daughter of Murshid Quli Jafar Khan (Hussein Khan, *Siyar*, trans. Manus, vol. 1: 274–275).

119. Hussein Khan, *Siyar*, trans. Manus, vol. 1: 281–282.

120. Salim, *Riyazu-s*, 304–305 and nn. 1, 3; also Hussein Khan, *Siyar*, trans. Manus, vol. 1: 340 (he referred to Nafisa Begam not as sister, but as the mother of Serferaz Khan, though at other place, he has given the name of his mother as Zinat-un-nisa; see reference 118 above).

121. Yusuf Ali, *Ahwal-i-Mahabat-Jang*, in *Bengal Nawabs*, trans. J.N. Sarkar (Calcutta: Asiatic Society, 1952), 89–90 (he also shows her as sister of Serferaz Khan); Salim, *Riyazu-s*, 320, note 2, 339, note 1; also Sarkar, ed., *History of Bengal*, 442; K.K. Datta, *Alivardi and His Times* (Calcutta: Calcutta University, 1939), 36–37.

122. Hussein Khan, *Siyar*, trans. Manus, vol. 1: 349–350; Stewart, *History of Bengal*, 449.

123. Salim, *Riyazu-s*, 329 and note 1, 339, note 1; Datta, *Alivardi*, 246–247.

124. Yusuf Ali, *Ahwal*, 116; Hussein Khan, *Siyar*, trans. Manus, vol. 2: 11; Sarkar, *Fall*, vol. 1: 76–77.

125. Salim, *Riyazu-s*, 363, 365, note 1, 381–382; Muhammad Ali Khan, *Tarikh-i-Muzaffari*, trans. Elliot and Dowson, in *History of India*, vol. VIII (Allahabad: Kitab Mahal, 1964), 328; Fakir Muhammad, *Jami'u-T-Tawarikh*, trans. Elliot and Dowson, in *History of India*, vol. VIII, 428–429; Hussein Khan, *Siyar*, trans. Manus, vol. 2: 185–186, 228, 281, 370–371.

6

Cultural Context

In the domain of culture, the common Muslim women had little to contribute because of their educational backwardness. The cultivation of fine arts, education and other aesthetic pursuits remained the privilege of the ladies of the high society. The queens, princesses and the wives of nobles played a significant role in these spheres.

Education

The medieval age did not provide conducive environment for the educational growth of the Muslim women in India. The social restrictions on these women, their confinement within harem and the prevalence of customs like early marriage and purdah had already clipped their wings and closed the outer world for them. Marriage became their highest goal in life and housekeeping, rearing up children and obeying the command of their respective husband were their greatest virtues. The horizon of education was virtually closed for them since it was considered a threat to their blissful innocence, as it exposed the womenfolk to undesirable literature.[1] With such social attitude and apathy, mass female education became practically unknown. It was confined to ladies of royalty and nobility and, to some extent, to those belonging to the middle class.

For the middle class ladies, arrangements to impart a little of primary education through *maktabs* in a Mosque or room or *verandah* of a mausoleum or house of a teacher were made. These *maktabs* were maintained through the donations of the rich people of the vicinity, although some even got help from provincial treasury. For example, it is mentioned that Jahangir promulgated a regulation that on the death of a rich man or traveller without any heir, his property would escheat to the crown, to be used for building and repairing madrasas and monasteries. It is also mentioned on the authority of *Tarikh-i-Jan-Jahan* that Jahangir, after his accession, got repaired those madrasas, which were of disuse for 30 years and 'filled them with students and professors'.[2] The girls were sent to *maktabs* with a ceremony, which was common for both boys and girls. When they commenced their education in *maktab*, besides the feasting, the teacher wrote an *Idi* (a verse on something relating to festival Id) or a blessing for the child on a coloured paper known as *Zarfishani*, which they were made to read to their parents. After this, the parents gave some presents to the teacher.[3] Although modern writers like J.N. Sarkar opine that there were no joint classes even for very small children, however, contemporary evidence shows that boys and girls studied together at the primary level in *maktabs*. There are paintings showing joint studies of boys and girls of the royal family at Kabul and also a female teacher, teaching a boy.[4] After primary education, secondary and higher education was imparted in *khanqahs* (mostly attached to mosques, being run by Muslim missionaries) and madrasas (mostly attached to mosques). But due to purdah, girls did not receive their education in these institutions. They were shifted to the higher schools, exclusively meant for girls thereafter, where they learnt practical arts concerning household duties like cooking, sewing, nursing children and spinning from some elderly ladies.[5]

The subjects taught in the *maktabs* were reading, writing, numerals, elementary arithmetic and ethics, reading Gulistan, Bostan and most important being the study of the Quran.[6] When they finished the reading of the Quran, the occasion was celebrated with great enthusiasm. The teacher was given presents by the parents and a half-day holiday was granted to the whole *maktab*.[7] At times, the *maktabs* were run in private houses by elderly ladies, especially widows of the middle class families, who imparted education to poor girls, considering it an act of piety.[8] Some others worked for girls' education out of their benevolence.[9] In general, while a number of educational institutions were opened both during the sultanate and Mughal periods for the boys, it appears that the schooling of the girls remained, more or less, a private affair in the Delhi empire and also in the adjoining Muslim principalities.[10] We get only a few exceptions. Ibn Batuta writes that the sultan of Hinwar was keenly interested in the education of his female subjects. He noticed 13 girls' schools in his capital and also informed that all the women of that place knew the Quran by heart.[11] Similarly, among the 15,000 ladies in the seraglio of Sultan Ghias-ud-din of Malwa (1463–100 A.D.), there were ladies who were apt in different fields like use of shield, use of musical instruments, wrestling, dancing, sewing, weaving, crafting, teaching and all other professions and trades. It is learnt that the king engaged tutors to train them and the presence of school mistresses within the harem is a testimony to this. About 70 women in his harem were so expert in reading of the Quran that they recited it at a stretch while the Sultan wore his garments.[12]

Higher education for ladies was confined to those belonging to royalty and upper class society. For this purpose, the well-to-do, as per their discretion, engaged at home scholarly ladies and learned old men while the royal harem inmates had matrons and superintendents within the harem.[13] There were many private institutions for imparting such education.[14] The main purpose of such education was moral and mental development of these ladies, so as to make them faithful wives, good mothers, efficient in household work and religious aspects. Therefore, Bakhtawar Khan, the author of *Mirat-i-Alam*, writes that the harem ladies in general were taught the tenets of religion only.[15] However, the ladies of royalty and nobility were taught subjects of their interest, ambition and future aims. They were fond of poetry, Shaikh Sadi's *Gulistan* and *Bostan*, books on morals, study of the Quran and *Hadis*, Persian and Arabic literature, elementary arithmetic, theology and mathematics. Some of them also acquired proficiency in calligraphy, others in medicine and treatment, by experience, family background or education and some in law. The art of administration was also taught to some royal ladies.[16]

The ladies of the poor and the lower classes mostly remained illiterate. Because of their poverty, they had to be busy with their household chores and rearing up of children. Those belonging to agricultural, artisan and working class also helped their menfolk in their respective activities. They hardly had time for intellectual pursuit. If, at all, they pursued anything, it was confined to reading Holy Quran.[17]

During the sultanate period, some of the royal ladies acquired proficiency in different fields including use of arms. Amir Khusrau has laid emphasis on royal ladies to have proficiency in military education.[18] Razia was one such person and was perfect in her military training, besides, being proficient in reading the Quran that she could do with correct pronunciation, affirmed Ferishta.[19] She was also known as a great patron of men of letters. She entrusted

Minhaj-us-Siraj with the task of looking after the *Madrasa-i-Nasiriya* in the capital. It was under her reign that Muizzi college at Delhi became a flourishing centre of learning.[20] She herself was a poetess and composed verses under the pen name of *'Shirin'*.[21] Another lady, Bibi Raji of Jaunpur, was known for her patronage to learned men and for encouraging the cause of education. She not only opened a number of madrasas and colleges, but also provided stipends to the students and teachers.[22] It was due to her efforts that Jaunpur became a centre of education during her lifetime.

The Mughals were keen on educating their women. The girls of the palace assembled together at one place within the palace to receive rudimentary knowledge. Sometimes, the school mistress and the governess were combined in one person called *Atun Mama*.[23] They have been mentioned by the contemporaries frequently in their narrations. Monserrate, for instance, writes, 'He (Akbar) gives very great care and attention to the education of the princesses.... They are taught to read and write and trained in other ways by matrons'. Similarly, Manucci narrated, 'Among them are some who teach reading and writing to the princesses, and usually, what they dictate to them are amorous verses. Or the ladies obtain relaxation in reading books called "*Gulistan*" and "*Bostan*"....' Still another contemporary Ishwar Dass Nagar, author of *Futuhat-i-Alamgiri*, mentioned about engagement of lady tutors.[24] Akbar opened a school in his palace at Fatehpur Sikri. The school was for the education of princesses and had learned women, particularly Persians, to teach them. There is a painting showing a Mughal princess taking her lessons.[25] Aurangzeb was very particular about training his daughters in the doctrines of religion and pious virtues, whom he himself taught. Not only them but all the ladies of his harem learnt doctrines of religion and reading of the Quran and acquiring virtues.[26] Since most of the Mughal princesses remained unmarried, they had sufficient time for learning.

Many princesses excelled in the educational field. The first known royal lady with literary pursuits was Gulbadan Begam. Well versed both in Persian and Turki, she had a poetic temperament and composed many verses; she was accomplished in calligraphy and is described as a 'pen woman'.[27] Her fame rested on her *Humayun Nama*, which is highly acclaimed by the contemporary and also by modern writers. So much so that Nizami considers it superior to even *Tuzuk-i-Jahangiri* and *Rukkat-i-Alamgiri* in its 'inimitable spontaneity, short and pithy sentences and colloquial touch'. Written in simple Persian, it is immortal as a piece of historical work.

Beveridge wrote, 'The book is its sole witness' and further praised her literary accomplishments by remarking,

> It is not only her book that lets us know she had a lively mind, but the fact of its composition at an age when wits are apt to be rusted by domestic peace. Only a light that was strong in childhood would have burned so long to guide her unaccustomed pen after half a century of life....[28]

To prop up her interest in studies, she maintained a big personal library with rich collection gathered from different parts of the country.[29]

The other educated ladies of times of Babur and Humayun, mentioned by Gulbadan, are Babur's second daughter Gulrukh Begam, Humayun's wife Bega Begam, Gulbadan's mother Dildar Begam and Aesha Sultan Begam. Gulbadan talks very highly of her mother, who was considered to be a very sensible woman.[30] Gulrukh Begam and Aesha Sultan Begam were accomplished poetesses.[31] Bega Begam founded a college near the tomb of her husband.[32]

Another distinguished lady was Salima Sultan Begam, daughter of Gulrukh Begam and Mirza Nur-ud-din Muhammad. Proficient in Persian, she was an accomplished and renowned poetess of her time under the pen name of *Makhfi* meaning 'concealed'. In *Babur Nama*, she has been referred to as a lady of charm and literary accomplishments. Abdus Hayy, author of *maasir-ul-Umara*, quotes one of her couplets:

> In my passion I called thy lock the 'thread of life'
>
> I was wild and so uttered such an expression.[33]

She had a great love for books and for that she not only maintained a personal library, but freely used Akbar's library as well.[34]

Hamida Banu had good knowledge of medicine and treatment.[35]

Next in line was Maham Anaga, who was well educated and a great patron of learning. She built a madrasa (college) called *Khair-ul-Manzil* that also had a mosque attached to it.[36]

Taj Begam, the wife of Akbar, and Begam Badshah Mahal, wife of Jahangir, were reported to be well versed in the Hindi poetry.[37]

Next important lady in this field was Nur Jahan. Well versed in Persian and Arabic languages, she had a great fascination for the Persian poetry and was herself a poetess under the pen name of *Makhfi*. She was adept in composing extempore verses and participated in poetic contests.[38] She was fond of reading books and maintained a rich library of her own.[39] Beni Prasad wrote:

> Nature had endowed her with a quick understanding, piercing intellect, a versatile temper and a sound common-sense. Education had developed the gifts of nature in no common degree. She was versed in Persian literature and composed verses, limpid and flowing, which assisted her in capturing the heart of her husband.[40]

Tuzuk-i-Jahangiri recorded that she was also having knowledge of medicine.[41] And with all her accomplishments, she rendered great service to the development of education during her time. Many of her courtiers were able poetesses who were patronised by her, one of them being Mehr Harwi (Hardi).[42]

Mumtaz Mahal was equally adept in Persian and Arabic as well as in writing poetry, besides being a patron of the learned and scholars. Vansidhara Mishra, a renowned Sanskrit poet of the time, was a favourite of the queen.[43] She utilised her knowledge as a mother by taking keen interest in the studies of her children.[44]

Jahanara Begam was one of the most talented literary personalities of the Mughal dynasty. Trained under the able guidance of Sati-un-nisa, the female *Nazir* to Mumtaz Mahal, she not only learnt the Quran and Persian, but became one of the most accomplished among the galaxy of poets of her time. Schimmel, a modern writer, considers her as one among the two best representatives of the literary talent of the Mughal dynasty, the other being Dara. Her self-written epitaph runs:

> Let no one cover my grave with anything but green grass
>
> For the covering of the grave of a lonely person should be only green grass.[45]

She learnt many other disciplines including the science of medicine, which has been testified by Lahori.[46] She also wrote *Munis-ul-Arwah*, a biography of Hazrat Chisti of Ajmer.[47] After being initiated into the Qudiri fold of Mulla Shah, she wrote a biography of Mulla Shah entitled *Sahabiya* in 1051 A.H., a hitherto unknown work. It contains 19 folios, 15 lines per page and is written in *Nastaliq* (it is a prominent style in Persian calligraphy) mixed with *Shikasta* (Persian calligraphic style).[48] She was also very popular for her generosity in patronising men of letters and helping the cause of education, so much so that Mir Muhammad Ali Mahir, entitled *Murid Khan*, wrote a *masnavi* (a long poem) eulogising her this trait.[49] She is said to have established a madrasa in the *Jama Masjid* of Agra.[50]

The most spectacular of all, however, was Zeb-un-nisa Begam, the eldest daughter of Aurangzeb. Brought up under the able guidance of Aurangzeb himself and also of the renowned scholars of the time—Hafiza Mariyam, Mulla Said Ashraf Muzanddrani (a great Persian poet) and Shah Rustam Ghazi—she came out to be one of the greatest educationists of her time. She was so talented that she became *hafiz* (one who knew the Quran by heart) at the tender age of 7 for which she was awarded 30,000 gold coins by her father.[51] She was a gifted poetess. It is reported that she wrote poems in Arabic in early youth that were so good that an Arab scholar remarked, 'it is a miracle for a foreigner to know Arabian so well'. Later on, she started composing in Persian under the pen name of *Makhfi* and won great laurels, not only for the high standard of her poetry, but also for being unrivalled in *mushaira*.[52] One of the most popular collection of poems attributed to her is entitled *Diwan-i-Makhfi*. If it is genuine in its present form, it contains 421 ghazals, some of them are of rare beauty. Fifty of these poems have been translated and placed in the book *The Diwan of Zeb-un-Nisa*.[53]

It is reported by *Maasir-i-Alamgiri* that she excelled in the field of calligraphy and could write Persian in *nastaliq, naskh* (a specific calligraphic style for writing in the Arabic alphabets) and *shikasta* with perfection.[54] Her language was so polished that her letters written in literary style were highly appreciated by Aurangzeb. She left behind a collection of her letters entitled *Zeb-ul-Manshat* for the posterity.[55] Her brilliance can be judged from the fact that besides poetry, she attained mastery in Mathematics and Astronomy.[56] She emerged as one of the greatest patrons of knowledge and the learned. After establishing a big library, 'the like of which no man has seen', wrote Must'ad Khan, she took up the work of translation of classical books. It was at her instance that Fakhr-ud-din Razi's commentary on the Holy Quran—*Tafsir-i-Kabir*—was translated from Arabic to Persian by Mulla Safi-ud-din Ardbeli and was entitled *Zeb-ut-tafasir* after her name.[57] She was wholly dedicated to the cause of knowledge and the distinguished educationists and scholars of her time looked towards her for rewards and recommendations.

Zinat-un-nisa, another daughter of Aurangzeb, was proficient in the tenets of Islam. She was also a great poetess and wrote her own epitaph that reads:

In my grave the grace of God is my only help.

It is enough if the shadow of the cloud of mercy covers my tomb.[58]

Aurangzeb's another daughter, Badr-un-Nisa from Nawab Bai, is also reported to have learnt the Quran by heart.[59] Nur-un-nisa, the wife of Prince Shah Alam, was a Hindi poetess.[60] The Mughals were also liberal in giving due respect and recognition to scholarly and learned ladies, irrespective of the class to which they belonged. As a result, many other ladies got chance to distinguish themselves. Dai Lado, Jahangir's foster mother, established a school in the Dai Lado mosque (her grave is situated there) in Lahore, which was presided over by Maulvi Asmatullah, a learned scholar of that place.[61]

There was a Persian lady named Sati-un-nisa in the service of Mumtaz Mahal who was a versatile genius. She was an expert in the Persian language, in the Persian poetry and the recitation of the Quran. She possessed profound knowledge in medicine. Her mistress recognised her talent and appointed her as the instructress of princess Jahanara. She held the post of *Sadr-un-nisa* also, as already discussed. It was at her recommendation that Mumtaz distributed grants and donations to the daughters of poor scholars, theologians and pious men.[62]

Another distinguished lady in this field was Hafiza Mariyam. She was the wife of Mirza Shukr-ullah of Kashmir and mother of Inayatullah Khan, who was one of Aurangzeb's nobles. It was in recognition of her great knowledge in different branches of learning, including the art of reading the Quran, that Aurangzeb appointed her as the lady tutor of Zeb-un-nisa. Zeb-un-nisa had so much regard for her that she exhorted her father to give an office to Inayatullah, her son.[63]

Another lady was Koki Jiu. She obtained proficiency in letters and also in handwriting and composition to such an extent that she excelled her brother. It was through her educational training only that she played an important role in Mughal politics.[64]

Following their royal masters, the nobles also paid due attention towards the education of their womenfolk. The wife of noble Tughral was a great scholar of Astrology. Tughral was Governor of Lakhnauti during the time of Balban.[65] The mother of Amir Khusrau was an educated lady and wrote frequently to her son.[66] Janan Begam, the daughter of Abdur Rahim Khan-Khana, was a great educationist. She wrote commentary on the Quran for which she was given a reward of 50,000 dinars by Akbar.[67] She was known for her generosity towards learned men.[68] Another lady was Sahibji. She took active part in the political and financial matters of Kabul and showed 'excellent sense in the conduct of business'.[69] Such examples, nonetheless, were not very many since early marriages of ladies thwarted their pursuits for higher learning.[70]

Some of the ladies of upper strata of the Muslim society in the states adjoining to the Delhi empire also made their mark. Gul Khatun, wife of Sultan Zain-ul-Abdin of Kashmir, was a great patron of education. She was credited with building a madrasa and for the study of medicine.[71] Hafiza Khadija, daughter of Mir Sayid Abdul Fattah, a liberal and learned man, mastered *The Quran*, the *hadith*, the *fiqh* (the knowledge and understanding of the Islamic law) and the Arabic and Persian literature. Being married to an equally great scholar named Zain-ud-din Mufti, she got an impetus for her pursuits of knowledge. She lives in history as a great teacher, full of zest for imparting education to the women of her homeland. She opened a madrasa at her own expense where she used to invite intelligent girls and teach them.[72] Habba Khatun, wife of Sultan Yusuf Khan (1579–1586 A.D.), earned a name in history as a great poetess, besides being a melodious singer and an efficient administrator. She introduced *Lol* lyric in Kashmiri poetry.[73] Lachhma Khatun, wife of Malik Jalal-ud-din, a minister of Sultan Bad Shah of Kashmir was known for her learning. She also founded a madrasa.[74] Bibi Bahat of the same time and a disciple of Shaikh Nur-ud-din, the patron saint of Kashmir, was also famous for her learning.[75]

Most of these ladies wrote under the assumed name of *Nihani* or *Makhfi*, that is, the hidden. Nur Jahan, Salima Sultan Begam and Zeb-un-nisa, all wrote under this name. Perhaps the society would not have accepted them in their original personality as women. Abul Fazl ignored to include them in the list of 50 topmost Persian poets of his time.[76] Badaoni made a list containing 168 names. It contains only one name of a poetess, but in that case also, her actual name is not known, since it appears under the name *Nihani*.[77] Women who had literary achievements to their credit formed a microscopic minority. It may be added that the women themselves were responsible for such a social apathy. Many of the princely ladies, with their vast resources, patronised learning and also distributed grants and allowances to men of letters. But none of the royal ladies of the sultanate or the Mughal period ever tried to promote the cause of women education exclusively. Hafiza Khadija of Kashmir, a commoner, only had this rare distinction of working for education of girls.

Artistic Creativity

The Muslim women were engaged in artistic pursuits. There was a gap between the extent of their achievements and the recognition they received in the society. The common women practised arts like cooking, sewing, embroidery, decorations as a part of their household routine. They attracted no notice of the society. The women in Bengal were experts in a special type of painting known as *Alipana* in which a kind of drawing was made on the floor with the paste of rice powder. Similarly, they made beautiful country blankets called *Kathas* from worn-out clothes and also embroidered them with pictures of flowers, leaves or different animals.[78]

About the aristocratic class of the sultanate period, hardly anything is known. However, the historians have adequately focused on the aristocratic women of the Mughal period. Painting was a popular pastime of the ladies of the Mughal harem. But Abul Fazl has not noted the name of any female painter in his list of 100 painters of Akbar's time. There are so many Mughal paintings that show in detail the different facets of the harem life. Since ladies of the harem were unapproachable, it seems, some of these paintings of the ladies must have been painted by the lady artists within the harem. There are evidences to show that these ladies practised this art. For example, there is a Mughal miniature depicting a lady painting her own portrait and she is being helped by an attendant, who sits facing her, holding the mirror.[79] Of late, a painting preserved in the Wantage Bequest in the Victoria and Albert Museum, London, belonging to the Mughal times, has also come to light that is signed by a woman painter named Sahifa Banu.[80] Nur Jahan shared interest in painting with her husband. There is a painting wherein one Hasan Ghulam is showing a portrait to her in *darbar*, which she is examining.[81] She herself was adept in this art and painted with expertise.[82] Unfortunately, her creations are not available.

In the field of music also, some of the Mughal ladies were proficient. Nur Jahan was an accomplished musician and she also composed lyrics.[83] Mumtaz Mahal, the wife of Shah Jahan, and Zeb-un-nisa, the daughter of Aurangzeb, were equally talented in this field.[84] Nadira Begam, the wife of Dara Shukoh, eldest son of Shah Jahan, was said to be expert in classical music. Shah Jahan liked her rendering of *Dhrupad* (a style of singing) and presented her a volume of *raga* and *raginis* (a term for the feminine counterpart or 'wives' to *ragas* [modal scale] in Indian Classical Music) composed by Mian Tansen.[85]

In the aesthetic decorations and adornments, the Mughal ladies were far ahead of their counterparts of the sultanate period. Nur Jahan excelled in many fields. She was expert in needle work and was also credited with having introduced many new designs and styles in dresses and decorations, replacing the old ones. For the bride and the bridegroom, she invented a full set of garments known as *Nur Mahali*, costing only ₹25.[86] In place of *peshwaz* (gowns), she brought *dudami* (floral patterned muslin), weighing just two *dams* and in place of *orhnis* (veils), she brought *panchtolia* (a cotton cloth, perfect for veil), weighing only five *tolas* (traditional unit of mass measurement in India. During Mughal period, 1 tola was = 185 grains [11.98 grams]). She also developed new designs for making carpet. Her *farsh-i-chandani* or carpets of sandalwood colour along with her new fashion in *badla* (brocade) and *kinari* (lace) were popular not only during her own times but also a century later. Khafi Khan informed that once she herself prepared covers for elephants with exquisite designs of flowers and leaves, and Jahangir highly praised her for this proficiency in needle work.[87] She also invented new patterns and designs for the gold ornaments.[88] The Muslim women of the higher strata and of royalty were, in general, very adept in embroidery work for which they were also given regular training. The female teachers called *Atuns*, engaged for teaching the royal ladies, also trained Mughal princesses in embroidery.[89]

One exclusive contribution of some of the Mughal ladies was the vast and beautiful gardens they laid out or maintained. Jahangir mentioned in his Memoirs about the gardens, which were built by different Mughal ladies like Bika Begam (Bega Begam), the widow of Babur, Mariyam Makani, Jahangir's grandmother and Shahr Banu Begam (daughter of Mirza Abu Said), who was Babur's aunt. Thevenot has also informed about Hamida Banu's garden situated on the road from Agra to Bayana.[90] Jahangir has also mentioned about a garden of his own mother, Mariyam Zamani, at the *pargana* of Jusat and another gifted by him to Rukayya Sultan Begam, his stepmother.[91] There are *Dehra Bagh* and *Zahara Bagh* at Agra that are said to have been built by Babur for his daughter named Zahra. Some writers are of the view that this is only one garden with two names. Some also opine that it was subsequently renovated by Nur Jahan and renamed *Nur Manjil*, the famous garden and rendezvous of many of Jahangir's excursions.[92]

Nur Jahan was credited with designing and inspiring the construction of many pleasure resorts and beautiful gardens, full of natural flora and fruit trees. She built a garden called *Dilamez* or *Dilkhusha* at Shahdara near Lahore. It was in this garden that Jahangir was buried after his death.[93] Her *vakil* built a lofty house and garden at Nur Sarai at Jalandhar.[94] There is another garden named *Moti Bagh* at Agra. Both Mundy and Pelsaert attributed this garden to have been built by Nur Jahan. It is explained that *Nur Mahal ki Sarai* of Agra stands between two gardens, one is *Char Bagh* and other *Moti Bagh*.[95] There was still other garden called *Nur Manzil (Bagh Dahra)* that has been discussed above. Then, there was *Nur-afshan* garden that also belonged to her.[96] Since Jahangir used to spend half the year in Kashmir, Nur Jahan showed her creativity in laying out gardens there. Her garden called *Begmabad (Sahibabad)* at Achchol with gushing springs and fruit-laden trees was very romantic. It was highly praised by Bernier:

> The garden is very handsome, laid out in regular walks, and full of fruit-trees.... Jets-d'eau in various forms and fish-ponds are in great number, and there is a lofty cascade which in its fall takes the form and colour of a large sheet, thirty or forty paces in length, producing the finest effect imaginable; especially at night, when innumerable lamps, fixed in parts of the wall adapted for that purpose, are lighted under this sheet of water.

He also praised the beauty of another garden at Vernag, which is reported to have been designed and laid out by Nur Jahan.[97] She is also said to have built another garden on the western side of Dal lake named *Bagh –i-Bahar Ara*, which no longer exists fully.[98]

Mumtaz Mahal was responsible for laying Mughal gardens in Delhi and Agra.[99]

Her daughter, Jahanara Begam, was equally fond of gardens. She got a garden called *Begam ka Bagh* built outside the Delhi Fort, which became a rendezvous for friends and lovers in her own time.[100]

Besides, she had three gardens namely *Bagh-i-Aishabad*, *Bagh-i-Nur Afshan* and *Bagh-i-Safa* laid out in Kashmir under the supervision of Jawahar Khan Khwajasra.[101] She got gardens laid out at Ambala[102], Surat[103] and Achchol.[104] In addition, she owned many gardens, either inherited or received as gifts by her. Lahori mentioned about her inheriting *Bagh-i-Jahanara* from her mother after the latter's death and having received *Bagh-i-Shaharara* as a gift from her father[105] Shah Jahan's other daughter, Roshanara Begam, also built the famous *Roshanara Bagh* along with her mausoleum in Delhi.[106]

Shah Jahan's wife, Akbarabadi (A'azz-un-nisa), built a splendid garden, in imitation of *Shalimar Bagh* of Kashmir, at Lahore at a high cost of ₹200,000.[107]

Zeb-un-nisa also planted her own garden at Lahore, where she was ultimately buried.[108] The famous *Charburj Bagh* of Lahore also belonged to her. But the princess gifted it to her favourite female attendant, Mian Bai, who had supervised its construction. The fact about this gift was recorded in the Persian verses on its gateway.[109]

Some of these ladies immortalised themselves by raising many edifices in the form of *sarais*, *khankahs* (a hermitage. It denotes a building where Sufis gathered for chanting and meditation sessions), mausoleums, mosques and other buildings, a few of which serve as monuments in their memory even to this day. Mother of Muhammad bin Tughlaq built many *khankahs* for free distribution of food to the travellers.[110] Bibi Raji of Jaunpur is credited with building a huge palace outside the city walls of Jaunpur. She also constructed *Lal Darwaza Masjid* at Jaunpur, which is considered to be 'one of the finest and the third biggest mosque in Jaunpur'. The mosque had attached *khanquas* and *madrasas* with endowments for students and teachers. The masjid is said to have been built for a saint named Syed Ali Daud and was subsequently demolished along with the *khanqas* and *madrasas* by Sultan Sikander Lodi. She also built another mosque at Etawah on the banks of Jamuna.[111]

During Mughal times, the first lady to have contributed to the field of architecture was Bega Begam (Haji Begam), the wife of Humayun. She got the mausoleum of Humayun built under her supervision after his death. Besides, she also built an *Arab Sarai* for the accommodation of Arab travellers and merchants.[112]

Akbar's mother, Hamida Banu, built a royal house on Agra–Bayana road.[113] His wife, Salima Sultan Begam, built her own tomb that had an attached garden. It was probably situated near Agra.[114]

Jahangir's mother constructed a *baoli* (stepwell) at a cost of ₹20,000 in the *pargana* of Jusat, the beauty of which was praised by her Emperor son. He wrote, 'Certainly the *baoli* was a grand building, and had been built exceedingly well'.[115] She also built a mosque at Lahore in 1614 A.D. (1023 A.H.).[116]

His wife, Nur Jahan, got a *sarai* built at Sikandra,[117] *Nur Mahal ki Sarai* near Jalandhar (famous as *sarai Nur mahal* during those days)[118] and another *Nur Mahal Sarai* near Agra, the last one, as per Mundy's estimation, could accommodate 2,000–3,000 people and 500 horses.[119] She also got built the tomb of Itimad-ud-daula, her father, at Agra that is highly praised for its magnificence. Fergusson, for instance, writes that it is 'the first, apparently and certainly one of the most splendid, examples of that class of ornamentation in India'.[120] Some authorities believe that she also built Jahangir's tomb at Lahore. Praising the construction of this mausoleum and also the acumen of Nur Jahan, Haig writes:

> [It manifests] in every part of it the imprint of the refined feminism of this remarkable queen. There is no other building like it in the entire range of Mughal architecture, the delicacy of treatment and the chaste quality of its decoration placing it in a class by itself.

Latif, however, attributes its construction to Shah Jahan.[121] She got her own mausoleum also built at Lahore.[122] She built a mosque called *Pathar Masjid* on the left bank of Jhelum in Kashmir. It is considered to be the largest of the surviving Mughal buildings in Kashmir. Built of polished gray limestone, it is constructed in a magnificent style with 'massive stone arches' and 'handsomely ribbed and vaulted' roof.[123]

Jahangir's wet nurse, Dai Lado, built her own grave at Lahore, where she was buried after her death in the first year of Aurangzeb's reign.[124]

Shah Jahan's daughter, Pur Hunar Banu Begam, got built her own mausoleum, where she was buried after her death.[125]

Jahanara Begam constructed a mosque in Agra at a cost of ₹500,000. Shah Jahan himself was interested in building this mosque. But, at her asking, the Emperor allowed her to do the same out of her personal allowances.[126] Another mosque is said to have been built by Jahanara Begam in Kashmir 'in an exquisite artistic style' at a cost of ₹40,000 from her own funds.[127] She built a *rabat* (monastery).[128] Catering to the needs of both rich and poor, she built many more buildings. For the poor, she built a house at Srinagar at a cost of ₹20,000.[129] For the well-to-do, she built a magnificent caravanserai called *Begam Sarai* in Delhi, which impressed even the foreigners. Bernier, for instance, compared it to the 'Palace Royal' in Paris. The *sarai* had lovely gardens and reservoirs of water and also arrangements of 'perfect security, the gates being closed at night'. Only great Mughals and rich Persian, Uzbeg and other foreign merchants were allowed to stay there. It has been highly praised by Manucci. He wrote, 'This is the most beautiful sarae in Hindustan, with upper chambers adorned with many paintings, and it has a lovely garden, in which are ornamental reservoirs'. As per him, even the Emperor was all praise for the *sarai*. The *sarai* was raised to the ground after 1857 revolt, and at present, the site is occupied by Queen's Garden.[130] She got built another famous caravanserai at Kirka near Bayana (Behana).[131] For herself, she built house at Achchol with gardens and fountains.[132] She also built her own tomb in her lifetime.[133] Jahanara is also credited with planning and supervising *Chowk Sarai Bazaar* in Lahore and *Chandani Chowk Bazaar* near Red Fort in Delhi.[134]

Zinat-un-nisa Begam, the daughter of Aurangzeb, built 14 caravanserais. Norris confirmed to have visited one of these caravanserais, when he arrived at Navapur.[135] She constructed *Zinat-ul-Masjid (Kuari Masjid)* at her own expenses and was buried there after her death. This masjid became the meeting place for Urdu poets in early 18th century.[136]

Qudsia Begam, mother of Emperor Ahmad Shah, built a garden named *Qudsia Bagh* on the banks of Jamuna (in 1748 A.D.), which also contained a big palace.[137]

Beyond Mughal ladies, there is a reference of Begam Saliha, the wife of King Muhammad Shah of Kashmir, who was also interested in architecture. She rebuilt *Khankah-i-Shah Hamdan*, which had been demolished by the Shias, on the bank of Vitasta. For meeting its expenses, she did not ask for any state help, but sold her own jewellery. Her creation is considered to be a 'precious specimen' of the Muslim architecture of the medieval times.[138] Lachhma Khatun also founded a *khankah*.[139]

These activities enhanced the social status of women. Such creative pursuits provided outlet for their smothered faculties and helped them add charm to the family life. Their presence was felt within their closed social circle. It was, however, unfortunate that the artistic pursuits of aristocratic ladies gradually petered out. After the reign of Aurangzeb, artistic contributions of the Mughal ladies vanished. In the decayed social milieu, economic bankruptcy and constant political upheavals, the ladies had neither the zeal nor the capability for creative art.

Dress and Aesthetics

The Muslim women, with the exception of those from the down South, were distinguished mainly by their *salwar* (trousers) and shirt with half-length sleeves or tight tunic, being of the same pattern, both for men and women, with belt round the waist, coming down to the knees, under which they wore breeches coming down up to their ankles. Manucci narrated that during Aurangzeb's reign, orders forbidding Muslim women from wearing tight-fitting trousers were passed, but they did not seem to have much impact.[140] Another important part of their dress was *dupatta* (scarf) to cover their head and upper part of the body. Manucci referred to it as a 'sheet of cloth' and Badaoni, as '*Chadar*'.[141] They wore their usual burqa (veil). *Ghanghara* (long and very loose shirt) was also popular among the Muslim women. De Laet also described that they wore fine cotton wrapping for head called *sash* (turban cloth). From his narration, it appears that both men and women were using it. These clothes were made of different materials, depending on the socio-economic background of the user. While the common women were satisfied with the coarser cloth like cotton, the women of the upper strata used costly gilded and jewelled items.[142] However, Muslim ladies of down south wore different dresses. Ibn Batuta informed that Muslim women in Malabar coast only wrapped 'unsewn garments', covering their down portion with one extreme and the upper portion up to head with the other.[143]

The aristocratic ladies had some exclusive dresses like *qabas* (a long coat), *kulah* (a high cap) and *lachaq* or *Qasaba* (a head dress). Minhas, author of *Tabqat-i-Nasiri*, described about Razia wearing *qaba* and *kulah*. From the narration of Thevenot, it appears that *qaba* had become a common dress by Aurangzeb's time and the women too were using it.[144] During the Mughal times, some of the princesses even wore turbans with the permission of the King. The poor women moved about barefoot. The rich ladies used shoes of varied designs and colours, often adorned with costly embroidery and studding.

There was a universal craze for aesthetics so as to look charming. Women were accustomed to putting on ornaments from their early childhood. Ibn Batuta observed about slave girls being awarded ornaments and that even women of down South, although scantily dressed, were fond of ornaments. Amir Khusrau has mentioned about the universal appeal of ornaments and even public women were having fondness for them.[145] But the rich upper class did maintain a difference in that they used costly ornaments, which were also better in quality and variety. While their ornaments were made of gold and studded with jewels, pearls, diamonds and other precious stones, the poorer people used ornaments of cheaper materials like silver, brass, iron, copper, ivory, glass and cowries. Fryer, for instance wrote, 'The rich (women) have their Arms and Feet Fettered with Gold and Silver, the meaner with Brass and Glass and Tuthinag, besides rings at their Noses, Ears, Toes and Fingers'. Similarly, Fitch mentioned about ornaments made of silver, copper and ivory; Careri about gold nose ring set with stone; Thevenot about silver and gold ear and nose rings and finger ring with a looking glass set in it; and Stavorinus about glass and cowry ornaments.[146] The bracelets or precious ring of the right thumb with a looking glass and pearls studded around it and the sweet smelling perfumes of different varieties were the distinct privileges of the ladies of royal and upper classes.[147] Likewise, the rich dresses, precious ornaments and pungent perfumes came to be regarded as 'signs of respectability and good breeding'. The one who looked different from the common women in attires and adoration received an automatic social distinction. In that age of sensuality and ostentation, glamour gained an upper hand and the ladies of higher class vied with one another to look more glamorous. Confined within their houses, these women did not have much else to achieve. So, such pursuits of self-adoration brought piquancy and zest in their dull, drab and secluded lives. They used a vast variety of ornaments for head, arms, nose, ears, fingers, neck, waist, thigh and numerous cosmetics and toilets they applied on their face, hands, feet and hair go to show that from head to toe, no part of their body remained undecked.[148] Since physical charm had the greatest attraction and was the easiest way for getting recognition in the society, there was a craze to use all kinds of methods and devices to look young and charming. Even the ladies, whose youth had long past, were no exception. Amir Khusrau, in *Matla-ul-Anwar*, has described how a middle-aged woman tried hard to retain her faded beauty by use of cosmetics and he also ridiculed the practice of dying of hair.[149] He was against excessive use of ornaments, and hence advocated against it.[150] He cautioned that beauty aids brought defame to the person and exhorted the need for cultivating beauty in chaste character and pious deeds, rather than in physical looks.[151] Considering excessive use of precious metals in ornaments and luxurious items particularly by royalty and nobility, Sultan Firoz Shah Tughlaq forbade the use of gold and silver for these things.[152]

Religious Pursuits and Beliefs

The women were, generally, religious minded and observed pre-scribed ceremonies and festivals. Hajj pilgrimage was popular among the ladies of means. Ibn Batuta informed that after the death of Khizr Khan, his mother visited Mecca in 1327 A.D.; Ferishta wrote about the mother of Muhammad Shah Bahmani I (1358–1377 A.D.) having gone for the *hajj* and Gulbadan wrote about Sultanam, the wife of Nizam-ud-din Ali Barlas Khalifa, having undertaken hajj pilgrimage along with Gulbarg Begam.[153] Mahchuchak Begam Arghun, the wife of Kamran, also undertook pilgrimage along with her husband.[154] Akbar arranged for the hajj of Bega Begam (Haji Begam). She is reported to have undertaken this journey twice.[155] Gulbadan Begam, accompanied by Salima Sultan Begam, Haji and Gulzar Begam (daughters of Kamran), Sultan (Sultanam) Begam (wife of Askari), Kulsum Khanam (granddaughter of Gulbadan), Gulnar Aghacha besides Bibi Safiya, Bibi Saru-qad and Shaham Aga (the royal servants of Humayun), undertook this journey in 1575 A.D. They returned in 1582 A.D., when Akbar personally came at Kanwah to receive them.[156] However, after the reign of Akbar, such journeys were discouraged because of disturbances caused by the Portuguese in the Arabian Sea.[157] Dai Lado, a wet nurse of Emperor Jahangir, performed this pilgrimage in the fourth year of Shah Jahan's reign.[158]

The presence of females in congregational prayers at the mosques, although not popular, was prevalent in the early medieval period. Islamic norms subjected the women visitors to certain restrictions. In the prayer, the Imam stood at the head. In the rows, men stood first of all, followed by children, eunuchs and finally women. Women could not speak, lest this would divert the attention of men. But, this order did not seem to have been followed strictly, as is also evident from the narrations of Mushtaqi, wherein he described women devotees praying by the side of men in the mosques.[159]

Acts of Piety and Charity

Inspired by *The Quran*ic dictum, many Muslim ladies undertook acts of piety and charity. The mother of Muhammad bin Tughlaq had a generous bent of mind and Barani considered none equal to her in charitable matters. She maintained a number of hospices, where she made provisions for feeding the wayfarers. She distributed grants and gifts liberally and many families thrived on her help alone. A separate department was organised to meet out these expenses and also to keep a record of the same.[160] Gulbadan informed that Maham Begam, after Babur's funeral, made 'allowance of food twice daily'.[161] Bega Begam spent her widowhood in distributing alms and supporting 500 poor people.[162] Alms were also distributed by them or on their behalf while they were on hajj. Abul Fazl, for instance, recorded that Haji Begam distributed alms after her hajj. Similarly, Monserrate narrates about distribution of alms by Akbar on Gulbadan's return from hajj.[163]

Nur Jahan brought relief to the destitute and the poor through her liberal grants. 'She was an asylum for all sufferers and helpless girls', wrote Muhammad Hadi, and thousands benefited from her generosity.[164] She had collected many maid servants in the palace, whom she got married to *ahadis* (gentleman troopers) and *chelas* (disciple or pupil). She distributed ₹3,000 as alms on prescribed days of bath.[165]

Mumtaz Mahal was also very generous. Helped by her *Nazir* Sati-un-nisa, she managed the marriages of many poor girls by arranging for their dowries. Qazwini narrated another incident as per which, on her recommendation, Hakim Rukna Kashi was given ₹24,000.[166]

Jahanara distributed a lot of money in charity on different occasions. Mannuci narrated that though in captivity, yet she sent 2,000 gold coins to be distributed among the poor after the death of Shah Jahan, although the guards did not allow the distribution, arguing that being imprisoned, she had no independence to do so.[167]

Aurangzeb's daughter, Zinat-un-nisa, was known for her piety and charity.[168] Jahanzib Banu, daughter of prince Dara, was also famous for her generosity and liberal attitude.[169]

In the later Mughal period, Lal Kanwar was known for generous charity of food and money, which she distributed among the poor and the needy.[170] Hazrat Qudsia Begam (Udham Bai) was also known for her generosity.[171]

Many notable women were fully devoted to religion and became *joginis* (lady ascetics), renowned saints and mystics. There is a painting given in Herman Goetz's book, depicting a *jogini* in the company of the court ladies.[172] Sufism was responsible for such a development. Sufis treated women with more respect and consideration, and opened the doors of religious upliftment for them. When a girl was purchased by one of the servants of Sufi saint, Amir Hasan, the latter purchased her back and handed her over to her parents.[173] Baba Farid, taking pity on a poor man, recommended a man for the marriage of his daughter.[174] They had great regard for mothers and treated even their maid servants and female slaves with kindness. One of the maid servants of Shaikh Jamal-ud-din Hansi used to carry letters of her master to Baba Farid. The latter called her 'mother of Momins', because of her sincere and sweet nature.[175] Hamid Qalander narrated another anecdote. Maulana Fakhr-ud-din and his guru, Shaikh Nizam-ud-din Auliya, had great difficulty once, when the former wanted to lead a life of celibacy while his mother wanted him to get married. They did not want to hurt the feelings of the mother by being adamant. So, the Shaikh took recourse to his mystic power to save his disciple from marriage. His mother did not force marriage on him thereafter.[176]

The Sufis readily accepted women as their *murid* (disciples), without making any discrimination on the basis of sex.[177] The initiation ceremony was almost similar and so were the restrictions and obligations required to be observed, for all. Rather, the Sufis depicted a softer corner for the ladies and rules were made less rigorous for them in some respects, considering their weak constitution.[178]

It is said that Bibi Zulaikha, the mother of Shaikh Nizam-ud-din Auliya, possessed unique intuitive power of foreseeing the future in her dreams. With deep faith in God, all her prayers were fulfilled.[179] Bibi Auliya, of the time of Muhammad bin Tughlaq, was a famous saint of her times and was deeply revered by the public.[180] Bibi Sara, mother of Shaikh Nizam-ud-din Abul Muid, also possessed mystic powers. It is narrated that the Shaikh even brought rains for Delhi after it had suffered a long dry spell, by praying after taking a thread from a garment worn by his mother.[181] Qarsum Bibi, mother of Baba Farid, was equally enlightened and exalted.[182] She used to pray throughout the night. There are numerous anecdotes popular about her piety and devotion. In one such case, when she was engrossed in her prayers one night, some thieves trespassed her house, but they were so much overwhelmed by her charismatic saintliness that they became changed persons and led honest lives thereafter.[183] She left indelible impression on the mind of her son and was responsible for giving him the spiritual bent of mind. Another known lady was Bibi Fatima Saam. She acquired a respectable place among the Sufi saints of the time, not only because of being an accomplished poetess, but also because of her virtues, devotion to God and charitable nature.

It is narrated that once Shaikh Najib-ud-din was visited by some guests and he had nothing to offer to them. At such a time, Bibi Fatima Saam came to his help by sending him some bread. She kept on helping the family of the Shaikh, off and on.[184] For his daughter, Bibi Sharifah, Baba Farid used to say, 'Had it been permitted to bestow *Khilafat Namah* of the Shaikh and his *Sajjadah* to a woman, I would have given them to Bibi Sharifah'. He also observed, 'If other women had been like her, women would have taken precedence over men'.[185] In Kashmir, Taj Khatun, the wife of Mir Muhammad Hamdani, son of famous saint Shah Hamdan and Lalla Arifa, also a contemporary of Shah Hamdan, were the known lady-saints of the time.[186] Nevertheless, the female Sufis were hampered in many ways. They were never allowed spiritual succession and hence, were never incorporated in *khankahs* and 'orders'. Thus, in spite of lack of encouragement from their male counterparts and Islam in general, some of them were still committed, in their individual capacities, to the cause of mysticism.

The visits to the shrines and tombs of the saints were one of the most popular practices. It was generally believed that prayers at the graves of the martyrs and saints were spiritually blissful and efficacious in averting ailments and misfortunes. When Shaikh Nizam-ud-din Auliya's mother fell ill, she sent her son to the tombs of many martyr saints, in order to pray for her recovery.[187] The ladies continued to visit them with full devotion. Firoz Shah Tughlaq ordered women not to visit the tombs in the vicinity of Delhi. Sikander Lodi also tried to enforce this regulation, but his efforts proved abortive. *Urs* or annual anniversaries of mystic saints were celebrated with great gusto and women participated in them. On every Thursday, or at some places on Friday, women along with men went to pay a visit to the *mazar*s (mausoleum or shrine, typically that of a saint or notable religious leader) of the *pir*s (sufi master or spiritual guide). The writings of the contemporaries are replete with such narrations. Badaoni mentioned about Gulbadan and other ladies visiting the shrine of Chisti after their return from the hajj; Abul Fazl and also Pelsaert narrate about ladies visiting tomb of Chisti along with Akbar; *Tuzuk-i-Jahangiri* referred to Hindal's daughter, Rukayya Sultan Begam, visiting her father's tomb at Kabul and Jahangir along with his harem visiting the tombs of Babur, Akbar, Humayun and Chisti. Kambo, the author of *Amal-i-Saleh*, recorded Jahanara's visit to Chisti tomb after recovery from her burns in 1644 A.D.[188]

Notes

1. Jamila BrijBhushan, *Muslim Women in Purdah and Out of it* (New Delhi: Vikas Publishing House, 1980), 98–99; N.N. Law, *Promotion of Learning in India During Muhammedan Rule*, rpt. (New Delhi: Idarah-i-Adabiyat-i-Delli, 1973), 200; S.M. Jaffar, *Education in Muslim India* (Delhi: Idarah-i-Adabiyat-i-Delli, 1973), 187; M.F. Billington, *Woman in India* (Delhi: Amarko Book Agency, 1973), 21–22.

2. M.L. Bhagi, *Medieval Indian Culture and Thought* (Ambala Cantt.: The Indian Publications, 1965), 158; R.C Majumdar, H.C. Raychaudhari and K. Dutta, *An Advanced History of India*, Part-II (New Delhi: Macmillan Publishers India Ltd., 2010), 571–572 (for Mughal Kings' interest in education).

3. Jafar Sharif, *Qanun-i-Islam*, in Islam in India, ed. William Crooke, rpt. (London, 1975), 43–44. See also Simmi Jain, *Encyclopaedia of Indian Women Through the Ages: The middle ages* (New Delhi: Kalpaz Publication, 2003), 95–97. J.N. Sarkar, *Studies in Aurangzib's Reign* (Kolkata: M.C. Sarkar & Sons, 1933), 302.

4. Rumer Godden, *Gulbadan-Portrait of a Rose Princess at Mughal Court* (London: MacMillan & Co., 1980), 34, also 35 (for painting of joint studies).

5. Jaffar, *Education*, 8, 191, note 7; S.M. Jaffar, *Some Cultural Aspects of Muslim Rule in India* (Delhi: Idarah-i-Adabiyat-i-Delli, 1972), 85.

6. Abul Fazl, *Ain-i-Akbari*, vol. 1 (New Delhi: Crown Publications, 1988), 288–289; John Fryer, *A New Account of the East Indies and Persia (1672–81)*, ed. W. Crooke, vol. 2, second series no. XX (London: Hak Society, 1912), 112; Jaffar, *Education*, 20; Yusuf Husain, *Glimpses of Medieval Indian Culture* (Mumbai: Asia Publishing House, 1957), 91.

7. Jafar Sharif, *Qanun-i-Islam*, 51; see also Jain, *Encyclopedia*, 96; Law, *Promotion*, 200; Jaffar, *Education*, 191.

8. Yusuf Husain, *Glimpses*, 91.

9. One such lady was Hafiza Khadija of Kashmir, who has been discussed in this chapter hereinafter.

10. Jaffar, *Some Cultural Aspects*, 85. For patronage of education by the then kings, see Abu-Umar-i-Usman Minhaj-ud-din Siraj, *Tabaqat-i-Nasiri*, trans. Elliot and Dowson, in *History of India*, Vol. II (Allahabad: Kitab Mahal, 1964)), 306–309; Firoz Shah Tughlaq, *Futuhat-i-Firoz Shahi*, trans. Elliot and Dowson, in *History of India*, Vol. III, 383; Muhammad Kasim Hindu Shah Ferishta, *Tarikh-i-Ferishta*, trans. J. Briggs, vol. 4 (New Delhi: Atlantic Publishers & Distributors, 1989), 277–278, 286; Abul Fazl, *Ain-i-Akbari*, vol. 1: 288–289; K.A. Nizami, *Royalty in Medieval India* (New Delhi: Munshiram Manohar Lal, 1997), 127–135.

11. Ibn Batuta, *The Rehla of Ibn Batuta*, trans. Mahdi Husain (Baroda: Oriental Institute, 1953), 179.

12. Ferishta, *Tarikh-i-Ferishta*, vol. 4: 143; Rizkullah Mushtaqi, *Waqiat-i-Mushtaqi*, trans. Elliot and Dowson, in *History of India*, vol. IV, 554.

13. Law, *Promotion*, 205; Jaffar, *Some Cultural Aspects*, 85; P.N. Ojha, *Some Aspects of Northern Indian Social Life*, 1st edn (Patna: Nagari Prakashan, 1961), 109; P.N. Chopra, *Some Aspects of Society and Culture During the Mughal Age (1526–1707)* (Agra: Educational Publishers, 1955), 161. See also Chapter 4 for role of matrons and superintendents in teaching the harem ladies.

14. Jaffar, *Education*, 192.
15. Bakhtawar Khan, *Mirat-i-Alam*, trans. Elliot and Dowson, in *History of India*, vol. VII (Allahabad: Kitab Mahal, 1961), 162; also Jaffar, *Education*, 23, 27–28.
16. Sarkar, *Studies*, 301; Jaffar, *Education*, 297; Syed Subah-ud-din Abdur Rahman, *Bazm-i-Taimuria* (Azamgarh: Daar-ul-Musannifeen, 1948), 456; Law, *Promotion*, 204; Yusuf Husain, *Glimpses*, 91. Contemporary references have also been given hereinafter while discussing proficiency of different ladies in different fields.
17. Bhagi, *Medieval India culture*, 361.
18. Amir Khusrau, *Matla-ul-Anwar* (Lucknow, 1884), 153.
19. Ferishta, *Tarikh-i-Ferishta*, vol. 1: 121; also K.M. Ashraf, *Life and Conditions of the People of Hindustan*, 2nd ed. (New Delhi: Munshiram Manoharlal, 1970), 170.
20. Abu-Umar-i-Usman Minhaj-ud-din Siraj (*Tabaqat-i-Nasiri*, trans. H.G. Raverty, vol. 1 (New Delhi: Oriental Books Reprint Corp., 1970), 637, 644; Law, *Promotion*, 21–22; U.N. Day, *Some Aspects of Medieval Indian History* (New Delhi: Kumar Brothers, 1971), 151; Jaffar, *Education*, 40; Rafiq Zakaria, *Razia: Queen of India* (Mumbai: Popular Prakshan, 1966), 86–87.
21. A.M.A. Shushtery, *Outline of Islamic Culture* (Banglore: The Banglore Printing and Publishing Co., 1954), 586.
22. Law, *Promotion*, 101, Jaffar, *Education*, 128; Yusuf Husain, *Glimpses*, 77; S.A. Halim, 'Harem Influence in the 15th Century Politics of India', *Muslim University Journal* II (October, 1938): 53.
23. A.S. Beveridge, Appendix A to Gulbadan's *Humayun Nama* (New Delhi: Idarah-i-Adabiyat-i-Delli, 1972), sr. no. XVI, 208 for *Atun Mama* (*Atun* is a teacher of reading, writing and embroidery, etc. Similarly, '*Mama*' seems to be title of old servants).
24. Zahir-ud-din Babur, *Babur Nama or Memoirs of Babur*, trans. A.S. Beveridge, vol 1, rpt. (New Delhi: Oriental Books Reprint Corpn., 1970), 148, note 4, 407, note 1; Gulbadan, *Humayun Nama*, 121; S.J. Monserrate, *The Commentary*, trans., ann. J.S. Hoyland and S.N. Banerjee (London: Oxford University Press, 1922), 203; Niccolao Manucci, *Storia Do Mogor or Mogul India*, trans. William Irvine, vol. 2 (New Delhi: Atlantic Publishers and Distributors, 1989), 308; Ishwar Dass Nagar, *Futuhat-i-Alamgiri*, trans., ed. Tasneem Ahmad (New Delhi: Idarah-i-Adabiyat-i-Delli, 1978), 282. See also S.K. Banerji, 'Some of the Women Relations of Babur', *Islamic Culture* IV (1937–1938): 53.
25. Law, *Promotion*, 202–203, 206, Pl. I (showing the painting of Mughal Princess taking her lessons); see also Sarkar, *Studies*, 301.
26. Must'ad Khan, *Maasir-i-Alamgiri*, trans., ann. J.N. Sarkar (Kolkata: Royal Asiatic Society of Bengal, 1947), 318; Bakhtawar Khan, *Mirat-i-Alam*, 162.
27. Beveridge, Introduction to Gulbadan's *Humayun Nama*, 76, 79 (mentions about Mir Mahdi Shirazi having preserved her two lines of poetry in his *Tazkit-ul-khwatin*); Abdur Rahman, *Bazm*, 436; Madhavanand and R.C. Majumdar, eds, *Great Women of India* (Almora: Advaita Ashram, 1953), 383; P.N. Chopra, *Life and Letters Under the Mughals* (New Delhi: Ashajanak Publications, 1976), 322; S.K. Banerji, *Humayun Badshah*, vol. 2 (Lucknow: Maxwell Company, 1941), 318–319; A. Schimmel, *Islam in the Indian Subcontinent* (Leiden: E. J. Brill, 1980), 78; also A.S. Beveridge, 'Life and Writings of Gulbadan Begam (Lady Rosebody)', *Calcutta Review* CVI (1898), Art. No. VIII: 346 (she is described as a 'pen woman').

28. K.A. Nizami, 'Persian Literature under Akbar', *Medieval Indian Quarterly* XII (Nos 3 and 4) (January and April, 1958): 317; Beveridge, Introduction to Gulbadan's *Humayun Nama*, 76, 22, resp.

29. Beveridge, Introduction to Gulbadan's *Humayun Nama*, 76; Law, *Promotion*, 201–202; J. M. Shelat, *Akbar*, eds K.M. Munshi and R.R. Diwakar, vol. 2 (Bombay: Bharatiya Vidya Bhavan, 1959), 341.

30. Beveridge, Appendix A to Gulbadan's *Humayun Nama*, 231, 218–219, 225, 211, resp.

31. Abdur Rahman, *Bazm*, 439; Rekha Mishra, *Women in Mughal India* (Allahabad: Munshiram Manohar Lal, 1967), 88 (for Gulrukh Begam); Beveridge, Appendix A to Gulbadan's *Humayun Nama*, 211(for Aesha Sultan Begam).

32. Banerji, *Humayun*, vol. 2: 317.

33. Babur, *Babur Nama*, vol. 2: 713; Samsam ud-daulah Shah Nawaz Khan and Abdul Hayy, *Maasir-ul-Umara*, vol. 1 (Patna: Janki Prakashan, 1979), 371. See also Beveridge, Introduction and Appendix A to Gulbadan's *Humayun Nama*, 58, 279; Blochmann, Notes to *Ain-i-Akbari*, by Abul Fazl, vol. 1: 321–322; F.E. Keay, *Indian Education in Ancient and Later Times* (London: Humphrey Milford, Oxford University Press, 1938), 80; Beni Prasad, 'A Few Aspects of Education and Literature under the Great Mughals', *Indian Historical Records Commission* V (1923): 48; Law, *Promotion*, 202.

34. Abdur Rahman, *Bazm*, 440 (for library). Abdul Qadir Al Badaoni, *Muntakhabu-t-Tawarikh*, trans. W.H. Lowe, vol. 2 (New Delhi: Idarah-i-Adabiyat-i-Delli, 1973), 389 (refers to her love of books); Beveridge, Introduction to Gulbadan's *Humayun Nama*, 76 (for her love of books).

35. Jain, *Encyclopaedia*, 93, 98.

36. Law, *Promotion*, 166, 202; Jaffar, *Education*, 194; Shelat, *Akbar*, vol. 2: 341–342; Keay, *Indian Education*, 80–81; Yusuf Husain, *Glimpses*, 82; Carr Stephen, *Archaeology and Monumental Remains of Delhi* (Allahabad: Kitab Mahal, 1967), 199–200. Some authorities like Percy Brown held that that the *madrasa* was meant for girls. But it is refuted by S. K. Banerji who held that because of purdah, the medieval Muslim women did not move out of the house ('The Historical Remains of Early Years of Akbar's Reign', *United Provinces Historical Society* XV, Part II (December, 1942): 89, note 5).

37. Rattan Pandauri, *Hindi Ke Mussalmaan Shora* (New Delhi: Shaan-e-Hind, 1982), 220–223, 253.

38. Sujan Rai Bhandari, *Khulasat-ut-Tawarikh*, ed. Maulvi Zafar Hasan (New Delhi: G & Sons, 1918), 449; Chittraman Kayath, 'Chahar Gulshan', Ms. (Aligarh: Azad Library, Aligarh Muslim University), f. 16a; Muhammad Hashim Khafi Khan, *Muntakhab-al-Lubab*, ed. Maulvi Kabir-ud-din Ahmad, Part I (Kolkata: Bibliothica Indica, 1869), 270–271 (he has also quoted her verses at page 270); Law, *Promotion*, 202; Jaffar, *Education*, 194; Shelat, *Akbar*, vol. 2: 342. Margaret Macnicol, ed., *Poems by Indian Women* (Calcutta: Association Press, 1923), 76–79 (for her verses). For poetic contest between Nur Jahan and Kalim, a poet of Jahangir's and Shah Jahan's court, refer to B.K. Sahay, *Education and Learning under the Great Mughals* (Bombay: New Literature Publishing Co., 1968), 90.

39. Abdur Rahman, *Bazm*, 443; P.N. Ojha, *North Indian Social Life During Mughal Period*, 1st ed. (New Delhi: Oriental Publishers, 1975), 132.

40. Prasad, 'A Few Aspects of Education and Literature', 157–158; Jaffar, *Education*, 194–195.
41. Nur-ud-din Jahangir, *Tuzuk-i-Jahangiri*, vol. 2 (New Delhi: Munshiram Manoharlal, 1968), 213–214.
42. Rekha Mishra, *Mughal India*, 89, note 7.
43. Law, *Promotion*, 202; Jaffar, *Education*, 195; J. N. Chowdhuri, 'Mumtaz Mahall', *Islamic Culture* XI (1937): 374; J.B. Chaudhury, *Muslim Patronage to Sanskrit Learning*, vol. 1 (Calcutta: Prachyavani, 1954),77.
44. Ila Mukherji, *Social Status of North Indian Women 1526–1707* (Agra: Shiva Lal Agarwala, 1972), 102.
45. Law, *Promotion*, 203–204; Jaffar, *Education*, 195–196; Abdur Rahman, *Bazm*, 448; A. Schimmel, *Islamic Literatures of India* (Wiesbaden: Otto Harrassowitz, 1973), 25; Ila Mukherji, *Social Status*, 103 (for her epitaph).
46. Abdul Hamid Lahori, *Badshah Nama*, ed. K.A. Ahmad and Abdal Rahim, vol. 2 (Kolkata: Bibliothica Indica, 1867/1872), 629–630.
47. Abdur Rahman, *Bazm*, 448; Ila Mukherji, *Social Status*, 103.
48. Bikrama Jit Hasrat, *Dara Shikuh, Life and Works* (New Delhi: Munshiram Manoharlal, 1982), 83, see also 85 (for her poetry written in the praise of Mulla Shah). The Ms. copy of the biography is preserved in Aparao Bholanath Library, Ahmadabad. Also J.N. Sarkar, *History of Aurangzib*, 1st Imp., vol. 1 (New Delhi: New Orient Longman Ltd., 1972–1974), 63.
49. M.A. Ansari, 'The Harem of the Great Mughals', *Islamic Culture* XXXIV (1960): 119.
50. Yusuf Husain Khan, 'The Educational System in Medieval India', *Islamic Culture* XXX, no. 1 (January, 1956): 117.
51. Must'ad Khan, *Maasir-i-Alamgiri*, 322; Zeb-un-Nisa, *Diwan-i-Makhfi*, in *The Diwan of Zeb-un-Nissa*, Introduction, trans. Magan Lal and Jessie Duncan (London: Westbrook, 1913), 8; Sarkar, *Studies*, 130.
52. Zeb-un-Nisa, *Diwan-i-Makhfi*, trans. Magan Lal and Duncan, Introduction, 9–10. *Mushaira* is a wit war, where one poet questions and other answers in poetic language using same metre and rhyme.
53. Some modern authors doubt her authorship of this book and consider it to have been written by a Khurasani poet under this pen name (Hafiz Shams-ud-din Ahmad, 'Zeb-un-nisa Begam and Diwan-i-Makhfi', *Journal of Bihar and Orissa Research Society* XIII, Part I (1927): 53; Khan Sahib A. Muqtadir, Diwan-i-Makhfi, Cat. III: Khuda Bakhsh Oriental Public Library, Bankipur, M.S. No.422, 250–52). See also Sarkar, *Studies*, 80.
54. Must'ad Khan, *Maasir-i-Alamgiri*, 322; Abdur Rahman, *Bazm*, 456; Sarkar, *Studies*, 79.
55. Ansari, 'The Harem', 119; Hafiz Shams-ud-din Ahmad, 'Zeb-un-nisa Begam and Diwan-i-Makhfi', 42; Jaffar, *Education*, 197.
56. Zeb-un-Nisa, *Diwan-i-Makhfi*, trans. Magan Lal and Duncan, Introduction, 8.
57. Must'ad Khan, *Maasir-i-Alamgiri*, 322; Sarkar, *Studies*, 79; Yusuf Husain, *Glimpses*, 193; Jaffar, *Education*, 197; Abdur Rahman, *Bazm*, 456; Madhavanand and Majumdar, eds, *Great Women*, 389; also Schimmel, *Islam*, 101–102 (he gives the title of the book as 'Zeb-i-tafasir').
58. Must'ad Khan, *Maasir-i-Alamgiri*, 323; also Macnicol, *Poems*, 79 for her poems and epitaph.

59. Sarkar, *Aurangzib*, vol. 1: 39.

60. Sarkar, *Aurangzib*, IV, 309.

61. S.M. Latif, *Lahore, Its History, Architectural Remains and Antiquities* (Lahore, 1892), 206.

62. Shah Nawaz Khan and Hayy, *Maasir*, vol. 1: 260–261; Sarkar, *Studies*, 21–22, 24; Chowdhuri, 'Mumtaz Mahall', 378.

63. Shah Nawaz Khan and Hayy, *Maasir*, vol. 1: 681; Aurangzeb, *Rukkat-i-Alamgiri*, trans. J.H. Bilmoria (New Delhi: Idarah-i-Adabiyat-i-Delli, 1972), 60, note 5; Sarkar, *Studies*, 79; G.M.D. Sufi, *Kashir*, vol. 2 (New Delhi: Light & Life Publishers, 1974), 391; N. Bazaz, *Daughters of the Vitasta* (New Delhi: Pamposh Publications, 1959), 162.

64. William Irvine, *Later Mughals*, vol. 2 (Kolkata: M.C. Sarkar & Sons, 1922), 264. Refer Chapter 5 for her role in politics.

65. Khwaja Abdul Malik Isami, *Futuh-us-Salatin*, ed. A. Mahdi Husain (Agra: Educational Press, 1938), 164.

66. M. Wahid Mirza, *The Life and Works of Amir Khusrau, rpt.* (Delhi, 1974), 73.

67. Abdur Rahman, *Bazm*, 442; Shushtery, *Islamic Culture*, 589; Chopra, *Some Aspects*, 123–124 (he names her Jan Begam).

68. Abdur Rahman, *Bazm*, 442.

69. Shah Nawaz Khan and Hayy, *Maasir*, vol. 1: 250.

70. Sarkar, *Studies*, 301–302.

71. P. N. K. Bamzai, *A History of Kashmir* (New Delhi: Metropolitan Book Co., 1962), 506; also Sufi, *Kashir*, vol. 2: 389.

72. Sufi, *Kashir*, vol. 2: 391; Bazaz, *Daughters of the Vitasta*, 162–163.

73. Sufi, *Kashir*, vol. 2: 389–390; Bamzai, *A History*, 521; Schimmel, *Islam*, 47.

74. Sufi, *Kashir*, vol. 2: 388–389.

75. Sufi, *Kashir*, vol. 2: 388.

76. Blochmann, Notes to *Ain-i-Akbari*, by Abul fazl, vol. 1: 617–680.

77. Badaoni, *Muntakhabu-t-Tawarikh*, trans. Wolseley Haig, vol. 3: 239–537, esp. 494 and nn. 3 and 4.

78. T.C. Das Gupta, *Aspects of Bengal Society*, Introduction (Kolkata: Calcutta University, 1935), xxxvii, 197 (for *kathas*).

79. A.J. Qaiser, *The Indian Response to European Technology and Culture* (New Delhi: Oxford University Press, 1982), Pl.7a (from *Khamsa*, BM. or.12208, f. 206a).

80. Enakshi Bhavnani, 'Creative and Fine Arts', in *Women of India*, ed. Tara Ali Baig (New Delhi: Ministry of Information and Broadcasting, 1957), 166.

81. Mishra, *Mughal India*, 92, note 5 (basing on Ivan Stchoukine's Pl. vii).

82. K.S. Lal, *The Mughal Harem* (New Delhi: Aditya Prakashan, 1988), 77.

83. Beni Prasad, 'A Few Aspects of Education and Literature', 172; J.J. Pool, *Famous Women of India* (Calcutta: Sushil Gupta (India) Ltd., 1954), 91–92.

84. Mishra, *Mughal India*, 95.

85. Soma Mukherjee, *Royal Mughal Ladies and their Contributions* (New Delhi: Gyan Publishing House, 2001), 222.

86. Beni Prasad, 'A Few Aspects of Education and Literature', 158.

87. Blochmann, Notes to *Ain-i-Akbari*, by Abul Fazl, vol. 1: 574; Khafi Khan, *Muntakhab-al-Lubab*, Part I, 269; also Beni Prasad, 'A Few Aspects of Education and Literature', 158; Pool, *Famous Women*, 99.

88. Blochmann, Notes to *Ain-i-Akbari*, by Abul Fazl, vol. 1: 574; T.H. Hendley, *Indian Jewellery*, rpt., vol. 1(Delhi: Cultural Publishing House, 1984), 10.

89. A.S. Beveridge, 'Life and Writings', 346–347. Also Banerji, *Humayun*, vol. 2: 310. (For Mughal ladies of Humayun's time practising different recreational activities.)
90. Jahangir, *Tuzuk*, vol. 1: 106; also M. De Thevenot, *Indian Travels of Thevenot and Careri*, ed. S.N. Sen (New Delhi: National Archives of India, 1949), 57.
91. Jahangir, *Tuzuk*, vol. 2: 64; vol. 1: 48, resp.
92. Peter Mundy *The Travels of Peter Mundy in Europe and Asia*, ed. R.C. Temple, second series no. XXXV, vol. 2 (London: Hak Society, 1914), 214, note 2; Sylvia Crowe and Sheila Hayhood, *The Gardens of Mughal India* (Delhi: Vikas Publishing House Pvt. Ltd., 1973), 63 (for view that Babur built it); Ellison Banks Findly, *Noorjahan, Empress of Mughal India* (New York: Oxford University Press, 1993), 249 (for one garden with two names and Nur Jahan rebuilt it); H. Beveridge in Jahangir's *Tuzuk*, vol. 2: 76 n. (*Dahra Bagh* is the same garden that has been mentioned as *Nur Manzil* Garden by Jahangir). See Jahangir, *Tuzuk*, vol. 1: 232, 252, vol. 2: 98 (for *Nur Manjzil* garden).
93. Latif, *Lahore*, 107, 250; C.M.V. Stuart, *Gardens of the Great Mughals*, rpt. (Allahabad: R. S. Publishing House, 1979), 130–131.
94. Jahangir, *Tuzuk*, vol. 2: 192; Latif, *Lahore*, 49.
95. Mundy, *The Travels*, vol. 2: 214 and 79 n.; Francisco Pelsaert, *The Remonstrantie or Jahangir's India*, trans. W.H. Moreland and P. Geyl, rpt. (New Delhi: Idarah-i-Adabiyat-i-Delli, 1972), 5.
96. Jahangir, *Tuzuk*, vol. 2: 199.
97. Francois Bernier, *Travels in the Mogul Empire, A.D. 1656–1668*, 2nd ed. (New Delhi: S. Chand & Co., 1968), 413, nn. 1 (for Achchol garden), 2, 414 and note 2 of 413 (for garden at Vernag); also Bamzai, *A History*, 365 (for Begamabad); Stuart, *Gardens*, 184–185.
98. Findly, *Noorjahan*, 255.
99. Enakshi Bhavnani, 'Creative and Fine Arts', 166.
100. Lal, *Harem*, 96; Stephen, *Archaeology*, 256.
101. Lahori, *Badshah Nama*, Part II, vol. 1: 27; Muhammad Salih Kambo, *Amal-i-Salih or Shah Jahan Namah*, ed. G. Yazdani, vol. 2 (Kolkata: Bibliothica Indica, 1927), 36.
102. Lahori, *Badshah Nama*, Part II, vol. 1: 7 and vol. 2: 115; Muhammad Amin Qazwini, *Badshah Nama*, Aligarh Transcript, Part III (Aligarh: Aligarh Muslim University), f. 584.
103. Thevenot, *Indian Travels*, 35–36.
104. Lahori, *Badshah Nama*, Part II, vol. 1: 51.
105. Lahori, *Badshah Nama*, vol. 2: 99, 587.
106. Stuart, *Gardens*, 108; Stephen, *Archaeology*, 260–261; S. Haywood, 'The Emperors and Their Gardens', in *The Gardens of Mughal India*, by Sylvia Crowe and Sheila Haywood (New Delhi: Vikas Publishing House Pvt. Ltd., 1973), 184.
107. Stuart, *Gardens*, 103–105.
108. Stuart, *Gardens*, 134–135; Latif, *Lahore*, 190.
109. Latif, *Lahore*, 188–190; Stuart, Stuart, *Gardens*, 134–135.
110. Ibn Batuta, *Rehla*, 118. *Khankahs* are religious establishments, popularly known as monasteries for the holy men like Sufis and *derveshes* (F. Steingass, *A Comprehensive Persian–English Dictionary* (London: Routledge and Kegan Paul, 1892), 443; J.T. Platts, *A Dictionary of Urdu, Classical Hindi and English*, vol. 1 (London, 1959), 446.

111. Halim, 'Harem Influence', 53.

112. Banerji, *Humayun*, vol. 2: 317; Monserrate, *The Commentary*, 96 and note 149; Stephen, *Archaeology*, 198–199.

113. Thevenot, *Indian Travels*, 57.

114. Jahangir, *Tuzuk*, vol. 1: 232–233.

115. Jahangir, *Tuzuk*, vol. 2: 64.

116. Latif, *Lahore*, 131.

117. Pelsaert, *The Remonstrantie*, 4, note 2 (This place is different from other Sikandra, where Akbar's tomb is situated and which lies some distance, west of the river).

118. Jahangir, *Tuzuk*, vol. 1: 192, 338; Findly, *Noorjahan*, 229.

119. Mundy, *The Travels*, vol. 2: 78, 79 and note 1.

120. Findly, *Noorjahan*, 230–232; James Fergusson, *History of Indian and Eastern Architecture*, vol. 2 (Darya Ganj, New Delhi: Rupa Publications India Pvt. Ltd., 2011), 305–306.

121. Fergusson, *History of Indian*, vol. 2: 304–305; Jaffar, *Some Cultural Aspects*, 107; Crowe and Hayhood, *The Gardens*, 131; Wolseley Haig, *The Cambridge History of India*, ed. Richard Burn, vol. 4 (London: Cambridge University Press, 1937), 552. See also Latif, *Lahore*, 107.

122. Shah Nawaz Khan and Hayy, *Maasir*, Part II, vol. 2: 1079; Latif, *Lahore*, 109; Findly, *Noorjahan*, 241–242; Crowe and Hayhood, *The Gardens*, 131.

123. Bamzai, *A History*, 537. He wrote that this mosque with all its magnificence, yet, did not become popular because of the insulting remark of the queen, who, when asked about the cost of the construction, was said to have replied, pointing to her jewel-studded slipper, 'as much as this'. Also see Findly, *Noorjahan*, 238.

124. Latif, *Lahore*, 206.

125. Must'ad Khan, *Maasir-i-Alamgiri*, 90.

126. Lahori, *Badshah Nama*, Part II, vol. 1: 252; Blochmann, Notes to *Ain-i-Akbari*, by Abul Fazl, vol. 1: 375.

127. Khafi Khan, *Muntakhab-al-Lubab*, Part I, 706; Soma Mukherjee, *Royal Mughal Ladies*, 201.

128. Lahori, *Badshah Nama*, vol. 2: 469.

129. Khafi Khan, *Muntakhab-al-Lubab*, Part I, 706.

130. Bernier, *Mogul Empire*, 280–281; Thevenot, *Indian Travels*, 60; Manucci, *Storia Do Mogor*, vol. 1: 213. Also see Stephen, *Archaeology*, 247; H.C. Fanshawe, *Delhi Past and Present* (London: J. Murray, 1902), 52.

131. J.B. Tavernier, *Travels in India by Jean Baptiste Tavernier*, trans. V. Ball, ed. William Crooke, vol. 1 (New Delhi: Oriental Books Reprint Corpn., 1977), 41, note 1.

132. Lahori, *Badshah Nama*, Part II, vol. 1: 51.

133. Stephen, *Archaeology*, 109.

134. Kambo, *Amal-i-Salih*, vol. 3: 47; Soma Mukherjee, *Royal Mughal Ladies*, 202.

135. Harihar Das, *The Norris Embassy to Aurangzib (1699–1702)*, Condensed and rearranged by S.C. Sarkar, 1st ed. (Kolkata: K. L. Mukhopadhyay, 1959), 236; see also Schimmel, *Islam*, 102, f. note 70.

136. Sarkar, *Aurangzib*, vol. 1: 38; vol. 3: 35; Stephen, *Archaeology*, 261–263; Schimmel, *Islam*, 102, f. note 70.

137. Stephen, *Archaeology*, 274–275.

138. Bazaz, *Daughters of the Vitasta*, 159; also Sufi, *Kashir*, vol. 2: 389.

139. Sufi, *Kashir*, vol. 2: 389.

140. Thevenot, *Indian Travels*, 53 and portrait facing 50; De Laet, *The Empire of the Great Mogol*, trans., ann. J.S. Hoyland and S.N. Banerjee, rpt. (New Delhi: Idarah-i-Adabiyat-i-Delli, 1975), 80–81; Edward Terry, in *Early Travels in India*, ed. William Foster (New Delhi: S. Chand & Co., 1968), 308; also K.P. Sahu, *Some Aspects of North Indian Social Life* (1000-1526), 1st ed. (Calcutta: Punthi Pustak, 1973), 78. See also Manucci, *Storia Do Mogor*, vol. 2: 139–140.

141. Manucci (*Storia Do Mogor*, vol. 2: 318) referred to it as a 'sheet of cloth'; Badaoni, *Muntakhabu-t-Tawarikh*, trans. S.A. Ranking, vol. 1: 503 (as '*Chadar*'); Meer Hassan Ali, *Observations of the Mussulmauns of India*, vol. 1, rpt. (New Delhi: Idarah-i-Adabiyat-i-Delli, 1973), 108–109 (as '*dupatta*'). See also Bernier, *Mogul Empire*, 170 for a portrait.

142. De Laet, *The Empire*, 81; also Della Valle, in *European Travellers under the Mughals*, by Ansari (New Delhi: Idarah-i-Adabiyat-i-Delli, 1975), 107. For details of dresses, see K.P. Sahu, 77–78; Ila Mukherji, *Social Status*, 55–57; Chopra, *Some Aspects*, 11–14; Ojha, *North Indian*, 30.

143. Ibn Batuta, *Rehla*, 179, 202.

144. Minhaj-ud-din Siraj, *Tabaqat-i-Nasiri*, trans. Raverty, vol. 1: 643; Gulbadan, *Humayun Nama*, 138, note 6; Manucci, *Storia Do Mogor*, vol. 2: 318; Thevenot, *Indian Travels*, 51, 53 see also Chopra, *Some Aspects*, 13; Jamila BrijBhushan, *The World of Indian Miniatures* (Tokyo: Kodansha International, 1979), 116.

145. Ibn Batuta, *Rehla*, 122, 179, 202; Amir Khusrau, *Ijaz-i-Khusravi*, vol. 5 (Lucknow, 1875–1876), 127; Amir Khusrau, *Nuh-Sipihr*, ed. M.W. Mirza, vol. 7 (Kolkata, 1948), 379.

146. Fryer, *A New Account*, vol. 2: 117; Ralph Fitch, in *Early Travels in India*, ed. William Foster (New Delhi: S. Chand & Co., 1968), 13, 28; J.F.G. Careri, *Indian Travels of Thevenot and Careri*, ed. S.N. Sen (New Delhi: National Archives of India, 1949), 248; Thevenot, *Indian Travels*, 53; J.S. Stavorinus, *Voyage to the East Indies (1768-1771)*, trans. Samuel Hull Wilcocke, vol. 1 (London: G. G. & J. Robinson, 1798), 416; see also J. Ovington, *India in the Seventeenth Century*, ed. J.P. Guha, vol. 1 (New Delhi: Associated Publishing House, 1976), 142–143.

147. Manucci, *Storia Do Mogor*, vol. 2: 317–318. See also Chapter 4.

148. For enumeration of ornaments and toilets, see Khusrau, *Matla-ul-Anwar*, 225, 228; *Nuh-Sipihr*, vol. 7: 383, 560; *Hasht Bahisht*, 30–31; Ibn Batuta, *Rehla*, 79, 122; Abul Fazl, *Ain-i-Akbari*, vol. 3: 341–345; Bernier, *Mogul Empire*, 223–224; De Laet, *The Empire*, 81; Careri, *Indian Travels*, Part III, 252; J.A. De Mandelslo, *The Voyage and Travels of J. Albert de Mandelslo... into the East Indies*, trans. John Davies (London: Printed for John Starkey, and Thomas Basset, 1669), 50; Jahangir, *Tuzuk*, vol. 1: 375, vol. 2: 99, 100, 101, 180; also K.P. Sahu, *Some Aspects of North Indian Social Life (1000–1526)*, 1st ed. (Kolkata: Punthi Pustak, 1973), 81–85; Ila Mukherji, *Social Status*, 63–78; Chopra, *Some Aspects*, 21–28; Ojha, *North Indian*, 36–45.

149. Khusrau, *Matla-ul-Anwar*, 186–194 and 173 resp. See also Ashraf, *Life and Conditions*, 215–216.

150. Amir Khusrau, *Dewal Rani Khizr Khan*, in *Khalji Kaleen Bharat*, trans. S.A.A. Rizvi, ed. R.A. Ansari (Aligarh: Aligarh Muslim University, 1917), 223.

151. Khusrau, *Matla-ul-Anwar*, 225, 194; Amir Khusrau, *Hasht Bahisht*, ed. Maulana Sayyid Suleiman Ashraf (Aligarh: Aligarh Muslim University, 1918), 29–31.

152. Firoz Shah Tughlaq, *Futuhat-i-Firoz Shahi*, ed. S.A. Rashid (Aligarh, 1954), Rule 14: 11.

153. Ibn Batuta, *Rehla*, 45; Ferishta, *Tarikh-i-Ferishta*, vol. 2: 185; Gulbadan, *Humayun Nama*, 159, also Beveridge,Appendix A, 230. (as per Gulbadan's description, Gulbarg Begam was Sultanam's stepdaughter).

154. Beveridge, Introduction and Appendix A to Gulbadan's *Humayun Nama*, 49, 260.

155. Abul Fazl, *Akbar Nama*, vol. 2 (New Delhi: Ess Ess Publications, 1977), 366–367; Beveridge, Appendix A to Gulbadan's *Humayun Nama*, 220.

156. Bayazid Biyat, *Tazkirah-i-Humayun-wa-Akbar*, ed. M. Hidayat Husain (Kolkata: Bibliothica Indica, 1941), 355; Abul Fazl, *Akbar Nama*, vol. 3: 205–206, 363; Beveridge, Introduction to Gulbadan's *Humayun Nama*, 69–70.

157. C.H. Payne, *Akbar and the Jesuits* (London: Harper & Brothers, 1926), 153, 269–270.

158. Latif, *Lahore*, 206.

159. Rizkullah Mushtaqi, *Waqiat-i-Mushtaqi*, in *Uttar Taimur Kaleen Bharat*, Part II, trans. Rizvi (Aligarh: Aligarh Muslim University, 1958–1959), 563.

160. Zia-ud-din Barani, *Tarikh-i-Firoz Shahi* (Kolkata: Bibliothica Indica, 1862), 482–483; Ibn Batuta, *Rehla*, 118, 127.

161. Gulbadan, *Humayun Nama*, 111.

162. Monserrate, *The Commentary*, 96.

163. Abul Fazl, *Akbar Nama*, vol. 2: 484; Monserrate, *The Commentary*, 205.

164. Muhammad Hadi, *Tatimma-i-Waqiat-i-Jahangiri*, trans. H.M. Elliot and John Dowson, in *History of India as Told by Its Own Historians*, vol. VI (Allahabad: Kitab Mahal, 1964), 399; also Mutamad Khan, *Iqbalnama-i-Jahangiri*, trans. H.M. Elliot and John Dowson, Vol. VI, 405.

165. Shah Nawaz Khan and Hayy, *Maasir*, Part II, vol. 2: 1078.

166. Sarkar, *Studies*, 11–12; Kambo, *Amal-i-Salih*, vol. 1: 249; also Qazwini, *Badshah Nama*, Aligarh Transcript, part II, f. 277; Chowdhuri, 'Mumtaz Mahall', 378.

167. Manucci, *Storia Do Mogor*, vol. 2: 117. See also Lal, *Harem*, 95.

168. Sarkar, *Aurangzib*, vol. 1: 38; Must'ad Khan, *Maasir-i-Alamgiri*, 323; also Schimmel, *Islam*, 102.

169. Manucci, *Storia Do Mogor*, vol. 4: 185.

170. Mirza Muhammad Bakhsh Ashub, 'Tarikh-i-Shahadat-i-Farrukhsiyar-wa-Julus-i-Muhammad Shahi Badshah', Rotograph, vol. 1 (Aligarh: History Department, Aligarh Muslim University), f. 35b.

171. Ashub, Tarikh-i-Shahadat, vol. 1: f. 36a; J.N. Sarkar, *Fall of the Mughal Empire*, vol. 1 (Kolkata: M.C. Sarkar & Sons, 1966), 209.

172. Herman Goetz, *The Art and Architecture of Bikaner State* (London: Oxford University Press, 1950), 172.

173. S.A.A. Rizvi, *A History of Sufism in India*, vol. 1 (Delhi: Munshiram Manoharlal, 1978), 166.

174. Hamid Qalander, *Khair-ul-Majalis*, ed. K.A. Nizami (Aligarh: Aligarh Muslim University, n.d.), 87, also see 218.

175. Amir Khurd, *Siyar-u'l-Auliya*, (Delhi: Muhib-i-Hind Press, 1302 A.H./1884 A.D), 180–81; see also A. Rashid, *Society and Culture*, 130.

176. Qalander, *Khair-ul-Majalis*, 63–65; See also Rizvi, *Sufism*, vol. 1: 401–402 (for Nizam-ud-din Auliya's and Baba Farid's regard for their mothers).

177. Dehlawi, Abdu'l-Haqq Muhaddis, *Akkbaru'l-Akhyar* (Delhi: Matba-i- Mujtabai, 1332 A.H./1914 A.D.), 295; see also Rizvi, *Sufism*, vol. 1: 401.

178. Qalander, *Khair-ul-Majalis*, 68, 134.

179. L.C. Nand, *Women in Delhi Sultanate* (Allahabad: Vohra Publishers and Distributors, 1989), 147–148; Rashid, *Society and Culture*, 138.

180. Dehlawi, *Akkbaru'l-Akhyar*, 298; also Rizvi, *Sufism*, vol. 1: 403.

181. Dehlawi, *Akkbaru'l-Akhyar*, 294; also Rizvi, *Sufism*, vol. 1: 401.

182. Dehlawi, *Akkbaru'l-Akhyar*, 136–137; Chishti, Allah Diyah, *Siyar-ul-Aqtab*(Lucknow: Newal Kishore, 1913), 163–64. See also See also Nizami, K. A., *The Life and Times of Shaikh Farid-ud-din Ganjishakar* (Delhi: Idarah-i-Adabiyat-i-Delli, 1973), 15. Rizvi, *Sufism*, vol. 1: 401–02.

183. Jamali, *Siyar-u'l-Arifin* 32; Sijzi, Amir Hasan, com., *Fawa'id-u'l-Fu'ad*, Lucknow: Newal Kishore Press, 1302 A.H./1884 A.D.), 136; see also Nizami, *Ganjishakar*, 15; Rizvi, *Sufism*, vol. 1: 139.

184. Jamali, *Siyar-u'l-Arifin*, 101–02; Sijzi, Amir Hasan, com., *Fawa'id-u'l-Fu'ad*, 245; see also K.A. Nizami, *Some Aspects of Religion and Politics in India During the Thirteenth Century*, 2nd ed. (New Delhi: Idarah-i-Adabiyat-i-Delli, 1974), 200; also Rashid, *Society and Culture*, 138.

185. Nizami, *Ganjishakar*, 65; Rashid, *Society and Culture*, 139.

186. Sufi, *Kashir*, vol. 2: 383–387.

187. Sijzi, Amir Hasan, com., *Fawa'id-u'l-Fu'ad*, 59; see also Nizami, *Religion and Politics*, 300.

188. Badaoni, *Muntakhabu-t-Tawarikh*, trans. W.H. Lowe, vol. 2: 320; Abul Fazl, *Akbar Nama*, vol. 2: 476–477; Pelsaert, *The Remonstrantie*, 70; Jahangir, *Tuzuk*, vol. 1: 110 and vol. 2: 101, 109, resp.; Kambo, *Amal-i-Salih*, vol. 2: 422.

Conclusion

The foregoing study highlights the social, economic, political and cultural dimensions of Muslim womanhood in the medieval period of the Indian history. The analysis takes into account the Islamic heritage on the one hand and the impact of Hinduism and its practices on the other. The changing status of Muslim women, both in ideology and in practice, emerges clearly.

In the social context, the overall position of Muslim women was dismal. Barring her role as a mother, where she commanded universal respect, she had a subservient position in social hierarchy. In those warring times, there was a universal craving for a son. Daughters were a security risk and a liability for Muslims. Therefore, the birth of a daughter was unwelcome for Muslims, both rulers and the ruled. They were married at a very early age, although this age was slightly higher for the aristocratic classes. Child marriage retarded physical and mental development of the women. They were discriminated against even in celebrations of birth and death. Muslims also adopted the dowry system of the Hindus. Daughters, therefore, became undesirable. The permission of divorce by Muslim society and its practice brought respite to some Muslim ladies. However, not many of them moved to courts for seeking divorce because of their weak social position. The male dominance and general social set-up dwarfed their personality. On account of the prevailing polygamy, the women had to bear with neglect and apathy, even if they were not divorced by their husbands. There were instances when divorced wives were also kept by their erstwhile husbands, even after the period of *iddat*. The institution of divorce, therefore, lost its value. It became rare under the Hindu impact. The practice of remarriage, as allowed by Islam, was followed in the beginning. Gradually, it also relegated to the background under the influence of Hinduism. Polygamy was a way of life with the affluent class, the number only varying according to the means, the requirement and the fancy of the man. The agricultural and labour class practised monogamy. Among other Muslim population, polygamy, though followed, yet came to be discouraged gradually. The Hindu practices of *sati* and *jauhar* made inroads into the Islamic practices, but they were not popular. A woman within the house was considered a man's possession. She was even sold for paying off taxes. Confined within her home, she had no other vocation in life except bearing and rearing of children and managing the home. Many restrictions were placed on women, which became stricter with increasing moral degradation of the society. Too many checks on them caused aberrations in their behaviour and deterioration in their moral values. Such tendencies grew more, as the restrictions imposed on women increased over a period of time. The common Muslim women generally safeguarded their chastity. The general sensual appeal brought a thriving business for the prostitutes, dancing and singing girls. Prostitution was taken as a necessary evil; this profession was not considered honourable. Gradually, the society developed tolerance for the harlots and they came to be patronised by the royalty and the aristocracy. The dancers and singers also enjoyed this patronage. They acquired proficiency professionally, but morally, they had to go down, because of the moral decline of their patronising masters. The menial female slaves were not treated well. But those slaves who were kept for entertainment tried to catch the fancy of their masters. Some of them succeeded and were able to rise to become centre of power in the later Mughal period. There was a soft corner for widows. The kings, queens and nobles provided for their living. The general behaviour towards the female relations was, more or less, good. Woman was considered the honour of the house and the man was to defend her. At times, she was also equated with social honour. However, the Muslim rulers were, generally, harsh towards the ladies of their opponents, irrespective of religion. There were some instances of good treatment meted out to them, but this reflected only the individual mood and not the general attitude of the society towards women. In general social estimation, they ranked very low and were considered helpless, dependent, short-sighted, cowardly and fit only for sensual entertainment.

The right of maintenance, provided to Muslim women by the Quran, was followed by the Muslim society of the medieval India. Some of the kings provided for the needy women by way of bestowal of *jagirs*, *suyurghal* grants (*madad-i-maash*), *wazifa*, land grants and right of collection of land revenue. *Madad-i-maash* grants originated with Mughals and could not be sold or transferred, except through inheritance. They were so extensive that Aurangzeb laid down a code of inheritance. The kings along with many nobles and royal ladies extended help to the destitute women financially. The ladies getting maintenance, generally, obeyed their masters. Such a surety of maintenance led to a sense of complacence among women, which smothered their quest for higher attainments.

Mahr was another economic right of Muslim women, provided by the Quran. In the early medieval period, the *mahr* was fixed at a low amount, and hence was paid in practice also. But gradually, as the *mahr* amount became high, the practice lost its importance and *mahr* became just a phony promise seldom fulfilled.

As regards the property rights, Muslim women owned and inherited property during this period. Some of the sultans followed the Shariat law in this regard, but mostly, Islamic rules were disregarded. The inheritance depended on the influence of the lady concerned or on the local customs. Often, they did not receive their share, unless there were no close male relatives or the parents were very wealthy. They could not afford to be assertive because of their weak position. Even those who inherited, their rights were, generally, infringed and women were not in a position to defend them. In most of the cases wherein courts were approached for redress, it was done mainly by their male guardians or male relatives. The society considered it worthy of a woman to remain in seclusion rather than to have economic independence. Many lower and middle class ladies came out of their houses for earning their living by working for others or through independent professions. They could not get a social standing for themselves, in spite of their economic viability, because of the prevalence of purdah. The Mughal ladies involved themselves in high-stake trades. But, the society did not look at it disparagingly. Their economic affluence and social aloofness generated awe and respect. The ladies also collected wealth through gifts and gratification, their possessions varying according to their economic and political involvement, closeness to the ruler, financial means of their respective masters and the period to which they belonged. The Muslim ladies of the Mughal time were much richer than their counterparts in the sultanate period.

The men of royalty and nobility maintained harem. In the pre-Mughal period, large harem was considered a status symbol. The sultans and nobles maintained big harems to enhance their prestige. Some of the sultans even framed rules for harmonious living within their harem and also for safeguarding its seclusion. During Mughal times, Babur and Humayun had small harems. With the coming of Akbar, the practice of keeping large harems was restored. He greatly improved upon the existing harem management and organisation. Dwelling was provided to all inmates of the harem; the size and type of accommodation depended upon the position of a particular lady within the seraglio. These women in harem had a very circumscribed life. They were lavishly provided. They squandered their time and money in wearing costly clothes, using various toilets and adornments, celebrating fairs and festivals and involving themselves in interior decorations, feasting, music, dance and other recreations. The Mughal ladies found time for going on excursions. They had fun in the celebration of *Khushroz*. They preferred everything fine, gilded, silvered, jewelled or precious stone-studded. In all their activities, ostentation was conspicuous. They enjoyed high-sounding epithets to be added to their names. Such pomp and show was more marked during the time of the Mughals than that of the sultanate period, particularly during the reign of Shah Jahan onwards, till the depletion of royal treasury in the later Mughal period. The male master remained the pivot of their activities. It was their constant endeavour to remain ever attractive for him. Women in harem were not sure of conjugal fidelity. They indulged in drinking and other vices. In short, they had all glamour and luxury. Yet, they could not carve out a permanent social standing for themselves. Their status depended either on their affluence or on the social position of their respective masters. Any variation in these two factors led to a change in their social recognition. At last, when both power and pelf deserted the royalty, their ladies also lost their position. The nobility, dependent on the royalty for its affluence and power, also faded away with the passage of time.

Purdah and seclusion of women had become a part and parcel of the Muslim society. It was considered a symbol of social prestige and a sign of modesty and decency. The women of the higher strata of society were, therefore, very rigid about its observance. Purdah norms were, generally, strict during the sultanate period, became relaxed during the time of Babur and Humayun, again became stringent from the reign of Akbar and were severest during the reign of Aurangzeb. In the later Mughal period, purdah came to be observed within the harem also because of the presence of *Khanazads, Salatins* and other *na-mahram* relations. The ladies of economically backward classes never observed purdah. They had to come out in order to earn their living. They only observed *ghunghat* (covering of head and a part of the face with *dupatta* or any other cloth) whenever they met a stranger. The other Muslim women, by and large, supported veil. The contemporary chroniclers eulogised purdah. Some of the kings, both of sultanate and the Mughal periods, brought ordinances to ensure observance of purdah and seclusion of the women. The practice proved most damaging for the overall development of the Muslim ladies. They were deprived of education and were prevented from mixing with the outside world. This retarded their mental growth, damaged their physical health, blunted their faculties, limited their horizon and made them susceptible to all sorts of superstitions and taboos.

Muslim women of royalty and nobility influenced the politics of the time. The early Turks accepted the sovereignty of Razia outwardly, because of the impact of Persian norms, which recognised a lady sovereign. But, inwardly, they remained averse to the idea of a lady ruling them. The Afghans generally kept their women in the background, yet allowed some participation. The policy of the Mughals was different. They never allowed the right of sovereignty to a lady. Even Jahangir guarded it zealously. But, beyond this, they were much more liberal than their counterparts in the sultanate period. In the sultanate period, except for Razia and a few others, the ladies, mostly, acted through their husbands or wards and were mainly involved in succession feuds or acted as reconciliators or instigators. During the Mughal time, many ladies were involved in active politics and administration and many others in reconciliatory role. The extent of this influence varied from one lady to the other, depending upon the thrust of their individual personalities and the outlook of the reigning king. The nature of their impact, good or bad, also depended on the upbringing and insight of the lady concerned. In the early medieval period, the ladies of royal blood dominated the scene. But during the later Mughal period, the dancing and slave girls outwitted the royal ladies. They exploited the prevailing licentiousness among the royalty and came to the forefront in the political field. They indulged in nepotism, court machinations and open gratification. They caused great harm to the decaying Mughal Empire.

Muslim women remained backward in the sphere of education. They were mainly taught the tenets of Islam and the practical arts like cooking, stitching, embroidery, concerning their household duties.

Only a few of the privileged ladies from among the royalty and nobility, particularly during the Mughal period, were fortunate to get education in subjects other than these. Razia and Bibi Raji patronised education during the sultanate period. Among the Mughals, many ladies maintained big libraries and were proficient in Persian and Arabic, calligraphy, tenets of Islam, composition of Hindi, Persian and Arabic poetry. They also patronised men of letters. The kings of the sultanate period were more conservative in their outlook and no mention is found about any general system of educating harem ladies. The Mughals started a regular system of imparting rudimentary knowledge to the ladies of the royal harem through the person of the school mistress called *Atun mama*. They also recognised the talents of the ladies not born in high families. Education of the common Muslim ladies remained largely a private affair and the state did not pay much attention towards it. Even none of the ladies of royalty, who otherwise worked for general educational development of men, ever thought of working exclusively for the promotion of the education of the fair sex. Consequently, educational opportunities for the Muslim ladies remained deficient.

Within the family sphere, the common women practised folk art and craft and, at times, their creations were of great artistic value. Yet, they could not attain the desired social recognition. The ladies of the higher strata got wider opportunities and large resources for their cultural pursuits. Their achievements in the sultanate period are not known. But some of the Mughal ladies produced works of creative art. They introduced new fashions and designs in dresses and ornaments, invented new perfumes, wrote books, constructed magnificent buildings and developed majestic gardens. Such pursuits earned for them a status in the society and a name in history. In the religious field, the ladies of well-to-do class undertook hajj, although such pilgrimage was discouraged after Akbar, due to Portuguese threat in the Arabian Sea. The visits to *mazars* of the *pirs* were also popular among Muslim ladies of all classes and clime. There were also Muslim ladies who were turning *joginis*. Sufi fold was the only exception, wherein women were given equal opportunities, along with men, for spiritual attainments. There were many lady mystic Sufi saints, who got highest regard and recognition in the society. However, Sufism did not allow spiritual succession to women.

Economic affluence, purdah and the class to which one belonged were the three factors that had a direct effect on the status that

Muslim women enjoyed in the society. Since money was mainly concentrated in the hands of the upper class of the society, the ladies of this class were rated high in the scale. Similarly, the ladies who could maintain their seclusion earned social respect for themselves. Others, who came out because of their economic need, became an object of social apathy. As a class, the women of the royalty and nobility got the highest social recognition, till they possessed pelf and position. Even breaking of purdah norms by some of them was overlooked by the society. Their involvement in trade activities was also not viewed adversely. Their commercial activities were of a high order and remained beyond the reach and comprehension of the common Muslim folks.

Purdah, the lack of proper education and over-sensuality of that period left a permanent mark on the development of Muslim women and adversely affected their social status. Their seclusion and educational backwardness rendered them helpless and dependent. The prevailing polygamy and over-sensuality of the age made them mere instruments of sexual gratification. The result was that the purdah rules were made stringent. The very birth of a girl became unwelcome and her existence became a burden. This brought, in its trail, the practices like early marriages, premature maternity, untimely aging and growing female mortality. Some of the Muslim rulers, like Ala-ud-din Khalji, Firoz Shah Tughlaq, Sher Shah Suri, Akbar and Aurangzeb, made some efforts to ameliorate the condition of women. Their impact was negligible.

Bibliography

Bibliographical Note

The study of Muslim women of medieval India is handicapped by the scanty and sketchy information available about them from the writings of the contemporary historians. A researcher has to gather relevant information from stray references, appearing here and there, in such literature.

The first important primary source of information is Minhaj's *Tabaqat-i-Nasiri*. The author provides an account of the political role of the royal ladies and brings to light the social conditions of the harem ladies and their cultural activities till 1259 A.D. Barani takes up the thread from him and carries it further to 1356 A.D. He is the most informative author for the history of the Khaljis and the Tughlaqs. His narration of the events, which took place around that time and his personal comments thereupon, as contained in his *Tarikh-i-Firoz Shahi* and *Fatawa-i-Jahandari*, throw ample light on the condition of Muslim women of that period. Equally important is Afif's *Tarikh-i-Firoz Shahi*. It covers the entire reign of Firoz Shah Tughlaq (1351–1388). Apart from the information about the lives of the harem ladies, he throws light on the common Muslim women and the burning issues like child marriage, dowry, dancing girls and the position of slaves as well. Sirhindi's *Tarikh-i-Mubarak Shahi* gives the most authentic account for 35 years, from 1400 to 1434 A.D. One gets a glimpse of the lives of the ladies in harem in this work. Isami's *Futuh-us-Salatin* (the history of Muslim conquerors and rulers of India from the Ghaznavites to the date of its composition in 1350 A.D.), Firoz Shah's *Futuhat-i-Firoz Shahi*, Rizkullah Mushtaqi's *Waqiat-i-Mushtaqi* (a detailed anecdote of the times of Lodi and Sur dynasties) and Sikander's *Mirat-i-Sikanderi* are also important.

Amir Khusrau's writings are especially helpful. Being a sensitive member of the society, he has vividly brought out the prevailing customs and practices regarding Muslim women and has elaborated all aspects of the contemporary feminine life. His works, namely *Hasht Bahisht, Ijaz-i-Khusravi, Matla-ul-Anwar, Khazain-ul-Futuh* (a history of reign of Ala-ud-din Khalji from his accession in 1296 to 1311 A.D.), *Nuh-Sipihr* (a poetic description of the court of Qutb-ud-din Mubarak Shah along with important events of his reign), *Qiran-us-Sadain and Dewal Rani Khizr Khan*, all provide useful information about different aspects of Muslim ladies.

For the Mughal period, the autobiographies of the members of the royal families are full of minute details of the harem activities. Babur's sentimental details, in his *Babur Nama*, about his female relatives, like grandmother, mother, sisters, wives, daughters and others, provide precious knowledge. Gulbadan Begam's *Humayun Nama* is much better. Being a lady and an inmate of the harem, her attention was essentially focused on feminine things and she wrote lucidly about them. The most important, however, is *Tuzuk-i-Jahangiri*, the autobiography of Emperor Jahangir. Being the master of the harem, his knowledge about it was intimate, and hence his account is very informative and authentic. He deals at length about the celebrations of *Nauroz* festival, weighing ceremonies, excursions with ladies, liberal allowances made to them, their clothes and their past times, about Nurjahan and his other wives and lady relations and many other subjects of interest.

Among the historians, Abul Fazl's *Ain-i-Akbari* and *Akbar Nama* and Nizam-ud-din Ahmad's *Tabaqat-i-Akbari* are valuable sources. They give concise account of Akbar's harem and its activities. Besides, the political roles played by ladies like Maham Anaga, Hamida Banu, Salima Sultan Begam and others find detailed mention in their writings. Abul Fazl also described events like Akbar's regard for his mother, his marriages with Indian princesses, his excursions with ladies and pilgrimages undertaken by these ladies. Badaoni's critical remarks about Akbar's reign in his *Muntakhabu-T-Tawarikh* balance the flattering observations made by Abul Fazl, a court historian. *Tarikh-i-Ferishta* was completed by Muhammad Qasim Hindu Shah, better known as Ferishta, towards the end of Akbar's reign (1606–1607 A.D.). It is a general history of India from the earliest times to the date of its composition. It is an important source to know about the activities of the Muslim ladies in different fields and also about their status in the society.

As regards the period of Jahangir, Mutamad Khan's *Iqbalnama-i-Jahangiri* and Muhammad Hadi's *Tatimma-i-Waqiat-i-Jahangiri* complete Jahangir's Tuzuk and throw light on different facets of Nurjahan's activities. Qazwini and Abdul Hamid Lahori are among the main sources of the time of Shah Jahan. They bring into focus the artistic pursuits and other activities of the Muslim ladies, and also their economic resources. Therefore, Qazwini's 'Badshah Nama' and Lahori's *Badshah Nama* (an official history of Shah Jahan from 1628 to 1647 A.D.) become important. Mirza Nathan's *Baharistan-i-Ghaybi* throws light on the *jauhar* committed by the Muslim ladies during the reign of Jahangir and Shah Jahan.

During the period of Aurangzeb, although restrictions were placed on writing official history, yet, the Persian chroniclers continued writing about the ladies and, at times, gave very saucy descriptions about the women in the harem. Hamid-ud-din Khan's description of Aurangzeb's attraction for Zainabadi in his *Ahkam-i-Alamgiri* and Khafi Khan's details of Jahandar's infatuation for Lal Kanwar are some of the examples. Hamid-ud-din also delved in the political role of the Muslim ladies. Khafi Khan, however, has the distinction of being a non-commissioned, non-official contemporary source for more than a century (1630–1732) and described, in his *Muntakhab-Al-Lubab*, not only the political role of Muslim ladies, but also the lavish living of the ladies and the fashions of the time. Must'ad Khan's *Maasir-i-Alamgiri* (the history of last 40 years of Aurangzeb's reign, with a prefix and a sketch of first 10 years, abridged from *Alamgir Nama* of Muhammad Kazim) is a useful source for varied information about the ladies of Aurangzeb's harem. *Rukkat-i-Alamgiri* (a collection of letters of Aurangzeb) and *Adab-i-Alamgiri* (a collection of letters written in the name of Aurangzeb by Munshi-ul-Mamalik Abul Fath, entitled Qabil Khan and collected by Sadiq Multalibi) also give information about political activities of Mughal ladies of Aurangzeb's time.

In the later Mughal period, since many royal and noble ladies came out of purdah and many of the dancing and singing women rose high in position, a number of chroniclers wrote first-hand account of these ladies. Thus, Gholam Hussein's *Siyar-ul-Mutakherin* brought out the political role of Muslim ladies and also other aspects of their lives like slackening of purdah rules, slackening of moral values and diminishing status of women. Shiv Das Lakhnawi's *Shahnama Munawwar Kalam*, a history mainly of Farrukhsiyar's reign, also confirms the degenerating values among women. Mirza Muhammad Bakhsh Ashub's *Tarikh-i-Shahadat-i-Farrukhsiyar Wa-Julus-i-Muhammad Shahi Badshah* is full of valuable details about the reign of Muhammad Shah and the harem activities. Dargah Quli Khan, through his personal diary entitled *Muraqqa-e-Delhi*, gave a detailed account of the different lady singers and dancers of Muhammad Shah's time. Among the regional histories, Ghulam Husain's *Riyazu-s-Salatin*, Yusuf Ali's *Ahwal-i-Mahabat Jang* and Karam Ali's *Muzaffarnamah* are important for Bengal and *Tahmas Nama* of Tahmas Beg Khan Bahadur Miskin for Panjab.

A number of European travellers, who happened to come to India, provide valuable accounts of Muslim women. Many of them lived in India for a long time, travelled widely and also remained in service of kings and nobles. Some of them were also favoured by the emperors and had an access to their harems. Akbar once provided special protection to Monserrate from the wrath of the Muslim courtiers. Jahangir insisted on Hawkins to remain at his court as Resident Ambassador. Manucci and Bernier, doctors of the ladies of their Mughal masters, had an access to their harems. They acquired first-hand knowledge about the way of life of Muslim women, which they penned down in their writings. These Europeans were not constrained to write with caution, lest they would hurt the vanity of any sovereign and nor did they need to write in a way so as to please and pamper any monarch. Hence, they wrote frankly and fearlessly.

These travellers are often charged of being gossipy, concocting stories and maligning the fair image of royalty and nobility or denigrating the Muslim social life by considering themselves superior. Such charges cannot be accepted on their face value. They cannot be suspected of deliberately indulging in sensational writings, because none of their accounts was designed for publication, which is clear from the lack of proportion in them. It should also be kept in mind that although the court historians could not write anything disparaging to the king, yet, such incidents did become the talk of the town and were whispered about all around. European travellers did not invent scandals and they wrote what they saw or heard. Consequently, the accounts of these Europeans are important from the point of supplementing the records of the Persian writers, and thus completing the picture of the harem life. Also, while the Persians chroniclers wrote mostly about the harem, the Europeans depicted different aspects of life of Muslim women in their narration. Therefore, their writings are of immense value for having a complete view of the life of Muslim women of that period.

Among the travel accounts, Ibn Batuta's *Rehla* is a mine of historical information. It gives an eyewitness account of Muslim women and their social worth. Monserrate wrote about education and journeys of the Mughal princesses. Hawkins described the financial resources of Mughal ladies and narrated the *Nauroz* celebrations. Finch gave details about commercial activities of the queens and princesses. Terry, Manrique, Thevenot, Careri, Tavernier, Bowrey and Stavorinus wrote about different aspects of the life in the harem. Among the travellers, Pelsaert, Manucci and Bernier wrote elaborately on subjects pertaining to feminine activities.

Primary Sources

Abdullah. *Tarikh-i-Daudi*. In *Uttar Taimur Kaleen Bharat*, Part I, translated by S.A.A. Rizvi.

Afif, Shams Siraj. *Tarikh-i-Firoz_Shahi*. Edited by Maulvi Vilayat Husain. Kolkata: Bibliothica Indica, 1891.

Ahmad, Khwaja Nizam-ud-din. *Tabaqat-i-Akbari*. Translated by B. De and Baini Prashad, vol. 1 and 2. Kolkata: The Asiatic Society, 1973; vol. 3. Kolkata: Bibliothica Indica, 1939–1940; also Translated by S.A.A. Rizvi, *Uttar Taimur Kaleen Bharat*,Part II.

Ali Muhammad Khan. *Mirat-i-Ahmadi*. Translated by M.F. Lokhandwala, 1st ed. Baroda: Oriental Institute, 1965.

Ali Khan, Muhammad. *Tarikh-i-Mazaffari*. Translated by H.M. Elliot and John Dowson, vol. VIII: Allahabad: Kitab Mahal, 1964.

Amir Khurd, *Siyar-u'l-Auliya*. Delhi: Muhib-i-Hind Press, 1302 A.H./ 1884 A.D.

Amir Khusrau, Abul Hasan. *Dewal Rani Khizr Khan*. In *Khalji Kaleen Bharat*, translated by S.A.A. Rizvi, also edited by R.A. Ansari. Aligarh: Aligarh Muslim University, 1917.

_____. *Hasht Bahisht*. Edited by Maulana Sayyid Suleiman Ashraf. Aligarh: Aligarh Muslim University, 1918.

_____. *Ijaz-i-Khusravi*. Vols II, IV, V. Lucknow: Newal Kishore, 1875–1876.

_____. *Khazain-ul-Futuh*. In *The Campaign of Ala-ud-din Khilji*, translated by Mohammad Habib. Mumbai: D.B. Taraporewala sons & Co., 1931.

_____. *Matla-ul-Anwar*. Lucknow: Newal Kishore, 1302 A.H./1884 A.D.

_____. *Nuh-Sipihr*. Edited by Mohammad Wahid Mirza, Vols. III, VII. Kolkata, 1948.

_____. *Qiran-us-Sadain*. Edited by Maulvi Mohammad Ismail and Syed Hasan Barani. Aligarh: Aligarh College Press, 1918.

Anonymous. *Intikhab-i-Jahangir_Shahi*. Translated by H.M. Elliot and John Dowson, Vol. VI.

_____. *Iqbal Nama*. Translated by S.H. Askari, *Iqbalnama by an Anonymous Contemporary Writer*. Patna: Janki Prakashan, 1983; also translated by H.M. Elliot and John Dowson, vol. VI.

_____. *Tarikh-i-Ahmad_Shah*. In *History of India*, translated by H.M. Elliot and John Dowson, vol. VIII.

_____. *Tarikh-i-Alamgir Sani*. Translated by H.M. Elliot and John Dowson, vol. VIII.

_____. *Tarikh-i-Salim Sahi*. In *Memoirs of the Emperor Jahangir Written_by Himself*, translated by David Price. New Delhi: Rare Books, 1904.

_____. 'Tarikh-i-Haqqi'. Persian Ms. No. 89, Cat. 537.Bankipur, Patna: Khuda Bux Oriental Public Library.

Asad Beg. *Wikaya-i-Asad Beg*. Translated by H.M. Elliot and John Dowson, vol. VI.

Ashub, Muhammad Baksh. 'Tarikh-i-Shahadat-i-Farrukhsiyar-wa-Julus-i-Muhammad Shahi Badshah'. Rotograph. Aligarh: History Department, Aligarh Muslim University.

Attar, Farid-ud-Din, *Tadhkirat-al-Auliya*, (*Memoirs of the Saints*), ed. Reynold A. Nicholson. Vol. I. Leiden: Luzac & Co, 1905.

Aurangzeb. 'Adab-i-Alamgiri'. Abdus Salam Collection. Aligarh: Azad Library, Aligarh Muslim University.

Aurangzeb. *Rukkat-i-Alamgiri*. Translated by J.H. Bilmoria. New Delhi: Idarah-i-Adabiyat-i-Delli, 1972; also Ms., Lytton Collection. Aligarh: Aligarh Muslim University.

Azfari, Zahir-ud-din. *Waqia-i-Azfari*. Translated by A. Satter. Madras: Oriental Research Institute, Madras University, 1937.

Babur, Zahir-ud-din. *Babur Nama* or *Memoirs of Babur*. Translated by A.S. Beveridge, 2 Vols., rpt. New Delhi: Oriental Books Reprint Corpn, 1970.

Bahadur, Tahmas Beg Khan. *Tahmas Nama*, Translated by P. Setu Madhava Rao. Mumbai: Popular Prakashan, 1967.

Bakhtawar Khan. *Mirat-i-Alam*. Translated by H.M. Elliot and John Dowson, vol. VII.

Baihaqi, Abul-Fadl. *Tarikh-i-Baihaqi*. Edited by W.H. Morley. Kolkata: Bibliothica Indica, 1862.

Badaoni, Abdul Qadir Al. *Muntakhabu-T-Tawarikh*. Translated by. S.A. Ranking, vol. I; W.H. Lowe, vol. II; Wolseley Haig, vol. III, rpt. New Delhi: Idarah-i-Adabiyat-i-Delli, 1973.

————. *Nijat-ul-Rashid*. Edited by Syed Moinul Haq. Lahore, 1972.

Barani, Zia-ud-din. *Tarikh-i-Firoz Shahi*. Kolkata: Bibliothica Indica, 1862; also translated by S.A.A. Rizvi, *Adi Turk Kaleen Bharat*. Aligarh: Aligarh Muslim University, 1956 (wherever specifically mentioned).

————. *Fatawa-i-Jahandari*. In *The Political Theory of the Delhi Sultanate*, by Mohammad Habib and Afsar, translated by Afsar Begam. Allahabad, n.d.

Bhandari, Sujan Rai. *Khulasat-ut-Tawarikh*. Edited by Maulvi Zafar Hasan. Delhi: G & Sons, 1918.

Bihamad Khani, Muhammad. *Tarikh-i-Muhammadi*. In *Tughlaq Kaleen Bharat*, Part I, translated by S.A.A. Rizvi. Aligarh: Aligarh Muslim University, 1956.

Biyat, Bayazid. *Tazkirah-i-Humayun-wa-Akbar*. Edited by M. Hidayat Husain. Kolkata: Bibliothica Indica, 1941.

Chishti, Allah Diyah, *Siyar-ul-Aqtab*. Lucknow: Newal Kishore, 1913.

Dargah Quli Khan. *Muraqqa-e-Delhi*. Translated by Chander Shekhar and S.M. Chenoy. New Delhi: Deputy Publication, 1989.

Dehlawi, Abdu'l-Haqq Muhaddis, *Akkbaru'l-Akhyar*. Delhi: Matba-i- Mujtabai, 1332 A.H./1914 A.D.

Dughlat, Mirza Mohammad Haidar. *Tarikh-i-Rashidi*. Translated by N. Elias and E. Denison Ross, rpt. Patna: Academica, 1973.

Fakir Muhammad. *Jami'ut_Tawarikh*. Translated by H.M. Elliot and John Dowson, vol. VIII.

Faruqi, Nur-ud-din. 'Jahandar Nama'. Rotograph. Aligarh: Aligarh Muslim University.

Fazl, Abul. *Ain-I-Akbari*. Translated by H. Blochmann, edited by D.C. Phillott, 2nd ed., vol. I; Translated by H. S. Jarrett, Vols II, III, rpt. New Delhi: Crown Publications, 1988.

————. *Akbar Nama*. Translated by H. Beveridge, 3 Vols, 2nd Indian rpt. New Delhi: Ess Ess Publications, 1977.

Ferishta, Muhammad Kasim Hindu Shah. *Tarikh-i-Ferishta* alias *Gulshan-i-Ibrahimi*. In *History of Rise of the Mahomedan Power in India*, translated by J. Briggs, Vols 1, 2, 4, rpt. New Delhi: Atlantic Publishers & Distributors, 1989.

Gholam Hussein Khan. *Siyar-ul-Mutakherin*. In *The History of Later Mughals Seir Mutaqherin*, translated by Nota Manus, Vols 1 and 2, 2nd rpt. Lahore: Oriental

Publishers and Book-sellers, 1975; also translated by J. Briggs, *The History of Mohamedan Power in India*, 3rd rpt. New Delhi: Idarah-i-Adabiyat-i-Delli, 1973.

Gulbadan Begam. *Humayun_Nama*. Translated by A.S. Beveridge. New Delhi: Idarah-i-Adabiyat-i-Delli, 1972.

Hadi, Muhammad. *Tatimma-i-Waqiat-i-Jahangiri*. In *History of India as Told by Its Own Historians* (Allahabad: Kitab Mahal, 1964). Translated by H.M. Elliot and John Dowson, vol. VI.

Hamid-ud-din Khan. *Ahkam-i-Alamgiri*. In *Anecdotes of Aurangzib*, translated by J.N. Sarkar, 4th ed. Kolkata: M. C. Sarkar, 1949.

Inayatullah. *Takmila-i-Akbar Nama*. Translated by H.M. Elliot and John Dowson, vol. VI.

Isami, Khwaja Abdul Malik. *Futuh-us-Salatin*. Edited by A. Mahdi Husain.Agra: Educational Press, 1938.

Jafar Sharif. *Qanun-i-Islam*. In *Islam in India*, translated by G.A. Herklots, edited by William Crooke, rpt. London: Oxford University Press, 1921.

Jahangir, Nur-ud-din. *Tuzuk-i-Jahangiri* or *Memoirs of Jahangir*. Translated by A. Rogers, edited by H. Beveridge, 2nd ed., 2 Vols. New Delhi: Munshiram Manhorlal,1968; also *Wakiat-i-Jahangiri*. Translated by H.M. Elliot and John Dowson, vol. VI.

Jamali, Maulana Fadl-u-llah, *Siyar-u'l-Arifin*. Delhi: Ridwi Press, 1311 A.H.

Kabir, Shaikh Muhammad. 'Afsana-i-Badshahan' or 'Tarikh-i-Afghani'. Ms, Photo print of Microfilm copy of B.M., Ms. Section. Patna: Patna University (It belongs to K. P. Jaiswal Research Institute, Patna).

Kambo, Muhammad Salih. *Amal-i-Salih* or *Shah Jahan Namah*. Edited by. G. Yazdani, 3 Vols. Kolkata: Bibliothica Indica, 1923, 1927, 1939.

Karam Ali. *Muzaffarnamah*. In *Bengal Nawabs*, translated by J.N. Sarkar. Kolkata: Asiatic Society, 1952.

Kayath, Chittraman. 'Chahar Gulshan'. Ms. Aligarh: Azad Library, Aligarh Muslim University.

Kazim, Mirza Muhammad. *Alamgir Namah*. Kolkata: Bibliothica Indica, 1865–1873.

Khafi Khan, Muhammad Hashim. *Muntakhab-al-Lubab*. Edited by Maulvi Kabir-ud-din Ahmad, 2 Parts. Kolkata: Bibliothica Indica, 1869.

Khwandamir. *Humayun Nama*. Translated by H.M. Elliot and John Dowson, vol. V (Allahabad: Kitab Mahal, 1964); also translated by Baini Prashad, *Qanun-i-Humayun of Khwandamir*. Calcutta: Royal Asiatic Society of Bengal, 1940.

Lahori, Abdul Hamid. *Badshah Nama*. Edited by K.A. Ahmad and Abdal Rahim, 2 Vols. Kolkata: Bibliothica Indica, 1867, 1872.

Lakhnawi, Shiv Das. *Shahnama Munawwar Kalam*. Translated by Syed Hasan Askari. Patna: Janki Prakashan, 1980.

Minhaj-ud-din Siraj, Abu-Umar-i-Usman. *Tabaqat-i-Nasiri*. Translated by H.G. Raverty, 2 Vols, rpt. New Delhi: Oriental Books Reprint Corpn., 1970; also translated by Elliot and Dowson, vol. II, wherever specifically mentioned.

Mirak, Yusuf. *Mazhar-i-Shahjahani*. Edited by Pir Husam-ud-din Rashidi. Hyderabad: Sindhi Adabi Board, n.d.

Mukhlis, Anand Ram. *Tazkira*. Translated by H.M. Elliot and John Dowson, vol. VIII.

Multani, Ain-ul-Mulk Abdullah. *Insha-i-Mahru*. Edited by S.A. Rashid. Lahore, Idarah-Yi-Tahqiqat-i-Pakistan, Danishgah-Yi-Punjab, 1965.

Mushtaqi, Rizkullah. *Waqiat-i-Mushtaqi*. In *Uttar Taimur Kaleen Bharat* Translated by S.A.A. Rizvi, 2 Parts. Aligarh: Aligarh Muslim University, 1958–1959; also translated by H.M. Elliot and John Dowson, vol. IV, wherever specifically mentioned.

Must'ad Khan. *Maasir-i-Alamgiri*. Translated and annotated by J.N. Sarkar. Kolkata: Royal Asiatic Society of Bengal, 1947.

Mutamad Khan. *Iqbalnama-i-Jahangiri*. Translated by H.M. Elliot and John Dowson, vol. VI.

Nagar, Ishwar Dass. *Futuhat-i-Alamgiri*. Translated and edited by Tasneem Ahmad. Delhi: Idarah-i-Adabiyat-i-Delli, 1978.

Nahavandi, Abd-ul-Baqi. *Massir-i-Rahimi*. Edited by S.M. Hidayat Husain, vol. I. Kolkata: Asiatic Society of Bengal, 1924.

Nathan, Mirza. *Baharistan-i-Ghaybi*. Translated by M.I. Borah, 2 Vols. Guwahati: Government of Assam, 1936.

Niamatullah. *Tarikh-i-Khan Jahani wa Makhzan-i-Afghana*. In *Niamatullah's History of the Afghans*, translated by N.B. Roy. Kolkata: Shantiniketan, 1958.

Qadri, Muhammad Ayub. *Majmua-i-Wasiya* (Collection of Wills). Hyderabad, Pakistan, 1964.

Qalander, Hamid. *Khair-ul-Majalis*. Edited by K.A. Nizami. Aligarh: Aligarh Muslim University, n.d.

Qalqashandi, Abu Al Abbas. *Subh al Asha*. In *An Arab Account of India in the Fourteenth Century*, translated by Otto Spies. Stuttgart, 1936.

Qazwini, Muhammad Amin. 'Badshah Nama'. Transcription of the Raza Library, Rampur Ms. in 3 parts. Aligarh: History Department, Aligarh Muslim University; also Persian Ms. Patna: Buhar Collection, wherever specifically mentioned.

Razi, Aqil Khan. *Waqiat-i-Alamgiri*. Edited by Maulvi Haji Zafar Hasan. New Delhi: Aligarh Historical Institute, 1946.

Razzaq, Abdur. *Matla-us-Sadain*. Translated by. H.M. Elliot and John Dowson, vol. IV.

Salim, Ghulam Husain. *Riyazu-s-Salatin* or (*A History of Bengal*). Translated by Abdus Salam, rpt. Delhi: Idarah-i-Adabiyat-i-Delli, 1975.

Sarwani, Abbas Khan. *Tarikh-i-Sher Shahi*. Translated by B.P. Ambashthya. Patna: K.P. Jayaswal Research Institute, 1974; also see translated by Imamuddin. Dacca, 1964. Used Ambashthya translation, unless specifically mentioned otherwise.

Shah Nawaz Khan, Samsam ud-daulah and Abdul Hayy. *Maasir-ul-Umara*. Translated by H. Beveridge, revised, annotated and compiled by Baini Prashad, 2nd ed., 2 Vols. Patna: Janki Prakashan, 1979.

Sijzi, Amir Hasan. Fawa'd-u'l-Fua'd. Lucknow: Newal Kishore Press, 1302A.H./1884 A.D.

Shirazi, Mulla Kami. 'Fateh Nama-i-Nurjahan Begam'. Ms. Aligarh: History Department, Aligarh Muslim University.

Sikander, Ibn-i-Mohammad. *Mirat-i-Sikanderi*. In *Uttar Taimur Kaleen Bharat*, translated by S.A.A. Rizvi, Part II. Aligarh: Aligarh Muslim University, 1959.

Sirhindi, Yahya Bin Ahmad. *Tarikh-i-Mubarak_Shahi*. Translated By K.K. Basu. Baroda: Abdullah Sirhindi Oriental Institute, 1932.

Timur. *Malfuzat-i-Timuri* or *Tuzak-i-Timuri*. Translated By H.M. Elliot and John Dowson, vol. III.

Tughlaq, Firoz Shah. *Futuhat-i-Firoz Shahi*. Edited by S.A. Rashid. Aligarh, 1954; also used translation by Elliot and Dowson, vol. III, wherever specifically mentioned.

Ulugh Khani, Abdullah Mohammad Bin Umar Al Makki Al Asafi. *Zafar-ul-Waleh be Muzaffar Wa Aaleh*. In *Khalji Kaleen Bharat; Uttar Taimur Kaleen Bharat*, Part II, translated by S.A.A. Rizvi.

Umari, Shahbu-d-din Abul Abbas Ahmad. *Masaliku-L-Absar_Fi_Mamaliku-L-Amsar*. In *Tughlaq Kaleen Bharat*, Part I, translated by S.A.A. Rizvi; also translated by I.H. Siddiqui and Qazi Mohammad Ahmad, *A Fourteenth Century Arab Account of India under Sultan Mohd.-bin-Tughlaq*. Aligarh: Siddiqui Publishing House, 1971; translated by H.M. Elliot and John Dowson, vol. III. All the three references specifically mentioned.

Yadgar, Ahmad. *Tarikh-I-Shahi or Tarikh-i-Salatin-i-Afghana*. In *Uttar Taimur Kaleen Bharat*, Part I, translated by S.A.A. Rizvi.

Yusuf Ali. *Ahwal-i-Mahabat Jang*. In *Bengal Nawabs*, translated by J.N. Sarkar. Calcutta: Asiatic Society, 1952.

Yazdi, Sharafu-d-din. *Zafar Nama*. Translated by H.M. Elliot and John Dowson, vol. III.

Zeb-un-Nisa. *Diwan-i-Makhfi*. Kanpur, 1345 H/1926. In *The Diwan of Zeb-un-Nissa*, translated by Magan Lal and Jessie Duncan. London: Westbrook, 1913.

Persian Documents and Farmans

Aligarh Farmans. University Collection, History Department, Azad Library. Aligarh: Aligarh Muslim University.

Bilgram Documents. Transcript no. 89. History Department Library. Aligarh: Aligarh Muslim University.

Farman-I-Salatin. Edited by Bashir-ud-din Ahmad. New Delhi, 1926. (Farman issued by Jahangir in his thirteenth year of reign).

Firangi Mahal Documents. Transcript. Aligarh: History Department Library, Aligarh Muslim University. These documents relate to the areas, for example, Haveli Bahraich, Sadrpur, Amethi Dongar, etc., where descendants and relatives of Mulla Qutb-ud-din of Sahali had their madad-i-maash.

Oriental Records. *A Calendar of Oriental Records*. Edited by B.P. Saxena, vol. I; S.A. Rashid, Vols II and III. Allahabad: Government Central Record Office, 1955, 1956, 1959.

Shamsabad and Bilhaur Documents. Transcript no. 104. Aligarh: History Department Library, Aligarh Muslim University.

Sharaif-i-Usmani Documents. Transcript no. 82. Aligarh: History Department Library, Aligarh Muslim University.

Foreign Travellers

Augustus, Frederick. *The Emperor Akbar–A Contribution Towards the History of India in the 16ᵗʰ Century*. Translated by A.S. Beveridge, 2 Vols, rpt. New Delhi: Atlantic Publishers and Distributors, 1989.

Barbosa, Duarte. *The Book of Duarte Barbosa*. Translated, edited and annotated by Mansal Longworth Dames, 2 Vols., rpt. New Delhi: Asian Educational Services, 1989.

Bernier, Francois. *Travels in the Mogul Empire (A. D. 1656–1668)*, 2nd ed. New Delhi: S. Chand & Co., 1968.

Bowrey, Thomas. *A_Geographical Account of Countries Round the Bay of Bengal (1669–1679)*. Edited by R.C. Temple. London: Hak Society, 1905.

De Laet. *The Empire of the Great Mogol*. Translated and annotated by J.S. Hoyland and S.N. Banerjee, rpt. New Delhi: Idarah-i-Adabiyat-i-Delli, 1975.

Della Valle, Pietro. *Travels of Pietro Della Valle in India*. Translated by G. Havers, edited by Edward Grey, Vol. I. London: Hakluyt Society, 1892; also in M.A. Ansari, *European Travellers under the Mughals*. New Delhi: Idarah-i-Adabiyat-i-Delli, 1975.

Downton, Nicholas. *European Travellers Under the Mughals*, by M.A. Ansari. New Delhi: Idarah-i-Adabiyat-i-Delli, 1975.

Foster, William, ed. *Early Travels in India* (1583–1619), rpt. in India. New Delhi: S.Chand & Co., 1968—for narratives of: Ralph Fitch (1583–1591), 1–47. William Hawkins (1608–1613), 60–121. William Finch (1608–1611), 122–187. Nicholas Withington (1612–1616), 188–233. Thomas Coryat (1612–1617), 234–287. Edward Terry (1616–1619), 288–332.

_____. *The English Factories in India (1618–1669)*. 13 Vols (each volume titled by the years it covers). Oxford, 1906–1927.

_____. *Letters Received by the East India Company from its Servants in the East, (1613–15)*. vol. II. London: Low, Marston &Co Ltd., 1897.

Fryer, John. *A New Account of the East Indies and Persia (1672–1681)*. Edited by W. Crooke, vol. II, second series no. XX. London: Hak Society, 1912.

Hamilton, Alexander. *Account of the East Indies* (1688–1723). vol. I. Edinburg: John Mosman, one of His Majesty's Printers, and sold at the King's printing house in Craig's Closs, MDCCXXVII (1927).

Ibn Batuta. *The Rehla of Ibn Batuta*. Translated by Mahdi Husain. Baroda: Oriental Institute, 1953.

Jourdain, John. *The Journal of John Jourdain (1608–1617)*. Edited by William Foster. London: Hak Society, 1905.

Mandelslo, J. A. De. *The Voyages and Travels of J. Albert de Mandelslo ... into the East Indies*. Translated by John Davies, 2nd ed. London: Printed for John Starkey, and Thomas Basset, at the Mitre near Temple-Barr, and at the George near St Dunstans Church in Fleet Street, 1669.

Manrique, F.S. *Travels of Fray Sebastien Manrique (1629–1643)*. Translated by Eckford Luard and S.J. Hosten, vol. II. London: Hak Society, 1927.

Manucci, Niccolao. *Storia Do Mogor or Mogul India*. Translated by William Irvine, Vols I, II, III, rpt. New Delhi: Atlantic Publishers & Distributors, 1989; also used London: Murray, 1907 publication. The 1989 print is generally used unless pointed otherwise specifically.

Marshall, John. *John Marshall in India*. Edited by Shafaat Ahmad Khan. London: Oxford University Press, 1927.

Monserrate, S. J. *The Commentary*. Translated and annotated by J.S. Hoyland and S.N. Banerjee. London: Oxford University Press, 1922.

Mundy, Peter. *The Travels of Peter Mundy in Europe and Asia*. Edited by R.C. Temple, vol. II, second series no. XXXV. London: Hak Society, 1914.

Nicoli Conti. *India in the Fifteenth Century*. Edited by R.H. Major. London: Hak Society, 1857.

Orme, Robert. *Historical Fragments of the Mogul Empire of the Morattoes, and of the English Concerns in Indostan, from the Year 1659.* Edited by J.P. Guha, rpt. New Delhi: Associated Publishing House, 1974.

Ovington, J. *India in the Seventeenth Century.* Edited by J.P. Guha, vol. I. New Delhi: Associated Publishing House, 1976.

Pelsaert, Francisco. *The Remonstrantie or Jahangir's India.* Translated by W.H. Moreland and P. Geyl, rpt. New Delhi: Idarah-i-Adabiyat-i-Delli, 1972.

Pyrard, Francois. *The Voyage of Francois Pyrard of Laval.* Translated and edited by Albert Grey and H.C.P. Bell, vol. I. London: Hak Society, 1888.

Roe, Thomas. *The Embassy of Sir Thomas Roe to the Court of the Great Mughal (1615-19).* Edited by William Foster, vol. II. London: Hak Society, 1899.

Roe, Thomas and John Fryer. *Travels in India in the Seventeenth Century.* London: Trubner & Co, 1873.

Stavorinus, J.S. *Voyage to the East Indies* (1768-71). Translated by Samuel Hull Wilcocke, vol. I. London: G. G. & J. Robinson, 1798.

Tavernier, J.B. *Travels in India by Jean Baptiste Tavernier.* Translated by V. Ball, edited by William Crooke, vol. I. New Delhi: Oriental Books Reprint Corpn, 1977.

Thevenot, M. De and J. F. G. Careri. *Indian Travels of Thevenot and Careri.* Edited by S.N. Sen. New Delhi: National Archives of India, 1949.

English Sources

Abbott, Jacob. *Makers of History Genghis Khan—Life And Conquests.* New Delhi: Heritage Publishers, 1975.

Ahmad, Imtiaz, ed. *Caste and Social Stratification Among Muslims in India,* 2nd ed. New Delhi: Manohar Publications, 1978.

Ahmad, Muhammad Aziz. *Political History and Institutions of the Early Turkish Empire of Delhi (1206–1290 A.D.).* New Delhi: Oriental Books Reprint Corpn, 1972.

Ahmad, Najma Perveen. *Hindustani Music.* New Delhi: Manohar Publishers, 1984.

Ahmad, S.M., com. *Islam in India and the Middle East.* Allahabad: Abbas Manzil Library, n.d.

Ahmad Ali, S.V. Mir. *Husain, the King of Martyrs.* Karachi: Grenich Pub. Co., 1964.

Ahmed, Akbar S. *Discovering Islam: Making Sense of Muslim History and Society.* New Delhi: Vistaar Publications, 1990.

Alam, Muzaffar. *The Crisis of Empire in Mughal North India; Awadh and the Punjab (1707–1748).* Delhi: Oxford University Press, 1986.

Altekar, A.S. *The Position of Women in Hindu Civilization.* 3rd ed. New Delhi: Motilal Banarasidass, 1962.

Ameer Ali, Syed. *A Short History of the Saracens.* London: MacMillan & Co., 1953.

_____. *Mahommedan Law.* 5th ed., vol. II, rpt. New Delhi: The English Book Store, 1985.

_____. *The Spirit of Islam,* rpt. Delhi: Idarah-i-Adabiyat-i-Delli, 1978.

Ansari, M.A. *European Travellers under the Mughals.* Delhi: Idarah-i-Adabiyat-i-Delli, 1975.

_____. *Social Life of the Mughal Emperors (1526–1707).* New Delhi: Shanti Prakashan, 1974.

Ashraf, K.M. *Life and Conditions of the People of Hindustan.* 2nd ed. New Delhi: Munshiram Manoharlal, 1970.

Aziz, Abdul. *Arms and Jewellery of the Indian Mughals.* Lahore: Ripon Printing Press, 1947.

Bach, Hilde. *Indian Love Paintings.* Varanasi: Lustre Press, 1985.

Baig, M.R.A. *The Muslim Dilemma in India.* New Delhi: Vikas Publishing House, 1974.

Baig, Tara Ali, ed. *Women of India.* New Delhi: Ministry of Information and Broadcasting, 1957.

Baljon, J.M.S. *Religion and Thought of Shah Wali Allah Dihlawi (1703–1762).* Leiden: E. J. Brill, 1986.

Bamzai, P.N.K. *A History of Kashmir.* New Delhi: Metropolitan Book Co., 1962.

Banaji, D.R. *Slavery in British India,* D. Mumbai: Taraporevala Sons & Co., 1933.

Banerjee, J.M. *History of Firuz Shah Tughlaq.* New Delhi: Munshiram Manoharlal, 1967.

Banerji, S.K. *Humayun Badshah.* vol. II. Lucknow: Maxwell Company, 1941.

Bazaz, P.N. *Daughters of the Vitasta.* New Delhi: Pamposh Publications, 1959.

Bevan, V.R., and L. Jones. *Women in Islam: A Manual with Social Reference to Conditions in India.* Lucknow: The Lucknow Publishing House, 1941.

Bhatty, Z. 'Status of Muslim Women and Social Change'. In *Indian Women from Pardah to Modernity,* edited by B.R. Nanda. New Delhi: Vikas Publishing House, 1976.

Bhagi, M.L. *Medieval Indian Culture and Thought.* Ambala Cantt: The Indian Publications, 1965.

Billington, M.F. *Woman in India.* New Delhi: Amarko Book Agency, 1973.

BrijBhushan, J. *Muslim Women in Purdah and Out of It.* New Delhi: Vikas Publishing House, 1980.

_____. *The World of Indian Miniatures.* 1st ed. Tokyo, 1979.

_____. *Sultan Raziya, Her Life and Times.* New Delhi: Manohar Publications, 1990.

Brown, Percy. *Indian Paintings Under the Mughals.* London: Oxford University Press, 1924.

Burn, R. *Census of India (1901) Report,* XVI. National Archives of India Library, New Delhi: Imperial Govt. of India.

Burton, Richard F.: *Sind Revisited.* vol. I. London: Richard Bentley & Sons, 1877.

Chandrababu, B.S. and Thilagavathi. *Woman: Her History and Her Struggle for Emancipation.* Chennai: Bharathi Pusthakalayam, 2009.

Chaudhury, J.B. *Muslim Patronage to Sanskrit Learning.* vol. I. Kolkata: Prachyavani, 1954.

Chandra, Satish. *Parties and Politics at the Mughal Court (1707–1740).* 3rd ed. New Delhi: People's Publishing House, 1979.

_____. *Medieval India From Sultanat to Mughals: Delhi Sultanat (1206–1526): Part 1.* 3rd edition, 2nd reprint. New Delhi: Har-Anand Publications Ltd, 2006.

Chopra, P.N. *Life and Letters Under the Mughals.* New Delhi: Ashajanak Publications, 1976.

_____. *Some Aspects of Society and Culture During the Mughal Age (1526–1707).* Agra: Educational Publishers, 1955.

Commissariat, M. S. *A History of Gujrat.* vol. II. Mumbai: Orient Longmans, 1957.

Cooper, Elizabeth. *The Harem and the Purdah: Studies of Oriental Women.* Reprint. New Delhi: Bimla Publishing House, 1983.

Crooke, William. *The Tribes and Castes of the North Western Provinces and Oudh.* vol. IV. Kolkata, 1896.

Crowe, Sylvia and Sheila Haywood. *The Gardens of Mughal India.* New Delhi: Vikas Publishing House Pvt Ltd, 1973.

Das Gupta, T.C. *Aspects of Bengal Society.* 1st ed. Kolkata: Calcutta University, 1935.

Das, Harihar. *The Norris Embassy to Aurangzib* (1699–1702). Condensed and rearranged by S.C. Sarkar, 1st ed. Kolkata: K. L. Mukhopadhyay, 1959.

Datta, K.K. *Alivardi and His Times.* Kolkata: Calcutta University, 1939.

Datta, K.K., ed. *Some Mughal Farmans, Sanads, Parwanahs, etc. (1578–1802).* Patna: Political Deptt, State Central Records Office, 1962.

Datta, V.N. *Sati.* New Delhi: Manohar Publications, 1988.

Davenport, John. *Mohammad and Teachings of Quran.* Edited by Mohammad Amin. Lahore: S.M. Ashraf, 1944.

Day, U. N. *Some Aspects of Medieval Indian History.* New Delhi: Kumar Brothers, 1971.

Desai, Neera and Krishnaraj Maithreyi. *Women and Society in India.* New Delhi: Ajanta Publications, 1987.

De Souza, Alfred, ed. *Women in Contemporary India.* New Delhi: Manohar Book Service, 1975.

Devee, Maharani Sunity. *The Beautiful Mogul Princesses.* Kolkata: Thacker & Spink, 1918.

Eglar, Z. *A Panjabi Village in Pakistan.* New York: Columbia University Press, 1960.

Elliot, H. M. and John Dowson. *History of India as Told by its Own Historians.* Vols II–VIII. Allahabad: Kitab Mahal, 1964.

Elphinstone, M. S. *The History of India.* Allahabad: Kitab Mahal, 1966.

Enakshi Bhavnani. 'Creative and Fine Arts'. In *Women in India,* edited by Tara Ali Baig. New Delhi: Ministry of Information and Broadcasting, 1957.

Erskine, W. *History of India under the Two First Sovereigns of the House of Taimur.* vol. I. Delhi: Idarah-i-Adabiyat-i-Delli, 1973.

Fanshawe, H. C. *Delhi Past and Present.* London: J. Murray, 1902.

Faruki, Zahir-ud-din. *Aurangzeb and His Times.* Delhi: Idarah-i-Adabiyat-i-Delli, 1972.

Fergusson, James. *History of Indian and Eastern Architecture.* vol. 2. New Delhi: Darya Ganj, Rupa Publications India Pvt. Ltd, 2011.

Findly, Ellison Banks. *Noorjahan, Empress of Mughal India.* New York: Oxford University Press, 1993.

Fitzgerald, V. *Muhammadan Law—An Abridgement.* London: Oxford University Press, 1931.

Fyzee, A.A.A. *Outlines of Muhammadan Law.* 3rd ed. London: Oxford University Press, 1964.

Gallichan, W.M. *Women Under Polygamy.* London: Holden & Hardingham, 1914.

Ganda Singh. *Ahmad Shah Durrani.* Mumbai: Asia Publishing House, 1959.

Gaudefroy Demombynes, M. *Muslim Institutions.* Translated by J.P. Macgregor. London: Allen & Unwin, 1950.

Gibbon, Edward. *The Decline and Fall of the Roman Empire.* vol. II, 22nd prt. Chicago: Encyclopaedia Britannica, 1978.

Godden, Rumer. *Gulbadan-Portrait of a Rose Princess at the Mughal Court.* London: MacMillan & Co., 1980.

Goetz, H. *Art and Architecture of Bikaner State.* London: Oxford University Press, 1950.

Gupta, H.R. *Studies in Later Mughal History of the Panjab (1707–1793).* Lahore, 1944.

———, ed. *Essays Presented to Sir Jadunath Sarkar.* Chandigarh: Punjab University, 1958.

Gupta, S. S., ed. *Women in Indian Folklore*. Kolkata: Indian Publications, 1969.

Habib, Irfan. *Agrarian System of Mughal India 1556–1707*. Bombay: Asia Publishing House, 1963.

———. 'Non-Agricultural Production and Urban Economy'. In *The Cambridge Economic History of India*, I, edited by T. Raychaudhuri, and Irfan Habib. London: Cambridge University Press, 1982.

———. 'Agrarian Economy'.In *The Cambridge Economic History of India*, I, edited by T. Raychaudhuri and Irfan Habib. London: Cambridge University Press, 1982.

Habib, Mohammad, and Afsar Umar Salih Khan. *The Political Theory of the Delhi Sultanate*. Allahabad: Kitab Mahal, n. d.

Habibullah, A.B.M. *The Foundation of Muslim Rule in India*. Allahabad: Central Book Depot, 1961.

Haig, Wolseley. *The Cambridge History of India*. vol. III. New Delhi: Concept Publishing Co., 1928; edited by Richard Burn, vol. IV. London: Cambridge University Press, 1937.

Halim, Abdul. *History of the Lodi Sultans of Delhi and Agra*, rpt. New Delhi: Idarah-i-Adabiyat-i-Delli, 1974.

Hardy, P. *Historians of Medieval India: Studies in Indo Muslim Historical Writing*. London: Luzac & Co., 1960.

Hasan, Mohibbul, ed. *Historians of Medieval India*. Meerut: Meenakshi Prakashan, 1968.

Hasan, Mushirul. 'Some Aspects of the Problems of Muslim Social Reform'. In *Muslims in India*, edited by Zafar Imam. New Delhi: Orient Longman, 1975.

Hasrat, Bikram Jit. *Dara Shikuh: Life and Works*. 2nd ed. New Delhi: Munshiram Manoharlal, 1982.

Haywood, Sheila. 'The Emperors and Their Gardens'. In *The Gardens of Mughal India*, by Crowe, Sylvia and Sheila Haywood. New Delhi: Vikas Publishing House Pvt Ltd, 1973.

Hendley, T.H. *Indian Jewellery*. vol. I, rpt. New Delhi, 1984.

Hitti, P.K. *History of the Arabs*. New York: Macmillan & Co Ltd., 1956.

Hoang, Michel. *Genghis Khan*. Translated by Ingrid Cranfield. London: Saqi Books, 1990.

Holt, P. M. et al., ed. *The Cambridge History of Islam*, Vols. I & II. London: Cambridge, 1970.

Husain, Sheikh Abrar. *Marriage Customs Among Muslims in India*. New Delhi: Sterling Publishers, 1976.

Hyder, Qurratulain. 'Muslim Women in India'. In *Indian Women*, edited by Devaki Jain. New Delhi: Ministry of Information and Broadcasting, 1975.

Indian Council of Social Science Research. *Status of Women in India*. New Delhi: Indian Council of Social Science Research, 1975.

Ikram, S.M. *Muslim Civilization in India*. London: Columbia University Press, 1964.

Imam, Zafar, ed. *Muslims in India*. New Delhi: Orient Longman, 1975.

Imtiaz Ali, ed. *Ameer Ali on Islam*. New Delhi: Amar Prakashan, 1982.

Irvine, William. *Later Mughals*. 2 Vols. Calcutta: M. C. Sarkar & Sons, 1922.

Jaffar, S.M. *Education in Muslim India*, rpt. Delhi: Idarah-i-Adabiyat-i-Delli, 1973.

———. *Some Cultural Aspects of Muslim Rule in India*. Delhi: Idarah-i-Adabiyat-i-Delli, 1972.

Jain, Devaki, ed. *Indian Women*. New Delhi: Ministry of Information and Broadcasting, 1975.

Jain, Simmi. *Encyclopaedia of Indian Women Through the Ages: The middle ages*. New Delhi: Kalpaz Publication, 2003.

Jauhri, R.C. *Firoz Tughlaq (1351–1388 A.D.).* 2nd ed. Jalandhar: ABS Publications, 1990.

Kabiraj, Shibnarayan. 'Hindu and Muslim Women in Folk Customs, Rites and Traditions'. In *Women in Indian Folklore,* edited by S.S. Gupta. Kolkata: Indian Publication, 1969.

Kapadia, K.M. *Marriage and Family in India.* 2nd ed., rpt. London: Oxford University Press, 1959.

Karim, Abdul. *Social History of Muslims in Bengal.* Dacca, 1959.

Kennedy, Pringle. *History of the Great Moghuls,* rpt. Kolkata: Thacker Spink & Co., 1968.

Keay, F.E. *Indian Education in Ancient and Later Times,* Humphrey Milford. London: Oxford University Press, 1938.

Keene, H.G. *History of Hindustan.* Delhi: Idarah-i-Adabiyat-i-Delli, 1972.

Khosla, R.P. *Mughal Kingship and Nobility.* Allahabad: The Indian Press, 1934.

Khuda Bukhsh, S. *Studies: Indian and Islamic.* 1st ed., rpt. Delhi: Idarah-i-Adabiyat-i-Delli, 1978.

Kidwai, S.M.N. *Women under Different Social and Religious Laws.* New Delhi: Seema Publication, 1976.

Lal, K.S. *Early Muslims in India.* New Delhi: Books & Books, 1984.

————. *Growth of Muslim Population in Medieval India, A.D. 1000–1800.* (S.I.) New Delhi: Delhi Research (Publication in Social Sciences), 1973.

————. *History of the Khaljis.* Allahabad: The Indian Press, 1950.

————. *The Mughal Harem.* New Delhi: Aditya Prakashan, 1988.

————. *Twilight of the Sultanate.* Bombay: Asia Publishing House, 1963.

Lane, E.W. *An Account of the Manners And Customs of The Modern Egyptians.* Vth ed. London: John Murray, 1860.

Lanepoole, Stanley. *Mediaeval India Under the Mohammedan Rule (A.D. 712-1764),* Delhi: Seema Publication, 1980.

Latif, S.M. *Lahore, Its History, Architectural Remains and Antiquities.* Lahore, 1892.

Law, N.N. *Promotion of Learning in India During Muhammedan Rule,* rpt. Delhi: Idarah-i-Adabiyat-i-Delli, 1973.

Levy, R. *The Social Structure of Islam.* London: Cambridge University Press, 1957.

Lockhart, L. *Nadir Shah.* London: Luzac & Co., 1938.

Macnicol, Margaret, ed. *Poems by Indian Women.* Calcutta: Association Press, 1923.

Madhavanand, and R.C. Majumdar, eds. *Great Women of India.* Almora: Advaita Ashram, 1953.

Majumdar, R.C., H.C. Raychaudhari, and K. Dutta. *An Advanced History of India,* Part II. 4th edition, rpt. New Delhi: Macmillan Publishers India Ltd, 2010.

Mahmud-un-nasir, Syed. *Islam, Its Concepts and History.* New Delhi: Kitab Bhavan, 1981.

Malik, Zahir-ud-din. *A Mughal Statesman of the Eighteenth Century.* Bombay: Asia Publishing House, 1973.

————. *The Reign of Muhammad Shah, (1719–1748).* New York: Asia Publishing House, 1977.

Maududi, S.A.A. *Purdah and the Status of Woman in Islam.* Translated and edited by Al-Ash' Ari. New Delhi: Markazi Maktaba Islami, 1974.

Mazhar-ul-Haq Khan. *Social Pathology of the Muslim Society.* New Delhi: Amar Prakashan, 1978.

Meer Hassan Ali. *Observations of the Mussulmauns of India.* 1st ed., 2 Vols, rpt. Delhi: Idarah-i-Adabiyat-i-Delli, 1973.

Menon, Indu. *Status of Muslim Women in India*. New Delhi: Uppal Publishing House, 1981.

Mikhail, Mona N. *Images of Arab Women*. Washington Inc.: Three Continents Press, 1979.

Mirza, M. Wahid. *The Life and Works of Amir Khusrau*, rpt. Delhi, 1974.

Mishra, Rekha. *Women in Mughal India*. Allahabad: Munshiram Manoharlal, 1967.

Moganan, Tatiel E.T. *The Arab Woman*. London, 1937.

Moin-ul-Haq, S. *Barani's History of the Tughluqs*. Pub. No. 13. Karachi: Pakistan Historical Society, 1959.

Moosvi, Shireen. *The Economy of the Mughal Empire, (C. 1595)*. New Delhi: Oxford University Press, 1987.

Moreland, W.H. *The Agrarian System of Moslem India*. New Delhi, 1968.

Morgan, David. *The Mongols*. 1st Pub. London: Basil Blackwell, Oxford, 1986.

Muhammad Ali, Maulana. *The Religion of Islam*. New Delhi: S. Chand & Co., n. d.

_____. *A Manual of Hadith*. Lahore: Ahmadiyya Anjuman Ishaat Islam, 1944.

Mujeeb, M. *The Indian Muslims*. London: George Allen & Urwin Ltd, 1967.

Mukerjee, R.K. *The Economic History of India* (1600–1800). Allahabad: Kitab Mahal, 1967.

Mukherji, Ila. *Social Status of North Indian Women* (1526–1707). Agra: Shiva Lal Agarwala, 1972.

Mukherjee, Soma. *Royal Mughal Ladies and their Contributions*. New Delhi: Gyan Publishing House, 2001.

Mukhia, Harbans. *The Mughals of India*. Oxford: Blackwell Publishing Ltd, 2004.

Mulla, D.F. *Principles of Mahomedan Law*. 15th ed. Calcutta, 1961.

Nand, L.C. *Women in Delhi Sultanate*. Allahabad: Vohra Publishers and Distributors, 1989.

Nanda, B.R., ed. *Indian Women from Pardah to Modernity*. New Delhi: Vikas Publishing House, 1976.

Nigam, S.B.P. *Nobility Under the Sultans of Delhi, A.D. 1206–1398*. New Delhi: Munshram Manoharlal, 1968.

Nizami, K.A. *Some Aspects of Religion and Politics in India During the Thirteenth Century*. 2nd ed. Delhi: Idarah-i-Adabiyat-i-Delli, 1974.

_____. *The Life and Times of Shaikh Farid-ud-din Ganjishakar*. Delhi: Idarah-i-Adabiyat-i-Delli, 1973.

_____, ed. *Politics and Society During the Early Medieval Period*. vol. I. New Delhi: People's Publishing House, 1974.

_____. *Royalty in Medieval India*. New Delhi: Munshiram Manoharlal, 1997.

Ojha, P.N. *North Indian Social Life During Mughal Period*. 1st ed. New Delhi: Oriental Publishers, 1975.

_____. *Some Aspects of North Indian Social Life*. 1st ed. Patna: Nagari Prakashan, 1961.

Pant, D. *Commercial Policy of the Mughals*. 1st ed., rpt. New Delhi: Idarah-i-Adabiyat-i-Delli, 1978.

Patricia, Jeffery. *Frogs in a Well, Indian Women in Purdah*. New Delhi: Vikas Publishing House, 1979.

Payne, C.H. *Akbar and the Jesuits*. London: Harper & Brothers, 1926.

Phillips, E.D. *The Mongols*. London: Thames and Hudson, 1969.

Pickthall, M. *The Meaning of the Glorious Quran*. New Delhi: Taj Company, 1986.

Pool, J.J. *Famous Women of India*. Kolkata: Sushil Gupta (India) Ltd, 1954.

Prasad, Beni. *History of Jahangir.* 3rd ed. Allahabad: The Indian Press Ltd., 1940.

Prasad, Ishwari. *The Life and Times of Humayun,* rpt. Mumbai: Orient Longmans, 1956.

_____. *A History of the Qaraunah Turks in India.* 1st ed., vol. I. Allahabad: Central Book Depot, 1974.

_____. *A Short History of Muslim Rule in India.* Allahabad: The Indian Press Ltd, 1939.

Pratapditya Pal. *Court Paintings of India.* New Delhi, 1983.

Prawdin, Michael. *The Mongol Empire: Its Rise and Legacy.* Translated from German by Eden and Cedar Paul, 2nd ed. New York: The Free Press, 1967.

Qaiser, A.J. *The Indian Response to European Technology and Culture (1498–1707).* New Delhi: Oxford University Press, 1982.

Qanungo, K.R. *Dara Shukoh.* 2nd ed., vol. I. Kolkata, 1952.

_____. *Sher Shah and His Times.* Mumbai: Orient Longmans, 1965.

Quamruddin, M. *Life and Times of Prince Murad Baksh* (1624–1661). Kolkata: Author himself, Syed Amir Ali Avenue, 1974.

Qureshi, I.H. *The Administration of the Sultanate of Delhi.* 5th revised ed. New Delhi: Oriental Books Reprint Corpn, 1971.

Qutb, Mohammad. *Islam The Misunderstood Religion.* New Delhi: The Board of Islamic Publications, 1964.

Randhawa, M.S. *Indian Miniature Painting.* New Delhi: Roli Books International, 1981.

Rashid, A. *Society and Culture in Medieval India (1206–1556 A.D.).* Kolkata: Firma K. L. Mukhopadhyay, 1969.

Rawlinson, H.G. *India, A Short Cultural History.* Revised ed. W. I. (Great Britain): The Cresset Press, 1948.

_____. *Five Great Monarchies.* vol. III. London: John Murray, 1871.

Raychaudhuri, T. *Bengal Under Akbar and Jahangir, An Introductory Study in Social History.* 2nd ed. New Delhi: Munshi Ram Manoharlal, 1969.

_____. 'The State and the Economy: The Mughal Empire'. In *The Cambridge Economic History of India c. 1200–1750,* edited by T. Raychaudhari and Irfan Habib, vol.1. London: Cambridge University Press, 1982.

Royal Asiatic Society of Bengal. *Introducing India,* Part I. Kolkata: Royal Asiatic Society of Bengal, 1947.

Rice, C. Colliver. *Persian Women and Their Ways.* London, 1923.

Richards, J.F., ed. *The Imperial Monetary System of Mughal India.* Delhi: Oxford University Press, 1987.

Rizvi, S.A.A. *A History of Sufism in India.* vol. 1. New Delhi: Munshiram Manoharlal, 1978.

Roberts, Robert. *The Social Laws of the Qoran.* New Delhi: Adam Publishers, 1978.

Roy, Shibani. *Status of Muslim Women in Northern India.* New Delhi: B. R. Publishing Corpn, 1979.

Sahay, B.K. *Education and Learning under the Great Mughals.* Mumbai: New Literature Publishing Co., 1968.

Sahu, K.P. *Some Aspects of North Indian Social Life (1000–1526).* 1st ed. Calcutta: Punthi Pustak, 1973.

Saksena, B.P. *History of Shahjahan of Dihli.* Allahabad: Central Book Depot, 1958.

Sardesai, G.S. *New History of the Marathas.* vol. I. Mumbai, 1946.

Sarkar, J.N. *Fall of the Mughal Empire.* 3rd ed., 2 Vols. Calcutta: M. C. Sarkar & Sons, 1964, 1966.

_____. *History of Aurangzib.* 1st Imp., Vols I–IV. New Delhi: New Orient Longman Ltd., 1972–1974.

Sarkar, J.N. *Studies in Aurangzib's Reign.* Kolkata: M. C. Sarkar & Sons, 1933.
———, ed. *History of Bengal.* Patna: Academica Asiatica, 1973.
Sastri, K.A.N. *A History of South India.* 4th ed. New Delhi: Oxford University Press, 1976.
Schimmel, A. *Islam in the Indian Subcontinent.* Leiden: E. J Brill, 1980.
———. *Islamic Literatures of India.* Wiesbaden: Otto Harrassowitz, 1973.
Sen, Geeti. *Paintings from the Akbar Nama.* New Delhi: Roli Books, 1984.
Shaikh, Abdur Rashid. 'Suyurghal Lands under the Mughals'. In *Essays Presented to Sir Jadunath Sarkar,* edited by H.R. Gupta. Chandigarh: Punjab University, 1958.
Sharma, S.R. *Mughal Empire in India,* rpt. Agra: Stoddard Press, 1971.
Shelat, J.M. *Akbar.* Edited by K.M. Munshi and R.R. Diwakar. vol. II. Bombay: Bharatiya Vidya Bhavan, 1959.
Sheowring, W., and C. W. Thies. *Religious Systems of the World.* New Delhi: Ajay Book Service, 1982.
Shushtery, A.M.A. *Outlines of Islamic Culture.* 2nd ed. Banglore: The Banglore Printing & Publishing Co., 1954.
Siddiqi, M.M. *Women in Islam.* New Delhi: New Taj Office, 1991.
Siddiqi, M.Z. *Sir Abdullah Memorial Lectures.* Kolkata: Calcutta University, 1971.
Smith, V.A. *Akbar: The Great Mogul (1542–1605).* 3rd Indian Print. New Delhi, 1966.
Smith, W.R. *Kinship and Marriage in Early Arabia.* London: Cambridge University Press, 1885.
Spain, James W. *The Way of the Pathans.* London: Robert Hale Ltd., 1962.
Spear, Percival. *Twilight of the Mughals.* London: Cambridge University Press, 1951.
Spuler, Bertold. *The Mongols in History.* London: Pall Mall Press, 1971.
Srivastava, A.L. *Akbar the Great.* vol. I. Agra: Shiva Lal Agarwala, 1962.
———. *The First Two Nawabs of Awadh,* 2nd ed. Agra, 1954.
———. *Studies in Indian History.* Agra: Shiva Lal Agarwala, 1974.
Srivastava, K.P., ed. *Mughal Farmans, 1540 A.D. to 1706 A.D.* vol. I. Lucknow: U. P. State Archives, 1974.
Stephen, Carr. *Archaeology and Monumental Remains of Delhi.* Allahabad: Kitab Mahal, 1967.
Stewart, Charles. *The History of Bengal.* New Delhi: Orient Publishers, 1971.
Stuart, C.M.V. *Gardens of the Great Mughals,* rpt. Allahabad: R. S. Publishing House, 1979.
Subbamma, Malladi. *Islam and Women.* Translated by M.V. Ramamurty. New Delhi: Sterling Publishers, 1988.
Sufi, G.M.D. *Kashir.* vol. II. New Delhi: Light & Life Publishers, 1974.
Suri, Pushpa. *Social Conditions in Eighteenth Century Northern India.* Delhi: University of Delhi, 1977.
Syed, A.J. *Aurangzeb in Muntakhab-al Lubab.* Bombay: Somaiya Publications, 1977.
Thomas, E. *The Chronicles of the Pathan Kings of Delhi.* 1st. Indian ed. Delhi: Oriental Publishers, 1967.
Thomas, F.W. *Mutual Influence of Muhammadans and Hindus in India.* Cambridge: Deighton, Bell, 1892.
Thomas, P. *Indian Women Through the Ages.* New York: Asia Publishing House, 1964.
Tirmizi, S.A. *Edicts of the Mughal Harem.* Delhi: Idarah-i-Adabiyat-i-Delli, 1979.
Tod, J. *Annals and Antiquities of Rajasthan.* 2 Vols. London: Smith Elder & Co., 1829, 1832.

Tewari, Yogeshwar. 'Influence of Harem on Politics in the Sultanate Period'. In *Region in Indian History*, edited by Mahendra Pratapa and S.Z.H. Jafri. New Delhi: Anamika Publishers & Distributors (P)Ltd, 1908.

Tripathi, R.P. *Rise and Fall of the Mughal Empire.* Allahabad: Central Book Depot, 1987.

_____. *Some Aspects of Muslim Administration*, rpt. Allahabad: Central Book Depot, 1966.

Tyabji, Faiz Badr-ud-din. *Muhammadan Law.* 3rd ed. Bombay: N.M. Tripathi, 1940.

Ward, Barbara E., ed. *Women in the New Asia.* Paris: UNESCO, 1963.

Wensinck, A.J. *A Handbook of Early Muhammadan Tradition*, rpt. Leiden: E. J. Brill, 1971.

Williams, Rushbrook. *An Empire Builder of the Sixteenth Century.* London: Longman, 1918.

Wright, Nelson. *Coins and Metrology of the Sultans of Delhi.* Delhi, 1936.

Yasin, Mohammad. *A Social History of Islamic India (1605–1748).* Lucknow: The Upper India Publishing House, 1958.

Yusuf Ali. *Medieval India, Social and Economic Conditions.* London: Oxford University Press, 1932.

Yusuf Husain. *Glimpses of Medieval Indian Culture.* Bombay: Asia Publishing House, 1957.

Zaidi, S.M.H. *The Muslim Womenhood in Revolution.* Calcutta, 1937.

_____. *Position of Women Under Islam.* Calcutta: Book Tower, 1935.

Zakaria, Rafiq. *Razia, Queen of India.* Bombay: Popular Prakshan, 1966.

Dictionaries and Encyclopaedias

Downey, Douglas W. et al., eds. *New Standard Encyclopedia.* vol. XVII. Chicago: Standard Educational Corpn, 1987.

Hastings, James, ed. *Encyclopaedia of Religion and Ethics.* 3rd edition, vol. II. New York: Charles Scribner's Sons, 1926.

Houtsma, M.T. et al., eds. *Encyclopaedia of Islam.* Vols I and II, London: Leyden, 1927, 1938.

Hughes, T.P. *Dictionary of Islam.* New Delhi: Rupa & Co., 1988.

Humphrey, Edward et al., eds. *The Webster Family Encyclopedia.* Vols I, VI, VII. Webster: Webster Publishing Co., 1984.

Platts, J. T. *A Dictionary of Urdu, Classical Hindi and English.* vol. I. London: Oxford University Press, 1959.

Steingass, F. *A Comprehensive Persian–English Dictionary.* London: Routledge and Kegan Paul, 1892.

Sanskrit Source

_____. *Atharva Veda*; also Eng. Trans. W. D. Whitney, *Atharva Veda Samhita.* London: Cambridge, Mass.: Harvard University 1905.

Hindi Sources

Bhushan. *Bhusan Granthavali.* Edited by Rajnarayan Sharma. Allahabad: Hindi Bhavan, 1950.

Dixit, Maya Shankar, ed. *Ratnavali.* 3rd ed. Varanasi: Sahitya Sewa Mandal, Vikrami Sambat 1995 (hereinafter V.S.).

Jayasi, Malik M. *Padmavat.* 2nd ed. Muhammad Chirgaon (Jhansi): Sahitya Sadan, V. S. 2018.

Rahim. *Rahim Bilas.* Edited by Brajratan Das. Allahabad: Ramnarayan Lal, 1948.

Rizvi, S.A.A., trans. *Adi Turk Kaleen Bharat.* Aligarh: Aligarh Muslim University, 1956.

_____. *Khalji Kaleen Bharat.* Aligarh: Aligarh Muslim University, 1955.

_____. *Tughlaq Kaleen Bharat.* 2 Parts. Aligarh: Aligarh Muslim University, 1956–1957.

_____. *Uttar Taimur Kaleen Bharat.* 2 Parts. Aligarh: Aligarh Muslim University, 1958–1959.

Vidyapati. *Kirtilata.* Edited by V.S. Agarwala, 1st ed. Chirgaon (Jhansi): Sahitya Sadan, 1962.

Urdu Sources

Abdur Rahman, Syed Subah-ud-din. *Bazm-i-Taimuria.* Azamgarh: Daar-ul-Musannifeen, 1948.

Pandauri, Rattan. *Hindi Ke Mussalmaan Shora.* New Delhi, 1982.

Journals

Ahmad, Hafiz Shams-ud-din. 'Zeb-un-nisa Begam and Diwan-i-Makhfi'. *Journal of Bihar and Orissa Research Society* XIII, Part I (1927).

Anonymous. 'Marriage in Islam'. *Mahjubah* 4, no. 7 (January–February 1986): 31.

Ansari, M.A. 'The Harem of the Great Mughals'. *Islamic Culture* XXXIV (January 1960).

Banerji, S.K. 'Some of the Women Relations of Babur'. *Islamic Culture* IV (1937–1938).

_____. 'The Historical Remains of Early Years of Akbar's Reign'. *United Provinces Historical Society* XV, Part II (December 1942).

Beveridge, A.S. 'Life and Writings of Gulbadan Begam (Lady Rosebody)'. *Calcutta Review*, Art. No. VIII, 106 (1898): 345–371.

Bilgrami, Rafat. 'Property Rights of Muslim Women in Mughal India'. Paper presented in *Proceedings of Indian History Congress*, 48th session, Goa, 1987.

_____. 'Women Grantees in the Mughal Empire'. *Quarterly Journal of the Pakistan Historical Society* XXXVI, Part III (July 1988): 207–214.

Bahadur, Bishan. 'Akbar as Depicted by Prominent Contemporary Hindu Poets'. Paper presented in *Proceedings of India History Congress*, 45th session, Annamalainagar, 1984.

Chowdhuri, J.N. 'Mumtaz Mahall'. *Islamic Culture* XI (July 1937): 373–381.

Farhat, Hasan. 'Two Official Documents of Jahangir's Reign Relating to East India Company'. Paper presented in *Proceedings of Indian History Congress*, 46th session, Amritsar, 1985.

Habibullah, A.B.M. 'Sultanah Raziah'. *The Indian Historical Quarterly* XVI, No. 1 (1940): 750–772.

Halim, S.A. 'Harem Influence in the 15th Century Politics of India'. *Muslim University Journal* II (October 1938): 50–60.

Hodivala, S.H. 'The Dirham-i-Sharai'. *Journal_of Asiatic Society of Bengal*, New Series, XIII (1917): 47–48.

Irvine, William. 'Ahmad Shah Abdali and the Indian Wazir Imad-ul-Mulk (1756-7)'. *Indian Antiquary* XXXVI (February 1907): 43-51.

Kozlowski, Gregory C. 'Muslim Women and the Control of Property in Northern India', *The Indian Economic and Social History Review* 24, Issue 2 (1987): 163–181.

Moosvi, Shireen. 'Mughal Shipping at Surat in the First Half of 17th Century'. Paper presented in *Proceedings of Indian History Congress*, 51st Session, Calcutta, 1990.

Nizami, K.A. 'Persian Literature Under Akbar'. *Medieval_Indian Quarterly* III, nos. 3 and 4 (Jan. and April 1958).

Prasad, Beni. 'A Few Aspects of Education and Literature under the Great Mughals'. *Indian Historical Records Commission* V (1923).

Ray, Anirudha. 'Last Memoir of Francois Bernier from Surat: March 10, 1668'. Paper presented in *Proceedings of Indian History Congress*, 42nd session, Magadh University, Bodhgaya, 1981:241–257.

Smith, V.A. 'Joannes De Laet on India and Shahjahan'. *Indian Antiquary* XLIII, Bombay (November 1914).

Temple, Sir R.C. 'Shahjahan and Jahan Ara'. *Indian Antiquary* XLIV (January 1915).

Yusuf Husain Khan. 'The Educational System in Medieval India'. *Islamic Culture* XXX, No. 1 (1956): 106–125.

Yazdani, G. 'Jahanara'. *Journal of Punjab Historical Society* II (1912): 153.

Author Index

Subject Index

About the Author

Sudha Sharma is on the Board of Directors, Indraprastha Gas Limited, New Delhi. She was former Chairperson of Central Board of Direct Taxes (CBDT), New Delhi. She has served as Director General (Vigilance) of the Income Tax (IT) department in the national capital before her appointment to the top body.

Dr Sharma has 37 years of experience in the fields of administration, different tax matters such as, assessment, appeals, printing, publishing and advertisement, promotion of official language, computerisation, investigation, international negotiations and signing treaties (Double Taxation Avoidance Agreement [DTAA] and Tax Information Exchange Agreement [TIEA]) and vigilance, both in the government and the public sector.

Dr Sharma did her PhD in History from Punjab University and started her career as a lecturer of History in Hans Raj Mahila Mahavidyalaya, Jalandhar.